FIRST READING

A Diary

Books by Janis Walker

ALLELUIA! A GOSPEL DIARY

FIRST READING: A DIARY

HALLELUJAH! A PSALM RESPONSE DIARY

SECOND READING: A DIARY

A TRIP TO GRACE

SHEPHERDS

MYSTERY!

FIRST READING

A Diary

BY

Janis Walker

Pallium Press

Scripture references, unless otherwise identified, are from The New Revised Standard Version Bible (NRSV), copyright 1989, Division of Christian Education of the National Council of Churches of Christ in the United States of America.

Scripture quotations marked KJV are from the The King James Version of the Bible.

Every effort has been made to insure accuracy of text and quotations, and any errors or omissions brought to our attention will be corrected in future editions.

SECOND PRINTING 2016

Pallium Press, P.O. Box 60910, Palo Alto, CA 94306-0910
We regret that Pallium Press cannot accept or return unsolicited manuscripts.

Check for new titles by Janis Walker at
www.palliumpress.com

Pallium Press books are available at
www.Amazon.com, www.BarnesandNoble.com,
or at your favorite local independent bookstore.

cover photos: Terry Walker
cover design: Janis Walker

Copyright © 2016 by Janis Walker

All rights reserved. No part of this book may be reproduced, transmitted, stored in a retrieval system, or otherwise copied by any means whether electrical, mechanical, optical, or recording without the express written consent of Pallium Press, except for brief excerpts as part of reviews as permitted under the 1976 United States Copyright Act.

Printed in the United States of America.

ISBN 978-0-9826883-5-9

for Terry

with

love

and

gratitude

Acknowledgements

Thank you to Terry, Christopher, and to all who inspire me to keep following the Lord in this journey of "a long obedience in the same direction."

I am very grateful to Father David Pettingill for his frequent references to "the Easter victory" of Jesus and also to St. Augustine, who said, "We are an Easter people and 'Alleluia' is our song."

As with <u>Alleluia! A Gospel Diary</u>, this book offers my personal reflections and prayers based on the daily Mass readings.

Unless otherwise indicated, the Scripture quotations are from the <u>The New Revised Standard Version Bible</u> (NRSV).

Please read the Scriptures slowly and prayerfully before reading the reflections.

A.M.D.G.

The Feast of St. Agnes
January 21, 2009

Year A

Advent 382

Christmas 392

Lent 412

Easter 435

Pentecost 461

Year B

Advent 1

Christmas 20

Lent 60

Easter 87

Pentecost 113

Year C

Advent 202

Christmas 212

Lent 241

Easter 264

Pentecost 290

Sunday, November 27, 2005 First Sunday in Advent, Year B
Isaiah 63, 16-17; 64, 2-7
Prayer for the Return of God's Favor

"Oh that thou wouldest rend the heavens, that thou wouldst come down …. (Isaiah 64, 1 KJV)."

The first reading for the first Sunday of Advent sets our house in order. Our Father will send his only Son to be our Redeemer. Our Father will answer the anguished cry of our hearts.

"… O LORD, you are our Father; we are the clay, and you are our potter; we are all the work of your hand (Isaiah 64, 8)."

God will truly tear the heavens to come to us. God is eager to break into our lives in a new way.

Late autumn. Leaves, dried leaves, are blowing everywhere in the wind. Sometimes we feel like those leaves, being blown about by the mysterious wind.

Lord Jesus, thank you that you did indeed come to us. You came to us and showed us the heart of our Father. You came to rescue us and to give us a fresh, new life, to forgive us and to remove our guilt. Thank you for all you are eager to do for us as we wait for you this Advent. Alleluia!

Monday, November 28, 2005
Isaiah 2, 1-5
Zion, the Messianic Capital

"In days to come the mountain of the LORD's house shall be established as the highest of the mountains, and shall be raised above the hills; all nations shall stream to it. Many peoples shall come and say, 'Come, let us go up to the mountain of the LORD, to the house of the God of Jacob; that he may teach us his ways and that we may walk in his paths.' For out of Zion shall go forth instruction, and the word of the LORD from Jerusalem (Isaiah 2, 2-3)."

Jerusalem! Zion! The Lord's house.

What happens in the Lord's house? Who is there?

The Lord is there! The Lord instructs us.

JANIS WALKER   FIRST READING

We learn, over time, to walk in the paths the Lord has chosen for us. We may stumble as we learn to walk and then to climb and eventually to run in the ways of the Lord.

The Lord is the one who will judge. Then, only then, will swords be transformed into plowshares. Only then will there be no more war.

Lord Jesus, thank you for the Holy Spirit who teaches us how to walk in the paths you have chosen for us. Thank you for the light we need to continue our pilgrimage to the new Jerusalem, to the house of our Father. Alleluia!

Tuesday, November 29, 2005
Isaiah 11, 1-10
The Rule of Immanuel; Union of Ephraim and Judah

From an unpromising stump springs forth a sprouting shoot! A bud and a blossom.

Our King will rule! The Messiah will come to set up his kingdom of peace on earth.

At last, there will be a reign of wisdom and peace. Knowledge, wisdom, and justice will be in perfect balance. The Holy Spirit will be manifested supremely in this reign.

The lamb will be safe and will invite the wolf. The baby goat will be safe to rest with the leopard. The little calf will feast on tender grass with the little lion cub, with a little child as their guide. The bear and the cow will live in close proximity. The regal lion may enjoy fragrant new-mown hay just as a simple ox does. Even a young child may safely play near the home of a cobra.

There will be no more harm on the earth. Immanuel, our royal Messiah, will reign with complete integrity.

Lord Jesus, thank you for the reality of your coming kingdom. Let us prepare daily for your reign by trusting you and obeying you. Alleluia!

Wednesday, November 30, 2005 St. Andrew
Romans 10, 9-18
Righteousness Based on Faith

Very physical. Mouth. Heart. Ears. Feet.

Very spiritual. Mouth. Heart. Ears. Feet.

Mouth! Acknowledge and proclaim with your mouth that Jesus is Lord.

Heart! Trust in your innermost heart that Almighty God raised Jesus from the dead.

You will be saved. You will be justified. You will be made whole.

Ears! To hear the Good News, we need someone to proclaim the Good News, the Gospel.

"The word is nigh thee, even in thy mouth, and in thy heart: that is, the word of faith, which we preach: That if thou shalt confess with thy mouth the Lord Jesus, and shalt believe in thine heart that God hath raised him from the dead, thou shalt be saved (Romans 10, 8,9 KJV)."

Feet! The preacher must be sent. In his letter to the Romans, Paul refers to the passage in Isaiah about the beautiful feet of those who bear the Gospel, the Good News of salvation (Isaiah 52, 7).

"How then shall they call on him in whom they have not believed? and how shall they believe in him of whom they have not heard? and how shall they hear without a preacher? And how shall they preach, except they be sent? as it is written, How beautiful are the feet of them that preach the gospel of peace, and bring glad tidings of good things (Romans 10, 14,15 KJV)."

Then, there's our response. We believe the message preached to us. We trust in the living Word of the living God.

Lord Jesus, give me ears to hear your word to me today, a heart to trust and believe your word. Give me a cleansed heart and a sanctified mouth to proclaim your word. Give me strong and beautiful feet to run with your word. Alleluia!

Thursday, December 1, 2005
Isaiah 26, 1-6
The Divine Vindicator

Singing! Strength. Walls. Ramparts. Gates controlled by the Lord, who protects us in this city. Jerusalem, the Jerusalem that is to come.

Our trust is in the Lord. The Lord is our everlasting Rock.

"Those of steadfast mind you keep in peace – in peace because they trust in you. Trust in the LORD forever, for in the LORD GOD you have an everlasting rock (Isaiah 26, 3-4)."

It is up to the LORD to vindicate. The Lord knows how to bring about justice for those who have been trampled and downtrodden in this life. They will sing for joy!

Lord Jesus, thank you for giving us patience as we wait for you to bring about restoration. Alleluia!

Friday, December 2, 2005
Isaiah 29, 17-24
Redemption

Redemption. Transformation. Restoration.

In the midst of injustice and oppression, we may believe that this intolerable situation will continue forever. We may wonder if and when God will ever show up to bring justice and redemption.

The Lord is tenderly reassuring us that wonders will soon unfold. Cedars will become orchards! The orchards will be regarded as forests.

The deaf will hear the words of a book. The blind will no longer be in darkness. They will see!

Tyrants who dared to oppress others will be no more. Those who slandered others will be silenced. Liars will be removed from the scene.

When? In a very short while, according to God's timetable.

To us it may seem a long time, but it's not. Soon. Very soon.

Lord Jesus, as we trust you to bring restorative justice, let us live in humility as we acknowledge our continual need of your mercy and forgiveness. Help us freely to forgive all who have wronged us as you have forgiven us. When we forgive, we are living out of a new love and a new strength. Alleluia!

Saturday, December 3, 2005 St. Francis Xavier
Isaiah 30, 19-21, 23-26
Futile Alliance with Egypt; Zion's Future Prosperity

"Truly, O people in Zion, inhabitants of Jerusalem, you shall weep no more … (Isaiah 30, 19a)."

When we cry out, the Lord will answer and give us the sustenance we need. We will be surrounded by the Lord's loving provision.

The Lord will be right there to teach us. We will hear the Lord's words instructing us exactly where to go.

"And thine ears shall hear a word behind thee, saying, 'This is the way, walk ye in it, when ye turn to the right hand, and when ye turn to the left (Isaiah 30, 21 KJV)."

We will sow seeds for an abundant harvest. There will be fresh, grassy meadows where the moo cows may happily graze to their hearts' content.

Water will stream from the mountains. Those who were our enemies will never again trouble us.

The moon will be bright and the sun will be even brighter! The Lord will heal the wounds and the scars inflicted upon us.

Lord Jesus, thank you for hearing every cry of our heart. Thank you for the time when we will no longer weep. You are not hidden from us. We know you are with us and that you are guiding us every step of the way to the house of our Father. Alleluia!

Sunday, December 4, 2005 Second Sunday in Advent
Isaiah 40, 1-5,9-11
Promise of Salvation

Jerusalem's time of exile is over! A time of gladness is here.

"The voice of him that crieth in the wilderness, Prepare ye the way of the LORD, make straight in the desert a highway for our God (Isaiah 40, 3 KJV)." The Lord's glory will be manifested for all to see.

"O Zion that bringeth good tidings, get thee up into the high mountain: O Jerusalem, that bringeth good tidings, lift up thy voice with strength; lift it up, be not afraid; say unto the cities of Judah, Behold your God (Isaiah 40, 9 KJV)!"

Good news at last! Here is God, our powerful God, who rules with strength.

Here is God, our powerful God, who tenderly carries his lambs in his arms, feeds his flock, and carefully leads his ewes.

Lord Jesus, thank you for tenderly speaking words of comfort to us. You are our Lamb who has taken away our sins and removed our guilt. You are our Good Shepherd and you are continuing to lead us Home, filling in the valleys and leveling the hills. You are our King who will come in glory. Alleluia!

Monday, December 5, 2005
Isaiah 35, 1-10
Israel's Deliverance

Hope is alive and thriving in this passage in Isaiah. The journey on the highway of holiness will culminate in joy.

"The desert and the solitary place shall be glad ... and the desert shall rejoice, and blossom as the rose. It shall blossom abundantly and rejoice, even with joy and singing ... (Isaiah 35, 1-2a KJV)."

Our weak hands and knees will be strong. Our frightened hearts will become fearless.

"Say to those who are of a fearful heart, 'Be strong, do not fear! Here is your God ... He will come to save you... (Isaiah 35, 4)."

The closed eyes of the blind will be opened to new wonders. The impediments in the ears of the deaf will be removed and they will hear. The lame will leap and the silent will sing! In the wilderness, streams of water will spring forth.

We, the ransomed of the Lord, have returned. We are home at last!

Lord Jesus, thank you for ransoming us, vindicating us, and leading us Home. Alleluia!

Tuesday, December 6, 2005 St. Nicholas
Isaiah 40, 1-11
Promise of Salvation

Back to where we were on Sunday! With the inclusion of the sixth, seventh, and eighth verses, this is the same passage from Isaiah that we heard on Sunday.

The extra three verses are a good reminder of the temporary nature of human glory in comparison to the everlasting glory of our God. God's word is forever.

"The voice said, Cry. And he said, what shall I cry? All flesh is grass, and all the goodliness thereof is as the flower of the field: The grass withereth, the flower fadeth: because the spirit of the Lord bloweth upon it: surely the people is grass. The grass withereth, the flower fadeth, but the word of our God shall stand forever (Isaiah 40, 6-8 KJV)."

The complete passage (Isaiah 40, 1-11) is a good place in which to camp out in Advent. It's an even better place in which to live.

"Behold, the LORD GOD will come with strong hand, and his arm shall rule for him: behold, his reward is with him, and his work before him. He shall feed his flock like a shepherd: he shall gather the lambs with his arm, carry them in his bosom, and shall gently lead those that are with young (Isaiah 40, 10-11 KJV)."

Lord Jesus, thank you for carrying us in your arms through this Advent. Alleluia!

Wednesday, December 7, 2005 St. Ambrose
Isaiah 40, 25-31
Power of the Creator To Save his People

Up! In the liturgy of the Eucharist, we are called to lift up our hearts. We lift them to the Lord.

In this passage, we are told to lift up our eyes. We are invited to see God in a new way.

When we are discouraged, we are down. We look down. We feel down. We sound down.

Look up! Our great, all knowing God is in control. He is not tired and is certainly not exhausted.

God is here to infuse us with strength! As we continue to place our hope in the Lord, our strength is being renewed. We will be refreshed, renewed, and restored.

I recall the passage below which was proclaimed by the actor, Ian Charleson, who played the Olympic runner, Eric Liddell, in my favorite film, "Chariots of Fire."

"Hast thou not known? hast thou not heard, that the everlasting God, the LORD, the Creator of the ends of the earth, fainteth not, neither is weary? there is no searching of his understanding. He giveth power to the faint; and to them that have no might he increaseth strength. Even the youths shall faint and grow weary, and the young men shall utterly fall: But they that wait on the LORD shall renew their strength; they shall mount up with wings as eagles; they shall run, and not be weary; and they shall walk, and not faint (Isaiah 40, 31 KJV)."

Lord Jesus, thank you that we will walk again. We will run even faster than ever. With eagles' wings, we will soar to new heights in your service. Alleluia!

Thursday, December 8, 2005 The Immaculate Conception
Genesis 3, 9-15,20
The Fall of Man

OK, the blame battle is over. The war is on!

Enmity. The snake against the woman!

Eve! The mother of all who live.

Mary! The mother of those will live forever, because of her Son.

Lord Jesus, we thank you for gift of your mother Mary. Thank you for her example to us in living out our vocation. Alleluia!

Friday, December 9, 2005
Isaiah 48, 17-19
Exhortations to the Exiles

Individual direction. Individual guidance.

This is a very personal passage. God, your Redeemer, will instruct you personally about what is for your good. You will be led in the way in which you personally should go.

"I am the LORD, your Redeemer, the Holy One of Israel: I am the LORD your God, who teaches you for your own good, who leads you in the way you should go (Isaiah 35, 17)."

Heeding God's commands is crucial. Your prosperity will be as a flowing river. Your vindication, even sweeter, will be as the waves of the mighty sea.

Descendants? Yes! You will have descendants as numerous as grains of sand. Your descendants will be forever in God's presence.

Lord Jesus, help us when we feel overwhelmed with what we are called to do. Strengthen us to do exactly what you call us to do and help us to discern when we are doing too much or too little. Thank you for gently guiding us in the way that is best for us. Alleluia!

Saturday, December 10, 2005
Sirach 48, 1-4,9-11
Elijah and Elisha

When our son, Christopher, was about four, we were outside a coffee house sitting on a bench in the December sunshine. Guess who walked by? Santa Claus! After Santa had walked by, Christopher said quietly, "I, for one, do not believe in Mr. Ho Ho Ho."

Instead of Mr. Ho Ho Ho, we read today about Mr. Woe Woe Woe. At least, that's the way the prophet Elijah must have appeared to those who experienced God's power surging through him.

Elijah! Fiery. Ferocious in his zeal for the Lord. He spoke the word of God and the heavens closed. He spoke and fire fell.

It would not be wise to cross someone like Elijah. He is so close to God. So close. God even sent a chariot of fire to escort this prophet to heaven.

Even so, God's tenderness is also manifested through the ministry of Elijah. It was Elijah who was chosen to bring reconciliation between fathers and children. Elijah was to be the one through whom the tribes of Jacob are reestablished. Happy are those who see "Elijah" before they die.

Elijah is also our example in how to pray. "Elijah was a human being like us, yet he prayed fervently that it might not rain, and for three years and six months it did not rain on the earth. Then he prayed again, and the heaven gave rain and the earth yielded its harvest (James 5, 17-18)."

Lord Jesus, help us to remember Elijah when we grow weary in prayer. Alleluia!

Sunday, December 11, 2005 Third Sunday in Advent
Isaiah 61, 1-2,10,11
The Mission to the Afflicted

"Rose" Sunday! Gaudete!

"The Spirit of the LORD GOD is upon me; because the LORD hath anointed me to preach good tidings unto the meek; he hath sent me to bind up the brokenhearted, to proclaim liberty to the captives, and the opening of the prison to them that are bound; To proclaim the acceptable year of the LORD, and the day of vengeance of our God; to comfort all that mourn; To appoint unto them that mourn in Zion, to give them beauty for ashes, the oil of joy for mourning, the garment of praise for the spirit of heaviness; that they might be called trees of righteousness, that planting of the LORD, that he might be glorified (Isaiah 61, 1-3 KJV)."

Rejoice! We are anointed! The Holy Spirit is here to anoint us.

As with the prophets of old and as with Jesus, we are also anointed. We are anointed to carry glad news to the poor of our world. We are to heal those who are crushed in spirit. We are to fling open the prison doors and tell all to go free!

A year of God's favor is at hand! Vindication from our God is here.

Rejoice! We rejoice in the Lord! God is our joy. God's joy floods our souls.

God has vested us. We are clothed in a robe purchased for us by the Anointed One, the Lord Jesus.

Jesus purchased this pure white robe by shedding his Blood. This is our vestment of salvation. God has wrapped justice around us as a mantle.

Like a bride, we are beautifully arrayed for our bridegroom. Jesus is our Bridegroom!

"I will greatly rejoice in the LORD, my soul shall be joyful in my God; for he hath clothed me with garments of salvation, he hath covered me with the robe of righteousness, as a bridegroom decketh himself with ornaments and as a bride adorneth herself with her jewels (Isaiah 61, 10 KJV)."

Springtime! New plants are springing forth all over the earth.

God will cause praise as well as justice to spring up before all the world. "For as the earth bringeth forth her bud, and as the garden causeth the things that are sown in it to spring forth; so the LORD GOD will cause righteousness and praise to spring forth before all the nations (Isaiah 61, 11 KJV)." Rejoice!

> Monday, December 12, 2005 Our Lady of Guadalupe
> Zechariah 2, 14-17
> The New Jerusalem

Called to rejoice. Called to silence.

Rejoice! Jerusalem is called to rejoice. The Lord is again choosing Jerusalem. The Lord is coming to dwell in her midst.

"Be silent, all flesh, before the LORD … (Zechariah 2, 13 KJV)."

Silence! Jerusalem and the land called holy belong to the Lord. The Lord is coming.

Silence. Remember the beautiful hymn "Let All Mortal Flesh Keep Silence."

Lord Jesus, thank you for teaching us to rejoice and for drawing us into silence. Alleluia!

> Tuesday, December 13, 2005 St. Lucy
> Zephaniah 3, 1-2, 9-13
> Reproach and Promise for Jerusalem

Remnant. After pronouncing judgment on the wrongs committed by the inhabitants of Jerusalem, God refers to the remnant of Israel. Humility, not arrogance, is the chief characteristic of this remnant.

"For I will leave in the midst of you a people humble and lowly. They shall seek refuge in the name of the LORD – the remnant of Israel; they shall do no wrong and utter no lies, nor shall a deceitful tongue be found in their mouths. Then they will pasture and lie down, and no one shall make them afraid (Zephaniah 3, 12-13)."

What is a remnant? I enjoy going to my favorite fabric store to look for cloth remnants. They are small bits of fine fabric that have been discounted. They are colorful and beautiful! I like to take them and think of new uses for them. Sometimes, I arrange them on the old dining table inherited from my grandmother. They may not be large enough for tablecloths, but they are lovely as table runners.

Remnants are survivors. Remnants remain. Fabric remnants are cut and placed on the remnant table instead of being thrown away.

God's remnant is a group of people who have survived. God is the refuge of this remnant. This purified remnant will live again in a happier place.

God's humble and holy remnant is promised a new destiny. This holy remnant is truthful and righteous. This beloved remnant will enjoy new pastures for their flocks.

Lord Jesus, thank you for purifying us so that we may serve you in humility and one day live in a happier place. Alleluia!

Wednesday, December 14, 2005 St. John of the Cross
Isaiah 45, 6-8,18,21-25
Cyrus, Anointed of the Lord, Liberator of Israel

The Persian King, Cyrus, was God's instrument to liberate the Jews to return to their land and to rebuild Jerusalem and the Temple. He was very important, but God was behind it all!

God is the supreme designer as well as the sole creator. Light! Darkness! All from God.

"Shower, O heavens, from above, and let the skies rain down righteousness; let the earth open, that salvation may spring up, and let it cause righteousness to sprout up also; I the LORD have created it (Isaiah 45, 8)."

There is no other. God saves. God is just.

"Turn to me and be saved, all the ends of the earth! For I am God, and there is no other (Isaiah 45, 22)."

We are wise and we are safe when we turn to God, our Creator. God has designed a place in which we may live.

God has also designed the way in which we are to live, remembering that, to God, justice is of utmost importance. Justice will descend as dew from heaven, as rain gently falling on the earth. God's justice will spring forth and salvation from God will blossom.

Everyone one day will answer to God. Our vindication rests with God. Our vindication is in God. God is our glory!

"The sun shall no longer be your light by day, nor for brightness shall the moon give light to you by night; but the LORD will be your everlasting light, and your God will be your glory (Isaiah 60, 19)."

Lord Jesus, let us live and flourish in the place you have specifically designed for us. Thank you for your action in our lives and for all you use as your instruments in our lives. Let us be your instruments to bless others. Alleluia!

Thursday, December 15, 2005
Isaiah 54, 1-10
The New Zion

"Sing, O barren, thou that didst not bear; break forth into singing, and cry aloud, thou that didst not travail with child: for more are the children of the desolate than the children of the married wife, saith the Lord. Enlarge the place of thy tent, and let them stretch forth the curtains of thine habitations: spare not, lengthen thy cords, and strengthen thy stakes (Isaiah 54, 1-2 KJV)."

This Advent, let us emerge from the cramped, dark place of low expectations. After all, GOD is coming!

No more fear. No more discouragement. No more shame.

"For thy Maker is thine husband; the LORD of hosts is his name; and thy Redeemer the Holy One of Israel; The God of the whole earth shall he be called (Isaiah 54, 5 KJV)."

The Holy God of Israel, our Maker, Redeemer, Lover, Spouse, is here with us. We are bold to ask the Holy Spirit to enlarge our expectations and to breathe new life into our sorrowful, listless spirits. It's time to prepare for joy!

The past is gone. God is here in our midst. God is enlarging our space.

Lord Jesus, thank you for the Holy Spirit who is breathing new life into us as we joyfully wait for you. Alleluia!

Friday, December 16, 2005
Isaiah 56, 1-3,6-8
The Lord's House Open to All

Maintenance! Maintenance can be a bore. Same old thing over and over and over!

In today's first reading, the Lord is telling his people to maintain justice and to continue to do what is right. Keep on keeping on.

"Thus says the LORD: Maintain justice, and do what is right, for soon my salvation will come, and my deliverance be revealed (Isaiah 56, 1)."

The Hebrew root of the word for maintain or keep on is "shamar." This word expands to mean to hedge about with protection and to preserve.

This definition can help us when it gets to be a bore or a chore to keep on. We are called by the Lord to protect and to preserve justice.

Soon! Soon, in the Lord's sense of soon, the Lord will make sure his salvation comes.

Salvation will come. Deliverance is on the way.

We are told to keep on keeping the Sabbath holy. We are to refrain from doing evil.

There are no outcasts in the Lord's eyes. All are welcome to the house of the Lord.

"Do not let the foreigner joined to the LORD say, 'The LORD will surely separate me from his people … (Isaiah 56, 3a)."

Remember, Jesus said, "I have other sheep that do not belong to this fold. I must bring them also, and they will listen to my voice. So there will be one flock, one shepherd (John 10, 16)."

The foreigner who is intent on ministering to the Lord in loving service, keeping the Sabbath, and honoring the Lord's name will be brought to the house of the Lord and will know joy in this holy house. The foreigner's sacrifice to the Lord will be welcome on the altar of this house.

The Lord is the gathering One. The Lord is gathering his beloved into his arms.

Lord Jesus, thank you that as you hold us close to your heart, you are also holding us close to one another. You are healing us all and reconciling us as you enfold us in your arms of mercy and love. Alleluia!

JANIS WALKER　　　　　　　　　　　　　　　　　　　　FIRST READING

Saturday, December 17, 2005
Genesis 49, 2,8-19
Jacob's Testament

Listen! In today's first reading, the patriarch, Jacob, is summoning his sons for some final words. How carefully they must have listened to their dying father.

"Then Jacob called his sons, and said: 'Gather around, that I may tell you what will happen to you in the days to come. Assemble and hear, O sons of Jacob; listen to Israel your father (Genesis 49, 1-2).'"

Jacob begins to speak individually to each of his sons. He describes their individual personalities and has something to say about their individual futures.

God, our loving Father, is summoning us, his children, to listen to him this Advent. Our loving Father knows, better than we, our individual personalities and all our flaws and foibles. He also knows the glorious future he has in store for us.

Let us listen to our loving, heavenly Father, who cares tenderly for us. His Son, the Anointed One, is coming to us. Alleluia!

Sunday, December 18, 2005 Fourth Sunday in Advent
2 Samuel 7, 1-5,8-12,14,16
David's Concern for the Ark; The Lord's Promises

King David's respect for the Lord's ark was genuine. However, the Lord's will in this matter was spoken through the prophet, Nathan.

The Lord reminded the king of his beginning as a shepherd lad. From guarding the sheep, David was promoted by the Lord to leading the nation of Israel.

The Lord God had always been with David. God took care of vanquishing David's enemies and then promoting David.

The Lord promised a place for the people of Israel, free from the torment of the wicked. The Lord promised David that his own heir would have a secure kingdom and would be the one to build a house for the Lord.

The Lord would be a strict, yet loving Father, with David's heir. The Lord's promise was that David's house, throne, and kingdom would endure.

God our Father, help us to respect you and yield readily to your will for us and for our children. May your kingdom come and your will be done in us and through us and through our children. Alleluia!

Monday, December 19, 2005 Late Advent Weekday
Judges 13, 2-7,24-25
The Birth of Samson

A difficult vocation was already mapped out for Samson. From the time of his conception in his mother's womb, the Lord knew his plan for Samson. It would be through Samson that the Lord chose to begin to deliver his chosen people, Israel, from the power of the Philistines.

Samson's mother had a crucial role to play in her son's life. The Lord sent a special messenger, an angel, to come to her to tell her that she who had been barren would bear a son. She was to follow carefully the Lord's commands to abstain from alcohol and from unclean food.

Samson was born and grew up with the Lord's blessing upon him. In a particular place, Mahenah-ddan, which was between Zorah and Eshtaol, at a particular time, the spirit of the Lord moved within Samson.

This passage shows no hint of Samson's future. All we see is a chosen woman, previously barren, who is called to give birth to a consecrated servant of the Lord.

Hannah? Elizabeth? Mary? We know their stories. They became the mothers of Samuel, John the Baptist, and Jesus.

Today, we ponder the faith of the nameless woman who was the mother of Samson. All we can do today or any day is to be open to the mysterious moves of the Lord. We pray to respond in trusting obedience, leaving the outcome in the hands of the Lord. Through flawed and frail instruments, the Lord's will is eventually accomplished.

Lord Jesus, thank you that you know how to use us in spite of ourselves. Forgive us when we make selfish decisions that hamper our vocation and the vocation of others. Thank you for bringing wholeness to us and to those for whom we pray. Thank you for bringing your plan to completion. Alleluia!

Tuesday, December 20, 2005 Late Advent Weekday
Isaiah 7, 10-14
Birth of Immanuel

"Therefore the Lord himself will give you a sign; Behold, a virgin shall conceive, and bear a son, and shall call his name Immanuel (Isaiah 7, 14 KJV)." The name, "Immanuel" means that God is with us.

Almighty God is coming to be right here with us on earth. Immanuel!

This treasured promise comes layered within layer. The Lord had previously spoken to Isaiah with a message for King Ahaz of Judah. Now the Lord is speaking again.

Prophecy and promise. The Lord is dealing with his people, using the Assyrians as his instrument.

The Lord is promising future deliverance. There is a message within a message.

Mary! In the midst of history is the Virgin.

The pure Virgin Mary bears a child. Immanuel. God is now with us.

God was with us. God is with us. God will be with us. The Eternal One who was and is and is to come again. Alleluia!

Wednesday, December 21, 2005 St. Peter Canisius
Song of Songs 2, 8-14
A Tryst in the Spring

"The voice of my beloved! behold, he cometh leaping upon the mountains, skipping upon the hills ... (Solomon's Song 2, 8 KJV)."

Our Beloved is coming to us! He can't wait to be with us. He is leaping. He is waiting at our window. He is gazing with longing upon us.

He speaks to us and invites us to arise and to come away with him. "My beloved spake, and said unto me, Rise up, my love, my fair one, and come away (Solomon's Song 2, 10 KJV)."

Winter is over! Spring is bursting forth. The flowers are blooming and the birds are singing. Fresh figs! Blossoming vines! Fresh air filled with the fragrance of spring.

Come away with your Beloved. Put down the lists. Put aside the expectations. Walk away with your Beloved. He has come to be with you now. Alleluia!

Thursday, December 22, 2005 Late Advent Weekday
1 Samuel 1, 24-28
Samuel is Offered to the Lord

When I wrote thank you notes to the people who gave baby gifts to Christopher, I quoted these verses from today's first reading: "For this child I prayed; and the LORD hath given me my petition which I asked of him: Therefore also I have lent him the LORD; as long as he liveth he shall be lent to the LORD (1 Samuel 1, 27-29 KJV)."

The first part is easy. I prayed and the Lord granted my request. The second part is more challenging. This is the part about giving or dedicating the child to the Lord for the Lord's purposes to be fulfilled.

Even more challenging is to worship! After Hannah left little Samuel in the temple with Eli, the priest, she worshipped the Lord.

The Lord had intervened in a powerful way in her life and she was now honoring the Lord with her trust and her worship. The Lord rewarded Hannah for her dedication of her first born child. She, who had been barren and then had given her child to God, was given more children (1 Samuel 1, 21)

Lord Jesus, thank you for strengthening us to give ourselves and all who are dear to us into your loving hands for your purposes. Alleluia!

Friday, December 23, 2005 St. John of Kanty
Malachi 3, 1-4,23-24
The Messenger of the Covenant

When I was studying the Hebrew scriptures in the seminary, I asked my professor's advice about the subject matter of our term paper. He suggested writing a paper about the times when the prophets really take the priests to task. Whew!

You say you want the Lord to come? Well, the Lord is indeed coming. Meek and mild? A little child? Yes.

The Lord is also coming as fire, the fire of a refiner. Who does he go after first?

The priests! Those in visible ministry.

The Lord will come suddenly! He will come, in power and with great determination, to the temple to purify and to refine.

Judgment! The apostle Peter, chief among the apostles, reiterated that judgment begins with God's own household (1 Peter 4, 17a).

Elijah! The Lord will send the fiery prophet Elijah to prepare his way. Elijah will set relationships straight before the Lord comes. In Matthew's Gospel (Matthew 11, 14), Jesus said that John the Baptist was "Elijah."

Lord Jesus, thank you for purifying and refining us. Let us yield to your fire so that we may be pure, shining vessels for your service. Alleluia!

> Saturday, December 24, 2005 Late Advent Weekday
> 2 Samuel 7, 1-5,8-11,16
> David's Concern for the Ark

King David was comfortably settled in a place of rest. Nice home, No enemies. It was in his cedar palace that he turned his attention wholeheartedly to the Lord and to his relationship with the Lord.

David looked at himself, a former shepherd lad, and he looked to the Lord God. The Lord had blessed him and he was now living very well. David was wondering how he could honor the Lord.

It is in the place of rest that we need to turn, with all our hearts, to the Lord. When some people have prospered and are in a good place, a place of prosperity, a place of rest, they dismiss the Lord, perhaps with a tip or even with a generous offering. Then they think they can do whatever they want to do.

The Lord does not want our tips. The Lord wants our time.

The Lord wants our trust. The Lord wants our hearts and our wills. The Lord wants our lives.

The Lord wants US! Anything we could ever do for the Lord will flow from this relationship of ever-growing trust in the Lord our God.

Lord Jesus, I offer myself to you and trust you to use me for your purposes. Alleluia!

Sunday, December 25, 2005 The Nativity of the Lord, Year B
Isaiah 52, 7-10
Let Zion Rejoice

"How beautiful upon the mountains are the feet of him that bringeth good tidings, that publisheth peace; that bringeth good tidings of good, that publisheth salvation; that saith unto Zion, Thy God reigneth (Isaiah 52, 7 KJV)!"

Feet. Beautiful feet! The runner on the mountains is proclaiming tidings of joy, peace, and salvation.

The runner says to captive Zion that the King is here! The Lord has come to restore, to comfort, and to redeem.

All over the earth! The salvation offered by God will be manifested all over the earth. All will see.

Lord Jesus, thank you for strengthening our feet and making them beautiful for your purposes. Let us be runners proclaiming that YOU are our King. You are our King and you have come to us. You are here to redeem us and to restore us. Alleluia!

Monday, December 26, 2005 St. Stephen
Acts 6, 8-10; 7, 54-59
Accusation against Stephen

You can debate facts. You cannot debate spirit. You certainly cannot debate the Holy Spirit.

"Stephen, full of grace and power, did great wonders and signs among the people (Acts 6, 8)."

Stephen's power and grace, worked out in signs and wonders, were the result of God's Holy Spirit living within him. These manifestations of the Holy Spirit infuriated the religious leaders who opposed Stephen. They could not successfully come against this kind of power and this kind of wisdom.

When Stephen spoke the truth, his opponents in the council were infuriated. Truth always infuriates those with an agenda. It gets in their way.

Stephen was, of course, lied about. False witnesses were procured to bring false accusations against him. Does this sound familiar?

"And all who sat in the council looked intently at him, and they saw his face was like the face of an angel (Acts 6, 15),"

Flesh rages against spirit! Stephen was so full of the Holy Spirit that he saw God's glory.

Stephen saw Jesus. He saw into the heavens!

"But filled with the Holy Spirit, he gazed into heaven and saw the glory of God and Jesus standing at the right hand of God. 'Look,' he said, 'I see the heavens opened and the Son of Man standing at the right hand of God' (Acts 7, 55-56)!"

The religious council of murderers stoned his body to death. They could not kill his spirit. His untouched spirit was already safe with Jesus.

"While they were stoning Stephen, he prayed, 'Lord Jesus, receive my spirit.' Then he knelt down and cried out in a loud voice, 'Lord, do not hold this sin against them ... (Acts 7, 59-60).''

Lord Jesus, let us gaze upon you, live as you call us to live, and leave the results with you. Alleluia!

Tuesday, December 27, 2005 St. John
1 John 1, 1-4
The Word of Life

"In the beginning was the Word, and the Word was with God and the Word was God. He was in the beginning with God (John 1, 1-2)." This is from the beautiful prologue to the Gospel of John.

Jesus came to us and illustrated the Father! We knew a little about God and yet we didn't really know. We had not seen.

Do you have a favorite book from your childhood? Have you read this book over and over both in illustrated versions and in versions without illustrations? The illustrations, especially if by a talented artist, make a huge difference.

The apostles actually saw Jesus! They saw the incarnate God. They saw God in human form. They saw and they told us.

"We declare to you what was from the beginning, what we have heard, what we have seen with our eyes, what we have looked at and touched with our hands, concerning the word of life – this life was revealed, and we have seen it and testify to it, and declare to you the eternal life that was with the Father and was revealed to us – we declare to you what we have seen and heard ... (1 John 1, 1-3a)."

We see Jesus in action in many ways. Jesus wants our lives to illustrate his presence in us. Those who do not read the Bible or go to church or receive the sacraments may begin to see Jesus illustrated by the way we live today.

Lord Jesus, let our lives be an illustration of you and bring you glory. Alleluia!

Wednesday, December 28, 2005 The Holy Innocents
1 John 1, 5 - 2, 2
God is Light; Christ and His Commandments

"This then is the message which we have heard of him, and declare unto you, that God is light, and in him is no darkness at all. If we say that we have fellowship with him, and walk in darkness, we lie and do not the truth: But if we walk in the light, we have fellowship with one another, and the blood of Jesus Christ his Son cleanseth us from all sin. If we say that we have no sin, we deceive ourselves, and the truth is not in us. If we confess our sins, he is faithful and just to forgive us our sins, and to cleanse us from all unrighteousness (1 John 1, 5-9 KJV)."

Walk in the light. Live in the light!

Breathe in the fresh air of honesty. Honesty with myself. Honesty with God. Honesty with others. The Lord does not want or need our efforts of self-justification.

What is required is to acknowledge God's supreme holiness. If we acknowledge God's holiness, then we see more clearly that our own efforts to defend ourselves are futile.

We don't need to defend ourselves. We can't defend ourselves.

Provision has already been made for our sins. All we have to do is to be realistic enough to acknowledge the times we have sinned.

"Therefore confess your sins to one another, and pray for one another, so that you may be healed. The prayer of the righteous is powerful and effective (James 5, 16)."

Jesus is the expiation for all our sins. Jesus has atoned for our sins all by himself. Jesus put an end to our sins. He paid the fine, death, all by himself. That's what Jesus did on the Cross.

Jesus made it possible for us to be free! Free to continue living in the radiant, pure, fresh light of the living God.

Lord Jesus, thank you for being our intercessor before the Father when we sin. Thank you for the privilege of confessing our sins and receiving your forgiveness. Thank you for the sacrament of reconciliation and for the priest who assures us that we are forgiven. Thank you for being the Lamb of God, the perfect offering for our sins and for the sins of everyone in the whole world. Alleluia!

Thursday, December 29, 2005 St. Thomas Becket
1 John 2, 3-11
Christ and His Commandments; The New Commandment

Someone once said that God spells "love" as O.B.E.Y. This is belief spelled out in active obedience.

At the Last Supper, Jesus told his followers, "If you love me, you will keep my commandments (John 1, 15)."

Love is the litmus test. This is love that loves with pure intent.

This is love that illustrates our unity with the Lord. We are learning to live as Jesus lives and to love as Jesus loves.

When we get to know ourselves a little better, we are faced with very unlovable aspects of ourselves that somehow we previously overlooked.

Jesus did not overlook these aspects. He saw us, knew what we were really like, and loved us anyway.

Now it's our turn to go and do likewise. We are learning to love ourselves and to love others with same generous love bestowed upon us.

Lord Jesus, I am very uncomfortable with having to face these aspects of myself I would prefer to ignore or to forget. Thank you for being with me and helping me to face them. As I am honest with you and with myself, you are eager to help me to change and to learn to love as you love. Help me to trust you and to obey you. Alleluia!

Friday, December 30, 2005 The Holy Family of Jesus, Mary and Joseph
Sirach 3, 2-6,12-14

There are lovely promises in this passage for those who honor their parents. These promises flesh out the fifth of the great Ten Commandments. This is the commandment to honor your father and your mother (Exodus 20, 12).

Sometimes it is hard for those who had less than happy childhoods to honor their parents. It's important to realize that honoring one's parents does not necessarily imply agreement with the way they lived or the way they treated their children.

If one's parents are deceased, it is still possible to honor them. We may remember the good that they did or that they tried to do. We may speak of them with respect and with love. After all, they gave us life!

A minister once had the privilege and the responsibility of forgiving an elderly relative. This relative had mistreated the minister in childhood and it had taken many years for the minister to begin to be healed. God has blessed this ministry for reaching out in compassion and offering forgiveness.

As we grow older, we are more and more aware of the good things our parents did for us that we did not realize at the time. It is never too late to thank God for those who gave us the gift of life and who worked to provide for us.

Lord Jesus, forgive us when it is so hard to forgive those who were not able to give us the love and the care we needed. Help us to forgive them and know that our forgiveness can reach them even now. Alleluia!

Saturday, December 31, 2005 St. Sylvester
1 John 2, 18-21
Antichrists

In the last day of the year, we are reading about "the last hour." It is getting closer and closer to the time Jesus will return to earth as King.

What's all this about antichrists? How do we recognize those who are false?

We are assured in this reading that we have been anointed and that we know. In the depths of our spirits, we know the truth.

Come, Lord Jesus. Come in glory!

Sunday, January 1, 2006 Mary, the Mother of God
Numbers 6, 22-27
The Priestly Blessing

"The LORD bless thee, and keep thee:
The LORD make his face shine upon thee, and be gracious unto thee:
The LORD lift up his countenance upon thee and give thee peace (Numbers 6, 2-26 KJV)."

What a beautiful way to begin the New Year! This blessing from God, spoken by Aaron and all the priests, breathes happiness into us.

The Lord wants us to be happy and safe in his care. The Lord is looking upon us and smiling. The Lord is the source of our peace and our joy.

Lord Jesus, we open our hearts to you to receive all that you long to give us this year. Enlarge our understanding and let us truly believe in your goodness and in your love for us. Let us blossom and bear fruit for you. Alleluia!

Monday, January 2, 2006 St. Basil, St. Gregory
1 John 2, 22-28
Antichrists; Life from God's Anointing; Children of God

"Who is the liar but the one who denies that Jesus is the Christ? This is the antichrist, the one who denies the Father and the Son. No one who denies the Son has the Father; everyone who confesses the Son has the Father also (vv. 22-23)."

We are continually learning. The Holy Spirit living within us is our teacher. The Holy Spirit teaches us what is true and what is false.

"But you have been anointed by the Holy One, and all of you have knowledge. As for you, the anointing that you received from him abides in you, and so you do not need anyone to teach you. But as his anointing teaches you about all things, and is true and not a lie, just as it has taught you, abide in him. (vv. 20, 27)."

We who have been baptized in the name of the Father, the Son, and the Holy Spirit are informed by the Holy Spirit. Our Teacher lives within us and is there to speak to us and to teach us. We are learning to live as God's children.

All through our lives, the Holy Spirit will teach us. The Holy Spirit, a wise Teacher, uses many different teaching methods.

In one sense, we are already living in the promised eternal life (John 17, 3). We are learning to be more and more sensitive to the Holy Spirit's voice.

Lord Jesus, thank you for the ways and methods you use in teaching us. Let us trust you and grow in joy and confidence as we prepare to greet you as our King. Alleluia!

Tuesday, January 3, 2006
1 John 2, 29 - 3, 6
Children of God; Avoiding Sin

"See what love the Father has given us, that we should be called children of God; and that is what we are. The reason the world does not know us is that it did not know him. Beloved, we are God's children now; what we shall be has not yet been revealed. What we do know is this: when he is revealed, we will be like him, for we will see him as he is (1 John 3, 1-2)."

The fact that you are choosing to act in a righteous way is a sure sign that you are God's child! Of course, we all make mistakes, but we aim at acting in the right way.

If we feel out of place here, it's because we are! The world doesn't like us any more than it likes God.

Why? God challenges. God confronts. So do we, if we follow God.

We remind ourselves that we are already God's children. Now. Not some day, when we are good enough. Now. Right now.

Sin is defined as lawlessness. It is defiance of God in order to do our own thing.

Lord Jesus, you were without sin in order to take away our sins. Let us live consciously in you, abiding in you, and choosing your plan for us. Teach us to purify ourselves in order to honor you. Alleluia!

Wednesday, January 4, 2006 St. Elizabeth Ann Seton
1 John 3, 7-10
Avoiding Sin

The test is quite plain. The person who acts righteously is righteous. The one who practices sin is acting in accord with the devil and indeed belongs to the devil.

Jesus! Jesus, Son of God, arrived on the scene to destroy the devil's works.

This passage says that those who are begotten by God do not habitually sin. It is simply not in their nature to sin.

God's children do not wish to sin. The devil's children make it a practice to sin, to act in unrighteous, unloving ways.

Lord Jesus, help us to remember who we are. We are God's dear children. You are our Brother. Thank you for the Holy Spirit who teaches us how to live righteously. Thank you that we may run to you and ask for forgiveness. Thank you for forgiving us and restoring us. Alleluia!

Thursday, January 5, 2006 St. John Neumann
1 John 3, 11-21
Avoiding Sin; Confidence before God

"Little children, let us love, not in word or speech, but in truth and action. And by this we will know that we are from the truth and will reassure our hearts before him whenever our hearts condemn us; for God is greater than our hearts, and he knows everything (vv. 18-20)."

Loving others is more than mere tolerance. It is actively serving those in need. When we seek God first, we will be shown how to reach out to others.

We can't expect applause from this world. The world is not going to affirm us in our vocation of following God.

We don't belong to the world. We belong to God. We are, even now, living a new life, a different life.

Our confidence is in God, not in ourselves. We are reassured that God is greater than we are, greater than our strengths and greater than our weaknesses. God knows absolutely everything about us, loves us tenderly, and is in complete control.

Lord Jesus, thank you that we are free to live and free to love. Alleluia!

Friday, January 6, 2006 Blessed Andre Besette
1 John 5, 5-13
Faith is Victory over the World; Prayer for Sinners

It's all over. Jesus won. Jesus won the victory for you!

If you believe that Jesus is truly God's Son, you are also the victor. Victor over the whole wide world.

How can that be? There is a three-fold witness or testimony to Jesus. There is the Holy Spirit, the water of Jesus' baptism, and the blood Jesus shed on the Cross.

We trust in Jesus, the Son of God. We are in him and his glorious Easter victory is in us. We are victorious!

Lord Jesus, thank you that your Easter victory is ours! We are now free to live and to love, since we have been assured of eternal life. Alleluia!

Saturday, January 7, 2006 St. Raymond of Penafort
1 John 5, 14-21
Prayer for Sinners

Our eternal life is assured since we are in Jesus. We have been given discernment to know Jesus.

We know that we have or that we will have what we ask for in accord and agreement with his perfect plan. We would not want to ask for anything else or for anything less.

"And this is the boldness we have in him, that if we ask anything according to his will he hears us. And if we know that he hears us in whatever we ask, we know that we have obtained the requests made of him (vv. 14-15)."

We are commissioned to pray for someone whose sin is not deadly. Our prayers are powerful. We are protected by God. We are God's own children.

Lord Jesus, thank you for giving us discernment as we follow you and intercede for others. Alleluia!

Sunday, January 8, 2006 The Epiphany of the Lord
Isaiah 60, 1-6
Glory of the New Zion

"Arise, shine; for your light has come, and the glory of the LORD is risen upon you (Isaiah 60, 1 KJV)."

I read this passage with a new understanding this morning. Somehow, the words "you" and "your" jumped out. In the past, I had somehow only applied these words to others.

It was liberating to read the passage with new eyes and a new heart and to realize that the Lord was really speaking to me!

"I" was to rise in splendor. "My" light had come. God's glory was shining on "me."

This is part and parcel of the lifelong process of really and truly believing that God loves us. We know God loves others, but what about us?

Do we really believe God loves us? We squirm away somehow from the divine love we so desperately yearn for and so desperately need.

Many years ago, Agnes Sanford was speaking with an elderly retired missionary who had never been able to accept God's forgiveness for a mistake she had made in her youth. Agnes asked the missionary if she believed that Jesus Christ forgives sins. With great indignation, the older lady exclaimed, "Of course, I believe that Jesus Christ forgives sins. I've been preaching it to the heathen for fifty years!" With gentleness and compassion, Agnes was able to speak the words that, at long last, set the missionary free to accept God's great love and forgiveness for her personally.

Light! Shining splendor! Radiance! Riches! Glory! This Epiphany, let us joyfully accept them all. Let us talk and walk and live them all.

Lord Jesus, thank you shining in us and through us. Alleluia1

Monday, January 9, 2006 Baptism of the Lord
Isaiah 42, 1-4,6-7
The Servant of the Lord

"I the Lord have called thee in righteousness, and will hold thine hand, and will keep thee, and give thee for a covenant of the people, for a light ... (Isaiah 42, 6 KJV)."

The true servant of the Lord, secure in the Lord's love, does not crush or oppress others. The true servant of the Lord does not crush the reed which is bruised. The true servant of the Lord does not extinguish a flickering flame.

"Here is my servant whom I uphold, my chosen, in whom my soul delights; I have put my spirit upon him; he will bring forth justice to the nations ... a bruised reed he will not break, and a dimly burning wick he will not quench; he will faithfully bring forth justice (vv. 1-3)."

The true servant of the Lord seeks justice! The true servant of the Lord liberates the imprisoned, gives sight to the blind, and brings those who have lived in dark dungeons out into radiant light.

Lord Jesus, thank you for healing us and restoring us when we have been bruised reeds and barely flickering lights. Thank you for restoring us to new life and new strength. Thank you for working in us and through us to liberate others. Alleluia!

Tuesday, January 10, 2006
1 Samuel 1, 1-20
Elkanah and His Family at Shiloh; Hannah's Prayer;
Hannah Bears a Son

Hannah, a childless wife, had had it! She was fed up with Peninnah's taunts. She was fed up with her husband's lack of understanding.

Hannah left home. She went directly to the Lord in the temple at Shiloh.

Hannah acknowledged her anguish to the Lord. She prayed. She wept. She told God all that was in her aching heart.

She even made a promise to God. Hannah promised that if the Lord gave her a son, she would give him into the Lord's service for life.

Eli, the priest, observed her distraught actions, but was unable to read her heart. He misinterpreted her actions and misunderstood her. After Hannah told him of her misery, Eli asked God to grant her petition.

Hannah returned home a different woman! Having turned the situation over to the Lord, she resumed her normal life. She was no longer sorrowful.

Samuel, the longed-for and prayed-for baby was born! And that, as they say, is another story. Alleluia!

Wednesday, January 11, 2006
1 Samuel 3, 1-10,19-20
Revelation to Samuel; Samuel Acknowledged as Prophet

Full circle! Hannah, Samuel's mother, had ministered to the Lord in a profound way. In her radical trust and in her radiant worship, she had ministered to the Lord.

Now, her prayed-for son, Samuel, was also ministering to the Lord. Samuel had lived since childhood in the temple in Shiloh, under the tutelage of Eli, the priest.

I have come to believe that our most important ministry is that of worship. This means more than singing or raising our hands.

True worship means casting our entire being upon the Lord, trusting the Lord, and then serving as the Lord directs. The saints, the angels, and the whole company of heaven are praising and worshipping the Lord at this very moment.

The young Samuel slept in the temple at Shiloh. The ark of God was there in the temple. The sanctuary light burned within the temple. It was in the temple that Samuel learned to hear the voice of God.

Samuel continued to grow in the Lord's presence. The Lord was watching over him and preparing him for ministry.

It was the Lord who would ultimately validate Samuel as prophet. All of Israel would one day acknowledge that Samuel was a true prophet of the Lord.

Full circle. Worshipping. Waiting. Training. Growing. Worshipping. More waiting. More training. Growing. In God's time, there will be a manifestation of vocation.

Lord Jesus, help us to continue to worship, to wait, to trust, and to grow in wisdom. Thank you that, at the absolutely right time, your plan for us will be evident to all. Alleluia!

JANIS WALKER FIRST READING

> Thursday, January 12, 2006
> 1 Samuel 4, 1-11
> Defeat of the Israelites; Loss of the Ark

The Israelites asked WHY. They asked why they had been defeated in battle, but they didn't wait for God to answer.

Instead, they took the ark, representing the presence of God, and tried to use the ark to fulfill their own purpose, namely, winning the battle. It didn't work. They lost.

Even so, the Israelites' enemy, the Philistines, had been frightened. They knew the significance of the ark. They were frightened, but they still fought the Israelites and won. Israel lost and the ark was captured.

What in the world could this mean for us today? Are we trying to use the presence of God for the purpose of God?

We bear God's presence within us. "Know ye not that ye are the temple of God, and that the Spirit of God dwelleth in you (1 Corinthians 3, 16 KJV)?"

Lord Jesus, help us to be increasingly sensitive to your presence within us and among us. Let us learn to listen to you and learn to wait for you to speak before we act. Thank you for strengthening us to trust you and to wait for you. Alleluia!

> Friday, January 13, 2006 St. Hilary
> 1 Samuel 8, 4-7,10-22
> Request for a King; God Grants the Request;
> Persistent Demand

There is a book called <u>Splitting Heirs</u> which is about inheritance. It has to do with how parents decide how much to bequeath to each child.

I haven't read this book and certainly Samuel, the prophet, had not read this book. He had to make decisions not only about his sons' future, but also about the future of Israel.

Tragically, Samuel's sons did not follow their father's example. That was the main reason that Israel's elders were scrambling to try to provide for the future of their nation while Samuel was still alive.

They decided to be like the other nations and to have a king. That turned out to be a terrible mistake.

How often do we try to provide for ourselves in our own way? Maybe God has a much better way, a way which had never occurred to us. Perhaps we need to ask for God's way before charging in to try to implement what might seem the obvious way.

Lord Jesus, please forgive me when I have begged you to answer my prayers in a certain way in and in a certain time. Thank you that, even now, you can give to me what you tried to give to me before and I was too frightened to accept. Thank you for continuing to teach me to trust in you and in your love and wisdom. Alleluia!

Saturday, January 14, 2006
1 Samuel 9, 1-4,17-19; 10, 1
Persistent Demand; The Lost Asses;
Samuel's Revelation about Saul

Well, here comes the answer to the people's nagging request for a king. Saul!

Saul even looked the part. He was very handsome.

Saul's concern at the time was about how to find his father's lost donkeys. Apparently he had no clue that his meeting with the prophet Samuel was about anything other than finding these lost animals.

Surprise! God seems to like surprises. God had told Samuel that Saul would be the future leader of Israel.

Samuel stayed within the parameters of Saul's understanding. He reassured Saul that the lost animals had been found.

Then came the real reason for the meeting of Samuel and Saul It wasn't really about finding lost donkeys. It was about Saul's future.

Samuel poured olive oil over Saul's head and announced that the Lord had anointed Saul to rule Israel, the Lord's own people.

How often are we fixated on looking for what is lost when the Lord has found something new for us?

Lord Jesus, help us to raise our minds and hearts to your purpose for us and to be open to surprises. Alleluia!

Sunday, January 15, 2006 2nd Sunday in Ordinary Time
1 Samuel 3, 3-10,19
Revelation to Samuel; Saul Acknowledged as Prophet

Samuel was about as close to God as you could get. He was born in answer to his mother's fervent prayer. From before birth, she had dedicated him to the Lord and for the Lord's service. "For this child I prayed; and the LORD hath given me the petition which I asked of him (1 Samuel 1, 27 KJV)."

From early childhood, Samuel had literally lived in God's house, the temple at Shiloh. The priest, Eli, had raised Samuel.

Samuel even slept in the temple. Daily he had been near the sanctuary lamp and the ark of the covenant of the Lord.

Even so, Samuel had to learn for himself how to hear the voice of the Lord. He still had to learn how to distinguish God's voice from the voice of his mentor, Eli, the priest.

No matter how godly our ancestry or our spiritual formation, we still have to meet God on God's terms. We still have to learn to wait for God and to discern God's voice.

We still have to learn to distinguish God's voice from our own desires and from the voices and opinions of others. The Holy Spirit lives within us and is eager to teach us.

Lord Jesus, thank you for your patience in continuing to teach me how to listen to you and to discern your voice. Alleluia!

Monday, January 16, 2006
1 Samuel 15, 16-23
Saul is Reproved

Well, here it is! A perfect example of the old saying, "Be careful what you pray for because you may get it." The people of Israel had whined for a king and the Lord had given them a king.

Saul! Saul was their king. Now even the Lord regretted making Saul king (1 Samuel 15, 11). How sad.

The prophet Samuel went to confront Saul about Saul's disobedience and prevarication. This wasn't going to be pretty.

Samuel reminded Saul that the Lord had anointed him as king and had given him a specific assignment. Saul rationalized and schmoozed around, trying to justify his lack of complete obedience to the Lord's clear command. Saul even bragged about offering sacrifices to the Lord.

Samuel quickly responded that the Lord valued obedience over sacrifice. Furthermore, the Lord regarded rebellion as just as heinous a sin as the sin of divination. As for the sin of presumption, the Lord compared it to the sin of idolatry.

The final blow was yet to come. Because Saul rejected the Lord's commands, the Lord rejected Saul from being king.

Seeing the progression of Saul's sins, we cannot feel complacent. We begin to see how we have justified and rationalized our way out of the Lord's blessings. God blesses our obedience, not our clumsy attempts at sacrifices.

Lord Jesus, have mercy. Help us to begin afresh to trust you and to obey you. You long to bless us. You have blessings ready to pour upon us as we step out today in obedience. Alleluia!

Tuesday, January 17, 2006 St. Anthony
1 Samuel 16, 1-13
Samuel Sent to Bethlehem

How long? We sometimes ask the Lord, "How long?"

The Lord also asks the same question of us. "How long?"

He asked Samuel how long he would continue to grieve over Saul. It was clear that the Lord had had it with Saul.

"The LORD said to Samuel, 'How long will you grieve over Saul? I have rejected him from being king over Israel. Fill your horn with oil and set out; I will send you to Jesse the Bethlehemite, for I have provided for myself a king among his sons (1 Samuel 16, 1)."

The Lord had rejected Saul from continuing as king. Now it was time for Samuel to continue his own ministry and to anoint another to be king.

The Lord also tells us, as he did Samuel to fill our horns with oil and get going. There is work for us to do.

When Samuel anointed God's chosen servant, David, with the anointing oil, the Holy Spirit came powerfully over the young shepherd lad. David, the youngest son, who seemed insignificant, would become the king from whose line sprang the Messiah.

Lord Jesus, you love to surprise us! Help us to be open to how you select your servants. Alleluia!

Wednesday, January 18, 2006
1 Samuel 17, 32-33,37,40-51
David Fights Goliath; Preparation for the Encounter; David's Victory

Before! Before the victory, there was the readiness on David's part to fight the giant from Philistine.

Before the victory, David also had to deal with Saul's doubt, negativity, and lack of support. To the young shepherd David's confident, "I can," there was the opinion of King Saul's, "You can't."

David reminded himself and Saul that the Lord, who had kept him safe from both bear and lion, was able to protect him from the big Philistine guy, Goliath. Saul then told David to proceed.

David still had to deal with Saul's attempts to stage the event. David could not fight his battle in Saul's armor (vv. 38,39).

David had to fight in his own way. What was his way? Into the bag that was part of his shepherd's equipment, David placed five stones from the stream.

To Goliath's sacrilegious taunts and curses, David spoke aloud his faith in God. "Then said David to the Philistine, Thou comest to me with a sword, and with a shield: but I come to thee in the name of the LORD of hosts, the God of the armies of Israel, whom thou hast defied (1 Samuel 17, 45 KJV)."

With his stones and his sling, David slew the giant. The real power came from David's firm trust in the power of God.

Our weapons have to be the ones we have personally experienced to be powerful. We fight our giants with our own trust in the Lord. The battle itself is the Lord's.

Lord Jesus, strengthen us to face and to defeat the giants who disdain us. You are our Lord and you are winning the victory for us. Alleluia!

> Thursday, January 19, 2006
> 1 Samuel 18, 6-8; 19, 1-7
> Saul's Jealousy; Persecution of David

Fair? It's just not fair!

Here David goes and risks his life to slay Goliath. Then he faithfully carries out King's Saul's military assignments.

Does Saul thank him? No!

Saul's becomes insanely jealous and plans to kill David. It didn't settle well with Saul that the women sang and danced David's praises. Saul got really bent out of shape about that.

Enter Jonathan, Saul's son, who happens to be a good friend of David. Jonathan tries to calm his dad down.

Jonathan reminds Saul that David has loyally served his king and his country. Saul cooled down and David was safe, for the present.

David's fate, as is our fate, may seem to be in the hands of those who do not wish us well. They may make decisions that are unfair.

God may allow this for a time and a season, but it is ultimately God who guides us in the direction in which we are to go. It is God who decides where we are to live and how we are to minister.

Lord Jesus, we place all our trust in you. In spite of others and in spite of ourselves, you will lead us to the place of ministry you have chosen for us. Alleluia!

> Friday, January 20, 2006
> Sts Fabian and Sebastian
> 1 Samuel 24, 3-21
> David Spares Saul; Saul's Remorse

David's great trust in the Lord was manifested in a dramatic way. Here was King Saul, vulnerable and within reach!

David could have easily killed the crazy king who was out to get him. Even David's advisors said to do so.

NO! David listened to the Lord, instead of to his advisors.

His advisors offered only temporary wisdom. The Lord's wisdom was eternal.

No matter how vicious Saul was, he was still occupying the office of king. In that sense, he was the Lord's anointed.

David would bide his time. The Lord would decide the matter.

The Lord's greatness and the Lord's gentleness were at work in a powerful way in David. David, the shepherd who would become king, respected the Lord too much to try to take matters into his own hand.

Lord Jesus, help us to honor and to respect you and your servants. You are in charge of them and you are in charge of us. No one can thwart your plan for us. Alleluia!

Saturday, January 21, 2006 St. Agnes
2 Samuel 1, 1-4,11-12,19,23-27
Report of Saul's Death; Elegy for Saul and Jonathan

Purity of heart. The purity of David's heart was again manifested.

When David learned of the deaths of King Saul and Saul's son, Jonathan, he mourned deeply. He wept. He fasted.

David chanted a beautiful elegy for Saul and Jonathan. There was no sign of rejoicing or gloating.

Only the pure in heart can respond as David responded. His love for Saul, who had been out to kill him, triumphed over the injustices he had suffered at Saul's hand.

Lord Jesus, forgive us, heal us, and purify our hearts. Let us honor all who serve you and leave all matters of judgment in your wise hands. Alleluia!

Sunday, January 22, 2006 Third Sunday in Ordinary Time
Jonah 3, 1-5,10
Conversion of Ninevah

Efficient! God is very efficient.

Nothing is ever wasted. God has a way of making everything turn out in the best way.

After his initial resistance, Jonah finally yielded to God's direction to go to the wicked city of Nineveh and to proclaim God's displeasure. Lo and behold, he had only traveled a third of the way through the large city when the inhabitants believed God's message, delivered by Jonah.

They fasted and wore sackcloth. God, seeing that they were serious about changing their ways, mercifully spared the city.

Sometime it really is scary to be used, knowingly or unknowing, to deliver a message from God. Confrontation is hard.

If God is truly telling us to do this, we simply obey and leave the outcome with God. It is so much easier for us when we finally learn that we only have to do our part.

Once, when I was all in a stew about another person's behavior, I sought advice from my wise friend, Bee. Bee told me, in no uncertain terms, "You are taking inappropriate responsibility." This was a relief for me to hear. I could back off and learn some more about trusting the Lord to solve the dilemma.

Lord Jesus, help me not to take inappropriate responsibility for others. Help me to focus on loving you by obeying you. Alleluia!

Monday, January 23, 2006
2 Samuel 5, 1-7,10
David King of Israel; Capture of Zion

At last! The day has come. The shepherd lad who had faithfully kept watch over the flocks on the hillside was now the king!

David was now the shepherd of the Lord's people, Israel. He was both king and commander.

David, as a shepherd, had already been anointed by the prophet, Samuel (1 Samuel 16, 13), but it had not yet been the proper time for him to rule Israel.

Now, however, it was the proper time! David, at the age of thirty, was publicly and officially anointed king.

When David was anointed by Samuel, the Holy Spirit had come upon David in a powerful way. Now, as king, David became even more powerful, because the Lord, who had called him to this position, continued to be with him.

Sometimes between the anointing and the manifestation of all the implications of the anointing, it is easy to become weary of waiting and weary of wondering. Will God's promise ever come to pass? Whatever God has truly promised will come to pass. In the "between" time, there is testing, trying, and training for all that lies ahead.

Lord Jesus, thank you for strengthening us to be patient and to wait for the full unfolding of your plan for us. Alleluia!

Tuesday, January 24, 2006 St. Francis de Sales
2 Samuel 6, 12-15,17-19
The Ark Brought Back to Jerusalem

Respect. Reverence.

Joy and dancing! Leaping and singing! David was bringing the ark back to Jerusalem. It was a time for celebration.

David danced before the Lord with joyful abandon. He was freely expressing his love and joy, caring not what others might think.

David gave peace offerings to the Lord and then turned to the people. To the people, he gave a blessing in the name of the Lord and then gave presents of bread, meat, and even raisin cakes. Each person in Israel was given these delightful gifts.

David had it right. Show reverence for God. Express joy in worship. Bless others. Give.

Lord Jesus, thank you for teaching us to love you, rejoice in you, and even to dance before you. Alleluia!

Wednesday, January 25, 2006 Conversion of Paul
Acts 22, 3-16
Paul's Defense before the Jerusalem Jews

The sun is a great light. Paul, however, at noon, saw an even greater light!

Paul saw Jesus Christ, the risen Lord. Jesus, the Light of the world, was shining upon Paul!

Jesus is here shining upon us today. It may be noon. It may be midnight.

Jesus is here! Jesus is shining! The light of Christ is greater than the light of our noon. The light of Christ is greater than the darkness of our midnight. The light of Christ is here to show us the Way. Alleluia!

Thursday, January 26, 2006 Sts. Timothy and Titus
Titus 1, 1-5
Greeting; Titus in Crete

Paul demonstrated in these few verses, his understanding of who he was and what his mission involved. This is a tight, compact mini-manual!

Paul referred to himself first of all as a servant of God. Then he referred to himself as an apostle of Jesus Christ.

Yes, he believed he was a servant of God before encountering the risen Christ on the road to Damascus. However, his ideas of serving God were terribly wrong. He was inflicting great harm on God's little ones.

The experience on the Damascus road changed all that. Paul was now in a place to know Jesus for himself and to know how Jesus wanted to be served.

Paul's mission was for the sake of others. He was chosen to minister to God's chosen ones, to help them to grasp the truth of eternal life. He was chosen to articulate the hope of eternal life.

It is possible to have a clinically correct faith, but to lack a vibrant and living hope. Paul, who had seen the risen Christ for himself, was now authoritatively telling others of the magnificent plan of the God who was indeed worthy of all trust.

He took seriously his responsibility of the promulgation of the faith. With care and concern, Paul instructed Titus about the way the church was to live.

Again, we see that so much of ministry must be based on knowing our true identity. If we know who we are, God's beloved children, we are ready to be entrusted with the specific assignment God has for each of us.

Lord Jesus, I am still so insecure. Help me to understand, on a deeper level, that God the Father really loves me, that you, my big Brother, are watching out for me, and that the Holy Spirit really can do something with my life. Alleluia!

Friday, January 27, 2006 St. Angela Merici
2 Samuel 11, 1-4,5-10,13-17
David's Sin

This passage goes from bad to worse. Sins, knowingly and deliberately committed. Tragedies. Death of an innocent.

David! David, God's chosen.

David, the shepherd lad who became the king of Israel. One's heart sinks and breaks.

David apparently had developed an attitude of invincibility. He did not seem to realize that God would hold him accountable for adultery and murder.

David had stayed back in Jerusalem at a time while other kings were engaged in military campaigns. He slept, he saw, he lusted, he took another's wife, he attempted to corrupt her husband, and, failing that, he made sure that Uriah, her righteous husband, was killed in battle.

Somewhere along the way, David had lost his single-hearted devotion to the Lord. Somewhere along the way, he started to choose self over God.

We do the same thing every day. Maybe not in such dramatic or obvious ways as David.

We have moment to moment choices. God? Self?

Simple, yes. Easy, no.

The Rev. Eric Milner-White, an Anglican, prayed, "Lord, reveal me to myself in the light of your holiness." This may seem frightening, but it is essential. We have to know ourselves as we really are.

Lord Jesus, thank you for the light of the Holy Spirit revealing us to ourselves as we truly are. Thank you for your readiness to forgive us and for the sacrament of reconciliation in which we are set free to continue to live and to serve you. Alleluia!

Saturday, January 28, 2006 St. Thomas Aquinas
2 Samuel 12, 1-7, 10-17
Nathan's Parable; David's Punishment; David's Repentance

As God's heart broke, so David's life was about to break. God was so displeased with David that he sent the prophet Nathan to confront David about his sin. Nathan told David a parable about a man who had behaved with avarice and cruelty.

After David had become righteously indignant over the unjust behavior of the man in the parable, Nathan turned to David and announced, " 'You are the man! Thus says the Lord, the God of Israel: I anointed you king over Israel, and I rescued you from the hand of Saul ... Why have you despised the word of the LORD to do what is evil in his sight (2 Samuel 12, 7, 9a).' "

God said that since David had despised God's commandment, "the sword" would never leave his house. God would bring about misfortune for David from within his own household.

Strife and tragedy would follow David for the rest of his life. The innocent child, conceived as a result of David's lust, would die.

Yes, David repented. However, the consequences of his sin were still there for the rest of his life.

Lord Jesus, how can we be smug and think we would never defy you or despise you? Help us to love you so much that we would never want to grieve you in any way. Keep our conscience pure and let us think, speak, and act, knowing that you are holding us accountable. Alleluia!

Sunday, January 29, 2006 Fourth Sunday in Ordinary Time
Deuteronomy 18, 15-20
Prophets

Moses told the people that God would raise up another prophet who would speak God's words to them. This was in accordance with the people's wishes that God not speak directly to them. They were afraid of the voice of God and of the fire of God.

Jesus is the Word made flesh. We are still sometimes afraid to hear his voice. Sometimes we still prefer to hear God speak through others.

How much do we lose? How much do we forfeit? What would happen if we opened ourselves to hear the voice of God?

Lord Jesus, thank you for all the ways you speak to us. Let us be silent and learn more and more each day how to listen to you, how to recognize your message spoken through others, and then to obey you. Alleluia!

Monday, January 30, 2006
2 Samuel 15, 13-14,30; 16, 5-13
David Flees Jerusalem; David and the Priests; David and Shimei

Tragedy. Shame. Death. Insults. Cursing. Dirt. Stones. This is not a very pretty reading.

David was reaping the results of his sins. Yes, God had mercifully forgiven him.

Still, since David had scorned the commandment of God, the consequences would continue. There would continue to be strife and tragedy in David's household.

Family tragedies and curses pursued David. He had to flee from his own son, Absalom. He covered his head, walked barefoot, and wept. He accepted the vile curses and accusations from Shimei, a disgruntled member of the clan of the former king, Saul.

David even thought that perhaps God has sent Shimei to deliver these curses. As David traveled, Shimei traveled nearby, throwing stones and dirt as he cursed his own king.

God's words to David were being fulfilled." Wherefore hast thou despised the commandment of the Lord, to do evil in his sight? thou hast killed Uriah the Hittite with the sword, and hast taken his wife to be thy wife, and has slain him with the sword of the children of Ammon. Now therefore the sword shall never depart from thine own house; because thou hast despised me, and hast taken the wife of Uriah the Hittite to be thy wife. Thus saith the Lord, Behold I will raise up evil against thee out of thine own house and I will take thy wives and give them unto thy neighbor, and he shall lie with thy wives in the sight of this sun. For thou didst it secretly: but I will do this thing before all Israel, and before the sun (2 Samuel 12, 9-12 KJV)."

Because David had despised the commandment of the Lord, "the sword" was falling and would continue to fall within David's own house. Uriah, the husband of Bathsheba, had been killed by the sword at David's command. The consequences of David's deliberate sins were being played out in all their shame.

Lord Jesus, thank you for the Holy Spirit who teaches us how to live a pure and holy life. Thank you that the Holy Spirit will confront us and convict us when we grow careless and begin to rationalize our thoughts, our words, and our deeds. Let us never trivialize your holiness and think we can get away with sin. Let us run to you, confess our sins, receive your forgiveness, and continue to follow you. You do not give up on us even when we sometimes give up on ourselves. Alleluia!

Tuesday, January 31, 2006
2 Samuel 18, 9-10,14,24-25,30 - 19, 3
Death of Absalom; David Told of Absalom's Death; Joab Reproves David

It's too much. It's too hard to read.

David's pain continued and seemed too much to bear. When would it all stop?

King David's son, Absalom, who had been pursuing him, was caught in the branches of a terebinth tree. Joab, who had been charged by David to protect Absalom (2 Samuel 18, 12) was the very one who brutally murdered him.

David, loving father that he was, wept and mourned. "O my son Absolom, my son, my son Absolom! would God I had died for thee, O Absolom, my son, my son (2 Samuel 18, 33b KJV)!"

Wednesday, February 1, 2006
2 Samuel 24, 2,9-17
Census of the People; The Pestilence

This is one of those passages which seems difficult to reconcile with the character of God. Why would God tell David to do something, and then get upset when David did it?

The key seems to lie in the first verse of this chapter. It seems the Lord was really angry with Israel and used David to chastise the people.

After the census, which required more than nine months to complete, David decided that he had made a mistake. He told God that he had sinned. Through a prophet, God told David of various consequences.

Mercy! What I am going to try to remember from this difficult passage is that David threw himself on the mercy of God. God then halted the destruction of the Israelites.

David, to his credit, held himself accountable, David, the shepherd, was willing to suffer in place of the sheep.

Lord Jesus, thank you for your mercy when I don't understand what I am to do. Thank you for helping me to trust you and to obey you as well as I know how. Alleluia!

Thursday, February 2, 2006 Presentation of the Lord
Malachi 3, 1-4
The Messenger of the Covenant

"Behold, I will send my messenger, and he shall prepare the way before me: and the LORD, whom ye seek, shall suddenly come to his temple ... (Malachi 3, 1 KJV)."

The messenger preparing the way of the Lord will first prepare and purify the descendants of Levi, the priests. They would be refined, like silver. They would be refined like gold.

Why? So that the priests would offer sacrifices which would be pleasing to the Lord, who will come suddenly to the temple.

Lord Jesus, let us yield to the Holy Spirit's refining fire in our lives in order to serve you as you deserve as we continue our pilgrimage to the house of our Father. Alleluia!

Friday, February 3, 2006 St. Blaise, St. Ansgar
Sirach 47, 2-11
Nathan, David, and Solomon

At last! After the angst of reading of David's victories, sins, and suffering, we see his life in perspective.

Here is David, the young giant-slayer. Here is David who knew how to call upon the Lord.

Here is David whose praises were sung. Here is David who takes on the Philistines.

Here is David who was chosen to be king. Here is David whose sins the Lord forgives.

David. "In all that he did he gave thanks to the Holy One, the Most High, proclaiming his glory; he sang praises with all his heart, and he loved his Maker. He placed singers before the altar, to make sweet melody with their voices (Sirach 47, 8-9)."

David. David was "...the man who was raised up on high, the anointed of the God of Jacob, and the sweet psalmist of Israel ... (2 Samuel 23, 1b KJV)."

Lord Jesus, thank you that one day we will see our life in your perspective. Thank you for teaching us how to love you and to trust you to lead us all the way Home. Alleluia!

Saturday, February 4, 2006
1 Kings 3, 4-13
Wisdom of Solomon

The Lord was pleased with young King Solomon, David's son. Solomon humbly acknowledged his need for understanding. He asked the Lord for understanding and discernment in leading the people of Israel.

The Lord was so delighted with this request for wisdom, that he granted the request. In addition, the Lord lavished upon King Solomon all that the young ruler had not requested. Riches! Glory! Long life was promised if the king adhered in obedience to the Lord

The Lord is always touched when we acknowledge of our need of wisdom. Knowledge may come from books, but the Lord's greater gift is the gift of wisdom.

Lord Jesus, thank you for the Holy Spirit who delights in giving us the wisdom and the insight we need in order to serve you. Alleluia!

Sunday, February 5, 2006 Fifth Sunday in Ordinary Time
Job 7, 1-4,6-7
Job's First Reply

Oh, dear! Poor Job. Here he is, pouring out his heart.

In graphic terms, Job is describing how he feels. His trials have been so overwhelming that he doubts he will ever again experience happiness.

Although Job is replying to his so-called friend, Eliphaz, it is God who is his real audience. It is God whose response matters.

As it finally transpired (Job 42, 7), God was angry, really angry, with Eliphaz and his friends, for how they misrepresented him to Job. They spouted self-righteous, preachy responses to Job's agony.

So with us. Sometimes, we pour out our hearts to those who either tell us that we "shouldn't" feel the way we feel. Or, we may unburden ourselves to others who put us down.

Either way, God is our true audience. It is God to whom we ultimately appeal.

When others pour out their hearts to us, let us listen with gentleness. We don't have to preach or to solve their problems. Let us listen with our hearts as well as our ears and then speak words that will strengthen and heal. Only God can bring the healing we need and the healing they need.

Lord Jesus, sometimes we have to experience being disappointed in our friends so that we learn that YOU are our best Friend. Help us to run first of all to you with all our concerns, big or little. You care about everything and everyone that concerns us. You are there when our heart is pierced and breaking. You alone have the answer. You know exactly how to help us. You alone are the Answer. Alleluia!

Monday, February 6, 2006 St. Paul Miki and Companions
1 Kings 8, 1-7,9-13
Dedication of the Temple

King David's desire to build God a temple (2 Samuel 7, 1-13) was now being fulfilled in the reign of his son, King Solomon. The priests carried the ark and the vessels to the beautiful new temple.

Glory! Splendor! God's radiant presence filled the temple! The priests were, for the time, unable to minister.

"And when the priests came out of the holy place, a cloud filled the house of the LORD, so that the priests could not stand to minister because of the cloud; for the glory of the LORD filled the house of the LORD (vv. 10-11)."

God was there! God was truly there in the temple.

God is truly here with us now! We are God's temple and God's Holy Spirit dwells in us (1 Corinthians 3, 16). God will not allow us to be destroyed. Alleluia!

Tuesday, February 7, 2006
1 Kings 8, 22-23,27-30
Solomon's Prayer

Standing before the altar of the beautiful new temple, in the presence of the Lord and of all of Israel, King Solomon prayed. His hands were lifted to heaven and his heart was bursting with gratitude to the Lord.

Although King Solomon knew that the Lord of all creation could not be confined to an earthly building, still this was the Temple in Jerusalem! This was the place where the presence of the Lord was manifested in a glorious way. Solomon yearned for the Lord to be honored and glorified in this place.

In this place! In the place where you dwell in my heart, O Lord Jesus, be honored and glorified today. Forgive the past and guide me this day to do your will with joy. Open wide the doors to the new Jerusalem, the heavenly Jerusalem, where I will see you face to face and dwell with you forever. Amen. Alleluia!

Wednesday, February 8, 2006 St. Jerome Emiliani,
St. Joseph Bekhita
1 Kings 10, 1-10
Visit of the Queen of Sheba

Sheba was in the region we now think of as Yemen. A hot spot in recent news!

The Queen decided to go and find out for herself about this famous King Solomon. She was apparently very skilled in asking hard, probing questions.

Observing Solomon's awesome wisdom and the beauty of his palace took her breath away! Her admiration of Solomon was transformed into praise of the Lord.

It was the Lord who had done all this for Solomon. Before returning home, she offered gifts of gold, jewels, and spices to the king.

Lord Jesus, please show me how to honor those through whom I see you working. Show me how to thank them and to acknowledge your presence in their lives. Alleluia!

Thursday, February 9, 2006
1 Kings 11, 4-13
The Sins of Solomon

From wisdom and wealth, Solomon then chose stupidity and spiritual bankruptcy. How? Why?

Simple. Disobedience!

The Lord had told the Israelites not to marry women from certain other nations. Solomon disregarded the Lord's command and did so anyway.

"Therefore the LORD said to Solomon, 'Since this has been your mind and you have not kept my covenant and my statutes that I have commanded you, I will surely tear the kingdom from you and give it to your servant (1 Kings 11, 11)."

The Lord knew that this practice would lead Israel into the worship of idols. That's just what happened. The women that Solomon married turned him from the worship of the one true God to the worship of idols.

We do the same thing when we choose to disobey the Lord. We are choosing our own way, which we think will satisfy us, over our relationship with the Lord who alone can satisfy our deepest longings.

Lord Jesus, have mercy upon us and forgive us. Thank you for strengthening us and giving us the grace continually to say yes to you and to your will. Help us to trust you and to know that your plan for us is what will bring us true joy. Alleluia!

Friday, February 10, 2006   St. Scholastica
1 Kings 11, 29-32; 12, 19
The Sins of Solomon

Tragedy after tragedy. Solomon's servant, Jeroboam, would be given Solomon's kingdom.

The prophet, Ahijah, dramatically illustrated what the future would hold. Ahijah removed his new cloak and tore it into twelve pieces.

There would be a tearing of the kingdom. Ten of the tribes would go to Jeroboam, who would be King of Israel.

For the sake of his beloved David and for the sake of Jerusalem, the Lord would allow David's son, Solomon, to keep one tribe. The consequences of King Solomon's disobedience to the Lord would have repercussions for the entire nation.

Whatever is done by one affects many. This is true of all of us.

In the Church, the body of Christ, we are meant to love and to serve one another. What we do and how we live matters to all.

Lord Jesus, thank you that we may repent, turn to you, and receive forgiveness. Lord, have mercy. Christ, have mercy. Lord, have mercy.

Saturday, February 11, 2006 Our Lady of Lourdes
1 Kings 12, 26-32; 13, 33-34
Religious Rebellion

King Jeroboam had been King Solomon's servant. He rebelled against his king and then continued in rebellion. He was afraid that the kingdom would go back to David's line, to King Solomon's son, King Rehoboam of Judah.

King Jeroboam rebelled against the Lord and the Lord's ways. Knowing that true worship of the Lord in Jerusalem would turn the people against him, he gave gold calves to the people and told them that these idols were to be worshipped.

Instead of followings the Lord's commands for the ordination of priests, the king consecrated on his own terms. Invalid ordinations, to say the least!

Defiance of the Lord always leads to division and leads many people astray. This kind of rebellion and defiance of the Lord results in spiritual leaders who were never appointed or approved by God.

Lord Jesus, we pray for ourselves and for our Church that we submit to your will. The Church belongs to you. You are the Head. Let us honor you by our trust and our obedience. Let us honor those in authority and trust you to bring about your perfect plan. Alleluia!

Sunday, February 12, 2006 Sixth Sunday in Ordinary Time
Leviticus 13, 1-2,44-46
Leprosy

Back then, people with skin problems did not head for the dermatologist. They headed for the priest.

If they really did have leprosy, the priest would say so. Then they would have to wear torn clothes and live apart from the community. They were required to call out and notify others of their condition.

They experienced terrible isolation. They were considered unclean and unfit.

Lord Jesus, thank you for cleansing us of all our sin and declaring us clean. Thank you for the sacrament of reconciliation in which we may experience the freedom of forgiveness and new life. Alleluia!

Monday, February 13, 2006
James 1, 1-11
Perseverance in Trial

St. James instructs us to "count it all joy" when our faith is tested (James 1, 1 KJV)." Joy!?

Joy, according to C.S. Lewis, is the "serious business" of heaven. Today's first reading gives us new insights into joy.

One way to prepare for joy is to learn to greet trials in a new way. Rather than dreading or fearing trials, James tells us actually to welcome them.

Even encountering trials may trigger joy. How on earth is that possible?

We are learning to see beyond what our senses tell us. We are learning to look ahead. We know where it all leads. It leads to a new level in our walk with God. It leads to endurance.

As our faith is tested and purified, we are stretched in the living out of our trust in God. We are learning to practice what we profess.

As we ask for wisdom, we give thanks that God is delighted with our trust. A good parent is always delighted when a toddler steps out in trust and takes another step and then another step. The Lord will grasp our hand and lead us into the joy already prepared for us.

Lord Jesus, help me today not to grow weary and irritated by the trials in this life. You are leading me, step by step, Home. Alleluia!

Tuesday, February 14, 2006 Sts. Cyril and Methodius
James 1, 12-18
Temptation

To those who love God, a crown, a crown of life eternal, is promised. God has ways to honor those who endure trials and temptations with a persevering trust.

Lord Jesus, let us learn to be happy as we endure our earthly trials. You are revealing to us areas in our lives that need to come under your sovereignty. Thank you for speaking to us the truth about ourselves. Let us be humble enough to thank you for caring enough for us to confront us and to correct us. You are drawing us closer to you in every trial. Alleluia!

Wednesday, February 15, 2006
James 1, 19-27
Doers of the Word

Ears. Mouth. Hands.

Hear the word of God. Speak in accordance with the holiness of God. Do what matters to God.

We are to be "…swift to hear, slow to speak, slow to wrath (James 1, 19 KJV)." Our blazing anger does nothing to accomplish God's purposes.

Lord Jesus, purify us to respond to our trials with humility Let us learn to be gentle, to hear your word to us, and to put it into practice. Purify our hearts to speak only words that are pure and to serve the defenseless among us. Alleluia!

Thursday, February 16, 2006
James 2, 1-9
Sin of Partiality

We are to show no partiality, but, instead, to favor the poor as we learn to love our neighbors as ourselves.

"Hath not God chosen the poor of this world [to be] rich in faith, and heirs of the kingdom which he hath promised to those that love him (James 2, 5 KJV)?"

Lord Jesus, thank you for your patience as you continue to teach us to love and to care for others as we love and care for ourselves. If we do not love ourselves, heal us and let us experience your tender love for us. The love you have poured into us will then overflow to others. Alleluia!

Friday, February 17, 2006
James 2, 14-24,26
Faith and Work

Unless my life reflects my faith, I am a fraud. My so-called faith is dead.

Abraham demonstrated his faith in God by his actions. He trusted God, believed God, and put his ultimate trust in God as he was prepared to offer his beloved son, Isaac, to God.

Lord Jesus, show me any way that I may be deceiving myself and thinking I have faith when in reality I do not. Show me how to put my faith into action by trusting you in a radical way and by serving others as you direct. Alleluia!

Saturday, February 18, 2006 Seven Servite Founders
James 3, 1-10
Power of the Tongue

"For every species of beast and bird, of reptile and sea creature, can be tamed and has been tamed by the human species, but no one can tame the tongue – a restless evil, full of deadly poison. With it we bless the Lord and Father, and with it we curse those who are made in the likeness of God. From the same mouth come blessing and cursing. My brothers and sisters, this ought not to be so (James 3, 7-10)."

The problem, as we know, originates in the heart, not in the mouth. "The good person out of the good treasure of the heart produces good, and the evil person out of evil treasure produces evil; for it is out of the abundance of the heart that the mouth speaks (Luke 6, 45)."

We pray with the psalmist, "Create in me a clean heart, O God, and put a new and right spirit within me (Psalm 51, 10)."

Lord Jesus, I really need your help to control my tongue and to use my tongue to bless others instead of hurting them or offending them. Please forgive me for the hasty and unwise and unloving things I have said. I cry out to you for mercy. Thank you for cleansing my heart and teaching me what to say. Thank you for your faithfulness to help me in this serious matter. Alleluia!

> Sunday, February 19, 2006
> Isaiah 43, 18-19,21-22,24-25
> Promises of Redemption and Restoration to Favor

"Remember not the former things, neither consider the things of old. Behold, I will do a new thing; now it shall spring forth; shall not ye know it? I will even make a way in the wilderness, and rivers in the desert. I, even I, am he that blotteth out thy transgressions for mine own sake, and will not remember thy sins (Isaiah 43, 18-19,25 KJV)."

Because God has chosen to remove and to forgive my past sins, I must now choose to release the past and to embrace the new life which is already bursting forth before me!

Lord Jesus, thank you for not only forgiving all my sins but also, amazingly, blotting them out! I don't understand how you do that, but I rejoice and give you thanks. Alleluia!

> Monday, February 20, 2006
> James 3, 13-18
> True Wisdom

"But the wisdom that is from above is first pure, then peaceable, gentle and easy to be intreated, full of mercy and good fruits, without partiality, and without hypocrisy. And the fruit of righteousness is sown in peace of them that make peace (James 3, 17-18 KJV)."

Lord Jesus, thank you that I may have wisdom, true wisdom, for the asking. I pray for your wisdom, mercy, and peace to be manifested in my life. Alleluia!

> Tuesday, February 21, 2006
> James 4, 1-10
> Causes of Division

"Submit yourselves therefore to God. Resist the devil, and he will flee from you. Draw nigh to God and he will draw nigh to you. Cleanse your hands, ye sinners; and purify your hearts, ye double minded. Humble yourselves in the sight of the Lord, and he shall lift you up (James 4, 7,8,10 KJV)."

To God. To God. It is to God that we submit our lives.

What does God do? God lovingly draws near to us. As we humble ourselves, God exalts us and lifts us up!

Lord Jesus, forgive us for craving what we cannot have and what we should not have. Forgive us for our rampant selfishness and perverse determination to have our own way. Thank you that your grace is greater than our greed and greater than our misguided desires. Thank you for cleansing us and gently leading us to see ourselves as you see us. Thank you for healing us and transforming us. Alleluia!

> Wednesday, February 22, 2006 The Chair of Peter
> 1 Peter 5, 1-4
> Advice to the Presbyters; Advice to the Community

Leaders in the Church are called to "...tend the flock of God that is in your charge ... as God would have you do it .... Do not lord it over those in your charge, but be examples to the flock. And when the chief shepherd appears, you will win the crown of glory .... And all of you must do clothe yourselves with humility ... for 'God opposes the proud, but gives grace to the humble (vv. 2-4,5b).'"

Lord Jesus, thank you that you are the Good Shepherd who gave your life for your flock. We pray that you will vest our earthly shepherds with gentleness and humility as they tend your flock. Alleluia!

> Thursday, February 23, 2006 St. Polycarp
> James 5, 1-6
> Warning to the Rich

This severe warning to the selfish and rich has to penetrate to the heart for a true change. This is possible!

Some with huge fortunes are known, not only for their huge contributions to worthy causes, but also for their huge hearts and their personal commitment to the poor. These are the rich who have a true heart for the poor.

As Christians, we are the richest of the rich. The Lord Jesus Christ lives within us! We are strengthened by the sacred scriptures and the sacraments. We pray with confidence for God's kingdom to come on earth. We pray for God to reign right here.

Lord Jesus, thank you for stretching our hearts to live as you call us to live. Thank you for showing us how to give ourselves completely into your service. Thank you that you know how to transform us and to give us to others. Alleluia!

Friday, February 24, 2006
James 5, 9-12
Patience and Oaths

"Take ... the prophets, who have spoken in the name of the Lord, for an example of suffering affliction, and of patience (James 5, 10 KJV)."

When we become impatient and when we complain about others, we are putting on judgment robes. Instead, we need to stay clothed in mercy robes, robes of humility.

We are not to judge. The real Judge, God, is here!

Lord Jesus, help us to continue to endure patiently, to persevere in our trust, and to speak only the words you wish us to speak. Alleluia!

Saturday, February 25, 2006
James 5, 13-20
Anointing of the Sick; Confession and Intercession,
Conversion of Sinners

We are to pray when we are afflicted and to sing when we are merry. If we are sick, we are to call for the elders of the church to pray for us and to anoint us with oil.

We are not simply to confess our sins and failings privately to God. "Confess your faults one to another, and pray for one another, that ye may be healed (James 5, 16 KJV)."

Our life is to overflow with prayer, praise, intercession for others, compassion for others, and a joyful knowledge that the true prayer of faith will be used of the Lord to heal.

We don't have to be perfect. We only have to be real before God and others. The great prophet, Elijah, was still a human being with his own problems, such as depression. When he prayed about rain, God answered in remarkable ways!

Lord Jesus, help me to be humble enough to receive your forgiveness in the sacrament of reconciliation. Help me to trust you enough to believe that you can use my prayers to heal others. Alleluia!

Sunday, February 26, 2006 Eighth Sunday in Ordinary Time
Hosea 2, 16-17,21-22
Israel's Punishment and Restoration

When we are in a "desert" time and place, hedged in by thorns and walls, we are assured of God's loving presence. We learn to experience God's justice, love, faithfulness, and mercy in new ways.

In the dry wildernesses of our lives, God seeks us out, speaks tenderly to us, calling us back, calling us home. We are renewed as we rest in the presence of our true Lover.

Lord Jesus, thank you for your tender love and understanding, even when I am so aware of how I have failed you and failed others. Thank you for bringing me through this wilderness and for bringing forth blossoms and fruit in my life. Alleluia!

Monday, February 27, 2007
1 Peter 1, 3-9
Blessing

"Blessed be the God and Father of our Lord Jesus Christ! By his great mercy he has given us a new birth into a living hope through the resurrection of Jesus Christ from the dead, and into an inheritance that is imperishable, undefiled, and unfading, kept in heaven for you .... In this you rejoice, even if now for a little while you have had to suffer various trials, so that the genuineness of your faith – being more precious than gold that, though perishable, is tested by fire – may be found to result in praise and glory and honor when Jesus Christ is revealed (1 Peter 1, 3,4, 6,7)."

Lord Jesus, thank you for teaching us to rejoice in the midst of our earthly suffering. You have a glorious inheritance waiting for us in heaven. Alleluia!

Tuesday, February 28, 2006
1 Peter 1, 10-16
Blessing; Obedience

You! Yours! You!

Prophets of old were like investigative reporters, eagerly digging into all they could discover about the unspeakable glory and grace that would belong to YOU!. Long before you were born, they were working for you and serving you by their extraordinary research.

The Good News, the Gospel, was coming to YOU! Even the angels were longing to peer into the good things that were coming YOUR way.

Lord Jesus, you have suffered and died for us. Thank you for teaching us self-control and self-discipline as we await your return in glory. Let us honor you by our trusting obedience. Alleluia!

Wednesday, March 1, 2006 Ash Wednesday, Year B
Joel 2, 12-18
The Day of the Lord; Blessings for God's People

"Therefore also now, saith the LORD, turn ye even to me with all your heart, and with fasting, and with weeping, and with mourning: And rend your heart, and not your garments, and turn unto the LORD your God: for he is gracious and merciful, slow to anger, and of great kindness ... (Joel 2, 12-13 KJV)."

Although the day of the Lord is portrayed as terrifyingly great, the Lord's compassion is still greater. Israel is summoned to return wholeheartedly to the Lord.

The people of Israel were called to a time of fasting, weeping, and mourning. The Lord was looking for inner repentance, the rending of the heart, not merely the outer tearing of the garment.

We, too, are called to return to the Lord and to make the Lord first priority in our lives. The Lord responds in tender compassion, promising restoration of favor.

Lord Jesus, thank you for healing our hearts torn by our own sins and by the sins of others. Thank you that you will mend us, renew us, and restore us. Let us emerge with new life this Easter.

Thursday, March 2, 2006 Lenten Weekday
Deuteronomy 30, 15-20
The Choice before Israel

"I call heaven and earth to record this day ... that I have set before you life and death, blessing and cursing: therefore choose life ... (Deuteronomy 30, 19 KJV)."

Life! The blessing of God. Prosperity.

Death. The curse. Destruction.

God gave the choice to Israel. God is giving the choice to us.

We all want good things, but we sometimes realize that we're in a toxic, cursed, deathlike existence which is destroying us. What do we do, then?

God is patiently telling us how we can live. We learn to love God in a conscious way by listening attentively to God and then obeying God.

We learn to cling like limpets to our strong, loving God. We are safe in God's embrace.

We learn to choose God. All that we are crazily running after in this brief moment of life on earth is already in GOD.

Life! Blessings untold! Prosperity which would make Wall Street blush.

It's all in GOD. God longs to give it all to us.

Lord Jesus, let the next step I take indicate that I am choosing you. Let your blessings of life descend upon all whose life I touch this day.

Friday, March 3, 2006 St. Katharine Drexel
Isaiah 58, 1-9
True Fasting

"Is this not the fast that I have chosen? to loose the bands of wickedness, to undo the heavy burdens, and to let the oppressed go free, and that ye break every yoke?

Is it not to deal thy bread to the hungry, and that thou bring the poor that are cast out to thy house? when thou seest the naked, that thou cover him; and that thou hide not thyself from thine own flesh?

Then shall thy light break forth as the morning and thine health shall spring forth speedily: and thy righteousness shall go before thee: the glory of the Lord shall be thy rereward [reward] (Isaiah 58, 5-8 KJV)."

Focusing on myself and promoting myself and my own agenda? Is that what I've been doing?

Have I been trying to get God's attention in ostentatious ways? We've all been there and done that.

Perhaps this Lent, we can learn to focus on the Lord and on others in a new way. How can we release the oppressed? How can we serve God by meeting the needs of others? How can we offer food and shelter? How can we be kinder in our thoughts and in our words?

True fasting goes beyond dietary discipline and self-denial, valuable though that is. True fasting involves experiencing God's heart of compassion and then letting that compassion become real in our lives.

A few weeks ago I realized that I had not really been praying about the survivors of the Hurricane Katrina tragedy. Yes, as a family we had given money. Yes, we had offered other forms of practical assistance. Still, I wanted to do more.

After praying with a friend about this, three days later I noticed in our church newsletter that my prayer was being answered. Our church will be helping a church in Louisiana this Lent. The church building is still under water and the pastor drowned trying to save his people. The parishioners are now worshipping with another parish, whose overwhelmed pastor asks for our help.

What is the reward for those who fast in the way chosen by the Lord? Light! Healing! Vindication! Sounds good to me. The Lord promises to come speedily to help us when we fast by serving others.

Lord Jesus, thank you for teaching us this Lent how to pray, fast, and to give.

Saturday, March 4, 2006
Isaiah 58, 9-14
True Fasting

When? Then!

"Then shalt thou call, and the Lord shall answer; thou shalt cry, and he shall say, Here I am. If thou take away from the midst of thee the yoke, the putting forth of the finger, and speaking vanity;

And if thou draw out thy soul to the hungry, and satisfy the afflicted soul; then shall thy light rise in obscurity and thy darkness be as the noon day:

And the Lord shall guide thee continually, and satisfy thy soul in drought, and make fat thy bones: and thou shalt be like a watered garden, and like a spring of water, whose waters fail not (Isaiah 58, 9-11 KJV)."

The Lord will answer our pleas for help. In our darkness, light will rise up to greet us. Our gloom will become our noon. The Lord will guide us continually. We will have abundance even when the land is parched.

Our strength will be made new. We will be like a bubbling spring and a garden refreshed with water.

Even the oldest ruins will rebuilt for us. We will raise again the foundations that were laid in the distant past. We will be known as the restorers of ruins. God will nourish us. We will ride and soar on the heights!

When? Are these promises automatic? No.

IF! The promises are for us if we choose to fast in God's prescribed ways.

The promises are for those who do not oppress others or permit oppression in their midst. The promises are for those who do not accuse others falsely. The promises are for those who do not speak with malice. Instead, they feed the hungry and fulfill the needs of the afflicted. They observe and honor the Sabbath. The Sabbath is a delight.

Lord Jesus, thank you for these clear directions about fasting. Thank you that the Holy Spirit will faithfully lead us into the most fruitful Lent we have ever experienced.

Sunday, March 5, 2006 First Sunday of Lent, Year B
Genesis 9, 8-15
Covenant with Noah

Animals! God's covenant was not only with Noah but also with the animals who came out of the ark after the flood.

Birds! Wild animals! Tame animals! Never again would a flood devastate the entire earth.

We saw, in the midst of all the devastation left by Hurricane Katrina, those who rescued animals as well as people. Life is precious. All life deserve our respect and care.

We are fashioned in GOD'S image. This Lent, let us pray that our thoughts, attitudes, words, and actions reflect more and more the loving God in whose image we were created.

Lord Jesus, when we get discouraged about ourselves, thank you for reminding us in whose image we are created. Let us stand tall and learn to love ourselves and to love others.

Monday, March 6, 2006
Leviticus 19, 1-2,11-18
Various Rules of Conduct

"And the Lord spake unto Moses, saying, Speak unto all the congregation of the children of Israel, and say unto them, Ye shall be holy: for I the LORD your God am holy.(Leviticus 19, 1-2 KJV)."

Holiness is not optional. God told Moses to inform the whole community that they were to be holy. They were a people set apart to love and to serve God.

Holiness is very practical. When we ask God to make us pure and holy, we will become increasingly aware of our inner selves, our attitudes as well as our actions.

We are not to practice any form of deception or theft. We are to be honest and impartial when we make judgments.

God forbids holding onto hatred in our hearts as well as the overt the spreading of slander. We are forbidden to hold grudges. We are not to stand by when someone's life is at stake.

God may require us to speak out or to be silent. We may be asked to speak up for someone who needs a wrong to be made right. If we remain silent, our silence could hurt the person suffering injustice.

Other times, it's hard to keep our mouths shut. We want to tell others how awful someone is. We may succeed in keeping quiet, but our emotions may be raging.

In that case, God may require a new silence, a silence of the heart. When we trust God, we know that when we are asked to be silent, God will eventually speak to us and for us.

The Lord has spoken The Lord is speaking. Let us pray this Lent to be made holy.

Lord Jesus, thank you for transforming us this Lent as we become more and more sensitive to the Holy Spirit. Let us honor you by our honesty, our trust, and our obedience.

Tuesday, March 7, 2006 Sts. Felicity and Perpetua
Isaiah 55, 10-11
An Invitation to Grace

"For as the rain cometh down, and the snow from heaven, and returneth not thither, but watereth the earth, and maketh it bring forth and bud, that it may give seed to the sower, and bread to the eater:

So shall my word be that goeth forth out of my mouth: it shall not return to me void, but it shall accomplish that which I please, and it shall prosper in the thing whereto I sent it (Isaiah 55, 10-11 KJV)."

Lord Jesus, thank you for helping me to be calm and quiet as I wait for the word you've spoken to come to pass in my life. Just as I do not control the rain from heaven, I cannot control the timing of your word being fulfilled. Just as when the rain comes, it will water the thirsty earth, so when your word at last comes to fulfillment in my life, I will become green and will blossom at last.

Wednesday, March 8, 2006
Jonah 3, 1-10
Conversion of Ninevah

Jesus referred to several times to Jonah in the context of his discussions with the scribes, Pharisees, Sadducees, and the crowds.

"For just as Jonah was three days in the belly of the sea monster, so for three days and three nights the Son of Man will be in the heart of the earth. The people of Ninevah will rise up at the judgment with this generation and condemn it, because they repented at the proclamation of Jonah, and see, something greater than Jonah is here (Matthew 12, 40-41)."

"An evil and adulterous generation asks for a sign, but no sign will be given to it except the sign of Jonah (Matthew 16, 4)."

"When the crowds were increasing, he began to say, 'This generation is an evil generation; it asks for a sign, but no sign will be given to it except the sign of Jonah. For just as Jonah became a sign to the people of Ninevah, so the Son of Man will be to this generation (Luke 11, 29,30)."

Ninevah was a huge city! It took the prophet Jonah three days to travel through it. The prophet began to proclaim God's message, however, after only one day.

Even so, God's purpose was fulfilled. Lo and behold, the residents of Ninevah all repented. They even fasted, from the king to the cattle!

They fasted. No food. No water.

We don't have to complete whatever we consider our own "three day journey" in order to follow God's call. We are not in charge. God is in charge. There are things we can do and things which, presently, we cannot do.

Let us continue with whatever we believe God is calling us to be and to do. Who knows? Maybe God's purpose is closer to fulfillment than we think.

Thursday, March 9, 2006 St. Frances of Rome
Esther C, 12, 14-16,23-24
Prayer of Esther

Beautiful Queen Esther prayed like a wild woman!. Knowing the life of the people of Israel was at stake, she immersed herself in the presence of the Lord.

She humbly acknowledged the Lord as King. She acknowledged that the Lord was her only hope and the only hope for the people of Israel. Without the Lord's intervention, they were all doomed to destruction.

Knowing that the Lord had chosen Israel and was always faithful to Israel, Esther cried out in anguish to the Lord in this time of distress. She prayed for courage. She prayed to speak the words that would be instrumental in saving her people.

We may think that all that was past history and does not apply to us. Really?

Lord Jesus, we desperately need you ! We are living in perilous times. We cry out to you to embolden us to speak the truth. We cry out to you to forgive us and have mercy on us.

Friday, March 10, 2006
Ezekiel 18, 21-28
Personal Responsibility

God is sovereign, yet generously gives us to us the ability and the freedom to make choices. We bear responsibility for each choice we make. We always affect others by our choices.

God is also merciful. God longs for us to live! Crying from the depths of our heart to God reaches the heart of God who longs to forgive us and to restore us to life again.

Lord Jesus, thank you for your tender mercy and compassion when we come to you in honesty, humility, and trust. Thank you for forgiving us and giving us life again.

Saturday, March 11, 2006 Lenten Weekday
Deuteronomy 26, 16-19
The Covenant

You and I are making a solemn agreement with the Lord and the Lord is making a binding agreement with us. It is the Lord! That is why we are to observe the agreement with all our heart and soul.

Lord Jesus, we pray to trust you to do for us and in us what only you can do. We pray to receive the grace to yield to you in a deeper way, a way that engages our entire being. You long to raise us high! You long for it to be obvious to all that we are a people holy and sacred to the Lord our God

Sunday, March 12, 2006 Second Sunday in Lent
Genesis 22, 1-2,9-13,15-18
The Testing of Abraham

Can we trust God when God asks us give what we perceive as the only means of fulfilling his will and his call? Can we sacrifice the very answer to our prayers?

Can we sacrifice ourselves for God's purposes through us and in us to be made real to us and to all? Can we believe that God loves us and has an even bigger answer than we could ever imagine?

Lord Jesus, sometimes it seems too cruel. It seems that we have come so close to the fulfillment of the vision you have placed within us and then it is snatched away. Help us to see that it is not snatched away. You are perfecting us. You are enlarging us to live an even larger vocation than we imagined. Help us to be quiet and patient as you work within us this Lent.

Monday, March 13, 2006 Lenten Weekday
Daniel 9, 4-10
Gabriel and the Seventy Weeks

Daniel is turning to the Lord with intense prayer, accompanied with fasting and other signs of contrition. He means business! Someone has said that fasting lends wings to our prayers!

Daniel gathers up the sins of Judah, the residents of Jerusalem, and all Israel. Then he goes before the Lord and confesses these sins. It's WE, not THEY. It is "we" who have sinned.

Instead of pointing the finger in accusation, Daniel realizes that he himself is involved. He lives in that culture and therefore bears responsibility. His is not a false, condescending humility.

After humbly acknowledging the sins of all Israel, Daniel turns to God and appeals to God's compassion. He implores God's forgiveness for all these sins of wrongdoing, disobedience, and failure to listen to the prophets. He intercedes for government leaders and for ancestors.

Lord Jesus, this Lent, help us to pray in humility for others, realizing that we are all sinful and need your mercy. We cry out as a nation and as a church for your mercy.

Tuesday, March 14, 2006 Lenten Weekday
Isaiah 1, 10,16-20
Israel's Sinfulness

Light shines! In the midst of this indictment of corrupt Israel, light shines.

God's people are commanded to stop their evildoing and to learn to live righteously. They are to strive for justice. They are to defend the helpless.

If they are willing and obedient, they will experience good. If they are rebellious and defiant, they will experience destruction.

God gets right in their face! There is the breathtaking promise (remember, this is centuries before the birth of Christ) that the people's sins, described as crimson, can become as white as snow.

Lord Jesus, you are the Lamb of God. You willingly shed your blood in order to cleanse us and to bring us into the light of a completely NEW life. This Lent, help us to believe this, truly believe this, perhaps for the first time, with all our heart. Cleansed, let us step into the light of a new day and reflect your purity and your holiness.

Wednesday, March 15, 2006 Lenten Weekday
Jeremiah 18, 18-20
Another Prayer for Vengeance

Speaking the truth has never been popular. Jeremiah, the faithful prophet, suffered terribly for speaking forth God's word.

"Give heed to me, O LORD, and listen to what my adversaries say! Is evil a recompense for good? Yet they have dug a pit for my life. Remember how I stood before you to speak good for them, to turn away your wrath from them (vv. 19-20)."

Jeremiah's enemies plotted to destroy him in a clever way. They would use his own words to incriminate him and then to destroy him. They gloated, "… Come, let us make plots against Jeremiah …. Come, let us bring charges against him, and let us not heed any of his words (v. 18)."

Does this tactic sound familiar? Jesus' enemies did the very same thing.

Jeremiah cried out to the Lord. Why, he cried, should the good he had done be reimbursed with such evil?

Why, indeed? Jeremiah had humbled himself before God and interceded for these very people who were out to destroy him. No wonder poor Jeremiah wanted God to step in and wreak vengeance on them.

Lord Jesus, thank you for strengthening us to choose to live for you and to be faithful to you in spite of opposition. You are sovereign! You still have the final word. Help us to trust you and to live courageously for you in this passing world.

Thursday, March 16, 2006 Lenten Weekday
Jeremiah 17, 5-10
True Wisdom

"Thus says the LORD: Cursed are those who trust in mere mortals … (v. 5)."

I really jumped when I read this passage this morning! Of course, we all know that it's unwise (stupid?) to put ultimate trust in human beings. We are created to trust, really trust, only God. Right?

Well, God is saying it's not only unwise to place ultimate trust in other people, but that we're actually cursed if we do.

Cursed? Execrated? Amazingly strong, powerful language here.

Why would God say that we were cursed? Because we're looking for help that God alone can give us.

We're looking in the wrong places. Our heart is turned away from God. All of us have deceitful (the Hebrew word is "aqob," meaning "swollen") hearts which God alone can understand and interpret.

We're trying to feel good and to find security in ways other than total reliance upon God. God doesn't like that. God is jealous for us in a righteous and holy way.

What do we do if any of this hits home? Rejoice!

God already has the answer waiting for us. We are happy and blessed by trusting and relying upon the Lord. We learn, day by day, to hope in the Lord. We begin to trust God more and more.

"Blessed are those who trust in the LORD, whose trust is the LORD. They shall be like a tree planted by water, sending out its roots by the stream. It shall not fear when heat comes, and its leaves shall stay green; in the year of drought it is not anxious, and it does not cease to bear fruit … (vv. 7,8)."

The imagery of a tree beside the water. stretching its roots to the stream. is beautiful and powerful. We needn't worry when drought is all around us. Our roots are in God. We are planted in God. We will still bear fruit for God.

Lord Jesus, sometimes I am so immature and insecure that I need constant reassurance that you love me and you are taking care of me. Help me to love others but to know that you and you alone are in control of my life.

Friday, March 17, 2006 St. Patrick
Genesis 37, 3-4,12-13,17-28
Joseph sold into Egypt

Just as you may have had a Judas and a Pilate in your life, so you may also have had a Reuben and a Judah. What does that mean?

Judas betrayed Jesus. Pilate washed his hands of Jesus.

Reuben tried to save Joseph. Judah was quick to betray Joseph.

Reuben initially tried to save the life of his brother Joseph. He suggested to his brothers that they merely throw Joseph into a pit rather than killing him outright. Reuben had planned to return to rescue Joseph and then to restore him to Jacob, their father.

That's not what happened, however. After stripping Joseph of the beautiful long garment his father had given him, his brothers threw him into a waterless pit.

The brothers, with the apparent exception of Reuben (Genesis 37, 29) had something to eat and then noticed the caravan headed for Egypt. Judah suggested selling Joseph for twenty silver pieces to the Ishmaelite traders. And so Joseph, the young dreamer, beloved of his father, was packed off to Egypt.

That's where the story ends today. Joseph seems doomed to captivity.

How does all that apply to us? We are learning to trust in God's purpose to be fulfilled in our life. God is still greater than any Reuben, Judah, Judas, or Pilate.

Lord Jesus, no matter how long it takes, you will bring me into the fulfillment of your plans for me. I place all my trust in you and wait with joyful expectation.

Saturday, March 18, 2006 St. Cyril of Alexandria
Micah 7, 14-15,18-20
Condemnation and Prayer

A promise of restoration! God's people, in exile, will again experience the loving care of their true Shepherd.

God not only forgives us, but also removes our sins and even eradicates our guilt. What a deal!

"He will turn again, he will have compassion upon us; he will subdue our iniquities; and thou wilt cast all their sins into the depths of the sea (Micah 7, 19 KJV)."

As Corrie the Boom loved to say, God then puts up a sign that says, "No fishing!"

Heavenly Father, this Lent, help us to understand, truly understand, that you have made complete provision for the forgiveness of our sins. Jesus, our Good Shepherd and our Lamb has been sacrificed for us. His blood has cleansed us from all our sins. Let us rejoice in the power of the Holy Spirit to give us new life!

Sunday, March 19, 2006 Third Sunday in Lent
Exodus 20, 1-17
The Ten Commandments

God did not bring us out of slavery in order for us to re-enter slavery. God made us to be truly free. God's commandments are the way to freedom, as we honor God and honor others.

Lord Jesus, thank you for teaching us how to live in true obedience and true freedom.

Monday, March 20, 2006 St. Joseph
2 Samuel 7, 4-5,12-14,16
David's Concern for the Ark; The Lord's Promises

God, through the prophet Nathan, redirected David's attention from the ark of the covenant to the Lord of the covenant. David's heir would be the one to build a new temple or house for God. David was promised that his own house would always endure.

Lord Jesus, thank you that sometimes you redirect our lives into new purposes. You broaden our vision as you purify us. You give us new hope for our future and for the future of those who come after us. May your name be glorified in us and in our descendants. Help us to remember that we are the temple of the Holy Spirit.

Tuesday, March 21, 2006 Lenten Weekday
Daniel 3, 25, 34-43
The Fiery Furnace

Thrown into a blazing furnace for refusing to bow down and worship a golden statue, Daniel's three friends sang praises to God! They implored God's forgiveness for the apostasy of their ancestors. Only then did they pray for their own deliverance from the flames.

Do we reverse the order? Do we pray for ourselves first, then perhaps for others, and only then think to praise and worship God?

Lord Jesus, thank you for purifying our hearts and our prayers this Lent.

> Wednesday, March 22, 2006 Lenten Weekday
> Deuteronomy 4, 1,5-9
> Advantages of Fidelity; Revelation at Horeb

Cling to God and live! We've been rescued from the flood waters. We cling to our loving God who has pulled us to safety.

We're meant, not only to survive, but also to enter into the land God gives us. We are to possess the land.

We're not to stand at the gate and stare. God calls us to enter in and to realize that it's all ours!

God gives us statutes so that we will be wise and know how to live our new life of freedom. We are cautioned to be very careful not to forget all that God has done for us. We are to teach our children and even our grandchildren.

Lord Jesus, this Lent, help us to remember that you have rescued us from sin and led us into a new land of forgiveness, love and light. Let us enter in and live fully this new life. Let us teach others by our words and our lives the joy of clinging to you in complete trust. You are holding us safely in your heart.

> Thursday, March 23, 2006 St. Toribio de Mogrovejo
> Jeremiah 7, 23-28
> Abuses in Worship

God has had it! Through the faithful prophet, Jeremiah, God had already spoken to the people.

Still, they refused to obey. At one point, God even told Jeremiah not to intercede for these stubborn people (Jeremiah 7, 16).

What had God been trying to tell the people all this time? Very simple.

The people had been told to listen to God's voice and obey God's commands. If they did so, they would prosper!

But, no, they turned their backs to God. They decided to follow the evil in their hearts, instead of following God.

God warned Jeremiah that the people would not listen to him, either. As far as God was concerned, the word "faithful" was not even in their vocabulary.

Lord Jesus, have mercy upon us. We have knowingly and unknowingly disobeyed you. Let us shrink from grieving you by not trusting you and not obeying you. Forgive us and help us to listen carefully to you and to honor you with our trust and our obedience. You know what is best for us and you will tenderly care for us as we obey you.

Friday, March 24, 2006 Lenten Weekday
Hosea 14, 2-10
Sincere Conversion

"O Israel, return unto the LORD thy God; for thou hast fallen by thine iniquity. Take with you words, and turn to the LORD: say to him, Take away all iniquity, and receive us graciously ... (Hosea 14, 1-2 KJV)."

Israel is implored to take raw, honest words of repentance to God. God is longing to forgive and to restore.

Do we take words of honesty to God? Do we still pretend with God?

Do we still seek our own way? Do we still think we can be happy without God?

Lord Jesus, we bring to you our honest selves, our real selves. We bring to you words of honesty from the depths of our hearts. We have avoided you, run from you, and tried to live without you. Have mercy on us. Forgive us. Help us to know that you love us and are ready to restore us. Shower, like dew, your tenderness upon us. Let us be refreshed and renewed in your love. Like pure, fragrant lilies, let us blossom forth in your time. Let us live and walk in the paths you already have planned for us.

Saturday, March 25, 2006 The Annunciation of the Lord
Isaiah 7, 10-14
Birth of Immanuel

Ahaz? Who was this Ahaz to whom the Lord was speaking?

Ahaz was king of Judah and, suffice it to say, he was not a good king (2 Kings 16; 2 Chronicles 28).

Nevertheless, the Lord chose to speak to Ahaz. The Lord even invited Ahaz to ask for a sign. Although Ahaz refused, the Lord gave the sign anyway.

"Therefore the LORD himself shall give you a sign: Behold, a virgin shall conceive, and bear a son, and shall call his name Immanuel (v. 14 KJV)."

Dear Father, thank you that you speak to us, whether or not we are worthy. You gave us Mary. You gave us Jesus. Immanuel! You are with us. You gave us the Holy Spirit to continue to teach us how to live.

Sunday, March 26, 2006 The Fourth Sunday of Lent
2 Chronicles 36, 14-16,19-23
Zedekiah; Decree of Cyrus

A very serious first reading for this Laetare Sunday. Still, we are to rejoice!

There was no remedy this time. God's people had stubbornly refused to listen to the prophets God had sent them. The priests and the people were unfaithful to God and even polluted the house of the Lord in Jerusalem.

They defiled what God had consecrated. The people would be given up to suffer the consequences of despising God.

The Chaldeans came and murdered young men in the sanctuary. Young and old, women and men were killed. The house of God with the sacred vessels, palaces, the wall around Jerusalem were all destroyed.

Those who escaped the sword were taken into captivity. All of this was a fulfillment of the prophetic words the Lord had given to Jeremiah.

After the years of desolation were completed, the Lord authorized King Cyrus of Persia to build a house in Jerusalem. This was a house for the Lord. The Lord's people were invited to return and to build the house.

Heavenly Father, you have given us a remedy. You have given your Son, Jesus, to take away our sins. Help us to listen to you and listen to those through whom you are trying to speak to us. Let us honor you in every way, keep a holy Lent, and come with rejoicing to your house.

Monday, March 27, 2006 Lenten Weekday
Isaiah 65, 17-21
The World Renewed

The weary world will rejoice! We will rejoice. If we have grown weary and listless this Lent, we may still rejoice.

Yesterday, the fourth Sunday in Lent, we were invited to rejoice and to remember that we are living on this side of the resurrection. Jesus did not stay on the Cross. Jesus did not stay in the tomb and neither shall we!

The future God has planned for us is full of rejoicing. Let's practice now.

Let's rejoice!. Let's rejoice in what the Lord has done for us.

Let's rejoice in the midst of trials. They are temporary.

God promises a new heaven and a new earth. We won't even remember the past. There will be happiness and rejoicing in what God has created.

God will also rejoice! God rejoices in us.

God rejoices in Jerusalem. No more weeping. No more lives cut short.

Homes. Vineyards. Joy

Thank you, Heavenly Father, for the brightness of the future you have ready for us. Thank you, Jesus, for dying for us and cleansing us of our sins. Thank you, Holy Spirit, for filling us with joy as we face this day.

Tuesday, March 28, 2006 Lenten Weekday
Ezekiel 47, 1-9,12
The Wonderful Stream

Water! In his vision, the priest and prophet Ezekiel saw water flowing from the temple in Jerusalem. The water brought life and healing wherever it flowed. Trees bearing fruit were watered from this stream.

We are God's temple and God's spirit dwells within us (1 Corinthians 3, 16). We pray that God's life flows through us this Lent so that we may bear fruit to nourish others.

Wednesday, March 29, 2006 Lenten Weekday
Isaiah 49, 8-15
The Liberation and Restoration of Zion

"Sing for joy, O heavens, and exult, O earth; break forth, O mountains, into singing! For the LORD has comforted his people, and will have compassion on his suffering ones (v. 13)."

This is just the encouragement we need if we've been in a time of darkness and desolation. If we have been in some kind of captivity, we will hear the Lord calling us to come out of the darkness and show ourselves at last!

Free! We will be free at last.

Free to be all that God has called us to be. Free to do all that God has called us to do.

God will bring complete restoration. We will know that nothing was lost in our time of darkness. God has not forgotten us.

"Can a woman forget her nursing child, or show no compassion for the child of her womb? Even these may forget, yet I will not forget you. See, I have inscribed you on the palms of my hands; your walls are continually before me. Your builders outdo your destroyers, and those who laid you waste go away from you (vv. 15-17)."

There will be new pastures and sparkling streams of fresh water. God will prepare new roads for us and level highways.

There will be singing and rejoicing. God has not forgotten us. We will emerge from darkness into God's triumphant light!

Thursday, March 30, 2006
Exodus 32, 7-14
The Golden Calf

Moses is having to pick up the pieces after Aaron was unfaithful to God. Aaron, the priest.

Aaron, priest though he was, had tragically allowed God's people to commit idolatry. Aaron had actually facilitated their sin (Exodus 32, 1-6).

God instructed Moses to descend Mt. Sinai, where the commandments had been engraved on tablets, and to return to the people. God was righteously wrathful!

God had faithfully led the people out of their bitter slavery in Egypt and here they were committing gross idolatry. God even referred to them as belonging to Moses.

Moses interceded, reminding God that these were indeed God's own people. Moses reminded God of the promises to Abraham, Isaac, and Israel (Jacob). Their descendents were to be numerous and the land was to be theirs. God honored the prayer of Moses and relented.

Dear Father, forgive us when our sins cause others to suffer. Thank you for those who intercede for us. Thank you that Jesus is our Great High Priest and knows just how to intercede for us. Thank you for forgiving us and redirecting our attention and our worship to you alone. Thank you for the Holy Spirit who warns us when we are not trusting you and obeying you.

Friday, March 31, 2006 Lenten Weekday
Wisdom 2, 1,12-22
The Wicked Reject Immortality and Justice Alike

The wicked exhibit incorrect thinking, uninformed reasoning, lack of discernment, and incorrect conclusions.

For all who suffer because of their trust in God and their passion to live for God, these words, written a hundred or so years before the birth of Christ, provide illumination and comfort.

Illumination. The faulty thought processes of the wicked will be exposed for what they are.

Comfort. God's children are counseled in ways hidden from the wicked. God has ways of rewarding the innocent.

Lord Jesus, purify our bodies, souls, and spirits this Lent. Let us cooperate with the work the Holy Spirit is doing within us. Let us be increasingly sensitive to your voice. Strengthen us to live for you, knowing that our true life is with you and our true home is with you. Thank you for the place you have already prepared for us in the house of our Father.

Saturday, April 1, 2006 Lenten Weekday
Jeremiah 11, 18-20
The Plot against Jeremiah

The prophet Jeremiah, as a gentle lamb, entrusted his cause to God. God alone could bring vindication from those plotting to destroy him.

Jeremiah understood that God was the ultimate Judge. His cause was safe with God.

Lord Jesus, when we follow you and are overwhelmed by the hostility of those who do not choose to follow you, come to us and strengthen us. Let us be as little lambs led by you into the pastures you choose. You are our shepherd, defender, and redeemer. You are the Lamb of God who was slain and yet rose triumphant.

Sunday, April 2, 2006 Fifth Sunday of Lent
Jeremiah 31, 31-34
The New Covenant

Tablets of stone can be broken and smashed. The words written on them are no longer easy to read.

Words breathed into our hearts are different. They are there because God put them there.

We have a choice. We may learn to listen to God's words imprinted on our hearts. As we listen and respond as God leads us to respond, we become increasingly sensitive to God's voice. We become tender and pliable in God's service.

Sadly, we may also choose to silence the voice of God within. We may choose to close our minds and our hearts to God. We may continue to ignore the gentle words of love from God.

God longs to speak to us and God is actually speaking to us. It is up to us be silent and to listen.

Lord Jesus, as we come into the final stretch of Lent, draw us aside to spend time in silence with you. Teach us to turn off the voices that would lead us away from you. Help us to be more sensitive and responsive to your voice. Let us carry this habit of spending time in silence with you into Eastertide and into the rest of our lives.

Monday, April 3, 2006 Lenten Weekday
Daniel 13, 1-9,15-17,19-30,33-62
Susannah's Virtue

Susannah, the pure, innocent, beautiful, and undefiled woman, was spared. Daniel spoke on her behalf and those who had lied about her were exposed and executed.

Jesus, the pure innocent, beautiful, and undefiled Son of God, was not spared. Those who lied about him seemed to win.

After all, he was crucified. He was dead. He was buried. He was gone.

Really? For us, he lived. For us, he died.

For us, he broke through all barriers of sin and suffering. For us, he rose, triumphant over death. For us, he will come again in glory.

Lord Jesus, thank you for being our Lamb and our Shepherd. Thank you for leading us through these last days of Lent. Thank you for transforming us. Thank you for opening our eyes to see you as you really are. Thank you that you will return in glory as our King!

Tuesday, April 4, 2006 Lenten Weekday
Numbers 21, 4-9
The Bronze Serpent

Out! I need to get out of this desert, stop complaining about the various snakes, and start looking, instead, at Jesus! After all, Jesus is the reason for the Lenten season.

In the desert, God sent snakes to bite the people because of their constant whining and complaining. God was just fed up with their ingratitude.

After the death of some of the people, the survivors had an "aha" moment. It was clear that God did not like their complaining.

God stepped in and told Moses what to do. Make a serpent out of bronze.

The people fixed their eyes on the bronze saraph serpent, wrapped round a pole, which Moses lifted high for all to see. They gazed at the bronze serpent and were healed.

Feeling stuck in the desert, I've been looking at snakes long enough. What I need is not a snake made out of bronze. I need JESUS!

It's time to focus on Jesus. High and lifted up, exalted on the Cross, Jesus took away my sins, including my sins of ingratitude and complaining. My sins are gone. It doesn't make any sense to complain about what is gone, does it?

Lord Jesus, we look to you. You are the one lifted high for our healing. Thank you for forgiving us and leading us out of the desert to streams of fresh, flowing water.

Wednesday, April 5, 2006 Lenten Weekday
Daniel 3, 14-20,91-92,95
The Fiery Furnace

"Dexify!" No need to defend. No need to explain. No need do justify.

"Dexify!" This composite (don't defend, don't explain, don't justify) popped into mind as I read the first reading this rainy morning.

Some years ago, I asked advice about a difficult situation from Helen, one of my professors in the seminary. She gave me one word of advice. "Dexify!"

The three friends of Daniel were in a life or death situation. If they wanted to live, they would have to violate their conscience and dishonor God.

They would have to bow down and worship a big golden statue. King's orders. Worship the statue or be thrown into a fiery furnace. Great choice.

"Dexify!" There was no need for these three men of God to defend themselves, to explain themselves, or to justify themselves.

They had already made up their minds. Come what may, they would not worship any statue.

Either God would rescue them or they would die. Either way, they would honor God. They would honor God through their life or in their death.

As we know, God did rescue the three. Bound, they were hurled into the fiery furnace. In the fire, they were not alone. The amazed king saw four, not three, in the flames.

They emerged unharmed from their ordeal, without even the smell of smoke (Daniel 3, 27). The power and the rage of the earthly king was no match for the power and the mercy of God.

Lord Jesus, you did not defend yourself before Pilate. You had no need to defend yourself, to explain yourself, or to justify yourself. Although you were the Son of God, you were not rescued from the Cross. Instead, you triumphed over the Cross. In you, we also triumph.

Thursday, April 6, 2006 Lenten Weekday
Genesis 17, 3-9
Covenant of Circumcision

Twenty-four years! Twenty-four years of waiting. Twenty-four years of going where God directed. Twenty-four years of wondering when God's promises would be fleshed out in his life.

In today's first reading, Abram (soon to be renamed Abraham) was ninety-nine years old. He was a mere lad of seventy-five when God called him to leave Haran, where his family was settled, and to hit the road and venture forth (Genesis 12, 1-5).

Venture forth where? Ah, that's where trust came in. Abram was to venture forth where God directed.

So, here he is at the age of ninety-nine and the promises still have yet to be fulfilled? Is it too late?

Abram made a few mistakes along the way, but God was still with him. God had not forgotten his servant.

God appeared to Abram, who promptly fell on his face. A good posture for the heart as well as for the body.

Abram would become a father, big-time. He would become the ancestor of a huge multitude. He would be known as Abraham.

Abraham was promised numerous descendants. as well as the land of Canaan. Abraham was charged with keeping the covenant, with the sign of circumcision (Genesis 17, 10).

This is both a challenging and a comforting passage to recall when we're in the in-between times in our lives. We have received God's promise, but it has not been fulfilled. We are living each day and following God as well as we can, while still waiting. We continue journeying forth, as Abraham did, and we keep trusting God.

Lord Jesus, thank you for strengthening us to continue to believe and to hope. Thank you for the new covenant given to us as we continue our pilgrimage to the heavenly Jerusalem.

Friday, April 7, 2006 Lenten Weekday
Jeremiah 20, 10-13
Jeremiah's Interior Crisis

Sooner or later, if we follow God and make God our priority, we will experience, to some degree, the anguish experienced by the prophet, Jeremiah. Jeremiah lamented that even his so-called friends were watching him and trying to see if they could trap him by his own words.

Jeremiah eventually shifted his focus from his false friends to God, his true Friend. God was with Jeremiah. It was God who had called Jeremiah to this difficult prophetic ministry.

It is God alone who is qualified to test and to probe the human mind and heart. Like Jeremiah and like our Lord Jesus Christ, let us entrust our cause to God and rejoice!

Saturday, April 8, 2006 Lenten Weekday
Ezekiel 37, 21-28
The Two Sticks

Sometimes God calls prophets to do weird things, in order to illustrate a truth. God told Ezekiel to take one stick and to write "Judah" on it and to take another stick and to write "Joseph" on it. Then he was to join the two sticks into one (Ezekiel 37, 16-17).

God was calling for Israel to be one true nation with one true shepherd. No more division. No more idols. No more apostasy.

"My tabernacle also shall be with them: yea, I will be their God, and they shall be my people .... I the LORD do sanctify Israel, when my sanctuary shall be in the midst of them for evermore (Ezekiel 37, 27-28 KJV)."

In his high priestly prayer, Jesus prayed that his followers would be one. "That they all may be one, as thou, Father, art in me, and I in thee, that they also may be one in us: that the world may believe that thou hast sent me (John 17, 21 KJV)."

Lord Jesus, cleanse us and purify us as we enter Holy Week. Let us, as Christians, live as you call us to live, in unity.

Sunday, April 9, 2006 Palm Sunday of the Lord's Passion
Isaiah 50, 4-7
Salvation Only through the Lord's Servant

"For the LORD GOD will help me; therefore shall I not be confounded: therefore have I set my face like a flint, and I know that I shall not be ashamed (Isaiah 50, 7 KJV)."

Lord Jesus, as Son of Man, you learned to make time to listen every day to your Father, your Abba. You learned how to speak the words your Father gave you to speak, words to refresh the exhausted. You manifested the perfect combination of humility and strength when you were cruelly insulted and abused. How often we want to defend ourselves or strike back when we are opposed. And yet you knew when to speak and when to remain silent. With firm determination, you set your heart and your mind and your face to Jerusalem, where your destiny lay. Help us during this Holy Week to adore you and to stay with you. Instead of brushing our unanswered questions away, let us bring them all to you this week. Let us live this Holy Week with you in a new way. Let us be transformed as we stay with you.

Monday, April 10, 2006 Monday of Holy Week
Isaiah 42, 1-7
The Servant of the Lord

"Behold my servant, whom I uphold ....A bruised reed shall he not break, and the smoking flax shall he not quench: he shall bring forth judgment unto truth (Isaiah 42, 1a,3 KJV)."

A true servant of the Lord brings about justice without violence. A true servant of the Lord is sensitive and strong. A true servant of the Lord does not crush the wounded or the injured. A true servant of the Lord brings light. A true servant of the Lord brings liberation.

Tuesday, April 11, 2006 Tuesday of Holy Week
Isaiah 49, 1-6
The Servant of the Lord

When feeling frustrated and useless, we need to remember that God has called us, even from our mother's womb. God's glory is manifested through us and will continue to be manifested through us, probably when we are least aware of it. Sometimes it's better if we don't know it.

We may identify with Jeremiah, who lamented "… 'I have labored in vain, I have spent my strength for nothing and vanity; yet surely my cause is with the LORD, and my reward with my God (v. 3bc).' "

When we are exhausted and are entertaining thoughts of futility, we may be refreshed with the certainty that our reward is safe with God. God is and will be our source of strength.

If we are especially weary this Tuesday in Holy Week, let us remember that we are not alone. We are walking with Jesus all this week in a special way, whether we feel we are or not. The God who called us into being is with us and is renewing us and leading us to a glorious future. Soon we will sing "Alleluia!"

Wednesday, April 12, 2006 Wednesday of Holy Week
Isaiah 50, 5-9
Salvation Only Through the Lord's Servant

Attacked, cruelly scourged, and disfigured, yet not disgraced. The Lord's servant endured terrible mistreatment, yet continued to trust the Lord.

When we are in a place of darkness, we remember that it is the Lord who is our light and it is the Lord who is our salvation (Psalm 27, 1). We are learning to be strong and firm in our faith.

Lord Jesus, you are the Light! You are the light shining in our darkness. Your light will never be extinguished. Shine in us and through us as we continue to trust in you and in your mercy.

Thursday, April 13, 2006 Holy Thursday
Exodus 12, 1-8,11-17
The Passover Ritual Prescribed

It is for the Lord alone to execute judgment. Because of the blood of the Passover lamb, the Lord passed over Israel while executing judgment on Egypt. It is because of the Blood of Jesus, our Passover Lamb, that the Lord mercifully passes over us, forgiving our sins and cleansing us.

>Friday, April 14, 2006 Good Friday
>Isaiah 52, 13 - 53, 12
>Suffering and Triumph of the Servant of the Lord

"Surely he hath borne our griefs, and carried our sorrows ... wounded for our transgressions ... bruised for our iniquities ... (Isaiah 53, 4a,5a KJV)."

Although "despised and rejected ... a man of sorrows (Isaiah 53, 3 KJV), the servant of the Lord did not remain in a state of suffering.

"Behold, my servant shall deal prudently, he shall be exalted and extolled, and be very high (Isaiah 52, 13 KJV)."

Rejected, mocked, scorned, abused, and defiled for a time, to atone for the sins of others, the servant of the Lord fulfilled the Lord's plan of redemption.

We are not called to remain in suffering. Jesus, who lived and died for us, is now calling us to breathe again, to live again, and to love again.

>Saturday, April 15, 2006 Holy Saturday, Easter Vigil
>Genesis 1, 1 - 2, 2
>First Story of Creation

God called forth light from the darkness! God called forth the sky, the seas, the sun, moon, and stars. God called forth trees and bees and all creatures.

God calls us forth. God calls you forth. God calls me forth. We were fashioned in God's image.

This Easter, God is calling us forth to be fruitful. New life is being poured into us to live and to love. Jesus has won the victory for us! Alleluia!

Sunday, April 16, 2006 Easter Sunday, Year B
Acts 10, 34,37-43
Peter's Speech

Peter! It's Peter again.

This time he is not denying that he ever knew Jesus. This time, Peter is glorifying and exalting the risen Lord Jesus Christ. Peter is preaching Jesus!

Earlier, John the Baptist had preached a baptism of repentance to prepare the way for Jesus. Then, he pointed to Jesus as the Lamb of God.

God the Father preached Jesus! God spoke and Jesus was the Word spoken by God.

"... God anointed Jesus of Nazareth with the Holy Ghost and with power: who went about doing good and healing all that were oppressed by the devil: for God was with him (Acts. 10, 38 KJV)."

After Jesus rose from the dead, Peter and others saw him. They actually ate and drank with the risen Lord. Jesus commissioned them to go out into the world and preach, to testify to Jesus, and to his power to forgive sins.

Lord Jesus, you are the Word made flesh, the one who will judge the living and the dead. Let us proclaim with our words and with our lives that you are with us. You are alive! Alleluia!

Monday, April 17, 2006 Easter Monday
Acts 2, 14,22-33
Peter's Speech at Pentecost

Peter has been to the ultimate speech therapist! Peter has been filled with the Holy Spirit and transformed by the Holy Spirit.

Peter is now free to fulfill the call of God on his life. Peter will faithfully proclaim the risen Lord Jesus Christ.

Peter portrays Jesus as triumphant! Death, even a terrible death at the hands of the merciless, could not restrain Jesus.

The Easter victory is now at work in Peter as he proclaims the risen Messiah. The Easter victory is at work in us today. The Holy Spirit is invigorating us and calling us to new life to proclaim the risen and glorified Lord Jesus Christ. Alleluia!

Tuesday, April 18, 2006 Easter Tuesday
Acts 2, 36-41
Peter's Speech at Pentecost

"Then Peter said unto them, Repent, and be baptized every one of you in the name of Jesus Christ for the remission of sins, and ye shall receive the gift of the Holy Ghost (Acts 2, 38 KJV)."

When we become aware of our sins, we have an assignment! There are three parts to this assignment.

Three "R's." Repent. Remind. Receive.

Repent! We repent. It is very helpful to celebrate the sacrament of reconciliation and to receive the assurance that God has forgiven us.

Remind! We remind ourselves of our baptism. In prayer, we may tap again into the cleansing waters of the sacrament of baptism. We do this every time we dip our hand into the holy water font at the door of church and make the sign of the cross.

Receive! We joyfully receive a fresh infilling of the Holy Spirit as we invite the Holy Spirit to have free rein in our thoughts, our words and our deeds.

Lord Jesus, thank you that we may come to you and receive the forgiveness of our sins. You have set us free. Alleluia!

Wednesday, April 19, 2006 Easter Wednesday
Acts 3, 1-10
Cure of a Crippled Beggar

Where? At the temple in Jerusalem.

When? Three in the afternoon. Time of prayer.

The poor, crippled man was in the right place at the right time! This was his day and his hour.

The passage begins and ends with the temple. Outside the temple. Inside the temple.

Outside the temple, the crippled man sat and begged. That was all he knew to do.

After he was cured, he leapt! He offered praise to God! Then he entered the temple with Peter and John.

Lord Jesus, thank you for transforming us during this time of prayer, this time when your grace and your mercy are poured forth upon all. Transform us from our distorted images of ourselves as crippled beggars into an awareness of our true strength and our true wealth which you died for us to enjoy. Alleluia!

Thursday, April 20, 2006 Easter Thursday
Acts 3, 11-26
Peter's Speech

Quite naturally, the newly healed man was clinging to Peter and John. They were the visible, human instruments through whom he had been healed.

Peter was very careful, however, not to touch the glory. The glory for this healing was all given to God! Peter made it clear that he and John were not the ones who had made the man walk.

Peter used this healing as an example of the power of God, the God of Abraham, Isaac, and Jacob.

It was because of the name of JESUS, the Son of God, that the crippled man was made whole. It was because of trusting in the name of JESUS that he was walking and leaping and praising God.

Peter carefully portrayed Jesus as the fulfillment of the promises made to the prophets of old. He assured his hearers that they had acted in ignorance when they demanded that a murderer be released and that Jesus be sent to his death.

God still triumphed! God still had and still has the final word. God raised Jesus! Jesus was alive. Jesus is alive.

Lord Jesus, you are alive! I trust in you. Thank you for healing me and healing those I bring to you in prayer. Alleluia!

Friday, April 21, 2006 Easter Friday
Acts 4, 1-12
Peter's Speech; Before the Sanhedrin

The fact that Peter and John were telling the people about Jesus disturbed the religious leaders. They were threatened, to put it mildly.

Jesus himself had been a threat to these leaders. He did not fit into their box. He did not play along with their strategies for power.

Jesus was dead and gone. Or, was he?

These leaders asked how the crippled man had been healed. Fair question.

Peter was filled with the power of the Holy Spirit. Wisely, he used this situation as an opportunity to glorify Jesus. It was in the name of the crucified and risen Jesus Christ of Nazareth that the crippled man had been made whole.

Peter referred to Jesus as the rejected stone who had become the cornerstone (Psalm 118, 22). Salvation was through Jesus alone.

Lord Jesus, when we are asked about our faith in you, let us use the opportunity to witness to you in a courteous and articulate manner. Let us tell others about you and then trust the Holy Spirit to lead them to you. Alleluia!

Saturday, April 22, 2006 Easter Saturday
Acts 4, 13-21
Before the Sanhedrin

Jesus! Being with Jesus had transformed Peter and John. Filled with the Holy Spirit, they were now doing the works that Jesus had promised they would do.

"Very truly, I tell you, the one who believes in me will also do the works that I do and, in fact, will do greater works than these, because I am going to the Father (John 14, 12)."

If I am living a boring, listless life, I am not living the life that Jesus died for me to live.

Lord Jesus, you said that we would do the same works you did and even greater works. Thank you for reminding us that the Holy Spirit is within us to be and to do all that you call us to be and to do. Help us to take a step of trust today, a step of trust that will surprise us and delight you. Thank you for transforming us to serve you as have called us to serve you. Alleluia!

Sunday, April 23, 2006 Second Sunday of Easter
Divine Mercy Sunday
Acts 4, 32-35
Life in the Christian Community

This early Christian community in Jerusalem shared their possessions as well as their faith. Sometimes it is easier for us to share our faith than it is to share our things.

Sometimes, however, it is easier for us to give away material things than it is to open our mouths and tell others about Jesus.

Come Holy Spirit. Teach us to testify to Jesus in both our words and in our deeds. Alleluia!

Monday, April 24, 2006 St. Fidelis
Acts 4, 23-31
Prayer of the Community

"And when they had prayed, the place was shaken where they were assembled together; and they were all filled with the Holy Ghost, and they spake the word of God with boldness (Acts 4, 31 KJV)."

God's hand is stretched out to heal as we courageously speak out and bear witness to the risen Jesus. Through the name of the risen Jesus, wonders will emerge in our lives and in the lives of those for whom we pray.

Risen Lord Jesus Christ, let us remember that you have raised us into a new realm, though we are still on this earth. We are filled with the power of the Holy Spirit to speak with confidence and boldness about you. Alleluia!

Tuesday, April 25, 2006 St. Mark
1 Peter 5, 5-14
Advice to the Community

In our dealings with others, we are to choose to be clothed in humility. God will then delight to pour grace upon us!

What matters to us matters to God. God will care for us. We don't have to be so concerned about ourselves.

"Humble yourselves therefore under the mighty hand of God, so that he may exalt you in due time. Cast all your anxiety upon him, because he cares for you (vv. 6-7)."

We are not fully free to serve God as long as we are anxious to protect and to defend ourselves. As we seek to please God and learn to be pliable in the hands of God, God is working on our behalf and will place us in the place already ready and waiting for us.

We will find this to be a place of restoration, a place where we are free at last to serve God as God has called us to serve. Our delight is in our relationship with the loving God who has so carefully led us and prepared us. Alleluia!

Wednesday, April 26, 2006
Acts 5, 17-26
Trial before the Sanhedrin

An angel may open the door of our prison, but we still have to choose to get up and walk out! We have to choose to go where God tells us to go and to do what God tells us to do.

The apostles were imprisoned because of the burning jealousy of the high priest and his associates on the Sanhedrin. Instead of trying to understand the mission of the apostles, it was easier to try to get rid of them. They had not counted on God's ability to intervene.

Lord Jesus, sometimes we stay in our dark prison, even when the doors are flung open and you are calling us forth. Maybe we think we no longer have a place where we may serve you. You know the place you have for us. Today, we arise from our prison and walk out into the sunshine with you. You will show us the next step. Alleluia!

Thursday, April 27, 2006
Acts 5, 27-33
Trial before the Sanhedrin

Obeying God rather than the religious authorities may elicit fury. That's what happened with the apostles.

The apostles stated their firm intention to obey God. They noted that, although the religious authorities had been responsible for killing Jesus, God had raised him.

This did not go over well! The Sanhedrin now wanted to kill the apostles.

Lord Jesus, you are alive! We are alive, also. Let us live this day to the fullest. Alleluia!

Friday, April 28, 2006 St. Peter Clavel; St. Louis de Montfort
Acts 5, 34-42
Trial before the Sanhedrin

Gamaliel, a wise teacher respected by all, was also heeded by all. His sound advice was so simple.

If the apostles of Jesus were out there on their own steam, their work would eventually fizzle. If, on the other hand, God was the source of their power, nothing could stop them.

If we try to serve God on our own, with our own limited resources, we will not endure. We may exhaust ourselves into a frenzy and then whine about our demanding ministry. Hogwash!

If, on the other hand, we are intelligent enough and humble enough to yield to the power of the Holy Spirit working within us and through us, watch out! We will go to places we never dreamed of and say things we never imagined we would say.

We will learn the challenge and exhilaration of flowing in the power of the Holy Spirit. No one can hinder God's work.

Lord Jesus, thank you for helping us to be confident in living for you. Thank you for helping us to be bold in believing your word to us and acting upon your word to us. Thank you for healing us in any way we need to be healed. Thank you for freeing us in any way that we need to be freed. Alleluia!

Saturday, April 29, 2006 St. Catherine of Siena
Acts 6, 1-7
Trial before the Sanhedrin

The Twelve were called to pray and to proclaim God's word. They were to do so with the attitude of a servant. Jesus had washed their feet, leaving them an example. Jesus had said he was in their midst as one who serves (Luke 22, 27).

Beginning with Stephen, a group of believers was selected for service which would free the Twelve to do their particular work. The result was that the word of God spread! Even a big crowd of priests became faithful to God's word.

There is great loss and great grief in the Body of Christ, the Church, when some are not able to fulfill the call of God on their lives.

Grief, because they suffer the loss and frustration of an unfulfilled vocation.

They spend years serving, yes, but it is not the work to which they are truly called. They serve as well as they can, but they doing ministry they were never intended to do and they are experiencing deep weariness of spirit.

Lord Jesus, thank you that you are the Head of the Church. Thank you for setting your Church in order, so each may serve as you have called. Alleluia!

> Sunday, April 30, 2006 Third Sunday of Easter
> Acts 3, 13-15,17-19
> Peter's Speech

Even if the author is killed, the words of the author still live and speak. Jesus, God's Word, is still speaking.

Jesus, the author of life, is still speaking. Wonder of wonders, Jesus can speak through you and me.

God raised Jesus from the dead. The crucified, risen Lord Jesus Christ spoke through his first apostles. Words of power brought healing. Words of power, proclaimed in the name of Jesus, still bring healing.

Lord Jesus, thank you for writing your message on our lives. Thank you for speaking through us today. Let our words, spoken in your name, bring healing. Alleluia!

> Monday, May 1, 2006 St. Joseph the Worker
> Colossians 3, 14-15,17,23-24
> Renunciation of Vice; The Christian Family

"Forbearing one another, and forgiving one another ... even as Christ forgave you, so also do ye, And above all these things, put on charity, which is the bond of perfectness. And let the peace of God rule in your hearts, to the which also ye are called in one body; and be ye thankful. And whatsoever ye do in word or deed, do all in the name of the Lord Jesus, giving thanks to God ... (Colossians 3, 13-15,17 KJV)."

Clothed in love, Controlled by peace. Thankful. Speaking in the name of Jesus. Acting in the name of Jesus.

Lord Jesus, help us to live for you and to love others with the love that flows from your heart into our hearts. Alleluia!

Tuesday, May 2, 2006 St. Athanasius
Acts 7, 51 - 8, 1
Conclusion; Stephen's Martyrdom

The Holy Spirit was coursing powerfully through Stephen! The Holy Spirit had empowered Stephen to speak the plain, unpalatable, unvarnished truth to those who would murder him.

The truth was that their ancestors had killed the prophets and that they had killed Jesus. The truth hurt so much that, instead of accepting the truth and repenting, they now sought to kill Stephen, the truth-bearer.

The Holy Spirit, who had empowered Stephen to serve as deacon and to preach the truth, now empowered him to die victoriously. Stephen saw the open heaven and Jesus, Son of Man, standing to God's right.

Lord Jesus, thank you that the same Holy Spirit who empowered Stephen to live for you and to die for you now lives in us. Thank you that we have the power to be bold in our witness to you. Alleluia!

Wednesday, May 3, 2006 Sts. Philip and James
1 Corinthians 15, 1-8
The Gospel Teaching

It is necessary, not only to receive the Gospel, but also to stand firmly in the Gospel. It is through the Gospel that we are continually being saved and made whole.

Paul saw himself as a transmitter, not as an originator. He simply passed on what he had himself received. With great precision, Paul articulated the essence of the Gospel.

The Messiah, the Lord Jesus, died for our sins, just as we were told in the scriptures. Jesus was buried and was raised on the third day, according to the account in the scriptures. Jesus appeared to Peter (Kephas), to the Twelve, to five hundred at one time, to James and then finally to Paul.

Paul was keenly aware that he was unworthy even to be called an apostle. Paul, who had persecuted Jesus (Acts 9, 5) was now preaching Jesus. Ministry happens and it happens on God's terms. Alleluia!

JANIS WALKER   FIRST READING

>Thursday, May 4, 2006
>Acts 8, 26-40
>Philip and the Ethiopian

It happened while on the path through the desert. It was on the desert road from Jerusalem to Gaza that Philip, a deacon, met an Ethiopian court official returning from a pilgrimage to Jerusalem. As he traveled in a chariot, the official was reading aloud from the prophet Isaiah.

It was while he was on this path through the desert that Philip broke open the Word of God to the Ethiopian. Philip explained that the passage in Isaiah referred to Jesus! Now the Ethiopian could understand the Scripture which had been such a mystery to him.

The Ethiopian, noticing a nearby source of water, asked for baptism. Philip baptized him at this place of water in the desert.

It was on the path through the desert that the direction of Philip's ministry was changed. Just as Philip emerged from the waters, after baptizing the Ethiopian, the Holy Spirit transported Philip to a new assignment. Instantly, Philip was in Azotus on a preaching mission which continued as he traveled on to Caesarea.

When we are in the desert, we may forget that we are also on a path. We need to remember that the path does indeed lead somewhere.

The Lord is leading us and guiding us. While on this desert path, we still have God's Word to offer to God's thirsting ones. When our time in the desert is complete, the Holy Spirit will direct us to a new place, a new assignment.

Lord Jesus, help me to keep moving on this puzzling path in the desert and not to grow weary or discouraged. Help me to be alert to opportunities to tell others about you. Thank you for the new place you have waiting for me when my time in the desert is complete. Alleluia!

>Friday, May 5, 2006
>Acts 9, 1-20
>Saul's Conversion; Saul's Baptism;
>Saul Preaches in Damascus

Increments. Saul's conversion, dramatic though it was, still occurred in increments.

Before his conversion, Saul was acting according to his lights. He truly believed that he was called to destroy Jesus' Church (Acts 8, 3). So naturally, he sought to find the followers of Jesus and imprison them. He had also been present at the martyrdom of Stephen and had completely approved (Acts 7, 58; 8, 1).

Saul was acting according to his lights. Jesus, however, was greater than Saul's mistaken ideas.

Jesus, the Light of the World, was about to shine upon Saul, this poor, misguided man. He identified himself simply as Jesus, the one being persecuted by Saul. By injuring the followers of Jesus, Saul was injuring Jesus himself.

Blinded, Saul was led by his companions to Damascus. In Damascus, the Lord had been speaking to a disciple, Ananias, telling him his part in Saul's conversion. Ananias was instructed by the Lord to lay his hands on Saul so that Saul could see again.

Saul was then baptized. Then, after three days without food or water, Saul took nourishment and regained strength.

Earlier, in Jerusalem, Saul had secured letters from the high priest to authorize the seizure of believers in the synagogues of Damascus. The men and women in these synagogues would then be forcefully taken to Jerusalem.

The Lord had other ideas! Saul had been transformed by his encounter with the risen Jesus. He was now preaching Jesus in the synagogues of Damascus.

He was telling people that Jesus was the Son of God! Saul had been transformed by the only One who can change people.

Lord Jesus, so often we try to change ourselves or change others. We may even try to do this impossible task all at once. We can't. Only you can change us, in increments. Only you can change those for whom we pray, in increments. You send others to lead us by the hand. You send others to pray for us, that our blindness may be removed and that we may see. Help us to trust you as you work in this incremental way of transformation. We give you all the glory. Alleluia!

Saturday, May 6, 2006
Acts 4, 8-12
Before the Sanhedrin

It was in the name of the crucified and risen Jesus Christ of Nazareth that the crippled beggar became strong and healthy. It was in the name of Jesus that he began walking and leaping and giving praise to God (Acts 3)!

Peter was filled with the power of the Holy Spirit as he spoke before the assembled religious leaders (elders, scribes chief priests) in the Sanhedrin. Peter referred to Jesus as the precious stone which was rejected by the builders and then became the cornerstone. Peter made it clear that salvation comes only through the name of Jesus.

Lord Jesus, we rejoice in you and in the power of your name. Let us learn to speak your name with increasing respect, reverence, and boldness. Alleluia!

Sunday, May 7, 2004 Fourth Sunday in Easter
Acts 9, 31-42
The Church at Peace; Peter Heals Aeneas at Lydda;
Peter Restores Tabitha to Life

The Church was growing numerically as well as spiritually. The Holy Spirit was working powerfully in the lives of the followers of Jesus.

Through the power of the Holy Spirit, Peter announced to Aeneas, paralyzed and bedridden for eight years, that Jesus Christ was healing him. When Aeneas instantly arose, all the residents of Lydda and Sharon turned to the Lord!

When Peter prayed over the dead body of Tabitha (Dorcas), the Lord restored her to life. Many in Joppa came to believe in the Lord as a result.

It is the Lord who heals us. It is the Lord who raises us to new life.

Lord Jesus, we ask you to heal us and to raise us to new life. We give you all the praise and the glory. We pray to be filled with the Holy Spirit and to be instruments of healing and life for others. Alleluia!

Monday, May 8, 2006
Acts 11, 1-18
The Baptism of the Gentiles Explained

Peter had to plunge into ministry without understanding it all. Peter was fashioned by God to minister in this way. After all, it was Peter who got out of the boat to go to Jesus!

This was water-walking of another nature. Peter had been prepared for this new adventure in ministry.

As Peter had prayed, God had showed him, three times no less, that God did not discriminate. What God called clean, Peter was not to call unclean.

The same Holy Spirit who had fallen upon the Jewish believers in Jesus was now at work in the Gentile believers in Jesus. They too had repented and were receiving new life.

Lord Jesus, help us to pray and to be open to you. Help us to realize that you may have ideas of how we are to minister that will greatly surprise us. Breathe upon us, Holy Spirit. Fill us with new power to fulfill God's call. Alleluia!

Tuesday, May 9, 2006
Acts 11, 19-26
The Church of Antioch

Persecuted. Scattered all over. Preaching! The early disciples of Jesus, far from hunkering down in bunkers of fear and self-pity, went everywhere, telling about Jesus.

If we suffer for living for Jesus, we are in good company. St. Paul told Timothy that everyone who really wants to live for Christ will be persecuted (2 Timothy 3, 12).

Lord Jesus, help us to focus on you rather than on ministry. It is our relationship with YOU that matters. Let us learn what it means to live for you and how to serve you. Let us learn how to tell others about you. Alleluia!

Wednesday, May 10, 2006 Bl. Damien de Veuster
Acts 12, 24 - 13, 5
Herod's Death; Mission of Barnabas and Saul;
First Mission Begins in Cyprus

Listen to the Holy Spirit! Go where the Holy Spirit says to go. Minister in the way, the time, and the place the Holy Spirit directs.

It was during a time of serving the Lord in worship and fasting that the Holy Spirit appointed Barnabas and Saul, who were prophets and teachers, be sent out on a particular mission. Once they were in Salamis, they preached the word of God in the local synagogues.

Lord Jesus, help us to begin, in silence and in prayer, to learn to listen for the Holy Spirit to give us direction in ministry. Let us learn to serve you by worshipping you and fasting in the way we are directed. Let us not charge off on our own, but stay quietly in prayer and in our daily tasks. Thank you that we will know how and when and where to minister. Let us be faithful in our present tasks and assignments as we are open to new direction. Alleluia!

Thursday, May 11, 2006
Acts 13, 13-25
Paul's Arrival at Antioch in Pisidia; Paul's Address in the Synagogue

When Paul was invited to speak in the synagogue, he gave a very compact outline of salvation history, how God has intervened on our behalf. Paul was ready!

We don't always know how much time we will have to speak to others about God. We may feel shy and inadequate, and yet there are people all around us who are starving to hear that they are beloved of God.

Lord Jesus, we pray, in advance, to be courageous and confident to speak the words that will be just the nourishment that the hungry in our midst need. We are able to go and put food in the food baskets in church for the hungry. Help us also to learn to speak words of nourishment to the spiritually hungry. Alleluia!

Friday, May 12, 2006 Sts. Nereus and Achilleus, St. Pancras
Acts 13, 26-33
Paul's Address in the Synagogue

God's promise will come true! God's promise has already come true.

Paul reminded the people in the synagogue on that day in Antioch that the promise God had made to their ancestors had been fulfilled. Jesus, the rejected, crucified Messiah, had been raised from the dead. God had raised him from dead, as promised.

When we become weary in waiting, we still need to maintain an active hope. We don't want to miss seeing the fulfillment of God's promise to us. God is faithful. What God has promised to us will indeed be fulfilled. Alleluia!

Saturday, May 13, 2006
Acts 13, 44-52
Address to the Gentiles

First, jealousy. Then, abuse. They seem to be evil twins, don't they?

Paul and Barnabas continued to speak with boldness, in spite of the jealousy and abuse which followed. This kind of calm determination makes those who are already jealous even more abusive.

Paul and Barnabas were persecuted and thrown out of that area. They simply shook the dirt from their feet and turned to their new assignment.

Filled with the power and light of the Holy Spirit, they turned to those who were more receptive to their ministry. The joy of the Lord was truly their strength as they continued in ministry.

Lord Jesus, help us not to cling to the past, but to press on to our new assignment. Thank you that the Holy Spirit is guiding us. Alleluia!

Sunday, May 14, 2006 Fifth Sunday of Easter
Acts 9, 26-31
Saul Visits Jerusalem; The Church at Peace

Poor Saul (Paul)! Those who did not accept Jesus were trying to kill him. Those who did accept Jesus were scared to death of him.

Barnabas to the rescue! Barnabas, good and wise soul that he was, took Paul under his wing and acted as his interpreter, in a sense. Barnabas interpreted the fiery new convert to the frightened apostles.

Paul started to move around and even spoke with the Hellenists who promptly attempted to kill him. His new brothers in Christ decided to send him back to Tarsus for a while

Peace! The church had a time of peace in which to be strengthened and to learn to walk reverently with the Lord. Enjoying the consolation of the Holy Spirit, the church grew numerically.

Lord Jesus, thank you for sending Barnabas to help Paul in his time of need. Please send a "Barnabas" to encourage us in the ministry which has been entrusted to us. Help us to be a "Barnabas" to assist others in their ministry. Alleluia!

Monday, May 15, 2006
Acts 14, 5-18
Paul and Barnabas at Iconium; Paul and Barnabas at Lystra

Paul could somehow tell that this particular crippled man, who had never walked in his life, had the faith to be healed. How could Paul discern this?

Some quality of continued trust in God must have shone through the eyes of the lame man. In spite of his terrible affliction, the lame man still reached out to God and had not given up his hope.

His trust was radically rewarded. When Paul told him to stand up, he not only stood up, but he also jumped and walked!

Lord Jesus, we are all lame and crippled in some way. In spite of our limitations, help us to continue to trust in you. Thank you for making us whole and strong. Alleluia!

Tuesday, May 16, 2006
Acts 14, 19-28
Paul and Barnabas at Lystra; End of the First Mission

What happens if you do the work God told you to do and you basically get killed? That's what happened to Paul!

Paul had faithfully preached the Gospel, instructed others in the Christian faith, and had been mightily used by God to bring healing. Suffering is always part of the discipleship package, however.

Those opposed to Paul's ministry bitterly resented the way God was obviously working through him. They hurled stones at him and left, licking their chops, no doubt, and thinking they had destroyed him.

Not so! Paul was not dead and his ministry had not been destroyed. After the disciples had gathered around him, he got up and continued in the work God had entrusted to him.

Even though their ministry had involved great suffering, Paul and Barnabas still reached out to other disciples, to encourage them to continue. Paul and Barnabas were supreme realists. They knew, from experience, that following the Lord would bring opposition.

Lord Jesus, thank you for opening the doors of ministry which you call us to enter, When we become discouraged, strengthen us to receive fresh energy to continue. Alleluia!

Wednesday, May 17, 2006
Acts 15, 1-6
Council of Jerusalem

"My way or the highway! Do things my way. Follow God my way. Pray this way. Observe this tradition. If it works for me, it will work for you and therefore you should do it this way."

This irritating, arrogant way of imparting one's faith is nothing new. The apostles Paul and Barnabas had to deal with it in the early church. They had to confront the group insisting on the necessity of circumcision as a requirement for salvation.

This hard-line view of circumcision was being promoted by a faction, a sect, within the Pharisees. It could almost be called sect bordering on heresy.

Having been rigid in their practice of Judaism, they were now rigid in trying to enforce their view of Christianity. They were believers, yes, but they still needed a great deal of faith formation.

In the old covenant, circumcision was God's command (Genesis 17, 11). Indeed, it was the sign of the covenant.

Modern Christians often have their infant sons circumcised for health reasons. It is not necessary, however, for salvation.

Paul later wrote that "… a person is a Jew who is one inwardly, and real circumcision is a matter of the heart - it is spiritual and not literal (Romans 2, 29)."

Lord Jesus, help us to reach out to others in ways that will draw them to you as you really are. You are our Savior. You are the Lamb of God. Your blood has washed away our sins. Alleluia!

JANIS WALKER   FIRST READING

> Thursday, May 18, 2006 St. John I
> Acts 15, 7-2
> Council of Jerusalem; James on Dietary Law

Shared ministry! Peter, Barnabas, Paul, and James all had specific issues to address.

Peter made it clear that we are all saved through grace. God, who alone knows all hearts, chose to give the Holy Spirit to the Gentiles, once considered the outsiders, as well as to the Jewish believers in Jesus.

God made no distinction. Therefore, this particular group within the Pharisees had no business making burdensome demands on the new Gentile converts. Even God did not make these demands!

Silence. For a time there was silence.

The Holy Spirit was clearly at work, inspiring and underlining the words of Peter. Barnabas and Paul related the mighty works of God on behalf of the Gentiles.

More silence. Then, James, representing the authority of the Jerusalem church, underscored their message by referring to ancient prophecy about the Gentiles seeking the Lord.

James then stated that the Gentiles who were coming to God should not be troubled. They should merely observe the usual dietary and sexual regulations.

Lord Jesus, thank you for this example of wisdom shining from the words of Peter, Barnabas, Paul, and James. Help us to listen with respect to the words of others and then to speak the words the Holy Spirit instructs us to speak. Let all our words be for the edification of the lambs of your flock. Alleluia!

> Friday, May 19, 2006
> Acts 15, 22-31
> Letter of the Apostles; Delegation at Antioch

An excellent example of wise pastoral care! The apostles addressed the Gentile Christians in Antioch by letter and then by a personal visit which restated the message of the letter.

The letter assured the new Gentile Christians that the ones who had upset them had spoken without instruction from the apostles.

Having confused ideas of the Christian faith, this misguided group within the Pharisees sought to propagate erroneous teaching.

The contents of the letter brought reassurance and joy to the new Christians in Antioch. It was tremendous relief to hear from the apostles themselves.

Lord Jesus, we pray for all who have been injured or confused by teaching which is not from you. Thank you for sending wise shepherds to tend your flock. Alleluia!

>Saturday, May 20, 2006 St. Bernadine of Siena
>Acts 16, 1-10
>Paul in Lycaonia; Through Asia Minor

I find this passage very comforting. Apparently, even for the sometimes idealized early church, divine guidance did not equal a divine zap!

When we hear people talking about getting back to the simplicity of the early church, it's wise to remember that, perhaps, it wasn't all that simple. As with the early Christians, we too are living within the confines of space and time.

Everyone in ministry knows what it is to struggle with puzzling circumstances and with a very wide variety of personality types within the church. The early Christians had these challenges, also.

We may think we're headed in one direction, and perhaps we're correct to head that way, only to discover a closed door at the last minute. Then, a totally unexpected door of ministry may open to us.

Lord Jesus, help us to follow you as simply as we can. You are at work in the lives of all those around us as well as in our own lives. You respect the free will of all to follow you or to forsake you. When we are puzzled, let us trust you and continue to travel on with you. Thank you that the Holy Spirit will lead us to the door we are to enter. Alleluia!

>Sunday, May 21, 2006 Sixth Sunday of Easter
>Acts 10, 25-26,34-35,44-48
>The Vision of Peter; Peter's Speech;
>The Baptism of Cornelius

God had carefully prepared Cornelius, a Gentile who prayed and gave alms, to send for Peter and to hear what Peter, a Jewish Christian, had to say. Cornelius had even invited his relatives and close friends to be present for Peter's visit (Acts 10, 24).

God had previously made it clear to Peter that he was not to consider the Gentiles unclean or defiled (Acts 10, 15) The graphic vision granted to Peter happened three times (Acts 10, 16).

Then, there was an on-site demonstration of the fact that God is not partial. The Holy Spirit descended on all the people in Cornelius' house that day. The Gentiles were giving glory to God and were speaking in other languages! This is just what had happened to Peter and the other Jewish believers on the day of Pentecost (Acts 2, 1-4).

Water baptism was the next obvious step. All the people in Cornelius' house were baptized. What a celebration that must have been!

Gracious God, thank you that are an expert at shattering our preconceived notions of other people. You are creatively at work preparing us and preparing others to serve you and to glorify you. Alleluia!

Monday, May 22, 2006 St. Rita of Cascia
Acts 16, 11-15
Into Europe

Outside the gate! God loves to surprise us, especially when we trust him enough to venture outside the gate.

It was outside the gates of the city of Philippi, on the Sabbath, that Paul and his companions found a place of prayer beside the river.

Of the women gathered there for prayer by the river, there was a particular woman named Lydia, a woman who revered God. She was a merchant who dealt with purple. The Lord had prepared Lydia to listen attentively the message of Paul.

As a result of this encounter, Lydia and her household were baptized! She then offered hospitality to Paul and his group.

Lord Jesus, today I need a place by the river to pray, a place of Sabbath peace and rest. Lead me beside the still waters. Open my heart to hear your voice. When you know I am ready, lead me outside the gate. Alleluia!

> Tuesday, May 23, 2006
> Acts 16, 22-34
> Imprisonment at Philippi; Deliverance form Prison

Falsely accused (Acts 16, 20-21), beaten, and imprisoned, Paul and Silas still prayed and sang praises to God! Their extraordinary trust touched the heart of God.

At midnight, an earthquake shook the very foundation of the prison. All the doors opened! All the chains were released!

The poor jailer, about to kill himself, instead entered into new life, taking his family with him. Leading Silas and Paul out of the prison, the jailer asked what he had to do to be saved.

Paul told the jailor that if he believed in the Lord Jesus Christ, he and his household would be saved (Acts 16, 31). Paul and Silas, still suffering from their wounds, then preached the word of God to the jailor and his household.

The jailer compassionately cleansed the wounds of Paul and Silas. Then, the jailer and his household were baptized.

With water, the jailer cleansed the wounds of the suffering Silas and Paul. Then, in the waters of baptism, the jailer and his household entered a new life, a life with Jesus as Lord.

A table was set in the home of the jailer. A time of feasting and rejoicing followed. I wonder how much time had gone by since the midnight earthquake.

What we do when we are mistreated affects others. If we respond by praising God, who is greater than everything and everyone, who knows what sort of earthquake might result?

Lord Jesus, let me praise you and trust you to release me and to bless others. Alleluia!

> Wednesday, May 24, 2006
> Acts 17, 15,22 - 18,1
> Paul in Beroea; Paul's Speech at the Areopagus; Paul in Corinth

Paul met the Athenians where they were, or at least where they thought they were, theologically. He even quoted from one of their poets!

Paul's great learning was blended with his profound sensitivity to the Holy Spirit. He knew what to say and what not to say quite yet to the Athenians. Paul respected their traditions, as he sought to tell them about Jesus.

How often do we rush in and try to cram Jesus down the throats and hearts and minds of others? Perhaps they begin to associate Jesus with our misguided efforts.

A friend told me yesterday of visiting relatives and the attempts to get the two year old to go to bed. He stoutly protested, "No bedtime and no Jesus!"

There are people all around us who may have great wealth and great learning, but yet are starving for Jesus. We may have to learn, as Paul did, to proceed with gentleness and wisdom.

Lord Jesus, you told your followers to go into the whole world and proclaim the Gospel. Thank you that the Holy Spirit will show us the words and the ways to proclaim you today. Alleluia!

Thursday, May 25, 2006 Ascension of the Lord
Acts 1, 1-11
The Promise of the Spirit; The Ascension of Jesus

Stay! Jesus instructed his disciples to stay in Jerusalem and wait for the promise of the Father, the powerful Holy Spirit. Jesus declined to answer tangential questions posed by the eager disciples.

The Ascension of Jesus. The promise of the Father. The Holy Spirit.

Lord Jesus, help us to stay, pray, and wait. The Father's promise will be fulfilled in our lives. The Holy Spirit will give us the power to be your witnesses wherever we are sent. Alleluia!

Friday, May 26, 2006 St. Philip Neri
Acts 18, 9-18
Paul in Corinth; Accusations before Gallio

Fear often brings silence. When it's been too hard for too long, we may withdraw into solitude and silence. Why speak out, we reason, when it all seems so futile?

The great St. Paul was not exempt from fear. One night, the Lord spoke to Paul and reassured him. The Lord told Paul not to be afraid, but to continue to speak.

Paul was reassured of the Lord's presence and protection. Paul was also reassured of the presence of many of the Lord's own people in that city.

Lord Jesus, thank you for your presence with us in the night seasons of our lives. When we feel like life has silenced us, speak to us, breathe new life into us, and give us a new message. Alleluia!

Saturday, May 27, 2006 St. Augustine of Canterbury
Acts 18, 23-28
Return to Syrian Antioch; Apollos

Paul's travels were in a sequence ordered by the Lord. To Paul himself, his travels may have appeared erratic, troubled, and incomplete. Not so.

The Lord had a specific plan for Paul in each place. When that work was complete, from the Lord's perspective, it was time for Paul to continue to a new assignment.

Lord Jesus, we look to you for strength to serve you in our present place. Let your work be accomplished in us and through us right where we are today. Let our presence bring hope and strength to those around us. Then, when it is time, lead us to the new place you have ready and waiting for us. Alleluia!

Sunday, May 28, 2006 Seventh Sunday of Easter
Acts 1, 15-17
The Choosing of Judas' Successor

Peter quoted from Psalm 109, 8, about the necessity of another taking the position, or office, which Judas had held. Peter was preparing the group of one hundred and twenty disciples to select a successor to Judas.

The office Judas had held was now empty. Judas' tragic betrayal of Jesus made it necessary to choose a successor.

Lord Jesus, you chose Judas to be with you as one the Twelve. He exercised his own free will to betray you. Let us be true to you in whatever place you have assigned to us. Let us serve you with love and fidelity. Alleluia!

Monday, May 29, 2006
Acts 19, 1-8
Paul in Ephesus

Paul was an wise teacher. He took this little group of twelve Ephesians, found out where they were in their understanding of the Holy Spirit, and then led them into a fuller understanding.

They had experienced the baptism of John the Baptist, which was a baptism of repentance. This baptism was to prepare them for belief in Jesus, the Messiah.

Paul led them immediately into the baptism of Jesus. Then, as Paul laid his hands on them, the Holy Spirit descended upon them! They spoke in other languages and prophesied.

Lord Jesus, help us to be honest about where we are in our understanding of you. Thank you for those who lead us into a deeper understanding. Alleluia!

Tuesday, May 30, 2006
Acts 20, 17-27
Paul's Farewell Speech at Miletus

Bearing witness to the Gospel was the essence of Paul's ministry. It is also the essence of our ministry. When we experience God's grace in our lives, we long to tell others.

Paul was leaving Ephesus, where he had had a very challenging time. His bearing witness to the Gospel had created a riot among the silversmiths (Acts 19, 23-40)! His truth telling was a threat to their business of making silver idols.

The power of the name of Jesus was evidenced in dramatic ways in Ephesus. Many who had been involved in occult practices became believers in Jesus (Acts 19, 13-20).

Paul, now preparing for his journey to Jerusalem, put his time in Ephesus in perspective. He openly stated that his own life was not what was most important.

Paul's deepest vocational goal was to complete the course and the ministry entrusted to him by Jesus. Paul was well aware of the suffering involved in this kind of ministry.

Lord Jesus, when I am restless or listless, strengthen me to continue. When I feel useless, let me know that you are still directing my life and guiding me to the place you have already prepared for me. Help me to be faithful to proclaim you this day. Alleluia!

> Wednesday, May 31, 2006
> The Visitation of the Blessed Virgin Mary
> Zephaniah 3, 14-18
> Reproach and Promise for Jerusalem

"Sing aloud, O daughter Zion; shout, O Israel! Rejoice and exult with all your heart, O daughter Jerusalem! The LORD has taken away the judgements against you, he has turned away your enemies. The king of Israel, the LORD, is in your midst; you shall fear disaster no more. The LORD, your God, is in your midst, a warrior who gives victory; he will rejoice over you with gladness, he will renew you in his love; he will exult over you with loud singing. (vv. 14,15,17)."

God's humble remnant will not always suffer. God has not forgotten. A time of rejoicing is approaching.

Sing! We will sing. We will rejoice. We will exult in the Lord. We will no longer fear or be discouraged or downcast.

Our King is here with us! Our strong, loving Savior is refreshing us and renewing us.

Lord Jesus, we forget these glorious promises sometimes. Raise our eyes to you, our glorious Redeemer, and let us live today in fresh joy and gladness. Alleluia!

> Thursday, June 1, 2006 St. Justin Martyr
> Acts 22, 30; 23, 6-11
> Paul before the Sanhedrin

Just say who you are, speak the truth, and a tumult may occur! That was what happened with Paul.

Paul stated that he was a Pharisee and that he believed in the resurrection of the dead. Then, the Pharisees and the Sadducees really began to argue.

The Sadducees absolutely did not believe in angels, spirits, or resurrection. The old joke is that that is why they were "sad, you see."

Paul, caught between the two opposing factions, was removed from the scene. The Lord came to Paul and instructed him to have courage. Paul had witnessed to Jesus in Jerusalem and would also witness in Rome.

Lord Jesus, you know we want to have people like us. However, we are not called to be cheerleaders for the approval of others. We are called to be witnesses to you. Our presence will cause division. Our witness to you will provoke some, perhaps many. Thank you for strengthening us to be steadfast and to complete the course you have assigned to us. Alleluia!

Friday, June 2, 2006 St. Marcillinus; St. Peter
Acts 25, 13-21
Paul before King Agrippa

Trapped! Paul seemed to be caught between warring factions. He had been deemed a nuisance who got people upset with each other (Acts 24, 5).

Those who did not wish him well had made unsubstantiated charges against (Acts 25, 7). Does this sound familiar?

Paul had been handed over, like a hot potato, from one ruler to another. One particular governor, Felix, had left Paul in prison for two years. Festus, the next governor, passed him along to Agrippa, the king.

Lord Jesus, you are our true King. When we seem to be caught in the issues and the agendas of others, thank you for coming to us and reminding us that we are free in you. Within your realm, the only realm that is eternal, we are free! We are free to live for you. Alleluia!

Saturday, June 3, 2006 St. Charles Lwanga and Companions
Acts 28, 16-20, 30-31
Arrival in Rome; Testimony to Jews in Rome

Within the limitations of his chains, encumbered with the stress of unjust accusations, and bearing up under all the hostility he had endured, Paul continued to witness to the living Christ.

Lord Jesus, within all the limitations we experience, let us still lovingly and boldly witness to you. Alleluia!

Sunday, June 4, 2006 Pentecost Sunday, Year B
Acts 2, 1-11
The Coming of the Holy Spirit

Lord Jesus, let us be filled with the mighty Holy Spirit and speak in such a way that all will understand your words to them. Alleluia!

Monday, June 5, 2006 St. Boniface
2 Peter 1, 2-7
Greetings; The Power of God's Promise

How amazing that we may actually share in the nature of God! God has given us everything to make this life worthwhile.

We are instructed, however, to exert efforts of our own to persist in supplementing our trust in God with a program of continuing education in the Christian life. We are growing, continuing in our knowledge, and empowered to learn to control ourselves and to love others with God's love.

Lord Jesus, let us not be discouraged when we realize we have a long way to go in your school of discipleship. Thank you for the Holy Spirit who lives within us and continues to teach as we continue our journey Home. Alleluia!

Tuesday, June 6, 2006 St. Norbert
2 Peter 3, 12-15
Exhortation to Preparedness

We live within the temporal realm as we await the full unfolding of the realm of the eternal. We seek wholeness for ourselves and for others as we recognize our need for quiet patience and trust. As we mourn the evidence of evil on this earth and seek justice, we know that God has prepared for us a new earth as well as new heavens, where righteousness will prevail.

Lord Jesus, it is hard to wait. Help us to know that, deep within, we are already living in that new realm of righteousness. Alleluia!

Wednesday, June 7, 2006
1 Timothy 1, 1-3,6-12
Greetings; Warning against False Doctrine;
Gratitude for God's Mercy

"And I thank Christ Jesus our Lord ... for he counted me faithful, putting me into the ministry (1 Timothy 1, 12 KJV)."

Paul reminded himself that it was the Lord Jesus who had chosen him for his particular ministry. Because the Lord considered him faithful to be entrusted with this ministry, Paul was confident as he lived out his vocation. It did not mean that absence of suffering, but it did mean that he knew the Lord was with him at all times.

Lord Jesus, you have called us to be faithful in following you. Let us remind ourselves that you count us faithful. Alleluia!

Thursday, June 8, 2006
2 Timothy 2, 8-15
Timothy's Conduct; Warning against Useless Disputes

"Remember Christ Jesus raised from the dead, a descendant of David – that is my gospel, for which I suffer hardship, even to the point of being chained like a criminal. But the word of God is not chained (vv. 2,8,9)."

What is your Gospel? What is my Gospel?

Yes, the Good News, the Gospel, is available to all. Yet, Paul referred to" his" Gospel. The Gospel was personalized for Paul.

He was able to understand that the Gospel was being worked out in his circumstances. Those who called Paul an evildoer and put Paul in chains were not able to put the Gospel in chains.

Lord Jesus, I want to learn more about my Gospel. How do you want the Gospel to be played out in my life? Even in the midst of difficult circumstances, help me to live the Gospel for others. Alleluia!

Friday, June 9, 2006 St. Ephrem
2 Timothy 3, 10-17
Paul's Example and Teaching

Paul glorifies God as he offers realistic counsel on the living out of our faith in Christ. It is taken for granted that all who choose to live all out for Jesus will suffer.

"Indeed, all who want to live a godly life in Christ Jesus will be persecuted (vv. 3, 12)."

Lord Jesus, let us glorify you as we seek to live for you in these difficult days. Thank you for the examples of those in our lives and in the past who have helped us to know what is really important in this life. Thank you for the Scriptures to teach us and train us. Alleluia!

Saturday, June 10, 2006
2 Timothy 4, 1-8
Solemn Charge; Reward for Fidelity

"In the presence of God and of Christ Jesus, who is to judge the living and the dead, and in view of his appearing and his kingdom, I solemnly urge you: proclaim the message; be persistent whether the time is favorable or unfavorable; convince, rebuke, and encourage, with the utmost patience in teaching (vv. 1,2)."

It was in the presence of God and of the Lord Jesus Christ, who will come to judge both the living and the dead, that Paul charged Timothy to preach God's word regardless of how it was received. Timothy was charged to complete his ministry.

Paul knew that his time to depart was imminent. He knew that he had kept the faith and finished his course.

"As for me, I am already being poured out as a libation, and the time of my departure has come. I have fought the good fight, I have finished the race, I have kept the faith (vv. 6,7)."

Lord Jesus, strengthen us to do our part to fulfill the vocation to which we are called. Let us bring joy to you as we trust you, especially in the times when we are weary and discouraged. Thank you that your word to us will be fulfilled. Alleluia!

Sunday, June 11, 2006 Most Holy Trinity
Deuteronomy 4, 32-34,39,40
Proofs of God's Love

The love of God. Experiencing God's love is foundational.

How can we ever trust God, if we are not convinced that God truly loves us? It is especially difficult if we have not experienced love and security from parents and other authority figures.

God chose us. God speaks to us. God' commandments are given out of God's love, so that we may enjoy our lives.

Lord Jesus, you came to show us what God is really like. Heal us of any lingering misconceptions we may have about the nature of God. Thank you, Father, Son, and Holy Spirit for continuing to whisper to us, speak to us, and shout to us of your amazing love. Let us learn how secure and safe we are in your love. Alleluia!

Monday, June 12, 2006
1 Kings 17, 1-6
Draught Prediction by Elijah

The prophet Elijah faithfully spoke forth the words God gave him to speak. Then, also following God's direction, Elijah withdrew to hide in seclusion by the brook called Cherith. In this secluded place, God provided for Elijah's needs.

In this our own era of intense competition and confrontation, we need to listen carefully to God. There are times to withdraw and to enter into seclusion.

Lord Jesus, in the midst of your ministry on earth, you knew how and when to withdraw into times of solitude and contemplation. Let us be sensitive and courageous to follow where you lead us. Alleluia!

Tuesday, June 13, 2006 St. Anthony of Padua
1 Kings 17, 7-16
Elijah and the Widow

When the brook Cherith dried up, the Lord provided another way to care for Elijah. He was directed to go to a new place, Zarephath of Sidon. God had already arranged for someone there to provide for Elijah.

In order to provide for Elijah, this chosen person in Zarephath, a widow, had to stretch her own faith in God's provision. She had to trust that if she first gave water and bread to Elijah, God would take care of her and her son.

She did her part and gave to Elijah first. God then faithfully kept her supplied with flour and oil until the drought was over.

Loving Father, help us to remember that you are our source. You are infinitely creative and you will continue to care for us wherever you send us.

Wednesday, June 14, 2006
1 Kings 18, 20-39
Elijah and the Prophets of Baal

Fire! Holy fire! Fire from heaven.

If life has rained on your parade, God can send not only sunshine, but also fire. New power!

God can vindicate you and raise you up. You will not be cast down forever.

As the prophet Elijah obeyed and honored God, God took care of all of Elijah's opponents, all worshipping false gods. As Elijah repaired the altar and prayed, the Lord showed up in dazzling ways. All present acknowledged that the Lord was indeed God!

Lord Jesus, we seek to honor you and to glorify you. Sometimes, though, we become so weary and discouraged. We get tired of fighting off the alligators. Let us go to your altar, pray to you, and receive you. You are GOD! You know how to heal us and to raise us up to new life. Alleluia!

> Thursday, June 15, 2006
> 1 Kings 18, 41-46
> Elijah and the Prophets of Baal

Elijah humbled himself before God and prayed. Then, with boldness, he spoke of heavy rain before there was even a tiny cloud in the sky!

Elijah directed his servant to go and look for clouds. This scenario was repeated over and over. At the seventh try, the servant reported seeing a very little cloud.

Hooray! That was enough.

Clouds! A blowing wind! Torrential downpours!

Lord Jesus, let us listen and receive your word to us. Your word to us will come to pass. Your will indeed will be done in our lives. Let us be steadfast as we look at the clouds. Let us open the umbrellas of our hearts as we await the showers of your blessings. Alleluia!

> Friday, June 16, 2006
> 1 Kings 19, 9,11-16
> Flight to Horeb

A gentle whisper. The Lord whispered new directions to the prophet Elijah for the course of his ministry.

Elijah had been exhausted, terrified, and depressed after the great victory at Mt. Carmel. The weary prophet, after sleeping, was given nourishment in order to travel to another mountain, Horeb.

Although the mighty wind tore the mountain and crushed the rocks, the Lord was said not to be in this particular manifestation of nature, nor in the subsequent earthquake and fire. Instead, the Lord spoke very quietly to Elijah, who was hiding his face in his coat and standing near a cave.

Lord Jesus, we run, we hide, and we sleep. We are terrified. Perhaps we think you won't speak to us or that you will speak something we don't want to hear. So we run, we hide, and we sleep. You long to speak to us and you are speaking to us. Lead us this day, gently, into a new awareness of your presence with us and your love for us. Alleluia!

Saturday, June 17, 2006
1 Kings 19, 19-21
Call of Elisha

Elisha, the prophet who would succeed Elijah, was called as he was going about his ordinary work of plowing. He knew what it meant when Elijah came to him and placed his mantle over him.

Lord Jesus, help us to continue in the ordinary, daily work you have given us to do. Let us live in a state of anticipation and readiness to follow where you lead. Alleluia!

Sunday, June 18, 2006 The Body and Blood of Christ
Exodus 24, 3-8
Ratification of the Covenant

Book. Body. Blood.

Book. Moses read aloud to the assembled people God's instructions in the book of the covenant. The people assented to the Lord's words of wisdom.

Body. The bodies of the sacrificial animals were burned. Destroyed. Total holocaust.

Blood. Moses sprinkled some of the blood of the sacrifice on the altar and sprinkled the rest of the blood on the people. They were covered with the blood of the sacrifice.

Lord Jesus, thank you for the Book, the Body, and Blood. Thank you for the words of the old and the new covenants. Thank you that you are the sacrificial Lamb of God. You were offered as a holocaust for our sins. You took our sins and when you died on the altar of the Cross, our sins were destroyed. Holy Spirit, help us to understand this with our hearts. Thank you, Father, for your love for us in offering your only Son, your Beloved, for our salvation. Now we can come with confidence into your very presence. Jesus, thank you for your Precious Blood. May we consume your words, your Body, and your Blood and be transformed to serve you. Alleluia!

> Monday, June 19, 2006 St. Romuald
> 1 Kings 21, 1-16
> Seizure of Naboth's Vineyard

Fortunately, this story is to be continued tomorrow. As it ends in today's reading, we are probably feeling tremendous horror and frustration at the apparent triumph of evil.

Poor Naboth lost. He lost his ancestral vineyard. He lost his life. He was falsely accused and then stoned to death. All was taken from Naboth because of the immaturity and greed of the wicked King Ahab and the vicious scheming of the King's wife, Jezebel.

Who really wins in this world? Who really loses?

Lord Jesus, you came to redeem us. Help us to look at our lives through the lens of the eternal redemption you died to give us. It seemed that you had lost. You suffered terribly and died upon the Cross. And yet, you did not lose. You rose from the dead! You triumphed over death. Thank you that we now live in your Easter victory. All that we seemed to have lost in this short life is safe with you. We are safe with you, our Redeemer. Alleluia!

> Tuesday, June 20, 2006
> 1 Kings 21, 17-29
> Seizure of Naboth's Vineyard

Time for accountability! The Lord was aware of the heinous crimes committed against Naboth and was about to pronounce judgment against King Ahaz. The prophet Elijah confronted the king and spoke forth the judgment.

"Then the word of the LORD came to Elijah the Tishbite, saying, Go down to meet King Ahaz of Israel, who rules in Samaria; he is now in the vineyard of Naboth, where he has gone to take possession. You shall say to him, 'Thus says the LORD: Have you killed and also taken possession?' You shall say to him, 'Thus says the LORD: In the place where dogs licked up the blood of Naboth, dogs will also lick up your blood (vv. 17-19).'" Whew!

Surprise! Instead of acting with hostility and defiance, King Ahaz, horrendous though his crimes had been, repented after hearing the full extend of his punishment. He wore sackcloth. He fasted. He behaved with deep humility. The Lord, who alone is capable of seeing into the mysterious recesses of the human heart, withdrew the judgment.

Instead of retribution or retaliation, Naboth's death was avenged in a powerfully gentle way. Naboth himself was with God and God was with the guilty King Ahaz.

Lord Jesus, help us to abandon ourselves to living in a new realm of trust. Thank you that you desire repentance rather than revenge. You promised to the repentant thief who was crucified beside you, that he would be with you that very day in Paradise (Luke 23, 43). Let us live for you and leave all matters of judgment in your hands. Alleluia!

Wednesday, June 21, 2006   St. Aloysius Gonzaga
2 Kings 2, 1,6-14
Elijah and Elisha; Elisha Succeeds Elijah

Chariot of fire! Grief. New power!

Chariot of fire! Elijah was taken to heaven in a chariot of fire. Sure beats the airport shuttle bus.

Grief. Elisha, who was still clinging to his esteemed mentor, tore his mantle (cloak) in two.

New power! A new ministry was beginning for Elisha. As he had requested, he received a double portion of Elijah's spirit.

Standing on the banks of the Jordan River, Elisha took up Elijah's mantle. The Lord's power now rested on Elisha in a new way.

Lord Jesus, when will the sweet chariot swing low to carry me Home? Will it really be a chariot of fire? I'm not Elijah, but I want my death as well as my life to glorify you and to bring new power to those I am temporarily leaving behind. I want them to minister in a powerful way for you. Alleluia!

Thursday, June 22, 2006 Sts. Thomas More and John Fisher
Sirach 48, 1-14
Elijah and Elisha

A couple of hundred years before the birth of Jesus, the author of Sirach wrote of the heroes of old. The power and glory of God working through the lives of Elijah and Elisha still shine forth.

Lord Jesus, when we are no longer living on this earth, let your achievement in our lives continue to shine through those whose lives we have touched. Alleluia!

Friday, June 23, 2006 Sacred Heart of Jesus
Hosea 11, 1,3-4,8-9
When Israel Was a Child; End of the Exile

This passage overflows with God's tenderness and compassion. It was God who called Israel out of slavery in Egypt. It was God who stooped to feed and to embrace. Israel was indeed lifted tenderly to the face of God.

"Yet it was I who taught Ephraim to walk, I took them up in my arms, but they did not know that I healed them. I led them with cords of human kindness, with bands of love. I was to them like those who lift infants to their cheeks. I bent down to them and fed them (vv. 3-4)."

How could we have such cruel ideas of God? How we not believe in God's tender love for us?

Lord Jesus, life has hurt us, but you are healing us. Let us learn to trust and to live again. Alleluia!

Saturday, June 24, 2006 Nativity of St. John the Baptist
Isaiah 49, 1-6
The Servant of the Lord

Hidden. Concealed. Exhausted Feelings of futility. The writer is being very honest.

"... I said, 'I have labored in vain, I have spent my strength for nothing and vanity; yet surely my cause is with the LORD, and my reward with my God (v. 4).'"

God was there all the time. God had called Isaiah from the womb. The very name Isaiah referred to the salvation of the Lord.

Strength, rewards, and recompense were all in the forecast for the weary Isaiah. God intended to use Isaiah to be a light. Isaiah was to be instrumental in raising up Jacob's tribes and in restoring Israel's survivors.

Lord Jesus, thank you for coming to us when we are about to give in to feelings of exhaustion and futility. Thank you that the Holy Spirit is breathing new life into us. Thank you for reminding us that you are not finished with us yet. There is still work you have for us to complete. Though hidden and concealed, we are indeed being used as swords and arrows for your purposes and for your glory. Alleluia!

Sunday, June 25, 2006 Twelfth Sunday in Ordinary Time
Job 38, 1,8-11
The Lord's Speech

The Lord is getting closer and closer to a most glorious restoration of poor, suffering Job, but not quite yet. There is still an adjustment in Job's attitude that only God can effect.

Job still needs to comprehend the awesome power of God. Job has been fixated on his own personal suffering. Job has been trying to defend himself.

No! God wants to take Job to a much higher level.

Although God is eager to restore Job, and to make up to him all that he has suffered. Job still needs to reach his own "aha" moment. This is about to happen at last.

It is from the storm that God speaks to Job. God knows how to set limits on the tempests. God is preparing Job for a joy that he would not have been able to fathom before all these trials.

Lord Jesus, thank you that you are speaking to us when we are in the storms of this life. Thank you that the storms will not last forever, but that your love and your power do last forever. We are safe in your presence. You will use even the wild winds of the storm to restore us and to bring us to the destination you have prepared for us. Alleluia!

Monday, June 26, 2006
2 Kings 17, 5-8,13-15,18
Hoshea of Israel

The Israelites did not actively and thankfully remember their wonder-working God who had rescued them from slavery in Egypt.

God had lovingly and carefully cleared the way for the Israelites to live in freedom.

Instead of living in reverence and gratitude, the Israelites began to blend into the culture around them. They dishonored God.

They actually despised God's statutes and the covenant God had made with them. They refused to listen to the warnings of the prophets God sent them.

Instead, they chose to worship idols. God then allowed his people to be taken into captivity in Assyria.

We have done the same thing. We have ignored God, or only paid lip service to God, as we too have blended into this corrupt, idolatrous culture.

Jesus called his followers to be the light of the world (Matthew 5, 14). Instead, we have chosen darkness.

Lord Jesus, have mercy upon us. Thank you for all you have done for us. Open our eyes. Let us turn back to you. Forgive us. Use us once again to bear your light in this dark world. Alleluia!

Tuesday, June 27, 2006 St. Cyril of Jerusalem
2 Kings 19, 9-11,14-21,31-36
Hezekiah and Israel; Punishment of Sennacherib

King Hezekiah of Judah was a king who trusted in the Lord in a remarkable way (2 Kings 18, 5-7). When he received this troubling letter from King Sennacherib of Assyria, he took the letter to the Temple, spread it out before the Lord, and prayed fervently.

First, Hezekiah worshipped the Lord and acknowledged that the Lord alone was God. God, the Creator, was the ruler of all the earth.

Then, Hezekiah prayed, in humility, asking the Lord to come to the rescue! He implored the Lord to listen and to see all that was transpiring.

The Lord assured Hezekiah that there would be survivors in Jerusalem. The Lord would protect and defend Jerusalem. The Assyrians were destroyed and King Sennacherib returned to Ninevah where he met his death.

Loving God, help us to come to you, spread out the details of our troubles before you, knowing that you will intervene on our behalf.

> Wednesday, June 28, 2006 St. Irenaeus
> 2 Kings 22, 8-13; 23, 1-3
> The Book of the Law

All the people stood. All the people listened. All the people participated.

Something momentous was happening. The high priest, Hilkiah, had just discovered the book of the law in the Temple.

Upon hearing the contents of the book, righteous King Josiah was mightily alarmed. He realized how terribly his ancestors had sinned against the Lord, disregarding the commandments set forth in this book of the covenant.

Hilkiah, the high priest, and several of the king's assistants hastened to consult a woman named Huldah, a prophet, who lived in the second quarter of Jerusalem (2 Kings 22, 14-20). Huldah relayed the Lord's message of comfort to the humble, penitent King Josiah.

The king summoned everyone to Jerusalem. All the people, the priests, and the prophets stood and listened as the book of the covenant was read aloud. King Josiah publicly made a covenant to follow the Lord and to keep the commandments of the Lord with all his heart and his soul. The people all joined their king in this covenant.

Lord Jesus, thank you that we may come to you, humble ourselves before you, and trust in you. Let us keep your commandments with our whole heart. Alleluia!

> Thursday, June 29, 2006 Sts. Peter and Paul
> Acts 12, 1-11
> Herod's Persecution of the Christians

The Lord can find me in any prison and set me free. The chains cannot hold me when the Lord comes to release me. The right gate will open and I will walk through into freedom.

Lord Jesus, thank you for showing us the power of the prayers of the faithful on behalf of Peter in prison. With all those soldiers guarding him, it seemed impossible for Peter ever to escape Herod's prison. Thank you that your power is greater, always greater. Thank you for your resurrection power flowing through us today to release us and to send us on to continue our witness to you. Alleluia!

> Friday, June 30, 2006
> 2 Kings 25, 1-12
> First Martyrs of the Roman Church

Some of the poorest people of the land were spared after the years of horror. They were left to work as vine dressers and farmers, while all the other survivors were taken into exile.

This passage reads like a math quiz interspersed with the atrocities of war. The months, the days, and the years when this awful thing or that awful thing happened was carefully spelled out.

Jerusalem was besieged, The king was arrested, blinded, after having seen his sons murdered.

The survivors in Jerusalem were forced into exile. All except the farmers and vine dressers.

Lord Jesus, whether we are left to be vine dressers, farmers, or forced into exile, you are still with us. Within the confines of our present life of exile on earth, let us live as you direct, knowing that you continue to lead us to the heavenly Jerusalem. Alleluia!

> Saturday, July 1, 2006 Bl. Juniperro Serra
> Lamentations 2, 2,10-14,18-19
> The Lord's Wrath against Zion

Terrible, terrible. The merited wrath of the Lord is unleashed against faithless Zion.

Silence. Weeping. Bowed heads. Hungry children with no food in sight. They die in the arms of their helpless mothers.

Can Jerusalem ever recover? Will the Lord ever show mercy again?

The prophets who spoke false words of comfort to the people did not do them a favor. They did not speak the harsh truth. They did not confront the Lord's people. False prophets speaking lies.

Lord Jesus, thank you that we may come to you, weep, tell you everything in our broken hearts, and ask for your mercy and forgiveness. You will forgive us, heal us, and even restore us. Alleluia!

Sunday, July 2, 2006 Thirteenth Sunday in Ordinary Time
Wisdom 1, 13-15; 2, 23-24
Exhortation to Justice, the Key to Life;
The Wicked Reject Immortality and Justice Alike

Have you heard it said that death is just part of life? Well, that's not what it says here!

Quite the opposite. It says quite clearly that God did not create death. Everything God made was good and God's justice does not die.

"Do not invite death by the error of your life, or bring on destruction by the works of your hands; because God did not make death, and he does not delight in the death of the living. For he created all things that they might exist; the generative forces of the world are wholesome …. for God created us for incorruption, and made us in the image of his own eternity … (Sirach 1, 12-14; 2, 23)."

Death is an enemy, but a temporary enemy which cannot hold us. As St. Paul reminds us, "The last enemy to be destroyed is death (1 Corinthians 15, 26)."

Even more startling is the flat-out statement that God made us to be imperishable! How can that be?

In the play based on the book <u>The Secret Garden</u>, little Colin, who had been so sick for so long, had a revelation. He realized that he would live forever and forever. He began to grow strong and well.

That's the way it really is. God did not originally intend for us to die. We are truly imperishable.

We will indeed live forever and ever because Jesus lived and died for us. Jesus overcame death and the devil.

So, it is true, after all, that we will live forever and ever. We will have beautiful, strong, new bodies and we will live forever. Alleluia!

Monday, July 3, 2006 St. Thomas
Ephesians 2, 19-22
One in Christ

How many people feel that they are nobodies who belong nowhere? Believing they are unwanted and rejected, they drift through life as tenants, not really belonging and not really living.

As Christians, we are not to live this way. Having been baptized into the Body of Christ on earth, the Church, we do count and we do belong.

St. Paul, in his letter to the Ephesians assured the Gentile Christians that they, too, belonged. The Gentiles were long accustomed to being considered as second-class citizens, when compared to the Jews. They were assured that they belonged in God's household, too.

As Christians, regardless of our ethnic origins, we count and we belong. We are part of God's family. We are part of the Church whose cornerstone is Christ and whose foundation was laid by the prophets and the apostles. We are in place.

'So then you are no longer strangers and aliens, but you are citizens with the saints and also members of the household of God, built upon the foundation of the apostles and prophets, with Christ Jesus himself as the cornerstone (vv. 19-20)."

Lord Jesus, when we feel insecure, help us to see ourselves as you see us. We are your sisters and brothers. You are leading us Home. On the way, let us rejoice in our relationship with you. All else will follow. Alleluia!

Tuesday, July 4, 2006 St. Elizabeth of Portugal
Amos 3, 1-8; 4, 11-12
First Word; Second Word

Amos, a shepherd called to a prophetic ministry, lived seven hundred years before Christ. He spoke hard words of truth, because his allegiance was to the Lord.

It was the Lord God who had sent Amos with this confrontational message to Israel. Although Amos was eventually removed by the local priest at Bethel (Amos 7, 10-17), God's word could never be removed.

Lord Jesus, you were both shepherd and prophet. You were the Good Shepherd and the Lamb of God, laying down your life for the sheep. Son of God and Son of Man, you were God's Word, the Word made flesh who came to dwell among us. You spoke God's words and the authorities of the time sought your life. Thank you for strengthening us, in our brief time on earth, to be bold to live the truth and to speak the truth. Alleluia!

Wednesday, July 5, 2006 St. Anthony Zaccaria
Amos 5, 14-15,21-24
First Woe; Second Woe

Truth-speaking and confrontational living were hated by the people Amos was addressing (Amos 5, 10). They were placidly content with external religious ceremonies and then living lives of utter selfishness.

Amos continued to challenge the people to seek and to love that which was good. Offering sacrifices to God without simultaneously seeking justice for others was a phony, baloney religion.

Lord Jesus, we want to be real as we come to worship you. We want to become the people you are calling us to be. Show us today how to reach out in prayer and in action to others. Alleluia!

Thursday, July 6, 2006 St. Maria Goretti
Amos 7, 10-17
Amos and Amaziah

Nasty. It always gets nasty when a prophet's message collides with a leader's agenda.

Shoot the messenger! That's what Amaziah, the priest in Bethel, did. He told the prophet, Amos, to get lost.

Amos was from Judah and here he was giving hard messages from the Lord to Israel. Very unpopular.

The prophet was very burdened. Even his name meant "burdensome."

"Hey," responded Amos, "this wasn't my idea to be a prophet. I was tending sheep and pruning sycamore trees when the Lord called me to go and prophesy to Israel." At least, that's my paraphrase.

Amos, the prophet, faithfully delivered the word of the Lord to the priest, Amaziah. The priest's wife would become a harlot. Then the sons and daughters of the priest would be killed. The land would be divided and the priest would die in an unclean land. Israel would be exiled.

Lord Jesus, you knew what it was like to be a sign of contradiction. You spoke the truth to religious and political leaders and they did not like it. You were God's Word and you spoke God's word. Thank you for your presence and your power as we live for you and as you speak your words through our lives. Alleluia!

> Friday, July 7, 2006 St. Maria Goretti
> Amos 8, 4-6, 9-12
> Against Greed

The Lord had had it with Israel and decided no longer to forgive (Amos 8, 2). This may be a shock to those who placidly assume that God ignores sin.

Time. Grace. The people of Israel had had plenty of time and plenty of grace. They chose to ignore God and to commit idolatry.

The word of the Lord. The time will come when people will hunger for the word of the Lord. Although they would search for a message from the Lord, they would not find it.

Lord Jesus, we take so much for granted. Let us listen with rapt attention to every word from you and pray for the grace to obey your word. Let us live with integrity before you and before others. Alleluia!

> Saturday, July 8, 2006
> Amos 9, 11-15
> Epilogue: Mission Statement

Although the Lord was watching the sinful kingdom of Israel and would destroy it, the house of Jacob would not be totally destroyed (Amos 9, 8). The house of Israel would be shaken and sifted; all the sinners would be killed (Amos 9, 10).

And yet, in the future, the Lord promised to raise, restore, and rebuild the house of David. Fallen Israel was to be restored. There would be cities, vineyards, and gardens again.

Lord Jesus, out of the destruction which comes from human sin, you still have a plan to restore. Let us not lose heart, but turn to you, trust you, and rejoice in the restoration which is to come. Alleluia!

> Sunday, July 9, 2006 Fourteenth Sunday in Ordinary Time
> Ezekiel 2, 2-5
> Eating of the Scroll

When God's Spirit comes into me, I stand! God is breathing life, new life into me. I am not dead, after all.

Life may have stifled me, but the life of God renews me. Now I am ready to hear from God.

Ezekiel, prophet and priest, was being prepared by the Lord for a very difficult assignment. After Ezekiel's brilliant celestial vision, the Lord came to the prostrate Ezekiel and spoke. The Lord told Ezekiel to stand up!

Then came the message from the Lord. The Lord was sending Ezekiel to the rebellious Israelites. Ezekiel was being sent as a prophet to these hardhearted people.

This was not going to be a popularity contest. This was simple obedience. The Israelites would know with certainty that a prophet of the Lord had been among them.

Lord Jesus, come to us. Holy Spirit, breathe new life into us. Father, dear Abba, let your holy will be done in us and through us. We are secure in your love. Let us deliver the message you have given us to live and to speak. Alleluia!

Monday, July 10, 2006
Hosea 2, 16-18
Israel's Punishment and Restoration

Israel's time of desolation will come to an end. God's mercy will triumph! God will tenderly bring Israel, pictured as a bride, back into favor.

After the desert, there will be the vineyard. The love relationship of mercy, justice, and fidelity will be back in place for suffering Israel. The valley which was filled with so many troubles will be seen as merely the door leading to renewed hope.

Lord Jesus, I've grown used to the desert. I've seen so many rocks and scraggly, struggling plants. I've observed other thirsty nomads wandering. Spring up as the well of living water for all of us who are thirsting for you. Restore us to your favor. Let us see ourselves, not as dusty, dispirited, exhausted desert nomads, but as your pure bride, dressed in dazzling purity. Let us rise to greet you as our eternal Spouse. Alleluia!

Tuesday, July 11, 2006 St. Benedict
Hosea 8, 4-7,11-13
Perversity of Israel

Whatever consumes your time and your attention is the object of your worship. Is God really God in your life?

Are you putting yourself first? Then you are your own God. You are an idolater.

Are you putting another human being first in your life? Then you are an idolater.

Are you putting your ministry first? Then you are not putting God first. You are an idolater.

Israel was not doing what God had said to do. Independent of God, Israel was making kings and setting up princes. This was done without the authorization and approval of God.

Making altars to try to get rid of the sin was no help at all. These very altars were considered by God to be the occasions of sin. Israel was on a path leading back to slavery.

Lord Jesus, in silence. we humble ourselves before you. Forgive us for striking out on our own to serve in our own way. Forgive us when we thought we were serving you and instead we were serving ourselves. Forgive us for committing idolatry. Let us submit to your authority in our life. Let us listen with respect to the instructions of those you have placed in authority in the Church. We are not here to do our own thing. We are here to glorify you. When we truly learn to live for you, our joy will be beyond all imagining. We will know that you are truly in charge. Alleluia!

Wednesday, July 12, 2006
Hosea 10, 1-3,7-8,12
Punishment of Idolatry; Time to Seek the Lord

Altars! Thistles on the altars.

Thorns growing on the altars. What happened?

Israel was meant to be a beautiful vine, bearing beautiful fruit for the Lord. The Lord who had delivered Israel from slavery was rewarded, not with gratitude and obedience, but instead with rebellion and idolatry.

God had had it with these altars. They were altars to false gods. God abhorred false gods and the worship of false gods, in case Israel hadn't noticed.

In case we haven't noticed, God still abhors false gods. God still abhors idolatry.

It is time to begin again. It is time to acknowledge and to forsake the sins of idolatry. It is time to plow new fields and to plant justice. It is time to seek God.

Lord Jesus, we see ourselves so clearly in this passage. We have slowly but surely turned from you. We have defended ourselves and our right to live as we choose. Thank you for reminding us that we are not our own. We belong to you. You purchased us with your Blood. You paid for us on the Cross. You redeemed us, you bought us back. Forgive us for our stupidity as we chase after the gods of this world. Turn our hearts and our eyes to you and to the true riches of the heavenly Jerusalem. Alleluia!

Thursday, July 13, 2006 St. Henry
Hosea 11, 1-4, 8-9
When Israel Was a Child; End of the Exile

God is the loving, but lonely Abba Father, reaching out over and over to rebellious, defiant children. It was God who drew Israel out of slavery in Egypt.

It was God who held his beloved children tenderly and stooped down to feed them. They still failed to recognize God as their healer.

Instead of destroying Israel in a wrathful fiery judgment, God's compassion triumphed. God responded in love and did not allow his beloved to be destroyed.

Lord Jesus, you took upon yourself the sins of all. You died for all so that all could live forever. Let us not try to bear our own sins or the sins of others. You have already borne our sins. When you died on the Cross, our sins died. Let us live as the free people we really are. Alleluia!

Friday, July 14, 2006 Bl. Kateri Tekakwitha
Hosea 14, 1-10
Punishment for Ingratitude; Sincere Conversion

Health! Sin which has never been confessed can lead to guilt which can, in turn, lead to eventual collapse.

We were not created to live in defiance of our loving God. God's commands are for our own health of body, soul, and spirit.

The Lord called Israel to return and to repent. Healing was promised.

God's love and forgiveness will be like the dew of early morning to parched, desolate Israel. It will be like the lily that blossoms into fullness and fragrance.

Lord Jesus, we run to you and bring our hearts of contrition and our awkward words of repentance. We acknowledge our idolatry. We have put ourselves and others before you. We have worshipped false gods. We are parched in spirit and we have inwardly collapsed. Thank you for forgiving us, healing us, renewing us, and releasing us to do your will in your way. Alleluia!

Saturday, July 15, 2006 St. Bonaventure
Isaiah 6, 1-8
Call of Isaiah

Isaiah, called by God to be a prophet, one who speaks forth God's words, felt doomed because he knew his own words were not pure. I know that my own words are not pure. I have criticized and condemned others. I have criticized and condemned myself.

To be called to be a prophet does not mean to be called to be a judge. Only God is the final Judge.

We are to love with God's love. We speak forth God's words, often when we do not realize that we so speaking.

We may not, however, attempt to execute judgment on ourselves or others. St. Paul said that he did not even judge or scrutinize himself (1 Corinthians 4, 3b).

The holiness of God dazzles us. The love of God melts us. The wisdom of God overwhelms us. In God's presence, we learn to be silent. In God's presence, we learn to speak. With purified hearts and lips, we learn to speak the words God wants us to speak. In God's presence, we offer ourselves for God's service. Alleluia!

Sunday, July 16, 2006 Fifteenth Sunday in Ordinary Time
Amos 7, 12-15
Amos and Amaziah

Ah, yes, shoot the messenger. Expel the prophet. Try and silence the visionary who dares to articulate the vision.

Amaziah, the priest in charge of the royal shrine in Bethel, ordered Amos, the prophet, to get out and go back to Judah. After all, Amos was from Tekoa in Judah. Why was he prophesying all this doom to Israel?

Amos, however, was no hireling prophet. Amos was the Lord's prophet!

The Lord had summoned Amos, who worked as a shepherd and a sycamore tree trimmer, to go and prophesy to Israel. This was the Lord's idea, not some bright idea of Amos.

Lord Jesus, you have called us to follow you. To follow you in silence is difficult when we know there is something you want us to speak. To follow you by speaking is difficult when we know that we will be disregarded and treated with contempt. Help us to continue to follow you in fidelity, in silence, in words, and in action. Alleluia!

Monday, July 17, 2006
Isaiah 1, 10-17
Israel's Sinfulness

The Lord was telling corrupt Israel to forget about prayer! Indeed, the Lord promised not to listen to these long, boring prayers.

Why? Because Israel had forsaken the Lord. Israel had gone into apostasy. The leader had become like the leaders of Sodom and Gomorrah.

Is this happening today? How does the Lord view our worship services? Does the Lord listen to our prayers?

The Lord instructed Israel to stop doing evil and to learn how to do good. It sounded obvious, but it needed to be stated again.

The Lord's people are to be active in reaching out to orphans and widows. The Lord's people are to be exemplary in seeking to redress wrongs and to bring justice.

Lord Jesus, you are coming again in glory as King. May your kingdom come and your will be done on earth as it is this moment being done in heaven. Alleluia!

Tuesday, July 18, 2006 St. Camillus de Lellis
Isaiah 7, 1-9
Birth of Immanuel

Isaiah took his son, Shear-jashub, with him when he journeyed to meet the king. What a name, Shear-jashub!

This name, however, contained a promise. The name referred to the return of a remnant of the Lord's people.

When we walk into a scary situation, the Lord with us and the Lord's promise is also with us. We do not walk alone.

The Lord told Isaiah to counsel the frightened king to be quiet and calm. The Lord knew the plots of the enemy would never come to pass. It was the king's part to stay in a state of trust.

Lord Jesus. I become frustrated and frightened when I seem to be trapped in a seemingly hopeless situation. Thank you for helping me to remain in a state of trust and to continue to believe in your presence with me and in your promise to me. Alleluia!

Wednesday, July 19, 2006
Isaiah 10, 5-7,13-16
Assyria the Unconscious Instrument of God

We don't always know when we are being used as God's instruments. God used Assyria to cause great suffering in Israel.

Only for a time, however. Israel belonged God and no one, no one, no one can touch Israel without experiencing God's judgment. Judging Israel is God's prerogative.

Lord Jesus, let us be instruments of peace and healing. Let us trust you that, when we suffer, you will rise up on our behalf. When you have wrought the change in us that you desire, you will then deal with those who caused our suffering. Alleluia!

Thursday, July 20, 2006 St. Apollinaris
Isaiah 26, 7-9,12,16-19
The Divine Vindicator

There is so much I can't yet understand, but this passage reassures me that God will triumph! God wins.

We win, also! Light and life will spring forth where there seemed to be only darkness and decay. All the while we were weeping, God was preparing a glorious resurrection.

Lord Jesus, let us awake and sing your praise even as we keep watch and await your vindication. Let us continue to trust in joyful expectation. Alleluia!

Friday, July 21, 2006 St. Lawrence of Brindisi
Isaiah 38, 1-6,21-22,7-8
Sickness and Recovery of Hezekiah;
Hezekiah's Hymn of Thanksgiving

Lord Jesus, you have so many ways to heal us. You are the Lord of life and you know when it is best to call us to our Father's house. Let us continue to trust in you and to live each day to the fullest. Come, Holy Spirit, fill us with new life for the rest of the journey. Alleluia!

Saturday, July 22, 2006 St. Mary Magdalene
Micah 2, 1-5
Social Evils

Time! The time will come for restoration.

All injustices will be addressed. God sees and knows. We follow the Holy Spirit's leading to address the wrongs in our time, but the ultimate restoration comes only from God.

Lord Jesus, sometimes we are so filled with frustration at the evil we see that we lose heart and retreat into our shell. Thank you for the gentle guidance of the Holy Spirit to redirect us in our thinking and in our action. Thank you that your will indeed will be done on earth as well as in heaven. Alleluia

Sunday, July 23, 2006 Sixteenth Sunday in Ordinary Time
Jeremiah 23, 1-6
Messianic Reign

"Woe to the shepherds who destroy and scatter the sheep of my pasture! says the LORD. Therefore thus says the LORD, the God of Israel, concerning the shepherds who shepherd my people: It is you have scattered my flock, and have driven them away, and you have not attended to them. So I will attend to you for your evil doings, says the LORD. Then I myself will gather the remnant of my flock out of all the lands where I have driven them, and I will bring them back to their fold, and they shall be fruitful and multiply, I will raise up shepherds over them who will shepherd them, and they shall not fear any longer, or be dismayed, nor shall any be missing, says the LORD (vv. 1-4)."

In God's meadow, the lambs who have suffered under unworthy, corrupt shepherds, will know joy and peace. God will personally assign true shepherds and will judge the wicked shepherds.

Lord Jesus, thank you that will come as the Royal Messiah. Thank you that the time of suffering will come to an end as we laugh and sing your praises. Alleluia!

Monday, July 24, 2006 St. Sharbel Makhluf
Micah 6, 1-4,6-8
Accusation and Answer

The Lord reminds. The Lord requires.

The Lord reminded his own people of his saving acts on their behalf. He delivered them from the degradation of their slavery in Egypt. Graciously, the Lord sent Moses, Aaron, and Miriam before them to guide them.

The Lord requires, not some outlandish sacrifice which we think will be impressive. We are required simply to do what is right, to love what is good, and to live in humility before our God.

Lord Jesus, sometimes our guilt consumes us and we try to think up ways to bargain with you. We dream up noble sacrifices which we hope will impress you. We try to outgod God. Thank you, loving Savior, that you are the Lamb of God who sacrificed your life for us. You are our Brother and you understand how we are to live. Thank you for showing us what the Father is really like. Thank you for the Holy Spirit who is teaching us how to live and how to love.

> Tuesday, July 25, 2006 St. James
> 2 Corinthians 4, 7-15
> The Paradox of the Ministry

In ministry, it's all about the Lord and it's all about others! Our ministry is for the benefit of others.

People are not fuel for our ego trips. Rather, we are here to be poured out and expended for them.

God calls us not to find ourselves, but to abandon ourselves. We are to abandon ourselves to God. If we are shaken up, wounded, disillusioned, rejected by others, and misunderstood, perhaps for a long time, we may become bitter and cynical

God has not forgotten us. God puts us back together and then sends us out again. And again. We cannot be destroyed, really. The resurrection life of Jesus surges through us!

Lord Jesus, correct any faulty notions we may have about ministry. Instead of elaborate processionals and dazzling vestments, show us your processional and your vestments. Show us your painful processional to the Cross. Remind us of your simple vestment of a towel wrapped round your waist as you washed the dirty feet of your ragtag, irritating disciples. After we have fallen on our faces before you, lift us gently to our feet and send us out again. Let your perfect plan for our ministry be fulfilled. Alleluia!

> Wednesday, July 26, 2006 Sts. Joachim and Anne
> Jeremiah 1, 1,4-10
> Call of Jeremiah

God's power flowed forth from Jeremiah's mouth. God's words flowed from Jeremiah's mouth. When Jeremiah spoke, God acted.

God acted long before Jeremiah spoke a word. Jeremiah was God's idea!

God had called Jeremiah even before Jeremiah was conceived in his mother's womb. "Before I formed you in the womb I knew you, and before you were born I consecrated you; I appointed you a prophet to the nations (vv. 4,5)."

How extraordinary to us, in our limited conception of God, and yet, how like God. God's ways are truly above our ways.

The Lord overruled Jeremiah's objections regarding his youth and his inability to speak. The Lord would take care of all that.

Lord Jesus, you said that as the Father sent you forth, so you also send us forth. Let us learn to be silent and to listen to you. Thank you for speaking your words of life to us to transform us. Thank you for speaking your words of life through us to transform others. Alleluia!

> Thursday, July 27, 2006
> Jeremiah 2, 1-3,7-8,12-13
> Infidelity of Israel

From the garden to the gutter! The Lord had rescued his bride, Israel, from slavery in Egypt.

The loving Lord then led Israel through the desert and into a beautiful, fruit-filled garden. Instead of responding in loving gratitude, the people and their leaders chased after idols.

The Lord accused his beloved people of two heinous evils. They had abandoned and forsaken the Lord God, their true source of life.

Pure, living water flowed from God. Instead of drinking from God, the people dug up cisterns for themselves to try to produce their own water. These pathetic cisterns were, of course, broken and useless.

Lord Jesus, we are just like these people. We run from you and try to live our own lives. We wither and perish from spiritual thirst. All the while, the Holy Spirit is offering us clean, fresh, living water. Thank you for the purifying waters of our baptism Let us come back to you and drink deeply from the well of life. Alleluia!

> Friday, July 28, 2006
> Jeremiah 3, 14-17
> Restoration of Israel

The Lord is inviting and preparing his beloved, yet still stubborn, children to enter into a new relationship with him. He will gather them and bring them to Zion and give them wise, understanding shepherds.

Jerusalem will be honored as the throne of God. All will follow the Lord and all will honor the Lord God.

Lord Jesus, as we travel each day closer to the heavenly Jerusalem, help us to let go of our stubborn agendas. Help us to relinquish our stubborn wills and run trustingly into your arms and into your heart. We have offended you and we have wounded you by our rebellion. Thank you for forgiving us and continuing to hold our hand as you lead us to the house of our loving Father. Let us love you and honor you with our trust and our obedience. Alleluia!

> Saturday, July 29, 2006 St. Martha
> Jeremiah 7, 1-11
> The Temple Sermon

"The word that came to Jeremiah from the LORD: Stand in the gate of the LORD's house, and proclaim there this word, and say, Hear the word of the LORD, all you people of Judah, you that enter these gates to worship the LORD. Thus says the LORD of hosts, the God of Israel: Amend your ways and your doings, and let me dwell with you in this place. Do not trust in these deceptive words: 'This is the temple of the LORD, the temple of the LORD (vv. 1-4).'"

Lord Jesus, help us to recognize the prophets who tell us to reform and to change our lives. We can't just live any way we want, ignoring and hurting others, and then think we're safe because we're in church. You search our hearts. You send all sorts of people to us. You send angels to us, whether or not we recognize them as your messengers. You speak to us through Scripture and sacraments. You call us to come to you, to repent, and to live honorably with all around us. Alleluia!

> Sunday, July 30, 2006 Seventeenth Sunday Ordinary Time
> 2 Kings 4, 42-44
> Multiplication of Loaves

A small amount of food and a large number of people. Elisha's servant was dubious when Elisha told him to give it to the people. How could it be enough?

Elisha, however, had heard from the Lord. The Lord had told his servant, the prophet Elisha, that there would even be leftovers from this food, this barley bread and fresh ears of grain. This was food from the first fruits.

Lord Jesus, we give you ourselves. When you have transformed us, we are enough. We are enough to be used for your purposes. Let us delight to be so consumed for your glory. Alleluia!

Monday, July 31, 2006 St. Ignatius of Loyola
Jeremiah 1, 1-11
Judah's Corruption

There was a lengthy interval between the times the Lord spoke to the prophet, Jeremiah. The Lord had told Jeremiah to do some rather unusual things. Jeremiah complied, but still had to wait for more understanding.

Stuck in the waiting? Maybe the Lord has told us to do various things which we've done. Then, there is silence.

The Lord is still with us in the silence. The Lord is preparing us. The Lord is preparing others.

It is so hard to wait. It is so hard to remember that the Lord's ways are not our ways.

In today's first reading, Jeremiah's strange actions, directed by the Lord, were to be illustrations. They were meant to be concrete reminders of how Israel and Judah were intended to cling to the Lord and to glorify the Lord.

Lord Jesus, it's hard to wait when we don't know how you're using us. In the waiting, let our clinging to you bring you joy. Alleluia!

Tuesday, August 1, 2006 St. Alphonsus Liguori
Jeremiah 14, 17-22
The Great Drought

In the midst of great suffering, the Lord's people finally began to face the truth. They had sinned. Their ancestors had sinned.

They confessed not only their own sins, but also the sins of their ancestors. They reminded the Lord of his promises. They reminded the Lord of his covenant with them.

The people acknowledged that all the idols could not end the drought and send rain. Only the Lord God could do that. The people placed their hope in God.

Lord Jesus, we are so self-centered that sometimes we don't bother to confess our own sins, much less the sins of our ancestors. You see the whole picture. We are in the picture, but those who have gone before us are also in the picture. Have mercy on us all. Forgive us. Forgive our ancestors. Thank you for interceding for us before your Father. Thank you that your Father is also our Father, our loving Father. Thank you that the Holy Spirit is restoring us. Alleluia!

Wednesday, August 2, 2006 St. Eusebius
St. Peter Julian Eymard
Jeremiah 15, 10,16-21

Oh, dear. Bad day. Jeremiah starts out by complaining that he was even born!

It seems that everyone is against him. He has tried to live for the Lord and look what a mess he's in.

Life is bad. On and on, the suffering prophet pours out his heart before the Lord.

The Lord knows exactly how to deal with Jeremiah, his chosen prophet. First, with a stern statement of the truth and then with tender promises of assistance.

"Therefore thus says the LORD: If you turn back, I will take you back, and you shall stand before me. If you utter what is precious, and not what is worthless, you shall serve as my mouth. It is they who will turn to you, not you who will turn to them. And I will make you to this people a fortified wall of bronze; they will fight against you, but they shall not prevail over you, for I am with you to save you and deliver you, says the LORD (vv. 19,20)."

Truth. Jeremiah has to repent in order to be restored. He has to speak differently.

Then, what? Then, a lot!

The people will come to Jeremiah. He won't have to go to them.

The Lord will make Jeremiah like a solid bronze wall. Others may fight against Jeremiah all they want, but they won't be able to destroy him. The Lord will be right there protecting Jeremiah and rescuing him from the evil ones.

Lord Jesus, I've been spouting a lot of nonsense, too. When I get frustrated, tired and discouraged, I just want to give up. You are telling me to repent and to change the way I speak. You will restore me and release me. Holy Spirit, I ask for a greater manifestation of the fruit of self-control in my life. Thank you, Father, for your loving and tender patience with me. Alleluia!

Thursday, August 3, 2006
Jeremiah 18, 1-6
The Potter's House

A new place! The Lord is sending his prophet, Jeremiah, to another place for a while. In this new place, Jeremiah will hear from the Lord.

In Jeremiah's case, it was to the house of the potter that the Lord sent him. As he watched the potter at work, Jeremiah understood the Lord's way of working with Israel. As the potter formed the clay, so the Lord was forming Israel.

Lord Jesus, I need a new place. I know you can speak to me in any place and in any way. I'm weary, however. Please send me to a new place, even if it is to a new place interiorly. Let me hear your voice within my heart. Form me into a vessel to honor you. Alleluia!

Friday, August 4, 2006 St. John Mary Vianney
Jeremiah 26, 1-9
Jeremiah Threatened with Death

Don't skip any of the words! Little children can always tell if you skip words when you're reading aloud one of the stories they know by heart.

Jeremiah did not skip any of the words of warning that the Lord told him to speak. He was sent to speak these serious words to the priests, the prophets, and all the people gathered in the court of the Lord's house.

Faithfully, Jeremiah spoke all the message the Lord had given him. He did not skip any of the words, nor did he mince any of the words. He told them that if they obeyed what the Lord had commanded them and heeded the warnings of the prophets, disaster might be averted.

If not, well, bad news. The Lord's house, the Temple, would be destroyed just as Shiloh, where the Ark of the Covenant had been kept, had been destroyed because of the people's iniquities.

So, what did this get him? The priests, the prophets, and the people surrounded him and threatened him with death. All this took place in the court of the Temple, the house of the Lord.

This was no popularity contest. This was a suffering prophet living out his difficult vocation with full awareness that the message he delivered might not be well received.

That was not Jeremiah's responsibility. His responsibility was to listen to the Lord and then to speak the message the Lord told him to speak.

Lord Jesus, we still want it both ways. We do want to serve you. We also want to be accepted and maybe even to be popular. Let us learn this day a little bit more what it means to desire to please you and to glorify you, regardless of the response we receive from others. Let us not skip any of the words we are to live and to speak. Alleluia!

> Saturday, August 5, 2006 Dedication of St. Mary Major Basilica
> Jeremiah 26, 11-16,24
> Jeremiah Threatened with Death; The Fate of Uriah

The rubber has hit the road! Again, Jeremiah boldly reminded the people that it was the Lord who commanded him to speak these hard words about the Temple and the city of Jerusalem. However, the people still had the opportunity to repent and to change their ways.

Jeremiah also acknowledged that he was in the hands of his accusers. If they killed him, however, his blood would be on them.

For the time being, he would not be killed. Recalling the fate of another prophet, Uriah, Jeremiah was being protected by Akiham, the son of one of the king's officials.

Lord Jesus, bring us to the place where serving you as you direct takes precedence over protecting ourselves, our reputations, our ministries, and our very lives. All that matters is that we stay close to you and stay true to you. Alleluia!

> Sunday, August 6, 2006 Transfiguration of the Lord
> Daniel 7, 9-10,13-14
> Vision of the Beasts

While reading Daniel's vision, we are transported into the heavenlies. The Eternal God, the Ancient One, is enthroned! Flames are flashing forth. Multitudes are worshipping. The court of heaven is in session, ready to judge.

Then, during Daniel's vision, a human being, surrounded with clouds, goes to the throne of God. There, at God's throne, he receives supreme authority. All the earth will serve him. He will be king forever.

Lord Jesus, thank you that we will not be tethered forever to this earthly existence. We are made to live forever and ever in the realm of the eternal. Today, as we walk through the temporal, attune our spirits to the eternal realm. Let the little things that used to irritate us be seen for what they are. Let us concentrate on loving you and loving others. Let us enter today into a new perspective of our lives. Alleluia!

> Monday, August 7, 2006 St. Cajetan, St. Sixtus II, and Companions
> Jeremiah 28, 1-17
> The Two Yokes

In the house of the Lord, the prophet Jeremiah listened, along with the priests and the people, to the prophecy of Hananiah. However, Jeremiah heard from the Lord also.

Bluntly put, the prophet Hananiah was not only wrong about his prophecy of peace but he was also guilty of leading the people to believe a lie. As Jeremiah prophesied, Hananiah soon died.

Lord Jesus, we want to believe good news. We're tired of all the bad stuff. Still, to live as your truthful and truth-filled followers, we must face the truth. Speak to us the truth we need to hear about our own lives. Forgive us. Pour your mercy upon us and fill us with your joy. Let us learn to discern your yoke and to carry only your yoke today. That will be very Good News! Alleluia!

> Tuesday, August 8, 2006 St. Dominic
> Jeremiah 30, 1-2,12-15,18-22
> The Restoration

Restoration! Restoration will eventually come to Israel because God is in ultimate control.

Exiled Israel has been in great pain and suffering which has been allowed by God. Israel had been unfaithful to God and so God, for a time, allowed this anguish.

However, enough already! The God of justice and correction is also the God of mercy and restoration.

There was to be restoration of joy, praise, and laughter as well as the restoration of the ruined cities. Most important of all is the restoration of Israel's relationship with God.

Lord Jesus, we too long for restoration. Restoration of innocence. Restoration of trust. Restoration of joy. Restoration of true life in you. Thank you that you have cleansed us from our sins by shedding your Precious Blood on the Cross. Thank you for restoring to us the joy of the deep understanding of our salvation. Thank you for restoring our health of spirit, soul, and body. Alleluia!

> Wednesday, August 9, 2006 St. Benedicta of the Cross
> Jeremiah 31, 1-7
> Good News of the Return; The Road of Return

GLORY! Shout glory, brothers and sisters! Plant vineyards! Dance! Shake those tambourines! Good news at last!

The God of all mercy is rebuilding and restoring Israel. Israel, eternally beloved of God, is emerging out of wilderness exile.

We too will emerge from our earthly exile. As God's beloved pilgrims, we will arrive at last in the family dwelling place Jesus promised to prepare for us (John 14, 2).

Lord Jesus, I want to keep on keeping on while still in exile. Fill me with new strength to finish the course. Let me learn to start to sing, shout, dance, and plant. Thank you that all that seemed lost here will be restored there. The seeds sown in prayer will bear a harvest. Alleluia!

> Thursday, August 10, 2006 St. Lawrence
> Jeremiah 31, 31-34
> The New Covenant

"The days are surely coming, says the LORD, when I will make a new covenant with the house of Israel and the house of Judah. It will not be like the covenant that I made with their ancestors when I took them by the hand to bring them out of the land of Egypt – a covenant that they broke, although I was their husband, says the LORD. But this is the covenant that I will make with the house of Israel after those days, says the LORD: I will put my law within them, and I will write it on their hearts; and I will be their God, and they shall be my people. No longer shall they teach one another, or say to each other, 'Know the LORD,' for they shall all know me, from the least of them to the greatest, says the LORD; for I will forgive their iniquity, and remember their sin no more (Jeremiah 31, 31-34)."

The new covenant God promised to Israel is right here for us to enjoy! Deep, deep within our hearts God's loving laws are written

We know, deep within. We know. We belong to God and God (how amazing!) belongs to us.

No class distinction. The greatest and the least all may know God in this intimate way.

God not only promises to forgive the evil we have done, but also to forget our sins. Not just to forgive, but also to forget. God can do that.

Lord Jesus, we still live as though we are staring at laws written in stone somewhere out there. Teach us to know the tender heartbeat of God within. Alleluia!

> Friday, August 11, 2006 St. Clare
> Nahum 2, 1,3; 3, 1-3,6-7
> The Lord's Coming in Judgment; Ruin Imminent and Inevitable

Why in the world should we be concerned about getting even with anyone? All matters of judgment are ultimately in God's hands.

Lord Jesus, let us live in trust and implore your mercy for ourselves and for all. You are our Advocate. You alone can restore us. You will care for the tendrils of our lives. You will set the record straight. We will blossom in your love. Alleluia!

> Saturday, August 12, 2006
> Habakkuk 1, 12 - 2, 4
> The Prophet's Complaint and Its Answer

The prophet Habakkuk poured out his anguished heart to the Lord, asking why, why, why. The Lord did not criticize or condemn Habakkuk for asking why.

Instead, the Lord reoriented Habakkuk's time frame. The Lord had not forgotten the suffering of Judah.

"I will stand at my watchpost, and station myself on the rampart; I will keep watch to see what he will say to me, and what he will answer concerning my complaint. Then the LORD answered me and said: Write the vision; make it plain on tablets, so that a runner may read it. For there is still a vision for the appointed time; it speaks of the end, and does not lie. If it seems to tarry, wait for it; it will surely come, it will not delay (vv. 2, 1-3)."

There was a vision yet to be fulfilled for the suffering people of Judah. The vision would indeed be fulfilled.

Carry on! The just were to carry on in trust.

Lord Jesus, thank you that your vision for us will also be fulfilled. When we are exhausted and discouraged, help us to carry on, to continue in calm, active trust. We will one day walk into the fulfillment of the vision you gave us. Alleluia!

> Sunday, August 13, 2006 Nineteenth Sunday in Ordinary Time
> 1 Kings 19, 4-8
> Flight to Horeb

"But he [Elijah] himself went a day's journey into the wilderness, and came and sat down under a solitary broom tree. He asked that he might die. 'It is enough; now, O LORD, take away my life, for I am no better than my ancestors. Then he lay down under the broom tree and fell asleep (vv. 4-5a)."

Elijah, the mighty prophet Elijah, prayed to die! He was exhausted and depleted. The Lord did not condemn Elijah for expressing such despair.

Instead, the Lord sent an angel, a messenger, to minister to Elijah, who had fallen into a deep sleep. The angel brought bread and water to strengthen the prophet. Energized, Elijah walked on to the mountain, God's mountain, Horeb.

Lord Jesus, you invite us to come to you and to be real about our lives. You invite us to come to you and to be refreshed. You invite us to come to you and to receive new strength to continue our journey. Alleluia!

> Monday, August 14, 2006 St. Maximilian Kolbe
> Ezekiel 1, 2-5,24-25
> The Vision: God on the Cherubim

"In the thirtieth year, in the fourth month, on the fifth day of the month, as I was among the exiles by the river Chebar, the heavens were opened, and I saw visions of God (Ezekiel 1, 1)."

The Lord's word. The Lord's hand.

In a place of exile, by the banks of a river, the word of the Lord came to the priest, Ezekiel.

The word of the Lord came to him. The hand of the Lord came upon him.

The word of the Lord comes to us. We are stopped.

We ask ourselves if we really heard from the Lord. We are learning to listen to the Lord.

The hand of the Lord comes upon us. We are moved. We are moved to respond.

We may be called to wait. And wait. And wait.

Most definitely, we will be called to trust. We will increasingly learn to act as the Lord directs.

We are no longer our own. We never were. The difference is that now we know this in a different way.

Lord Jesus, Ezekiel saw creatures within a cloud within the winds of the storm. Today, let me see you in action within the clouds and the winds and the storms of my life. Let your word come to me. Let your hand be upon me. Let me learn to trust, to wait, and to act according to your will. Alleluia!

Tuesday, August 15, 2006 Assumption of the Blessed Virgin Mary
Revelation 11, 19; 12, 1-6,10
The Two Witnesses
The Woman and the Dragon

In the writer's vision, recorded in the first part of Revelation 11, the writer is instructed to measure the temple and the altar with a staff-like measuring rod. Only the inner court would be measured.

Later, there would be another rod, a rod of iron. This would be the rod with which the son of the sun-clothed woman would rule the nations.

The dragon, waiting to devour her son would not be successful. The child would be protected by the God of all power. The woman would be protected, also, in a place of safety prepared for her by God.

Lord Jesus, you are truly Son of God and Son of Mary. As the gentle Good Shepherd, you still guide your flock. As the royal Messiah, you will rule and reign forever and ever. Measure us today. Fit us to serve you in your temple and at your altar. Let us be your witnesses. Let us testify to you, believing that even if we are silenced, you will continue to speak your message through us and you will restore us. Alleluia!

Wednesday, August 16, 2006 St. Stephen of Hungary
Ezekiel 9, 1-7; 10, 18-22
Slaughter of the Idolaters; God's Glory Leaves Jerusalem

In Ezekiel's vision, the linen-clad man with the writer's case marked an "X" (the Hebrew letter "tau") on those who abhorred the sacrileges committed in Jerusalem. All others would be slain.

The holy city had become corrupt. God's glory would soon depart from the Temple. What could be more tragic?

In Baptism, we too are marked. We are marked, we are signed with the sign of the cross.

"You are sealed by the Holy Spirit in Baptism and marked as Christ's own forever (The Book of Common Prayer, p. 308)."

We belong to God. We are not our own.

Lord Jesus, from the bronze altar in Ezekiel's vision, agents of destruction were sent to slaughter the wicked. As we leave your altar where we have been fed with your true Body and Blood, let us be agents of your life. Marked with the sign of the cross, let us live in peace as we pray for the peace of Jerusalem. Alleluia!

Thursday, August 17, 2006
Ezekiel 12, 1-2
Acts Symbolic of the Exile

The Lord speaks directly to the prophet Ezekiel, preparing him for his assignment. The Lord reminds Ezekiel that he is living amongst rebellious people.

These were people who were capable of seeing and hearing, but they did not see and did not hear, because of their rebellion against the Lord. The Lord spoke to Ezekiel and said, "Therefore ... prepare for yourself an exile's baggage, and go into exile by day in their sight; you shall go like an exile from your place to another place in their sight. Perhaps they will understand, though they are a rebellious house (Exekiel 12, 3)."

Lord Jesus, we also live among people who choose to ignore you and to rebel against your sovereignty. Help us not only to love them, but also to be very sensitive to your voice. You have forgiven us over and over. Let us also be merciful in our dealings with others. You will tell us how to live while we are in this place of exile. Alleluia!

Friday, August 18, 2006 St. Jane de Chantal
Ezekiel 16, 1-5,60,63
The Faithless Spouse

In vivid imagery, the Lord reminds Jerusalem of her origin. She was nothing. From infancy, the Lord had cared tenderly for her.

When she was ready, the Lord entered into a covenant relationship with her. Everything beautiful was bestowed upon her. Exquisite silk gowns. The finest food.

Instead of gratitude, Jerusalem began to become infatuated with herself. She grew proud and conceited, thinking first of herself. She entered into idolatrous relationships, thus becoming unfaithful to the Lord who had called her and loved her.

Yet the Lord remembered. The Lord remembered the covenant with the beautiful young bride.

What the grieving Lord did was to arrange an everlasting covenant. Jerusalem would fall silent and ashamed as she remembered her faithlessness.

Lord Jesus, thank you that you are our Bridegroom and we are your Bride, your Church. We will rejoice one day with you at the Marriage Feast of the Lamb. You are the holy Lamb of God who offered yourself as the perfect sacrifice for our sins. Remind us today of who you are, who we are, and whose we are. We belong to YOU! Alleluia!

Saturday, August 19, 2006 St. John Eudes
Ezekiel 18, 1-10,13,30-32
Personal Responsibility

Responsibility! The Lord is very clear about this matter.

Each person will be judged individually, regardless of the conduct of other family members. Each is responsible before the Lord.

The Lord says to turn away from past evil deeds and to make new hearts and new spirits.

Turn to the Lord. LIVE!

Lord Jesus, thank you that this is a new day. We don't have to be burdened with the sins and the mistakes of the past. We don't have to blame our genes. Forgive us. Cleanse us. Set us free to live and to serve you today with joy. Alleluia!

> Sunday, August 20, 2006 Twentieth Sunday in Ordinary Time
> Proverbs 9, 1-6
> The Two Banquets

Where do we like to hang out and eat? With the mindless who choose poison or with the wise who feast with joy?

Lord Jesus, we are invited to the table of wisdom which gives life. Let us discern what is good for us. Thank you for feeding us at your altar and sending us into the world to nourish others. Alleluia!

> Monday, August 21, 2006 St. Pius X
> Ezekiel 24, 15-24
> Symbol of the Destruction of the Temple

No rivals. Not even the Temple.

As a prophet, Ezekiel has been given the tragic task of being a sign. The Lord is about to destroy the Temple in Jerusalem.

Ezekiel is told that even when his wife dies he is not to make an outer show of mourning. In just the same way, the sinful people of Jerusalem are not to mourn when the Temple is destroyed. They themselves will also be destroyed because of their sins.

Lord Jesus, the people back in Ezekiel's time thought that nothing could destroy the Temple and yet it was not spared. Have mercy on us. Forgive all our sins and help us to forgive others. Teach us to delight in you. You are our treasure. Thank you for setting all our priorities in your order. Alleluia!

> Tuesday, August 22, 2006 Queenship of Mary
> Ezekiel 28, 1-10
> The Prince of Tyre

The Lord had a thing or two to tell the Prince of Tyre. The Lord instructed Ezekiel exactly what to say to the prince.

Basically, Ezekiel told the prince, "You're toast. You've believed your own press. You're not as great as you think you are. You are going to die a terrible death."

Lord Jesus, thank you for sending prophets to speak to us the hard, but true words we need to hear to set us free. Let us be open to hearing your message today, regardless of the messenger. Alleluia!

Wednesday, August 23, 2006 St. Rose of Lima
Ezekiel 34, 1-11
Parable of the Shepherds

The wicked shepherds of Israel have fleeced the sheep, but have not fed the sheep. They used the sheep for their own purposes, instead of serving the sheep.

The Lord, outraged by this betrayal of trust, will remove these unworthy shepherds. The Lord God will personally care for the sheep.

Lord Jesus, you are the Good Shepherd. We may safely entrust ourselves into your loving care. Thank you for leading us, feeding us, guarding us, and guiding us safely Home. Alleluia!

Thursday, August 24, 2006 St. Bartholomew
Revelation 21, 9-14
The New Jerusalem

"Then I saw a new heaven and a new earth; for the first heaven and first earth had passed away, and the sea was no more. And I saw the holy city, the new Jerusalem, coming down our of heaven from God, prepared as a bride adorned for her husband (vv. 1,2)."

We are invited to lift our eyes and our hearts to the heavenly Jerusalem, the Church, the Bride of Christ, the Lamb. We are looking at ourselves as we will be!

We will be living with Jesus. We will be transformed. The radiance of God will, at last, shine through us completely.

Lord Jesus, let us enter this day with rejoicing and thanksgiving. Thank you for leading us through new gates. We are still learning to yield to you, our gentle Shepherd. We are beginning to see you as the Lamb of God whose blood has cleansed us. We are no longer stuck in the mundane. We are beginning to live in the heavenly reality which awaits us and which is already within us. Alleluia!

Friday, August 25, 2006 St. Louis Calasanz
Ezekiel 37, 1-14
Vision of the Dry Bones

All of Israel had been speaking words of death. All of Israel had been saying that they were dead. They said that there was no hope.

The Lord stepped in by sending the prophet, Ezekiel, to speak words of life and hope. The dry bones won't stay dry! The Lord tells Ezekiel to prophesy new words to the dry bones.

"Then he said to me, 'Prophesy to these bones, and say to them: O dry bones, hear the word of the LORD. Thus says the LORD GOD to these bones: I shall cause breath to enter you, and you shall live (vv. 4,5)."

The Lord will bring spirit into these dead, dry bones. The bones will be brought together.

Flesh and skin will cover the bones. Spirit will enter into the bones.

These bones will live! What the Lord promises, the Lord will accomplish.

Lord Jesus, when we have felt dead for so long, we are without hope. Thank you for coming to us and speaking words of life to us. Teach us also to begin to speak words of life to ourselves and to others. Thank you for reminding us of your promises to us. We are beginning to breathe again and to arise to new life and to new hope. We know that your words of life to us will come to us and we live in joyful expectation. We speak forth words of life and hope. Alleluia!

Saturday, August 26, 2006
Ezekiel 43, 1-7
The Return of the Lord

"Then he brought me to the gate, the gate facing east. And there, the glory of the God of Israel was coming from the east; the sound was like the sound of mighty waters; and the earth shone with his glory. The vision I saw was like the vision that I had seen when he came to destroy the city, and like the vision I had seen by the river Chebar; and I fell upon my face. As the glory of the LORD entered the temple by the gate facing east, the spirit lifted me up, and brought me into the inner court; and the glory of the LORD filled the temple (vv. 1-5)."

The priest and prophet, Ezekiel, was granted a vision of the glory of the Lord filling the temple. The spirit of the Lord lifted Ezekiel and brought him into the inner court of the temple. The glory and the majestic holiness of the Lord was shining forth!

Lord Jesus, when you died on the Cross, the veil in the temple was torn asunder. We now have free access to come into the presence of God. You died to make all this possible. Let the light of the glory of God shine upon us and shine forth from us today. Alleluia!

Sunday, August 27, 2006 Twenty-first Sunday in Ordinary Time
Joshua 24, 1-2,15-18
Reminder of the Divine Goodness; Renewal of the Covenant

The elderly Joshua gathered the tribes of Israel to ask for a definite commitment. He reviewed what the Lord had done for Israel and then challenged the people to decide.

"Now if you are unwilling to serve the LORD, choose this day whom you will serve ... but as for me and my household, we will serve the LORD (v. 15)."

Would the people of Israel serve the Lord and get rid of any competition to the Lord's sovereignty? Joshua and his family were committed to serving the Lord.

Lord Jesus, we choose again today to serve you. It is so easy to think we are serving you when, in reality, we are serving ourselves. Thank you for your mercy and your forgiveness. Let us hold fast to you and follow you closely as you lead us Home. Alleluia!

Monday, August 28, 2006 St. Augustine
2 Thessalonians 1, 1-5,11-12
Greeting; Thanksgiving; Prayer

Paul commends the Christian community at Thessalonica for not only for growing in the faith, but also for growing in the ability to love each other. These two cannot be separated.

What good is it to say what a strong believer I am if it cannot also be said of me that I reach out in loving concern to other Christians? Am I harboring resentment to another Christian? My thoughts need to be brought into alignment with God's love for that particular person.

God is inviting us to practice this love for other Christians. It is not easy. They are still people and we are still people. We are not angels!

The love of God has most certainly not yet been perfected in any of us. As a child practices scales at the piano, we need to ask for God's help as we practice patiently our loving concern for other Christians.

We do this by focusing on Jesus, our Lamb and Shepherd who gave himself up entirely for us. With this proof of the love of God, we are secure enough to reach out and to try again to love others.

Lord Jesus, sometimes it seems easier to think of going to the cross than to go across the street to reach out to someone we would rather ignore. Let us live this day in a manner worthy of our vocation to follow you and to care for others. Alleluia!

Tuesday, August 29, 2006
The Martyrdom of St. John the Baptist
2 Thessalonians 2, 1-3,14-17
Christ and the Lawless One

Communication. Words.

Spoken words. Written words.

The spoken word and the written word can cause great confusion and misunderstanding. The spoken word and the written word can also create clarification and a deep rapprochement. This is true in both temporal matters and in matters of eternity.

Lord Jesus, let us learn to take all words which have been spoken to us or written to us to YOU. Thank you that you will communicate the truth to us. Alleluia!

Wednesday, August 30, 2006
2 Thessalonians 3, 6-10,16-18
Neglect of Work

Paul urges the Christians at Thessalonica to avoid anyone acting in a disorderly way. Paul is stressing the requirement of normal, everyday work.

Lord Jesus, thank you for strengthening us to conduct ourselves as your followers in this stressed-out world. Calm us and help us to work faithfully at the task you have set before us. Thank you for your peace. Alleluia!

Thursday, August 31, 2006
1 Corinthians 1, 1-9
Greeting; Thanksgiving

In union with Christ, we are rich! Jesus is in charge of keeping us steadfast to the very end. We are learning to trust completely in God who has called us into this deep relationship with Jesus, his beloved Son.

Lord Jesus Christ, Son of the living God, thank you for reminding us that we live in union with you. You have not abandoned us to plod wearily through this life. We have free, unlimited access to you, to your wisdom and to your wealth. Alleluia!

Friday, September 1, 2006
1 Corinthians 1, 17-25
Groups and Slogans

The message we proclaim is CHRIST. We tell of Christ crucified. We teach with our words and with our lives.

Paul knew that his assignment was not primarily to baptize but to preach. He didn't worry at all about being polished. He just launched out into the mercy and power of God.

Lord Jesus, thank you for helping me today to launch out into your mercy and your power. Give me loving eyes with which to look upon others. Give me simple words with which to speak of you. Thank you for showing me how to serve others today. Alleluia!

Saturday, September 2, 2006
1 Corinthians 1, 26-31
The Corinthians and Paul

It is not until we are able to realize our desperate need of God that God can lift us, transform us, and gloriously fill us with new life. The trouble is that it hurts to realize our need. It hurts our pride, which must eventually give way and die.

We are terrified to face ourselves, much less to face God. It's so much easier to survive on the surface, than to dive deep into the depths of God.

"Consider your own call, brothers and sisters: not many of you were wise by human standards, not many were powerful, not many were of noble birth. But God chose what is foolish in the world to shame the wise; god chose what is weak in the world to shame the strong;

God chose what is low and despised in the world, things that are not, to reduce to nothing things that are, so that no one might boast in the presence of God. He is the source of your life in Christ Jesus, who became for us wisdom from God, and righteousness and sanctification and redemption, in order that, as it is written, 'Let the one who boasts, boast in the Lord' (1 Corinthians 1, 26-31)."

God's ways are not our ways. God deliberately chose those considered weak and worthless to startle and to put to shame those who are considered bigwigs.

God chose us to be in union with Jesus Christ, his beloved Son. We are in right standing with God because Jesus made it possible. Jesus redeemed us. We share in the very wisdom and holiness of the Lord Jesus.

Lord Jesus, we rejoice because we finally are realizing that, with you, we have it all. YOU are our all in all. We are redeemed, holy, righteous and wise because of you. We glory in you! Alleluia!

Sunday, September 3, 2006
Twenty-second Sunday in Ordinary Time;
Deuteronomy 4, 1-2, 6-8
Advantages of Fidelity

Fidelity to God and obedience to God. Carefully observing God's decrees lead to life and to true freedom.

Lord Jesus, we have not entered the land of freedom that is ours, much less taken possession of this promised land. We stand on the edge and cringe. We stay cooped up in our cage, even though you have flung open the door. Help us to step out and to explore this new land you died for us to enjoy. Help us to leave the cage and learn to spread our wings. Alleluia!

Monday, September 4, 2006
1 Corinthians 2, 1-5
The Corinthians and Paul

"When I came to you, brothers and sisters, I did not come proclaiming the mystery of God to you in lofty words or wisdom. For I decided to know nothing among you except Jesus Christ, and him crucified. And I came to you in weakness and in fear and in much trembling. My speech and my proclamation were not with plausible words of wisdom, but with a demonstration of the Spirit and of power, so that your faith might not rest on human wisdom but on the power of God (1 Corinthians 2, 1-5)."

Paul concentrated on Jesus and specifically on the death of Jesus Christ on the cross when he addressed the Christians in Corinth. He did not choose to focus on himself and to try to polish his speaking skills. Neither did he focus on the Corinthians and what they would think of him.

Although Paul was frightened, he was determined to focus on Jesus and to allow the Holy Spirit to take control. The people would then base their faith on the power of God rather on the eloquence or the wisdom of Paul himself.

Lord Jesus, we have it all backwards. When we are insecure in our relationship with you, we tend to focus on ourselves and on others. We need to learn to start by focusing on YOU! We look to you, knowing that you are gazing upon us with love and understanding. You will not fail us. We are learning each day to trust you a little more. You will tell us what to say and what to do. Come, Lord Jesus. Be glorified in us today. Alleluia!

Tuesday, September 5, 2006
1 Corinthians 2, 10-16
The True Wisdom

" 'For who has known the mind of the Lord so as to instruct him?' But we have the mind of Christ (v. 16)."

If the Holy Spirit of God is teaching me, how will I live? The Holy Spirit living within me is a spiritual bloodhound searching out the secret recesses of my spirit.

We are carefully fashioned to understand the treasures freely given to us by God. God has given us discernment.

We have been given the mind of Jesus Christ. It must be possible, then, to learn to think as Jesus thinks! Amazing.

Without the Holy Spirit, it is not possible to recognize or to understand that which has been freely given to us. The Holy Spirit lives within us to teach us and to open our hearts and our minds to unimaginable gifts. Even when we begin to recognize the treasures of the Holy Spirit, we still need the Holy Spirit to instruct us.

Lord Jesus, thank you for showing us, by your life, death, resurrection, and ascension what it means to be completely filled with and controlled by the Holy Spirit. Thank you that the Holy Spirit will instruct us today. Let us take a new step in learning to listen to the Holy Spirit and to live according to the guidance of the Holy Spirit. Alleluia!

>Wednesday, September 6, 2006
>1 Corinthians 3, 1-9
>The Corinthians and Paul; The Role of God's Ministers

Last week-end, we went to a very lively Greek Festival. Terrific music, drama, dancing, food, chanting, and an excellent lecture.

What do I remember the most? The mosaic of Jesus! The beautiful mosaic of Jesus, surrounded by the saints, in the dome of the church.

At the festival of our Christian life, Jesus is above us, among us, with us, and in us. Jesus is working patiently through all of us.

Lord Jesus, as I gazed upon the mosaic of you in the dome of the church, let me also recognize you today. Let me honor all those who serve you. Let me accept the way you have called me to serve you. You alone are the Lord! Alleluia!

>Thursday, September 7, 2006
>1 Corinthians 3, 18-23
>The Role of God's Ministers

We belong to God! Everything belongs to us and we belong to God.

When we grasp this truth, everything else will fall into place in our lives. We will learn the wisdom born of humbly acknowledging who God is and who we are. We will be at peace with God, with ourselves and with others.

Lord Jesus, forgive us for idolizing others and looking up to others in an unhealthy way. You alone are the Lord. We will one stand before you and you will be our judge. You are the Lamb of God who died to take away our sins. You are the wise and loving Good Shepherd leading us Home along the route that you know is best for us. Let us live simply today, looking to you and serving others. Alleluia!

Friday, September 8, 2006 Nativity of the Blessed Virgin Mary
Micah 5, 1-4
Restoration through the Messiah

"But you, O Bethlehem of Ephrathah, who are one of the little clans of Judah, from you shall come forth ... one who is to rule in Israel, whose origin is from old, from ancient days (v. 2)."

Small. Insignificant. Unnoticed.

From little Bethlehem would come Jesus. The Baby born to the Virgin Mary.

Jesus, the Son of God. The King. The Messiah. Jesus, our Lord.

Lord Jesus, you are our peace in this troubled world. Let us trust in you today as our strong, loving Shepherd leading us home. We are not too small or too insignificant for you to notice us. Alleluia!

Saturday, September 9, 2006 St. Peter Claver
1 Corinthians 4, 6-15
Paul's Life as a Pattern

Poor Paul seems to be quite weary of it all. The sufferings which accompany his apostolate combined with the immature whining of the Corinthians were weighing heavily upon him.

Lord Jesus, when we are weary of it all, thank you for coming to us and speak ing peace to us. You yourself are our peace. Help us to endure and to triumph. Alleluia!

Sunday, September 10, 2006
Twenty-third Sunday in Ordinary Time
Isaiah 35, 4-7
Israel's Deliverance

"The wilderness and the dry land shall be glad, and the desert shall rejoice and blossom; like the crocus it shall blossom abundantly, and rejoice with joy and singing. The glory of Lebanon shall be given to it, and the majesty of Carmel and Sharon. They shall see the glory of the LORD, and the majesty of our God. Strengthen the weak hands, and make firm the feeble knees. Say to those who are of a fearful heart, 'Be strong, do not fear! Here is your God. He will come with vengeance, and terrible recompense. He will come and save you (Isaiah 35, 1-4)."

What will it be like when God comes to deliver us and to vindicate us? We will, at last, live as we were intended to live.

We will live without fear. We will be strong. God, who has already secured our salvation, will vindicate us.

We will see and perceive clearly. We will hear and understand clearly. We will leap! We will sing!

Streams of water will spring forth in the wilderness. The scorched sands will welcome pools of cool water.

Lord Jesus, please come soon! It is so hard to wait. Before you come in glory, let us patiently learn to practice. Let us learn to praise and to rejoice. You have promised us vindication. You have promised us a glorious future. Thank you for the purification process to which we gladly submit in order to be prepared for you. Let us live today as if we truly believe your promises. Alleluia!

Monday, September 11, 2006
1 Corinthians 5, 1-8
A Case of Incest

Christ our Passover Lamb has indeed been sacrificed for us. We are called to keep and to celebrate the feast in purity and with truth.

We are called to speak the truth and to confront wrongdoing. We are to love other Christians enough to confront them when they are "tolerant" to the point of ignoring flagrant immorality.

Lord Jesus, thank you for removing the old hidden yeast of sin in our lives. Thank you that you are eager to forgive us. Thank you for the joy and freedom in living in transparency before you and before others. Alleluia!

Tuesday, September 12, 2006 Holy Name of Mary
1 Corinthians 6, 1-11
Lawsuits before Unbelievers

"Who says they're Christians?" Someone asked me this question after I decided not to pursue legally a serious matter involving people who were presumably Christians. It turned out to be more fun to wait and see what God would do.

St. Paul called it a failure for Christians, who will one day judge the world and the angels, to pursue lawsuits in which the decision will be rendered by unbelievers. Better to put up, for now, with the injustice, knowing that the Lord will render the final judgment. Pope John Paul II said, "I forgive all who have injured me and ask pardon of all I have injured …."

Lord Jesus, we have been washed in your Precious Blood, cleansed in the waters of Baptism, sanctified, and justified. Since we have been made right with Almighty God because of what you did for us, we trust you to make everything else right. Thank you for strengthening us to forgive all and to ask forgiveness from all. Alleluia!

> Wednesday, September 13, 2006 St. John Chrsysostom
> 1 Corinthians 7, 25-31
> Advice to Virgins and Widows

The world as we know it will not remain as it is. It is going to pass away.

We, however, are not going to pass away, in a final sense. We are going to be changed into the image and likeness of Christ. We are going to live forever and forever.

Lord Jesus, help us to live this day fully, knowing that your kingdom will come on earth and your plan will be carried out on earth as it is already being carried out in heaven. Alleluia!

> Thursday, September 14, 2006 The Exaltation of the Holy Cross
> Numbers 21, 4-9
> The Bronze Serpent

Snakes! Many people are afraid of snakes. Being bitten by certain snakes may be fatal.

The bronze serpent in this reading is different. This is the serpent, designed by God, for healing!

Moses told the complainers in the wilderness to look at this serpent and live! The merciful Lord provided this bronze serpent as a means to bring healing to the repentant Israelites.

My own patience has been worn thin by the journey and I have really been complaining a lot. After reading this passage, I realize that this is a serious sin to complain. It shows me that my faith is out of focus.

Lord Jesus, please forgive me for complaining. I have been looking at difficult circumstances and not looking at you. Today, let me look to you. You were lifted high upon the Cross so that we could all look upon you and live. Thank you for healing the root cause of what is bothering me. Thank you for forgiving me and freeing me to live and to continue the journey with new strength and joy. Alleluia!

> Friday, September 15, 2006 Our Lady of Sorrows
> 1 Corinthians 9, 16-19,22-27
> Reason for Not Using his Rights; All Things to All

Paul yielded himself completely to the vocation to which he was called. He was humble and did not pull rank.

It was the Lord who called him to preach the Gospel. The Lord entrusted Paul with this ministry.

"If I proclaim the gospel, this gives me no ground for boasting, for obligation is laid on me, and woe to me if I do not proclaim the gospel (v. 16)!"

The Lord has entrusted each of us with a particular ministry. If we desire to be faithful to the Lord and to fulfill this ministry, we will suffer. We will be a contradiction to others.

As we die to our own ideas of ministry, the Lord is free to stretch us. We are learning to desire what is the very best for others, even if we have to suffer and to sacrifice in ways we had not anticipated. We may have to give up legitimate rights in order to become broken bread and wine poured forth to nourish others.

Lord Jesus, we long to win the prize you have waiting for us. Help us to accept hardships and to continue to trust you to bring us to the finish line. Alleluia!

> Saturday, September 16, 2006 Sts. Cornelius and Cyprian
> 1 Corinthians 10, 14-22
> Warning against Idolatry

"Therefore, my dear friends, flee from the worship of idols. I speak as to sensible people; judge for yourselves what I say. The cup of blessing that we bless, is it not a sharing in the blood of Christ? The bread that we break, is it not a sharing in the body of Christ? Because there is one bread, we who are many are one body, for we all partake of the one bread. You cannot drink the cup of the Lord and the cup of demons. You cannot partake of the table of the Lord and the table of demons (vv. 14-17, 21)."

As Christians, we have participated in the altar. We have participated in the body of Christ. We have participated in the blood of Christ.

We are now one because we have all partaken of the same loaf. Holy Communion. Body of Christ. Blood of Christ.

We cannot now go out and have unholy communion with demons. We belong to God.

Lord Jesus, thank you for the Holy Spirit who confronts us when we, knowingly or unknowingly, commit idolatry by putting anyone or anything in first place in our lives. You and you alone belong in first place. You and you alone are the Lord. Thank you for forgiving us and cleansing us to continue to follow you and to serve you. Alleluia!

Sunday, September 17, 2006
Twenty-fourth Sunday in Ordinary Time
Isaiah 50, 5-9
Salvation Only through the Lord's Servant

Jesus gave himself totally to Almighty God, his heavenly Father. He gave himself totally to us.

He was tortured. He was crucified.

With the spittle of his persecutors upon his face, he could affirm his total trust in God. His face was still steadfastly set as flint. He knew he could never be disgraced before God.

"The LORD GOD helps me; therefore I have not been disgraced; therefore I have set my face like flint, and I know that I shall not be put to shame; he who vindicates me is near (v. 7)."

Lord Jesus, we can never completely comprehend your suffering on our behalf. We can only throw ourselves at your feet and thank you. We can only run into the recesses of your heart and learn to trust you to lead us the rest of the way Home. Let us follow you with joy and with confidence. Alleluia!

Monday, September 18, 2006
1 Corinthians 11, 17-26,33
An Abuse at Corinth; Tradition of the Eucharist

The members of the church at Corinth were not properly living out their vocation of love. They were not living together as a community of love. There was rampant self-interest at work.

The Christians at Corinth did not belong to themselves. We do not belong to ourselves, either.

We belong to God. We are called to love other Christians and to place their concerns above our own.

Lord Jesus, you do not call us to be doormats, but to be disciples. Thank you for showing us how to speak the truth in love and how to live the truth in love. Alleluia!

Tuesday, September 19, 2006 St. Januarius
1 Corinthians 12, 12-14,27-31
One Body, Many Parts; Application to Christ

"For just as the body is one and has many members, and all the members of the body, though many, are one body, so it is with Christ. For in the one Spirit we were all baptized into one body – Jews or Greeks, slaves or free – and we were all made to drink of one Spirit (vv. 12-13)."

We are collectively the Body of Christ, the Church. We are individually members of the Body of Christ, the Church.

Lord Jesus, help us to honor you by honoring each member of your Body. When we hurt other members in your Body, the Church, we are hurting you. Help us to honor ourselves, also, by learning to speak for you and to live for you with new confidence. Alleluia!

Wednesday, September 20, 2006
St. Andrew Kim Taegon, St. Paul Chong Hasang and Companions
1 Corinthians 12, 31 - 13, 13
Application to Christ, The Way of Love

"For now we see in a mirror, dimly, but then we will see face to face. Now I know only in part; then I will know fully, even as I have been fully known. And now faith, hope, and love abide, these three; and the greatest is love (vv. 12-13)."

Hope. That's what I think I still need the most.

Hope is part of the whole painting of love. The painting includes splashes of patience, kindness, and unselfishness. No room for grudges on this canvas.

Bearing. Believing. Hoping. Enduring.

What am I hoping for? A strong hope means that I KNOW God will triumph in my life.

We don't know much right now. The canvas still has blurry edges. One day we will see clearly. One day we will know.

Lord Jesus, thank you that you know us through and through. Let us live this day in eager anticipation of seeing you clearly. Let us grow in trusting you, putting our hope in you and loving ourselves and others. Alleluia!

Thursday, September 21, 2006 St. Matthew
Ephesians 3, 1-7,11-13
Unity in the Body; Diversity of Gifts

One, One. One.

Three Persons. One God.

One. One. One. One. One. One. One. Seven "ones" in today's reading.

Old math is out. The new math is all about unity. Seven times one still equals one in God's economy.

We are called to live in radically organic unity. We are called to unity with God and with others in the Body of Christ, the Church.

Lord Jesus, we can't do old math anymore. We can't keep on keeping track of all our past hurts and grievances. You are calling us to learn the new math. You are calling us to stop keeping score. You are calling us to love and to respect one another. Help us to be patient with ourselves and with others as we learn to be one with you and with our brothers and sisters in your Body. Forgive us when we wound you by wounding your little sisters and brothers. Have mercy on us. Thank you for the Holy Spirit who lovingly teaches us this new math. Thank you that we will understand it all one day when we are Home with our Father in heaven. Alleluia!

Friday, September 22, 2006
1 Corinthians 15, 12-20
Results of Denial; Christ the First fruits

"If for this life only we have hoped in Christ, we are of all people most to be pitied. But in fact Christ has been raised from the dead, the first fruits of those who have died. For since death came through a human being, the resurrection of the dead also came through a human being; for as all die in Adam, so all will be made alive in Christ (vv. 19-22)."

Everything hinges on the resurrection of Jesus Christ from the dead. Paul boldly asserted that we would be miserable if our trust in Christ was meant for this life only.

Lord Jesus, you are alive! You have indeed been raised from the dead. You were born into this world, you lived among us, you suffered, died, and were raised from the dead. God will raise us also from the dead. You don't want us to live this life, believing a lie. You don't want us to live this life thinking that this is all there is. You want us to live this life fully, knowing that we will live forever, Alleluia!

Saturday, September 23, 2006 St. Pio of Pietrelcina
1 Corinthians 15, 35-37,42-49
Practical Arguments; The Resurrection Body

I awoke this morning praying for restoration, asking the Lord to restore the "lost" years. Maybe the years weren't really lost, though. Maybe the suffering of those years was necessary for the joy and victory to come.

Making a new garment requires a precise pattern, the sticking of pins to attach the pattern to the new garment material, and a number of fittings. Then comes the moment. The beautiful new garment is ready!

When God, in mercy, sees that I am as ready as I can be, the pattern and the pins will no longer be necessary. I will slip into my shimmering resurrection ball gown and dance throughout eternity!

Lord Jesus, help me to be patient as little and big death and resurrection experiences occur throughout this life. Thank you that you have already redeemed me and that you will bring about a glorious restoration of what seemed to be lost forever. Alleluia!

Sunday, September 24, 2006
Twenty-fifth Sunday in Ordinary Time
Wisdom 2, 12,17-20
Exhortation and Justice, the Key to Life;
The Wicked Reject Immortality and Justice Alike

Yes, God will tenderly care for the just one who has suffered at the hands of the unjust. God will also deal with those who seemed to succeed in putting the just one to death.

Pilate will stand before Jesus. We will stand before Jesus.

Jesus will judge. Jesus knows how to judge.

Lord Jesus, forgive me for not being patient and gentle when I meet with injustice. Forgive me for not being a good witness to you. You have been most gentle and patient with me. Help me to continue in my lessons of trusting you. Thank you that you will sort it all out and bring healing, redemption, and restoration. Alleluia!

Monday, September 25, 2006
Proverbs 3, 27-34
Attitude toward Fellow Men

"Do not withhold good from those to whom it is due, when it is in your power to do it (v. 27)."

I could hardly bear to read beyond the first verse of today's first reading. We are not to refrain or to hold back from helping another when we are able to do so. We have been given so much to share with others.

It is also very sad when someone offers to do good and is refused. How ungracious. How unlike our gracious God who delights in us and in our efforts to serve.

Lord Jesus, help us to bless those who refuse to do good and who refuse to allow others to do good. You alone see into their troubled, and fearful hearts. Have mercy on us all. Thank you that you will open new doors for all who long to serve you. Alleluia!

Tuesday, September 26, 2006 St. Cosmos and St. Damien
Proverbs 2, 1-6,10-13
The Blessings of Wisdom

"My child, if you accept my words and treasure up my commandments within you, making your ear attentive to wisdom and inclining your heart to understanding; if you indeed cry out for insight, and raise your voice for understanding; if you seek it like silver, and search for it as for hidden treasures – then you will understand the fear of the LORD and find the knowledge of God. For the LORD gives wisdom; from his mouth come knowledge and understanding; he stores up wisdom for the upright; he is a shield to those who walk blamelessly …. Then you will understand righteousness and justice and equity, every good path; for wisdom will come into your heart, and knowledge will be pleasant to your soul … (vv. 1-7,9-10)."

Wisdom will lead us to a knowledge of God we have never known. We will be increasingly in awe of GOD. As we seek God's wisdom and God's wisdom comes into our lives, we will begin to know God and to know ourselves in new ways.

Lord Jesus, let us pursue, not merely knowledge, but also wisdom. Guide our thoughts and our actions as we submit ourselves to the wise leadership of the Holy Spirit. Alleluia!

>Wednesday, September 27, 2006 St. Vincent de Paul
>Proverbs 30, 5-9
>The Words of Agur; Numerical Proverbs

The writer of this proverb, Agur, son of Jakeh, refers to God as a shield. He prays that he may live in truth and be neither too rich nor too poor. God's honor is a utmost importance to this person.

"Two things I ask of you; do not deny them to be before I die: Remove far from me falsehood and lying; give me neither poverty nor riches; feed me with the food that I need, or I shall be full, and deny you, and say, "Who is the LORD?' or I shall be poor, and steal, and profane the name of my God (vv. 7-9)."

Lord Jesus, thank you for shielding us and for strengthening to speak the truth and to live the truth. Alleluia!

>Thursday, September 28, 2006
>St. Wenceslaus, St. Lawrence Ruiz and Companions
>Ecclesiastes 1, 2-11
>Vanity of Toil without Profit

If nothing else, the book of Ecclesiastes gives expression to our own times of gloom and doom. Every honest person, at one time or another, experiences a sense of futility.

It is healthy and wise to acknowledge that we, at times, feel this way. Life is not all a joy ride.

However, joy is a fruit of the Holy Spirit, a result of our abiding in Jesus, the True Vine. Whatever our gloomy circumstances, we may always find a calm joy in our relationship with the Lord, who understands every single one of our emotions.

Lord Jesus, as we ride the waves of changing circumstances, let us be brave and step out of the safety of the boat. With Peter, let us walk on the waves to you. Thank you that you are always with us and you are reaching out to grasp our hand. Alleluia!

Friday, September 29, 2006
St. Michael, St. Gabriel, and St. Raphael
Revelation 12, 7-12
The Woman and the Dragon

Every time I open the book of the Revelation, I remember my son's words. As a child, he read the book of the Revelation and found it very cool. I asked him what he thought it all meant. His answer was, "God wins!"

Yes, God wins! When reading these puzzling, frightening passages, we have to remember that God wins. When experiencing accusations from the old dragon devil, we have to remember that God wins.

Lord Jesus, thank you that we conquer through the blood you shed for us as the Lamb of God. Let us bear testimony to you and love you better than we love this life. You are our life! Alleluia!

Saturday, September 30, 2006 St. Jerome
Ecclesiastes 11, 9 - 12, 8
Poem on Youth and Old Age

"Remember now thy Creator in the days of thy youth ... (Ecclesiastes 12, 1 KJV)."

Koheleth, also known as the "Preacher," is definitely living in the here and now. He cautions us to remember our Creator, not only in the days of our youth, but in all our days, knowing that "...the spirit shall return unto God who gave it (v. 7b KJV)."

"The end of the matter ... Fear God, and keep his commandments; for that is the whole duty of everyone. For God will bring every deed into judgment ... (v. 13)."

Lord Jesus, we rejoice in the beauty of the birds, the blossoms, the sun, moon and stars. We rejoice in all of creation. Most of all we rejoice in you, our Savior and Redeemer. Alleluia!

Sunday, October 1, 2006
Twenty-sixth Sunday in Ordinary Time
Numbers 11, 25-29
The Spirit on the Elders

Lots of room! There's room for your ministry. There's room for my ministry.

Moses rejoiced that the Spirit came to rest on seventy elders, on Eldad and Medad, and they began to prophesy. Moses' aide, Joshua, did not like this and wanted them to stop.

Moses reproved Joshua and said, "Are you jealous for my sake? Would that all the LORD's people were prophets, and that the LORD would put his spirit on them (Numbers 11, 29)!"

The Holy Spirit is lavishly poured out upon us. The LORD's Spirit dwells within us, longing to express the life of Jesus through us.

Lord Jesus, thank you for the Holy Spirit who fills us and empowers us to serve you. Thank you that there is room for all of us to serve you. Alleluia!

Monday, October 2, 2006 The Guardian Angels
Job 1, 6-22
Job's Wealth and Piety; The First Trial

Although Satan was the sender of Job's trials, Job still needed to learn to enlarge his personal frame of reference. Instead of dwelling on the devil or on his losses, Job looked to God and referred all to God.

Job recognized that he had come into the world with nothing and would leave the world with nothing. Everything was given or taken with God's knowledge.

Lord Jesus, we rejoice that you will bring true justice into our lives. We think we are always right, but we are not always right. Show us how to live in this world, trusting that you have a better place for us. Thank you for the protection of the guardian angels. Alleluia!

> Tuesday, October 3, 2006
> Job 3, 1-3,11-17,20-23
> Job's Plaint

Up until this time, even though he had suffered greatly, Job had not said anything at all that was sinful (Job 2, 10). With the arrival of his three friends, however, he began to speak.

Job began to spew forth words of utter desolation. He cursed the day of his birth. He asked why he had not died at birth. He poured out his heart before God (Psalm 62, 8).

Why? Why? Why?

Instead of the darkness of oblivion, Job was given light that was even more puzzling. Why?

At that time, Job did not want light. He did not want life. He longed for death.

Truly, Job's path was currently a mystery. It was a path in which he was hedged in by God. No escape.

Lord Jesus, in the midst of trials, we too cry out with wild words straight from our crushed hearts. Thank you that, in the midst of our misery, we are hedged in by your love. Our circumstances may be trying, but they are not sovereign. You are sovereign! We praise you in the midst of our tears. Alleluia!

> Wednesday, October 4, 2006 St. Francis of Assisi
> Job 9, 1-12,14-16
> Job's Second Plaint

Silence! We fall silent or search awkwardly for words as we gaze upon God. God's power and majesty are beyond our comprehension.

Lord Jesus, thank you for coming from heaven to show us what God is truly like. Thank you for your tenderness and understanding. You are always near us when we call. When we are experiencing desolation, we cry especially to you. Thank you for the Holy Spirit who dwells within us reassuring us of your love. Alleluia!

Thursday, October 5, 2006
Job 19, 21-27
Job's First Reply

Do we prey or pray? Job definitely felt preyed upon by his so-called friends.

Instead of praying for him, they fell upon him with their self-righteous, destructive words. What kind of friends were they, anyway!

Then there was an "aha" moment! Truth!

Job bursts out with his declaration that his divine Vindicator is alive and will stand right here on the earth. Job will see God for himself.

"For I know that my Redeemer lives, and that at the last he will stand upon the earth; and ... I shall see God (vv. 25,26)."

Lord Jesus Christ, thank you that you are coming as our King! We will see you. You died as Victim, as the sacrificial Lamb of God, but you will return as Vindicator of those who trust in you. Alleluia!

Friday, October 5, 2006 St. Bruno, Bl. Marie-Rose Durocher
Job 38, 1,12-21; 40, 3-5
The Lord's Speech

Out of the storm, God spoke to Job. Job's wild words were beginning to subside. He was beginning to choose silence.

At the beginning of his trials, Job had not sinned in word. It was at the advent of his so-called friends that he became defensive.

Lord Jesus, you know that when we are threatened in any way, we want to defend ourselves. Give us wisdom to choose our words carefully or to choose to remain silent. You will speak on our behalf in many creative ways. Alleluia!

Saturday, October 7, 2006 Our Lady of the Rosary
Job 42, 1-3,5-6,12-17
Job's Restoration

Repentance. Intercession. Restoration

Repentance. Job repents. He thinks again. And again.

Job had heard about the Lord. Job had been a righteous man, but now it was different. Job had seen the Lord in action!

Job 42, 7-10 tells of the Lord's anger with Job's so-called friends. These self-righteous men had misrepresented the Lord to Job

Intercession and restoration. It was after righteous Job interceded for his friends that the Lord brought a glorious restoration to Job.

This was truly an astonishing restoration for Job. New possessions! Seven more sons and three more daughters, Jemimah, Keziah, and Kerenhappuch.

Lord Jesus, thank you for Job. He suffered, cried, and even cursed the day he was born. Yet he was gloriously restored. In the midst of our earthly trials, help us to remember that there will be restoration and there will be resurrection. Alleluia!

Sunday, October 8, 2006
Twenty-seventh Sunday in Ordinary Time
Genesis 2, 18-24
Second Story of Creation

In the first story of creation, God created humanity male and female. We were created in the image of God.

In the second story of creation, there is a very tender element. God's intentions of completion and unity are beautifully described.

Lord Jesus, thank you that we are now living out the "third" story, as we follow you in our daily lives. Thank you for healing us at the places where creativity seems to be blocked in our lives. Thank you for coming into those hurt places and making us whole. Alleluia!

Monday, October 9, 2006
St. Denis and Companions; St. John Leonardi
Galatians 1, 6-12
Greetings; His Call by Christ

Paul was an apostle called by God. He was not called to be a people pleaser. He was called to serve the Lord Jesus Christ.

Lord Jesus, deliver us from our obsessive need to be needed and appreciated. When we are so preoccupied with pleasing other, we are actually hurting them in the long run. We can never be their savior. We will always disappoint them. When we learn to look to you, obey you, and then serve others as you direct, we become strong and secure in you. Then we may safely serve others in the way you have called us to serve. Alleluia!

> Tuesday, October 10, 2006
> Galatians 1, 13-24
> His Call by Christ

Is our zeal really for God alone or is it for ancestral tradition? Do we get the two mixed up?

If so, we're in good company. Paul did the very same thing.

However, there came a time when God revealed Jesus IN Paul and Paul was never the same. The one who had once violently persecuted the church was the same one who would powerfully proclaim the faith.

Not yet, though. Although God had set Paul apart even before his birth for his vocation, it was not yet time for Paul to move in the fullness of that vocation.

After his personal encounter with the risen Jesus, Paul did not seek human counsel. He went to Arabia and then back to Damascus.

Not until three years later did Paul go to Jerusalem to meet with Kephas (Peter) and James, the brother of Jesus. No one else in the churches of Judea personally knew Paul during this time of intense formation. They had, of course, heard about him and glorified God.

Lord Jesus, come to us and reveal yourself to us and in us. You are alive! You are the crucified and risen Lord Jesus Christ. Holy Spirit, breathe new life into us. Let our lives glorify God. Alleluia!

> Wednesday, October 11, 2006
> Galatians 2, 1-2,7-14
> The Council of Jerusalem; Peter's Inconsistency at Antioch

Fourteen years! After fourteen long years, God decided to turn Paul loose on the church again. God sent Paul back to Jerusalem.

Paul clearly understood Peter's ministry and his own ministry. Peter had been charged with proclaiming the Gospel to the Jews. Paul was charged with proclaiming the Gospel to the Gentiles.

Paul was not shy about confrontation. He confronted Peter face to face.

Why? Out of fear, perhaps, Peter had acted with hypocrisy.

Peter had behaved one way with the Gentiles and then another way with the Jews. He was leading others into his error.

This didn't settle well with Paul. Since the matter needed immediate attention and correction, Paul publicly confronted Peter.

Lord Jesus, help us to be patient during our long years of formation. Help us to be strong and bold to live and to speak as you direct us. Alleluia!

Thursday, October 12, 2006
Galatians 3, 1-5
Justification by Faith

The Holy Spirit is freely given to us. We do not need to work up a sweat to receive the Holy Spirit.

We do not earn the Holy Spirit. We do not flaunt the Holy Spirit.

Lord Jesus, thank you for praying to your Abba, Father, to send us the Holy Spirit to be our Teacher. Where we realize that we are off the track of trust and on the track of legalism, help us to return to you in simplicity. Alleluia!

Friday, October 13, 2006
Galatians 3, 7-14
Justification by Faith

Abraham had radical trust in God! The belief in his head and the trust in his heart gave him amazing power as he glorified God (Romans 4, 20).

We are told in this passage in Galatians that we, too, are children of Abraham. We are blessed right along with Abraham.

We receive the gift of God's Holy Spirit. Could there ever be a greater gift?

Lord Jesus, our Redeemer, sometimes we drag through this life as if we had no faith and no future. Come, Holy Spirit, and reawaken the resurrection life of Jesus within us! Let us be bold to live and to love as people of radical faith as we travel Home to our Abba, our Father. Alleluia!

Saturday, October 14, 2006 St. Callistus
Galatians 2, 22-29
The Law Did Not Nullify the Promise;
What Faith Has Brought Us

If we have been baptized into Jesus Christ, we are wearing Christ. We are clothed with Christ. We are living in Christ Central Station!

Our racial identity, social standing, and our gender are not of primary importance. We belong to the Lord Jesus Christ.

Lord Jesus, if we don't know who we are, we will flounder all through life. Let us realize our freedom to live boldly for you and to love and serve others as you direct. Alleluia!

Sunday, October 15, 2006
Twenty-eighth Sunday in Ordinary Time
Wisdom 7, 7-11
Solomon Prays and Wisdom and Riches Come to Him

Solomon asked for wisdom first of all. He preferred wisdom to all that the world could offer. He even preferred wisdom to health.

Jesus told us to seek, first of all, God's kingdom and God's righteousness (Matthew 6, 33). We are to seek to live God's way. Then, everything else we need will be given to us as well.

Lord Jesus, we run after the things we think we need or want. Let us run to you and seek from you the wisdom to live your way. You our treasure. You will make sure that we have what we need to live this life while we wait for your coming in glory. Alleluia!

Monday, October 16, 2006 St. Hedwig,
St. Margaret Mary Alacoque
Galatians 4, 22-24,26-27,31 - 5, 1
An Allegory on Christian Freedom; The Importance of Faith

We may choose to live expansive lives of freedom in Christ! Yet we often live cramped lives filled with fear. Do we not yet know who we are?

Consider Abraham's two sons. Ishmael, son of the slave Hagar, was born because of human initiative.

Isaac, however, son of the elderly Sarah, was an "impossible" child! It was "impossible" for Sarah and Abraham to have a child at their age.

Yet, Isaac, whose name means "laughter," was born! Isaac was born because God had taken the initiative and had promised this birth.

Lord Jesus, help us to laugh in joyful expectation of the fulfillment of your promises to us. Let us live in the faith-filled freedom you died to give us. Let us honor you this day by trusting you. Alleluia!

Tuesday, October 17, 2006 St. Ignatius of Antioch
Galatians 5, 1-6
The Importance of Faith

We will be exhausted if we have faith in Christ and then try, frantically, to justify ourselves. That's just not our job.

Jesus has already done the hard part. Jesus took all our sins to the Cross. They're gone.

Our part? Believe.

Trust. Learn to live in the freedom Jesus died to give us.

Lord Jesus, I ask for the grace to believe you, to believe you with all my heart as well as with all my mind. Alleluia!

Wednesday, October 18, 2006 St. Luke
2 Timothy 4, 10-17
Paul's Loneliness

Paul was suffering and was able, at least, to describe his suffering, in writing, to Timothy. He was suffering both personally and professionally.

Paul was suffering personal loneliness. Several of his ministry partners had gone off for various reasons. Only Luke was still with him.

A coppersmith, Alexander, had done great evil to Paul. Paul trusted the Lord to bring justice in this matter. However, he still cautioned Timothy about Alexander.

Paul was suffering an acute form of professional loneliness, known to those who attempt to live up to their calling in the midst of opposition from within their own institution. When Paul needed supporters, no one was there for him. He experienced abandonment.

The Lord, however, had not abandoned him. The Lord strengthened his weary servant to continue to proclaim the Gospel. The Lord rescued Paul, as it were, from the lion's mouth.

Lord Jesus, it is hard to trust people as friends and as professional colleagues and then to have them misunderstand us and harm us. Help us to be cautious without being cynical. We are learning each day to trust you more and more. Thank you for strengthening us to continue the particular work you have entrusted to us. Alleluia!

Thursday, October 19, 2006
St. John de Brebeuf, St. Isaac Jogues and Companions
Ephesians 1, 1-10
Greetings; The Father's Plan of Salvation;
Inheritance through the Spirit

This is the kind of math I can learn to love. God's math is to sum up everything in Christ.

Everything! Earth and heaven all included.

I don't have to count on my fingers or push buttons on a calculator or a computer in order to understand. God has it all under control.

So what do I do while I'm here on earth? Pray to rejoice in my adoption.

What does it really mean that I am adopted by God? How does this knowledge affect how I live?

We have relatives who have spent great amounts of love, time, and money in order to adopt their beloved children. God's beloved Son was freely given for us, so that we could be God's children.

We are chosen by love. We are chosen to be holy, to be whole. We belong. We belong to God.

Lord Jesus, thank you for redeeming us by shedding your Blood for us. Thank you for this new math based on love. It is beyond our understanding, but you have made it within our reach. Alleluia!

Friday, October 20, 2006 St. Paul of the Cross
Ephesians 1, 11-14
Inheritance through the Spirit

Remember! With the Holy Spirit we have been sealed.

There is a manifestation of our redemption yet to come. There is a promise yet to be realized.

Lord Jesus, thank you are Head of the Church and you are in control of everything. Thank you that you will come again in glory to rule and to reign. Thank you that we will have all eternity in which to enjoy our inheritance. Alleluia!

Saturday, October 21, 2006
Ephesians 1, 15-23
The Church as Christ's Body

Hope is attached to our call! We have the hope of glory. It will not always be the drudgery, the committees, the politics, and the other petty stuff.

Jesus is Lord! Jesus, the crucified and Risen Christ, is the head of the church. The enormous power of the Lord Jesus Christ is available to us right now

Lord Jesus, thank you for strengthening us to believe in your power in us as well as your love for us. Alleluia!

Sunday, October 22, 2006
Twenty-ninth Sunday in Ordinary Time
Isaiah 53, 10-11
Suffering and Triumph of the Servant of the Lord

"Out of his anguish he shall see light; he shall find satisfaction through his knowledge. The righteous one, my servant, shall make many righteous, and he shall bear their iniquities (v. 11)."

Distilled suffering. Anguish.

Through the unspeakable suffering of the Lord's Servant, many are justified and made righteous. This happened through no effort of their own.

Another sprang into action on their behalf! The Servant who suffered bore their guilt.

Lord Jesus, we know that you bore our sins on the Cross. You suffered unspeakable anguish in order to cleanse us and to make us righteous. Let us live this life in daily gratitude for your sacrifice. Let us bring you joy by our trust in you today. Alleluia!

Monday, October 23, 2006 St. John of Capistrano
Ephesians 2, 1-10
Generosity of God's Plan

When we were spiritually dead, we lived by following our own desires and impulses. That was the only way we knew how to live.

All of us once lived … following the desires of flesh and senses …. But God, who is rich in mercy, out of the great love with which he loved us even when we were dead through our trespasses, made us alive together with Christ - by grace you have been saved – and raised us up with him and seated us with him in the heavenly places in Christ Jesus (vv. 3-6)."

Our merciful God, however, had already made provision for us to live in a new way. Even when we were spiritually dead, God lifted us to a new realm.

By God's grace, we are saved. What does that mean?

God has touched us and made us whole. This is the work of GOD!

"For by grace you have been saved through faith, and this is not your own doing; it is the gift of God – not the result of works, so that no one may boast (vv. 8,9)."

What is our part? Faith. And yet this trusting faith is still God's gift.

Lord Jesus, let us begin to realize more fully what you have done for us. Thank you that all our transgressions have been forgiven. Thank you for showing us the new way of living that is available to us. We are alive! We are free to follow you and to do good. Let our lives reflect your action on our behalf. Alleluia!

Tuesday, October 24, 2006 St. Anthony Mary Claret
Ephesians 2, 12-22
One in Christ

Love won! God took us in.

We were outside. God took us inside.

The heart of God. We are now invited into the innermost recesses of the loving heart of God.

How did God do this? Jesus.

The blood of Jesus. The blood of the Lord Jesus Christ.

There is no enmity now between Jew and Gentile. Provision has been made for us to be one.

Jesus abolished the Law in order to "... create in himself one new humanity ... (v. 15). He fulfilled what we could never fulfill.

We are no longer outsiders. We belong. We are now "... citizens with the saints and also members of the household of God ... (v. 19)."

We are one within God's household. The prophets and the apostles are the foundation. Jesus is the cornerstone holding us all together.

Lord Jesus, thank you that we do belong. Help us to stop trying to prove ourselves. We have nothing to prove. You did it all. You proved your love for us by dying for us. Thank you that we will live, live, and live. Today, tomorrow, and throughout eternity. Praise and glory to you forever. Alleluia!

Wednesday, October 25, 2006
Ephesians 3, 2-12
Commission to Preach God's Plan

We're not just preaching to the choir or even to the world. As church. we are making a proclamation even unto entities in the heavenly realms.

Gentiles share equally with Jews in all that is promised in the Messiah. The Gentiles are now in the same family and share in the same privileges.

What we think, say, and do is noted in the heavenly realm. We don't have to be so obsessive about being people pleasers. Our audience is far more extensive than we realize.

Lord Jesus, help me to forget my insecurities long enough to thank you for all that you have done. You have made it possible for all of us, whether or not we are Jewish, to be in God's family. Let our thoughts, words, and actions today be illustrations of your Easter victory. Alleluia!

> Thursday, October 26, 2006
> Ephesians 3, 14-21
> Prayer for the Readers

Within. Within. Within.

Paul prays that his readers become strong within through the power of the Holy Spirit. Because Christ lives within us, we may be strong and understand his amazing love for us.

This is an inside job. It happens because of God's power within us.

Lord Jesus, let us believe that all these promises of inner strength are really true! Let us learn to live this truth as we reach out to others with love. Let us draw on your power within us. Thank you for transforming us. Alleluia!

> Friday, October 27, 2006
> Ephesians 4, 1-6
> Unity in the Body

Paul writes, "I therefore, a prisoner in the Lord, beg you to lead a life worthy of the calling to which you have been called, with all humility and gentleness, with patience, bearing with one another in love, (vv. 1-2)."

We are to live in a way that is consonant with our call. We not only believe intellectually in Jesus, but we also follow him with our whole being. We will have to learn how to love others and not merely tolerate them. After all, others have been so patient with us!

Lord Jesus, thank you for transforming our emotions, our thoughts, our words and our actions. Thank you for transforming us to serve as you are calling us to serve. Alleluia!

> Saturday, October 28, 2006 St. Simon and Jude
> Ephesians 2, 19-22
> One in Christ

We are not alone. We are together, not only with other contemporary Christians, but also with the foundation of the prophets and apostles.

We are truly in the communion of saints. The cloud of witnesses (Hebrews 12, 1) is cheering us on!

I remember Rev. James Niles, our Rector at the Church of the Transfiguration in Dallas. He loved to refer to the Church Militant, the Church Expectant, and the Church Triumphant.

Jesus is holding us all together as we grow up. Jesus is holding us all together as we grow into the fullness of God's plan for us.

We recall that "there is one Body and one Spirit ... one Lord, one faith, one baptism, one God and Father of all, who is above all and through all and in all (Ephesians 4, 4-6)."

Our Father is watching over us. Jesus, our Brother, is holding our hand. The Holy Spirit is energizing us to continue our journey Home.

Lord Jesus, thank you that we will not be exiles forever. You are working within us individually and corporately to form us into a holy temple. Alleluia!

Sunday, October 29, 2006 Thirtieth Sunday in Ordinary Time
Jeremiah 31, 7-9
The Road of Return

Group travel. This is group travel at its best. With the vulnerable in our midst, we are traveling Home together.

We wept tears as we left, but the Lord will replace those tears with brooks of fresh, flowing water to refresh us. There will be no stumbling or falling on this road which has been made level for us.

Lord Jesus, thank you for guiding us and comforting us as you lead us Home We rejoice in you. Alleluia!

Monday, October 30, 2006
Ephesians 4, 32 - 5, 8
Rules for the New Life; Duty to Live in the Light

We are called to live in a new way. The light of Christ is now shining upon us!

Lord Jesus, let your light shine in us and purify us of all sin. Let your light heal us of all wounds and hurts of the past. Let your light shine through us to others. Let us be gentle and forgiving, remembering how you have forgiven us and are healing us. Alleluia!

JANIS WALKER   FIRST READING

> Tuesday, October 31, 2006
> Ephesians 5, 21-33
> Wives and Husbands

"Be subject to one another out of reverence for Christ (v. 21)."

The perfect blend of love and respect is what Paul is describing. The unity of Christ and the church is illustrated for us on earth in the sacrament of marriage.

Lord Jesus, you gave yourself totally for the church. Let us give ourselves totally to you. Alleluia.

> Wednesday, November 1, 2006 All Saints
> Revelation 7, 2-4,9-14
> The 144,000 Sealed; Triumph of the Elect

Years ago in a prayer group, I remember praying for a woman who was able to attend only a couple of times, due to serious illness. As I silently prayed, I saw her clothed in white and holding a palm branch.

She came to mind when reading this passage this morning. Quite ill at the time, she has since died, having been cared for most tenderly by her husband.

It is extraordinary to contemplate the heavenly praise of God. The multitudes of every background. The throne of God. The Lamb of God. The angels. Continuous worship and adoration. White garments. Palm branches,

Lord Jesus, you are the Lamb who continues to be our Shepherd to lead us to the springs of living water. Thank you that all our tears will cease. We will continually learn to worship and to praise. Help us today to practice our praise. Alleluia!

> Thursday, November 2, 2006 All Souls
> Wisdom 3, 1-9
> The Hidden Counsels of God

Comforting words for All Souls' Day. In God's hands. Peace. Untouched by torment. Future blessings. A time to shine! Allusions to future ministry.

Lord Jesus, help us to trust in you in order to comprehend truth. Let us cling to you in love. Thank you for your tender mercy.

Friday, November 3, 2006 St. Martin de Porres
Philippians 1, 1-11
Greeting; Thanksgiving

"I am confident of this, that the one who began a good work among you will bring it to completion by the day of Jesus Christ (v. 6)."

This is a good passage to ponder when we're discouraged about our spiritual progress. We are assured that God's work begun in us will be continued and completed.

It is not all up to us! We may rest in God and trust.

Lord Jesus, let us trust that the good work begun is us will blossom, bud, and bear wholesome fruit. Thank you for cleansing us and purifying us to live as you call us to live. Alleluia!

Saturday, November 4, 2006 St. Charles Borromeo
Philippians 1, 18-26
Thanksgiving

"For to me to live is Christ, and to die is gain (v. 21 KJV)."

For some people, life is all about money. For others, life is all about power. Fot still others, life is all about ....

For the apostle Paul, life was all about Christ. Period!

Paul was willing to live or to die for Christ. His consuming desire was that his life and death would magnify the Lord Jesus Christ.

Paul's personal preference was to leave this life in order to experience union with Christ. However, for the sake of those who still needed him on earth, he was willing to remain.

Lord Jesus, you are the only one worthy of our worship. We become fatigued watching the power players of this world. Your power, when you walked this earth, was the power to serve. Let us rejoice in you, serve you as well as we are able while we're here, and then spend all eternity rejoicing in you and with you. Alleluia!

Sunday, November 5, 2006
Thirty-first Sunday in Ordinary Time
Deuteronomy 6, 2-6
Moses as Mediator; The Great Commandment

"Hear, O Israel: The LORD is our God, the LORD alone. You shall love the LORD your God with all your heart, and with all your soul, and with all your might. Keep these words that I am commanding to you today in your heart. Recite them to your children and talk about them when you are at home and when you are away, when you lie down and when you rise. Hear therefore, O Israel, and observe them diligently, so that it may go well with you, and so that you may multiply greatly in a land flowing with milk and honey … (vv. 4-7,3)."

God's commands are not capricious, nor or they meant to constrict us. Following God's commands empowers us to live and to enjoy prosperity in a land of milk and honey.

Obvious though it seems, God alone is God. When we become fearful and insecure, we may think that the opinions of others are God. They are not.

We may cringe in servile fear of others, thinking that they are in charge of our lives. They are not.

We slowly begin to serve, not God, but our fear. This is not God's way. We were meant to conquer (Deuteronomy 6, 1)!

Lord Jesus, thank you that we are free to be your followers. You lived for your Father. You lived to carry his plans. You boldly served him, regardless of the consequences. Your fidelity to your Father led you to the Cross and to your resurrection. Thank you that the Holy Spirit dwells within us and longs to surge powerfully within us so that we long to live for God alone. Come, Holy Spirit, release your power within us! We will then be free to serve others in a way that is healthy. Thank you that we will enter the land of promise. Alleluia!

Monday, November 6, 2006
Philippians 2, 1-4
Plea for Unity and Humility

"Do nothing through selfish ambition or conceit: but in humility regard others as better than yourselves (v. 3)."

The third verse in this passage has popped into my mind many times, just as I was about to say something better left unsaid. Many years ago, this was one of the verses our Scripture study group decided to memorize.

It's a quick motivation check. We are to do nothing with selfish motives. Nothing!

We are not to show off. Well, that advice alone would eliminate a lot of trouble.

We are to be very concerned about others. We are to consider the worth and value of others. We are to look after others.

Lord Jesus, when we are truly thinking of others and living for others, we are most like you. Forgive us when we begin to act out of insecurity instead of out of love. Let us look up to you and reach out with love and humility to others. Alleluia!

Tuesday, November 7, 2006
Philippians 2, 5-11
Plea for Unity and Humility

Jesus was not going to a costume party. He did not dress up as a slave.

Jesus actually became a slave in order to secure our freedom. Jesus, Son of God, actually became a human being! He refused all divine prerogatives in order to serve.

We are to choose this same mind-set. Are we able to forget about our so-called rank and rights long enough to die? If we can die to the way we think life should be, we will be raised to a new life even while we are still on earth.

Lord Jesus, let us relax our tense hold on our own bright ideas of how things should be. Let us relinquish ourselves into your strong, loving hands to be formed by you and then sent back into the world to serve you. Alleluia!

Wednesday, November 8, 2006
Philippians 2, 12-18
Obedience and Service in the World

"Do all things without murmuring and arguing, so that you may be blameless and innocent, children of God without blemish in the midst of a crooked and perverse generation, in which you shine like stars in the world (vv. 14-15)."

Aha! We're not to complain or to argue. Most of us do far too much of both.

We're to live out our wholeness in Christ with great reverence. God is truly at work in us. In the darkness of this world, we are called to shine and to rejoice.

Lord Jesus, forgive all our complaining and our arguing. You want us to thank you as we walk in the light we have. Let us rejoice in you! Alleluia!

Thursday, November 9, 2006
Dedication of the Lateran Basilica in Rome
Ezekiel 47, 1-2, 8-9, 12
The Wonderful Stream

The water flowing from the temple purified even the salt water of the Dead Sea. Life resulted wherever this water flowed.

Animals. Fish. Trees on the stream's banks, which continually bore fresh fruit. Mysteriously, the leaves from these fruit trees did not wither or fade. Instead, they had healing qualities.

Lord Jesus, we pray for Ezekiel's vision of the stream to come to full fruition in our lives. Let the living water of the Holy Spirit bring healing to us and to all for whom we pray. Alleluia!

Friday, November 10, 2006 St. Leo the Great
Philippians 3, 17 - 4, 1
Wrong Conduct and Our Goal; Live in Concord

Our true citizenship is not on earth, but in heaven. We are to enjoy the good things of this life, but not to live for them or to be controlled by them. We belong to God.

Jesus, who now lives in a glorified body, will change our bodies to be like his body. Glorified! Everything will become subject to Jesus.

Lord Jesus, help us to stop living as though this life is all there is. It is so easy to get stuck in our own woes and in the woes of the world. Lift our hearts to you today. Let us practice praising you! Alleluia!

Saturday, November 11, 2006 St. Martin of Tours
Ephesians 4, 10-19
Joy and Peace

An uninterrupted flow. Giving. Receiving. Gratitude.

Reciprocity. Paul and the Christians at Philippi enjoyed a healthy reciprocity in their relationship.

It is very difficult to keep on giving when no appreciation is expressed. Do we keep giving? Do we give elsewhere instead?

Paul offers comfort and counsel. He was comfortable with both poverty and prosperity. He experienced both humiliation and honor. Paul knew that God was his strength and his supply.

Lord Jesus, purify our motives when we give. Let us give joyfully to others as you direct and leave the results with you. Let us look to you for our strength and our supply. Alleluia!

Sunday, November 12, 2006
Thirty-Second Sunday in Ordinary Time
1 Kings 17, 10-16
Elijah and the Widow

It was time for the prophet Elijah to leave Cherith, the brook where the Lord had cared for him. The brook was now dry. The Lord directed Elijah to a new place, Zarephath.

A widow in Zarephath agreed to give Elijah water, as he had requested. When he also asked for a bit of bread, she told him that she was running out of flour and oil.

She fully expected that, after she and her son had eaten the last of the bread, they would die of starvation. She listened to Elijah, however, and gave him something to eat.

Then came the message from God! For a year, there would be a constant supply of flour and oil. The flour and oil would last until the drought was over.

Lord Jesus, help us to trust you to care for us. There is enough of everything we need if we look first to you. Alleluia!

Monday, November 13, 2006 St. Frances Xavier Cabrini
Titus 1, 1-9
Greetings; Titus in Crete

Paul began this letter by reminding himself as well as Titus and other readers of his own identity. Who was Paul, anyway?

Paul described himself as God's slave and as Jesus' apostle. He had been sent out on a mission!

Only then does Paul start to give pastoral direction about church leadership. From his vantage point of humility, he describes the kind of leaders who are to serve as presbyters (priests) and bishops.

"For a bishop, as God's steward, must be blameless; he must not be arrogant or quick-tempered or addicted to wine or violent or greedy for gain; but he must be hospitable, a lover of goodness, prudent, upright, devout and self-controlled. He must have a firm grasp of the word that is trustworthy in accordance with the teaching, so that he may be able both to preach with sound doctrine and to refute those who contradict it (vv. 7-9)."

Lord Jesus, we pray for all leaders in the church. Let there be wise and loving leaders who know their constant need of you and who have experienced your mercy. Alleluia!

Tuesday, November 14, 2006
Titus 2, 1-8,11-14
Christian Behavior; Transformation of Life

Self-control is required of all us. We don't have to gobble up everything we see or want in this world.

We are not living for this world. We are living for God.

We are in training, learning to live a certain way here on earth, as we wait joyfully for the coming of our Lord Jesus Christ.

Lord Jesus, thank you for all the good and beautiful things we may enjoy here on earth. Let self-control be more and more evident in our lives, as we trust you and realize that you are in control. You gave yourself to free us and to make us your own. Let us live to please you. Alleluia!

Wednesday, November 15, 2006   St. Albert the Great
Titus 3, 1-7
Transformation of Life

Here's that "control" word again! Paul, writing to Titus on the island of Crete, continues to give wise direction to the Christian community. The Christians are to live under the authority and control of the local government leaders and to be at peace with one another.

"Remind them to be subject to rulers and authorities, to be obedient, to be ready for every good work, to speak evil of no one, to avoid quarreling, to be gentle, and to show every courtesy to everyone. For we ourselves were once foolish, disobedient, led astray, slaves to various passions and pleasures, passing our days in malice and envy, despicable, hating one another. But when the goodness and loving kindness of God our Savior appeared, he saved us, not because of any works of righteousness that we had done, but according to his mercy, through the water of rebirth and renewal by the Holy Spirit. This Spirit he poured out on richly through Jesus Christ our Savior, so that, having been justified by his grace, we might become heirs according to the hope of eternal life (vv. 1-7)."

We are all in need of realizing that God is in ultimate control. We pray to cooperate with the Holy Spirit, but we are not in ultimate control of our lives. We recognize some of our failings, but we need God's mercy in order to change.

Lord Jesus, you are our loving Shepherd and Savior. You came to us because we needed you. We did not love ourselves and we did not love others. Thank you for making it possible for us to be truly reborn. Let us live joyfully, confidently trusting that you are in control. Alleluia!

Thursday, November 16, 2006
St. Margaret of Scotland, St. Gertrude
Philemon 7-20
Plea for Onesimus

Paul interceded and intervened on behalf of Onesimus, a runaway slave soon to be returned to his master. Onesismus, although still a slave, was now free in Christ.

Paul generously offered restitution to the master of Onesimus. More importantly, Paul appealed to the master to welcome Onesimus as he would welcome Paul himself, as a brother in Christ.

Lord Jesus, we are all runaways in some sense. Thank you for reminding us that we are your beloved brothers and sisters. You paid the price for our freedom You welcome us back with open arms. Alleluia!

Friday, November 17, 2006 St. Elizabeth of Hungary
2 John 4-9

"Everyone who does not abide in the teaching of Christ, but goes beyond it, does not have God; whoever abides in the teaching has both the Father and the Son (v. 9)."

We are to stay tightly within Christ's teaching. Within this boundary, we are free and safe.

Lord Jesus, thank you that you protect us from deceivers. Thank you, Holy Spirit, for giving us discernment. Thank you, Father, for giving us the power of the Holy Spirit to live in the truth. Alleluia!

Saturday, November 18, 2006
Dedication of the Basilicas of St. Peter and St. Paul;
St. Rose Philippina Duchesne
3 John 5-8

Gaius, the recipient of this letter, is commended for his faithful, loving service. The writer urges him to continue to support those who are ministering in the name of Jesus.

Lord Jesus, help us to remember to pray for and to support missionaries. Open our eyes to ways we may encourage all who minister in your name. Alleluia!

Sunday, November 19, 2006
Thirty-third Sunday in Ordinary Time
Daniel 12, 1-3
Vision of the Hellenistic Wars

" 'At that time [the angel] Michael, the great prince, the protector of your people, shall arise. There shall be a time of anguish, such as has never occurred since nations first came into existence. But at that time your people shall be delivered, everyone who is found written in the book. Many of those who sleep in the dust of the earth shall awake, some to everlasting life, and some to shame and everlasting contempt. Those who are wise shall shine like the brightness of the sky, and those who lead many to righteousness, like the stars forever and ever (vv. 1-3).' "

This is a scary passage. Distress. Suffering. It would be easy to give into fear, especially fear of the unknown.

What we do know is that God is in control. There is light in the darkness. Indeed, the wise will be as shining lights. Those who work for justice will be as eternal stars.

Lord Jesus, there is so much in the big world that frightens us. Help us not to live lives of lazy, cringing fear. Let us live lives of disciplined service. Let us shine brightly for you. Alleluia!

Monday, November 20, 2006
Revelation 1, 1-4; 2, 1-5
Prologue; Greeting; To Ephesus

It is not enough to read the book of the Revelation and to engage in endless theological speculation. We are to read, to listen, and to heed.

John is simply the reporter and recorder of the vision Jesus gave to him. The one who reads aloud the Revelation is blessed, as are those who listen and heed the message.

Jesus is seeking more than mere work in his service. Jesus is seeking those who will put him first and who will love him wholeheartedly.

Lord Jesus, thank you for rekindling in us the love we have for you. Sometimes we become so weary and discouraged. Let us read your words to us, listen to the message, and heed what you tell us. Alleluia!

Tuesday, November 21, 2006
Presentation of the Blessed Virgin Mary
Revelation 3, 1-6,14-22
To Sardis; To Laodicia

Rich and poor. Alive and dead.

The church in Sardis was not alive, but dead. Jesus said, "I know your works; you have a name for being alive, but you are dead. Wake up, and strengthen what remains and is on the point of death, for I have not found your works perfect in the sight of my God (v. 1c,2)."

The church at Laodicia was not rich, but was wretchedly poor in what matters to Jesus. It was also so disgustingly lukewarm that Jesus said he wanted, literally, to spit it out of his mouth.

Jesus said to the lukewarm, wishy-washy church in Laodicia, "I reprove and discipline those whom I love. Be earnest, therefore, and repent (v. 9)."

Lord Jesus, we repent and cry to you for mercy and forgiveness. You are standing before us and longing for us to invite you into our lives. Please come to us and speak the words we need to hear. Thank you for strengthening us to follow you faithfully Alleluia!

Wednesday, November 22, 2006 St. Cecelia
Revelation 4, 1-11
Vision of Heavenly Worship

Now! I want to live now, this hour, this day, in a greater awareness of the awesome, dazzling worship that is going on in heaven at this very moment.

" 'You are worthy, our Lord and God, to receive glory and honor and power, for you created all things, and by your will they existed and were created (v. 11).' "

Worship! This is worship so profound that John, in his vision, was only able to describe it in similes.

A voice like a trumpet. An appearance dazzling as jewels. Elders clothed in white with golden crowns. Thunder and lightening! A floor like a sea of crystal. Amazing creatures resembling a lion, a calf, a human being, and a flying eagle.

The holiness of the eternal God is being endlessly proclaimed. The elders in white cast their crowns before the throne of God.

Lord Jesus, we get so caught up in the living of each day that we sometimes lose sight of heaven. Let us be conscientious to do the work that you have given us to do, yet remember that this is not all there is. You beckon us to lift our spirits to a new level of worship. Alleluia!

Thursday, November 23, 2006 St. Clement I, St. Columban,
Blessed Miguel Agustin Pro
Revelation 5, 1-10
The Scroll and the Lamb

Lion and Lamb. Christ the Lion and Christ the Lamb.

Jesus is the Lion from Judah. Jesus is the Lamb of God whose blood shed for us frees us to live.

Our sins are removed by his Blood. Because the Lamb died and rose, we too will live forever.

Lord Jesus, thank you that we may join in the prayers of heaven. You opened the scroll and fulfilled its conditions. Let our prayer this day rise as sweet incense to you. Alleluia!

> Friday, November 24, 2006
> St. Andrew Dung-Lac and Companions
> Revelation 10, 8-11
> The Angel with the Small Scroll

Eat the scroll! What in the world?

Eat the scroll without reading it first. It will be sweet at first and then turn sour. Again, go forth and prophesy! That was John's perplexing assignment.

God sometimes tells us to undertake a mission without our complete understanding of what it's all about. That's putting it mildly!

It is sweet to hear God's words to us. However, the living out of God's words may turn sour.

The mission may appear to sour because it is a hard message we deliver and it may be rejected. Living and speaking as a prophet is never popular.

John's prophetic task, as writer of the Revelation, was of cosmic proportions. He was instructed to convey God's message to many nations and rulers.

Lord Jesus, help us to take the "scroll," your words to us, into our inner being. Let us say yes to you, receive your message, and live it out as well as we are able. We leave the results with you. Alleluia!

> Saturday, November 25, 2006 St. Catherine of Alexandria
> Revelation 11, 4-12
> The Two Witnesses

Go ahead and live for God! As with the two witnesses, you may be either silenced or slain.

No problem. God will raise you to new life!

In the case of the two witnesses, they were indeed slain. However, "... after three and a half days, the breath of life from God entered them, and they stood on their feet, and those who saw them were terrified. Then they heard a loud voice from heaven saying to them, 'Come up here!' And they went up to heaven in a cloud while their enemies watched them (vv. 11-12)."

Lord Jesus, we just don't want to suffer. We want to be like you, but we want it to be easy. Let us look to you, then look to ourselves, and trust you to transform us. Let us live as a bridge for others. Alleluia!

Sunday, November 26, 2006 Christ the King
Thirty-fourth Sunday in Ordinary Time
Daniel 7, 13-14
Vision of the Four Beasts

Jesus, fully human, the baby in Bethlehem, shepherd and servant, the Crucified the Risen Christ, will return as King. All will serve him. His kingship will be eternal.

Lord Jesus, forgive me when I try to live as though you are not in charge of my life. Forgive me for growing profoundly weary and yielding to discouragement. Thank you that you conquered death. Thank you that you are coming back to earth to reign forever. As Advent approaches, help me to make the changes in my interior life as well as in my exterior life that will be evidence that you are my King. Alleluia!

Monday, November 27, 2006
Revelation 14, 1-3,4-5
The Lamb's Companions

To be with the Lamb on the mountain. Mount Zion. Jerusalem!

To be marked with the name of the Lamb. Coursing water. Reverberating thunder. Joyful singing. The music of harps. True worship before the throne of God.

John cannot tell us exactly what he saw in this revelation. He can only make comparisons. He can only attempt to convey this scene in the heavenlies.

Lord Jesus, thank you for being the true Lamb of God. Thank you for this foretaste of worship in the heavenly realm. Thank you for the purity and the joy that awaits us. Help us to practice now, while we're still here on earth. Thank you for purifying our hearts so that we speak the truth with gentleness and love. Alleluia!

Tuesday, November 28, 2006
Revelation 14, 14-19
The Harvest of the Earth

Time!. When it was exactly the right time, God sent Jesus into the world to ransom us (Galatians 4, 4).

Time! John, in his vision, saw the harvest of the earth ready to be harvested. With a swing of the sickle, the harvest was accomplished.

Time! With another swing of the sickle, the ripe grapes of the vines of the earth were cut and cast into God's wine press to be destroyed.

Lord Jesus, thank you for showing us what time it is in our lives. Let us hasten to cry to you for mercy while there is still time. We pray for mercy for ourselves, our loved ones, and for all. Alleluia!

Wednesday, November 29, 2006
Revelation 15, 1-4
The Seven Last Plagues

Shimmering sea and fiery flames! Angels. Beast. Victors. Harps. Singing. Seven angels. Seven plagues.

The victors, those who suffered and overcame, are now singing God's praises. Their time of martyrdom is over. Their witness is complete. They are with the Lamb.

"And they sing the song of Moses, the servant of God, and the song of the Lamb: Great and amazing are your deeds, LORD GOD the Almighty! Just and true are your ways, King of the nations! Lord, who will not fear and glorify your name? For you alone are holy. All nations will come and worship before you, for your judgments have been revealed (vv. 3-4)."

Lord Jesus, thank you for this glimpse into the heavenly realm where you are even now being worshipped and adored. Our little worries and our big worries are being put into proper proportion as we contemplate your holiness. You are the Lamb of God whose blood had purified us. Let us walk into this Advent waiting for you and trusting you to transform us. Alleluia!

JANIS WALKER   FIRST READING

Thursday, November 30, 2006 St. Andrew
Romans 10, 9-18
Righteousness Based on Faith

" 'The word is near you, on your lips and in your heart' (that is, the word of faith we proclaim) because if you confess with your lips that Jesus is Lord and believe in your heart that God raised him from the dead, you will be saved (Romans 10, 8-9)."

Mouth. Heart. Feet. Ears. All are involved in our relationship with Jesus.

We say with our mouth that the Lord of our lives is Jesus. We are made whole.

We trust in our deepest heart that God, our Father in heaven, raised the crucified Christ from the dead. God considers us righteous!

God sends people to tell, to preach, to proclaim the Gospel of peace! The very feet of the preachers are beautiful because they are being used in God's service.

"How beautiful are the feet of them that preach the gospel of peace, and bring glad tidings of good things (v. 15b KJV)!"

Faith comes into our lives as we listen with our ears and respond. The very word of God has found an entrance into our lives.

We have a new confidence. God has promised that all who call out to Jesus will be saved and made whole.

Lord Jesus, thank you that your word is permeating our entire being. Today, we give you our ears, our hearts, our mouths, and our feet. Let us be filled with your word and walk it out in our lives. Let your word flow forth to all we meet today. Alleluia!

Friday, December 1, 2006
Revelation 20, 1-4,11 - 21, 2
The Thousand Year Reign; The Large White Throne

It is most tempting to run from this passage. Angel. Dragon. Abyss. Books. Death. Resurrections. A throne set for judgment.

We do know that God will require an accounting from each of us. What did we do in this life?

"For we will all stand before the judgment seat of God. For it is written, 'As I live, says the Lord, every knee shall bow to me, and every tongue shall give praise to God.' So then, each of us will be accountable to God (Romans 14, 10c-11)."

Lord Jesus, thank you that you alone know how to judge us. We call to you and put our trust in you. Let us not trouble ourselves trying to figure out things that are beyond our current understanding. Let us trust you and, with all simplicity, love you and love others. Alleluia!

Saturday, December 2, 2006
Revelation 22, 1-7
The New Jerusalem

Sparkling water which gives life is flowing from God's throne. There is a wonderful tree, with medicinal leaves to heal nations, which offers fruit every month.

Worship! John tries to describe what he saw in the vision.

There will be no more night. No more darkness. No more curses.

"But the throne of God and of the Lamb will be in it, and his servants will worship him; they will see his face, and his name will be on their foreheads. And there will be no more night; they need no light of lamp or sun, for the LORD GOD will be their light, and they will reign forever and ever (vv. 3b,4,5)."

Lord Jesus, thank you that you will come again in glory. We will one day be living in the fullness of the vision granted to John in the book of the Revelation. Help us to keep your words and to live this day on earth knowing that we will live with you forever. Alleluia!

Sunday, December 3, 2006 First Sunday of Advent, Year C
Jeremiah 33, 14-16
Restoration of Jerusalem

God's promises will be fulfilled because God is faithful. Jerusalem will have a new name, a name which exalts God's justice. There will be safety and security.

Lord Jesus, we are frightened as we look about our world. Thank you for teaching us to trust you more and more. You are faithful and just. We rejoice now in the restoration you have promised. Alleluia!

Monday, December 4, 2006 St. John of Damascus
Isaiah 2, 1-5
Zion, the Messianic Capitol

A preview of our ultimate Homegoing. Jerusalem! The heavenly Jerusalem.

From Jerusalem will flow God's words of instruction. There will be peace. From Jerusalem will stream the Lord's light.

Lord Jesus, I long to see the fulfillment of your word to me for my time on earth. Even more, I long to go to the heavenly Jerusalem. Let me be conscientious and diligent to follow you today, knowing that you are leading me Home. Alleluia!

Tuesday, December 5, 2006 Advent Weekday
Isaiah 11, 1-10
The Rule of Immanuel; Union of Ephraim and Judah

Another glimpse into the joy of the reign of the royal Messiah. The baby from Bethlehem will take his rightful place as King. There will be peace, innocence, and security.

Lord Jesus Christ, you came to us as a helpless infant and you will return as our King. Let us not lose heart while we are still in exile. Let us exalt you as our King. Alleluia!

Wednesday, December 6, 2006 St. Nicholas
Isaiah 25, 6-10
A Remnant Saved

"On this mountain the Lord of hosts will make for all peoples a feast of rich food, a feast of well-aged wines, of rich food ... of well-aged wines.... And he will destroy on this mountain the shroud that is cast over all peoples ... he will swallow up death forever. Then the LORD GOD will wipe away the tears from all faces, and the disgrace of his people he will take away from all the earth, for the Lord has spoken. It will be said on that day, Lo, this is our God; we have waited for him, so that he might save us. This is the Lord for whom we have waited; let us be glad and rejoice in his salvation (vv. 6-9)."

Mount Zion! The heavenly Jerusalem.

It is in the heavenly Jerusalem that we will feast. There will be no more death, no more tears, and no more reproach for the people of God. The Lord's own hand rests on Mount Zion.

Lord Jesus, thank you for this breath of springtime, of Easter, in early Advent. We rejoice in you! We are waiting, yes, but you are waiting, too. You are waiting for us to realize who we are and where we are going. Alleluia!

Thursday, December 7, 2006 St. Ambrose
Isaiah 26, 1-6
The Divine Vindicator

We are strong when we know God is our strength. We may trust God to exalt, to humble, and to set the record straight.

Lord Jesus, we are safe and secure with you. You hold us and fold us in your arms. Thank you that we are learning to trust you and to rejoice in you as we wait. Alleluia!

Friday, December 8, 2006 Immaculate Conception
Genesis 3, 9-15,20
The Fall of Man

Adam and Eve sinned and hid from God. Adam blamed Eve. Eve blamed the serpent.

Adam and Eve offered God excuses for their disobedience. Mary offered God herself.

At the Annunciation, "... Mary said, 'Here am I, the servant of the Lord; let it be with me according to your word (Luke 1, 38).'"

Lord Jesus, forgive us when we blame others for our actions. Let us not hide from you, but run to you and receive forgiveness. Let us offer ourselves completely to you. You have made it possible for us to live in victory. Alleluia!

Saturday, December 9, 2006 St. Juan Diego
Isaiah 30, 19-21,23-26
Future Alliance with Egypt; Zion's Future Prosperity

Sometimes it does seem that our Teacher is hidden. We grow perplexed and frustrated. We may even weep.

We are comforted in this passage with God's own reassuring words. We will see our Teacher and hear very clear direction. We will know the way in which we are to walk.

"Though the Lord may give you the bread of adversity and the water of affliction, yet your Teacher will not hide himself any more, but your eyes shall see your Teacher. And when you turn to the right or when you turn to the left, your ears shall hear a word behind you, saying, 'This is the way; walk in it (v. 20-21).'"

Lord Jesus, thank you that you are our wise Teacher and our Shepherd. Thank you for the spacious land of meadows and streams where we will live. Thank you that we will be healed at last and weep no more. Alleluia!

Sunday, December 10, 2006 Second Sunday in Advent
Baruch 5, 1-9
Jerusalem Consoled; The Captivity about to End

A glorious change of attire! Off with the widow's weeds. On with the bridal gown!

Off with the black mourning veil. On with the beautiful mitre!

God is leading us through fragrant forests. Our time of captivity is coming to its conclusion. The ones led by foot into captivity will return, borne aloft in triumph.

Lord Jesus, thank you that you are our Bridegroom and we are your Bride. Thank you that we will one day rejoice at the wedding supper of the Lamb. You are our Lamb! You shed your blood to make us righteous. Let us spring up this Advent and live joyfully for you. Let our heavy hearts, weighed down with sorrow, become light as we honor you with our joyful trust. Alleluia!

Monday, December 11, 2006 St. Damasus I
Isaiah 35, 1-10
Israel's Deliverance

"The wilderness and the solitary place shall be glad for them; and the desert shall rejoice, and blossom as the rose (v. 1 KJV)."

God is here to vindicate us and to bring us to wholeness. God is here to open our eyes to see and our ears to hear. God is here to strengthen the lame to leap and the mute to sing!

We have a journey to accomplish. Jesus has redeemed us so that we may walk along this holy way with joy and singing. We will see the desert bloom. We will behold our God.

"Say to them that are of a fearful heart, Be strong, fear not: behold, your God will come with vengeance, even God with a recompense; he will come and save you (v. 4 KJV)."

Lord Jesus, thank you for pouring the living water of the Holy Spirit upon our parched lives. Let us receive the strength you long for us to enjoy. Let us reach forth with strong hands and strong hearts to receive the abundance you have prepared for us. Thank you for removing our pauper mentality, our victim mentality, and our trampled expectations. You have made us victors with you! Let us walk through this Advent with eyes and hearts ablaze with your glory. Alleluia!

Tuesday, December 12, 2006 Our Lady of Guadalupe
Zechariah 2, 14-17
The New Jerusalem

God chooses us and chooses us again and again. We may rejoice that God chooses us, knowing our weaknesses much better than we do.

God chooses us, already aware of exactly where we will fail. God chooses us, knowing our final destiny.

Lord Jesus, we sing and rejoice because you are with us. We also rejoice in silent wonder. Alleluia!

Wednesday, December 13, 2006 St. Lucy
Isaiah 40, 25-31
Power of the Creator to Save His People

We are learning to lift our eyes to God! Our Creator is the One who knows how to replenish us and to strengthen us.

"But they that wait upon the LORD shall renew their strength; they shall mount up with wings as eagles; they shall run, and not be weary; and they shall walk, and not faint (v. 31 KJV)."

We are promised that, as we place our hope in the Lord, our strength will be renewed. We will walk, run, and fly with the strength of God.

Lord Jesus, thank you for showing us how to wait expectantly this Advent. Thank you for showing us how to hope. Alleluia!

Thursday, December 14, 2006 St. John of the Cross
Isaiah 41, 13-20
The Liberation of Israel

"For I the LORD thy God will hold thy right hand, saying unto thee, Fear not; I will help thee. Behold, I will make thee a new sharp threshing instrument ... (vv. 13, 15 KJV)."

New life! New strength! The Lord is surrounding us with signs of life.

Water! Rivers and fountains. Marshes and springs.

Trees! Even in the desert, God is planting trees. Cedars. Acacias. Myrtles. Olives. Cypresses. Planes and pines.

Lord Jesus, you know where to plant us. You know how to pour the water of the Holy Spirit upon us to give us new life. Thank you for renewing us this Advent and making us instruments of your grace. Alleluia!

Friday, December 15, 2006 Advent Weekday
Isaiah 48, 17-19
Exhortation to the Exiles

"Thus says the LORD, your Redeemer, the Holy One of Israel: I am the LORD your God. who teaches you for your own good, who leads you in the way you should go (v. 17)."

God promises to teach us what is for our own good. God will teach us the specific ways in which we should proceed in our lives.

Obedience is the key. Obedience to the Lord, regardless of our feelings and regardless of the cost, results in prosperity, vindication, and countless descendants.

Lord Jesus, when we are being fearful and stubborn, clinging to our own ways, please help us. Let us trust that our obedience will result in benefits which will overflow to us and to many others. You know what is best for us and for those we love. Alleluia!

Saturday, December 16, 2006 Advent Weekday
Sirach 48, 1-4,9-11
Elijah and Elisha

"Then Elijah arose, a prophet like fire, and his word burned like a torch (v. 1)."

Mission accomplished, Elijah was escorted to heaven in a chariot of fire! While on earth, his very words had been words of fire. God's words of power flowed through this prophet in a powerful way, in spite of the prophet's personal fears and foibles.

Lord Jesus, let us speak the words you give us to speak, pray the prayers you give us to pray, and do the work you give us to do. Let us trust that you are indeed using us. Let us trust that you are being glorified in our lives. Let your purpose for our lives be accomplished. Alleluia!

Sunday, December 17, 2006 Third Sunday in Advent
Zephaniah 3, 14-18
Reproof and Promise for Jerusalem

This is Gaudete Sunday! Rejoice! Rose-coloured vestments.

"Sing aloud, O daughter Zion; shout, O Israel! Rejoice and exult with all your heart, O daughter Jerusalem! The LORD has taken away the judgments against you, he has turned away your enemies. The king of Israel, the LORD, is in your midst; you shall fear disaster no more. On that it shall be said to Jerusalem: Do not fear, O Zion, do not let your hands grow weak. The LORD your God is in your midst, a warrior who gives victory; he will rejoice over you with gladness, he will renew you in his love; he will exult over you with loud singing as on a day of festival. I will remove disaster from you, so that you will not bear reproach for it (vv. 14-18)."

Lord Jesus, thank you that you are here with us. We are free to sing and to rejoice and to be glad. You will come as our King and you will rejoice over us! You have forgiven us. You will remove our enemies. You tell us not to fear and not to be discouraged. You are with us. Thank you for renewing us. Thank you for your love for us, especially when we are discouraged with ourselves. Thank you for the victory you have won for us. We adore you as our beautiful King. Alleluia!

Monday, December 18, 2006 Late Advent Weekday
Jeremiah 23, 5-8
Messianic Reign

"Woe to the shepherds who destroy and scatter the sheep of my pasture! says the LORD. Therefore thus says the LORD, the God of Israel, concerning the shepherds who shepherd my people: It is you who have scattered my flock, and have driven them away, and you have not attended to them. So I will attend to you for your evil doings, says the LORD. Then I myself will gather the remnant of my flock out of all the lands where I have driven them, and I will bring them back to their fold, and they shall be fruitful and multiply. I will raise up my shepherds over them who will shepherd them, and they shall not fear any longer, or be dismayed, nor shall any be missing, says the LORD (Jeremiah 23, 1-4)."

After deploring the behavior of the unworthy shepherds who scattered the flock, the Lord promised to bring his flock back to their own meadows with good shepherds. The Good Shepherd will be acknowledged as the royal Messiah.

The King will rule with justice and wisdom. The ones who were driven away by wicked leaders will return home.

Lord Jesus, thank you that you are coming as our King. You will be the One to secure justice for your flock. We love you and trust you and long to live for you as we wait for you to return in glory. Alleluia!

Tuesday, December 19, 2006 Late Advent Weekday
Judges 13, 2-7,24-25
The Birth of Samson

A woman in Zorah was promised a son who would be instrumental in the deliverance of Israel. Her role was crucial.

During her pregnancy, she was to abstain from alcohol and from unclean food. From her womb, her son was to be consecrated to the Lord.

Lord Jesus, during our "pregnancy," our time of waiting for your promise to us to be fulfilled, strengthen us to abstain from all that would be harmful to the new life within us. Thank you for forgiving us when we fail. Thank you for bringing to birth your promise to us. Alleluia!

Wednesday, December 20, 2006 Late Advent Weekday
Isaiah 7, 10-14
Birth of Immanuel

In the midst of political turmoil, the Lord spoke to King Ahaz of Judah. Earlier, the Lord sent the prophet, Isaiah, to tell the king not to fear (Isaiah 7, 4).

Then the Lord invited the King to request a divine sign. This will be the Sign of signs, given by the Lord.

"Therefore the LORD himself shall give you a sign; Behold a virgin shall conceive, and bear a son, and shall call his name Immanuel (v. 14 KJV)."

A virgin! A pregnant virgin will give birth to a son who will be called Immanuel.

Lord Jesus, you are Immanuel! You are God with us. You came to us through the Virgin Mary. You yourself are the Sign. Let our lives be signs to all around us that you are with us. You are the explanation of our lives. You are with us. Alleluia!

Thursday, December 21, 2006 St. Peter Canisius
Zephaniah 3, 14-18
Reproach and Promise for Jerusalem

We visited this passage four days ago. Today, we are returning for a longer visit. We may even decide to settle down and live here.

Where? In a new place! A new place in our relationship with God.

Perhaps we have believed in God, yet lived in fear. It is not too late to move to a new place in our understanding of God.

Lord Jesus, this is moving day! We choose to arise and to move into a new place in our relationship with you. We are moving into a place of strength and trust. You have reversed our fortunes. We are no longer living under condemnation and judgment. You came to set us free! You are Immanuel. You are with us and you are rejoicing over us. Alleluia!

Friday, December 22, 2006 Late Advent Weekday
1 Samuel 1, 24-28
Samuel is Offered to God

She was the one! Hannah identified herself to Eli, the priest, as the woman who had once been in the Temple and had been so misunderstood as she prayed.

Now, her prayer had been answered. Hannah was back in the Temple with the answer to her prayer, Samuel!

This was the child for whom she had prayed and the Lord had answered her prayer. She, the barren one who had suffered such reproach, was now a mother.

"For this child I prayed; and the LORD has granted me the petition that I made to him. Therefore I have lent him to the LORD; as long as he lives, he is given to the LORD (vv. 27-28)."

Hannah's focus remained on the Lord, rather than on Samuel, her child. The Lord had given her Samuel in answer to her prayer. Hannah was now making the supreme act of gratitude in dedicating her child to the Lord's service for life.

Lord Jesus, someday we will be identified as the ones who prayed. You prompted us to pray and you answered our prayers. You are in charge of our whole lives, our reputations, and our relationships. Thank you that one day our suffering will be forgotten as we rejoice in you and see the glorious way in which our prayers were answered. Alleluia!

Saturday, December 23, 2006 St. John Kanty
Malachi 3, 1-4,23-24
The Messenger of the Lord

"Behold, I will send my messenger, and he shall prepare the way before me: and the Lord, whom you seek, shall suddenly come to his temple, even the messenger of the covenant, whom ye delight in: behold, he shall come, saith the LORD of hosts. But who may abide the day of his coming? and who shall stand when he appeareth? for he is like a refiner's fire ... (vv. 1-2 KJV)."

Suddenly! To the Temple.

The Lord will come very suddenly into the Temple. His first order of business will be to purify the leaders in order for their sacrifice to be acceptable.

Lord Jesus, let us recognize the prophets, the priests, and the process of purification. Come in glory and let our worship be acceptable to you. Alleluia!

Sunday, December 24, 2006 Fourth Sunday in Advent
Micah 5, 1-4
Restoration through the Messiah

"But you, O Bethlehem of Ephrathah, who are one of the little clans of Judah, from you shall come forth for me one who is to rule in Israel, whose origin is from old, from ancient days. And he shall stand and feed his flock in the strength of the LORD, in the majesty of the name of the LORD his God. And they shall live secure, for now he shall be great to the ends of the earth; and he shall be the one of peace (vv. 2,4,5a)."

Come forth! Come forth for God!

The world may think we're small and of no account, but that's not the way God sees us. God calls us and will call us to come forth.

Come forth for God! Bethlehem, too little even to be counted among Judah's clans, was not overlooked by God. Jesus, who was to rule Israel, was called to come forth for God from Bethlehem.

Lord Jesus, thank you that you are our permanent peace in this passing world. You are our Shepherd calling us forth. Alleluia!

Monday, December 25, 2006 The Nativity of the Lord, Year C
Isaiah 52, 7-10
Let Zion Rejoice!

"How beautiful upon the mountains are the feet of the messenger who announces peace, who brings good news, who announces salvation, who says to Zion, 'Your God reigns (v. 7).'"

Beautiful feet! We think even the messenger's feet are beautiful when we receive good news.

This is the best news ever! News of peace and salvation. Our God is our King!

The Lord is restoring Zion right before our eyes. The Lord is comforting his people.

The Lord is redeeming Jerusalem. All will see the Lord's restoration.

Lord Jesus, thank you for lifting us from the mire of our misery to behold you in your glory. We will see you! We will be restored. We will sing and shout. Let us begin now to carry the great news to all. You have given us beautiful feet with which to run with the glorious news. Alleluia!

Tuesday, December 26, 2006 St. Stephen
Acts 6, 8-10; 7, 54-60
Accusation against Stephen; Stephen's Martyrdom

"Stephen, full of grace and power, did great wonders and signs among the people (v. 8)."

A double-track life with a single-track focus. Stephen was focused on the Lord Jesus Christ.

Power and grace. Stephen was full of the power of God and the grace of God.

Signs and wonders. The people saw Stephen doing signs and wonders. These were a result of his faith-filled trust.

Spirit and wisdom. When Stephen spoke, it was by the power of the Holy Spirit. Stephen's words were words of wisdom. His opponents could not withstand his words.

When Stephen suffered for his single focus, he saw the heavens opened. Jesus was there, standing at the right of God.

Lord Jesus, thank you for strengthening us to focus on you and to live on the tracks you have chosen for us. Alleluia!

Wednesday, December 27, 2006 St. John
1 John 1, 1-4
The Word of Life

Eyes of love! We are being told, not by someone who consulted a dusty theology textbook, but by someone who actually saw Jesus, that Jesus is real! Jesus is alive and well!

We trudge on in this life, step by step, day by day. We can't live on the mountain top everyday. There is the valley through which we all have to travel.

We have the assurance and the reassurance that Jesus is real! He lives not only in our hearts when we consciously experience his presence, but he lives, period! He came into our world, lived with us and among us and has now returned to his home in heaven to prepare a place for us.

Lord Jesus, let your life and your light so shine in us today that you will become visible to others. Let your eyes of love shine through us today. Alleluia!

Thursday, December 28, 2006 Holy Innocents
1 John 1, 5 - 2, 2
God's Light; Christ and His Commandments

'If we say that we have no sin, we deceive ourselves, and the truth is not in us. If we confess our sins, he who is faithful and just will forgive us our sins and cleanse us from all unrighteousness (vv. 8-9)."

Just be real! We are called to live in the stream of God's light and truth.

If we turn aside and wander into darkness, we don't have to stay there, confused and sad. We may return to our loving Shepherd, whose blood is continually cleansing us.

Lord Jesus, you call us to wholeness and to truth. Let us be quick to acknowledge what you already know about us. You know all about us. You loved us to death and you are loving us to life. Alleluia!

Friday, December 29, 2006 St. Thomas Becket
1 John 2, 3-11
Christ and His Commandments; The New Commandment

"Whoever says, 'I am in the light,' while hating a brother or sister, is still in the darkness. Whoever loves a brother or sister lives in the light, and in such a person there is no cause for stumbling. But whoever hates another believer is in the darkness, walks in the darkness, and does not know the way to go, because the darkness has brought on blindness (vv. 9-11)."

Love and truth are eye-openers. Hatred and lies make it impossible to see.

We need to see the truth about God, about ourselves, and about others. It's a package deal

According to the Gospel of John, "… those who do what is true come to the light, so that it may be clearly seen that their deeds have been done in God (John 3, 21)."

We can't see the truth about ourselves if we are squinting at God. If we perceive God in a distorted way, we will also see ourselves and others in a distorted way.

We cannot see ourselves and love ourselves if we are afraid of God and live in this unwholesome fear. We will dislike and distrust ourselves and will dislike and distrust others because we don't yet see God.

When we begin to obey God, much will fall into place. We will begin to grasp God's love and will begin to trust God more and more. We will begin to accept and to love ourselves and begin to accept and to love others. We are growing healthier and healthier!

Lord Jesus, thank you for helping us to trust you enough to obey you. Thank you for leading us on and on into more and more light and freedom. Alleluia!

Saturday, December 30, 2006
1 John 2, 12-17
Members of the Community

All that seems so enticing in this world is temporary. The post-Christmas sales, the glitz and glamour, and all the perks are all temporary.

"And the world and its desire are passing away, but those who do the will of God live forever (v. 17)."

Lord Jesus, let us be fixed on you, loving you by obeying you. Thank you that we live in you now and will live with you forever. Alleluia!

Sunday, December 31, 2006 The Holy Family
Sirach 3, 2-6
Duties toward Parents

"Listen to your father, O children; act accordingly, that you may be kept in safety. For the Lord honors a father above his children, and he confirms a mother's right over her children. Those who honor their father atone for sins, and those who respect their mother are like those who lay up treasure. Those who honor their father will have joy in their own children, and when they pray they will be heard. Those who respect their father will have long life, and those who honor their mother obey the Lord .... (Sirach 3, 1-6)."

Honoring our parents is noticed by God and rewarded by God. This is very important to the Lord.

Even when parents have not properly loved or cared for their children, the Lord still honors those who find some way to honor their parents. God is ultimately the one who calls all life into existence.

Lord Jesus, thank you for helping us to honor our parents and to encourage others to honor their parents. Let there be healing for all as we offer our respect and our loving care to our parents. Alleluia!

Monday, January 1, 2007 Mary, Mother of God
Numbers 6, 22-27
The Priestly Blessing

Once, on a retreat, someone told me that one of the saints pictured God smiling upon her. This helps me to relax and to slow down. I don't have to be so frantic!

The Christian life is not supposed to consist of endless labor for God. We don't need to knock ourselves out trying to earn merit badges.

The Lord instructed Moses to tell Aaron and the priests to bless the people with very specific words. The priests prayed that the Lord's face would shine upon the people.

"The LORD bless thee, and keep thee:
The LORD make his face shine upon thee,
    and be gracious unto thee:
The LORD lift up his countenance upon thee, and give thee peace
(Numbers 6, 24-26 KJV)."

Lord Jesus, I need this particular blessing today and every day. Bless me. Keep me. Let your face shine upon me. Smile on me. Be gracious to me. Look upon me and give me peace. Thank you for smiling upon me. Alleluia!

Tuesday, January 2, 2007 St. Basil the Great,
St. Gregory Nazianzen
1 John 2, 22-28
Antichrists; Life from God's Anointing; Children of God

Stay close to Jesus and you will be fine. As Kathryn Kuhlman used to say, in her inimitable gentle drawl, "As long as God is still on the throne and as long as your faith in him is still intact, everything will come out all right."

Lord Jesus, we acknowledge that you are the Christ, the Messiah, the Anointed One. Thank you for calling us to remain in you and in the Father. Come, Holy Spirit, and fill us with fresh faith and trust to live unafraid this day and this year. Alleluia!

Wednesday, January 3, 2007 Holy Name of Jesus
1 John 2, 29 - 3, 6
Children of God; Avoiding Sin

"See what love the Father has given us, that we should be called children of God; and that is what we are. The reason the world does not know us is that it did not know him. Beloved, we are God's children now; what we will be has not yet been revealed. What we do know is this: when he is revealed, we will be like him, for we will see him as he is. And all who have this hope in him purify themselves, just as he is pure (1 John 3, 1-3)."

As God's children, we are called to live a holy life. We are called to live a pure life, a life of righteousness.

This is a blunt passage. The world will not recognize who we are. The world did not recognize who Jesus was.

If we are already God's children now, what shall we be later? Wonders await us!

Lord Jesus, let us remember that we are indeed God's children. Let us live and love and rejoice. Our hope is based on you. Alleluia!

Thursday, January 4, 2007 St. Elizabeth Ann Seton
1 John 3, 7-10
Avoiding Sin

If you act righteously, you are righteous. You belong to God and God is righteous.

If you choose to sin habitually, you belong to the devil. The devil has been sinning from the beginning.

Scary? Yes. However, the good news is that Jesus destroyed all the devil's schemes.

We belong to God. We are called to live in love and to act in righteousness. If are realistic about ourselves and openly confess our sins, God promises to forgive us and to cleanse us (1 John 1, 9).

Lord Jesus, thank you for the cleansing waters of Baptism. Thank you that you meet us in the cleansing sacrament of reconciliation. Thank you for reminding us that we belong to God. Alleluia!

Friday, January 5, 2007
St. John Neumann
1 John 3, 11-21
Avoiding Sin; Confidence before God

Love is the password. Love is the key. Love is the litmus test.

Are we living in death or in life? How do we tell?

Love.

If we are learning to act in love rather than to react in hate, we may rejoice! We are learning to be more and more like Jesus, our big Brother.

Lord Jesus, thank you for giving your life for us. You gave us the password of love. You gave us the key of love. Thank you for your patience with us as you continue to teach us to love. Alleluia!

Saturday, January 6, 2007 Blessed Andre Bessette
1 John 5, 5-13
Faith is Victory over the World; Prayer for Sinners

"For the love of God is this, that we obey his commandments. And his commandments are not burdensome, for whatever is born of God conquers the world. And this is the victory that conquers the world, our faith. Who is it that conquers the world but the one who believes that Jesus is the Son of God (1 John 5, 3-5)."

Do you feel like a victor? Feelings aside, if you believe that Jesus is God's Son, you are indeed a victor! You are conquering and overcoming the world because of Jesus.

God testified on his Son's behalf. The Holy Spirit testifies. The water of his baptism (Matthew 3, 16-17) and the blood of his cross also testify to Jesus.

Life! Life everlasting is in Jesus. If we have Jesus, we have life. We are victorious.

Lord Jesus, we pray to know deep within that we have this life. We place our trust in you. Alleluia!

Sunday, January 7, 2007 Epiphany of the Lord, Year C
Isaiah 60, 1-6
Glory of the New Zion

"Arise, shine; for your light has come, and the glory of the LORD has risen upon you …. the LORD will arise upon you, and his glory will appear over you. Then you shall see and be radiant; and your heart shall thrill and rejoice … (vv. 1,2b,5a)."

The light is on! We don't have to stumble around in the darkness any longer. God's glory is shining on us.

Lord Jesus, thank you for these promises of consolation and restoration. Let us rejoice, even before we see the complete fulfillment of these glorious promises. Alleluia!

Monday, January 8, 2007 Baptism of the Lord
Isaiah 42, 1-4,6-9
The Servant of the Lord

"I am the LORD, I have called you in righteousness, I have taken you by the hand and kept you; I have given you as a covenant to the people, a light to the nations, to open the eyes that are blind, to bring out the prisoners from the dungeon, from the prison those who sit in darkness (vv. 6-7)."

Lord Jesus, you walked right into the dungeon to slay our dragons. You came into our darkness and led us into your light.

When we are swaying back and forth as a fragile reed in the storm, you will not allow us to be broken. When the flame of our life is flickering, you will not allow us to be extinguished.

Thank you, Lord Jesus, for opening our eyes. Thank you for bringing about justice and restoration in your own way. Alleluia!

Tuesday, January 9, 2007
Hebrews 2, 5-12
Exaltation through Abasement

"It was fitting that God, for whom and through whom all things exist, in bringing many children to glory, should make the pioneer of their salvation perfect through sufferings. For the one who sanctifies and those who are sanctified all have one Father. For this reason Jesus is not ashamed to call them brothers and sisters, saying, 'I will proclaim your name to my brothers and sisters, in the midst of the congregation I will praise you (v. 10-12)."

If even Jesus was perfected through sufferings, we need not shrink in terror from our own sufferings. God is using our sufferings in ways that currently mystify us. We are being consecrated for God's purposes.

Lord Jesus, we join the angels in worshipping you. Thank you, dear big Brother, for yielding to suffering on our behalf. Thank you for going through death and for triumphing over death. We are not afraid because we know that you are with us. We sing to you and we praise you. Alleluia!

Wednesday, January 10, 2007
Hebrews 2, 14-16
Exaltation through Abasement

Jesus suffered. "For it is clear that he did not come to help angels, but the descendants of Abraham. Therefore he had to become like his brothers and sisters in every respect, so that he might be a merciful and faithful high priest in the service of God, to make a sacrifice of atonement for the sins of his people. Because he himself was tested by what he suffered, he is able to help those who are being tested (vv. 16-17)."

If you are being tested and if you are suffering, you are in good company. Jesus was tested. Jesus suffered.

Jesus is here to help us He understands testing, He understands suffering. He understands us. He is our High Priest.

Lord Jesus, you even went through death so that we don't have to fear death. Set us free today. Let us not fear death. Let us not fear life. Alleluia!

>Thursday, January 11, 2007
>Hebrews 3, 7-14
>Israel's Infidelity a Warning

God is grieved when we see his power, experience his love, and yet still choose not to trust him. It is a grief laced with exasperation.

Lord Jesus, let us hear your voice today. Let us confront our fears and then learn to disregard our fears. You are guarding us and guiding us. Let us joyfully follow you in trust and love. Alleluia!

>Friday, January 12, 2007
>Hebrews 4, 1-5,11
>The Sabbath Rest

We long to experience more deeply what it means to enter this sabbath rest. If we believe, we have already entered.

Perhaps it's simply a matter of relinquishing ideas of our own of how to please God. Perhaps it is a call to complete simplicity.

Lord Jesus, continue to teach us to rest in you. Thank you for your gentleness and your willingness to lead us into a heart knowledge of this rest. Alleluia!

>Saturday, January 13, 2007 St. Hilary
>Hebrews 4, 12-16
>The Sabbath Rest; Jesus, Compassionate High Priest

"Indeed, the word of God is living and active, sharper than any two-edged sword, piercing until it divides soul from spirit, joints from marrow; it is able to judge the thoughts and intentions of the heart (v. 12)."

Just as the surgeon makes an incision, opens us up, and peers carefully inside, so we are opened with the scalpel of God's word.

Everything within us is visible to God. Body, soul, and spirit. What a relief to know that we are known through and through!

"And before him no creature is hidden, but all are naked and laid bare to the eyes of the one to whom we must render an account (v. 13)."

We don't have to shrink in terror from the One who knows us. It is Jesus, our Brother, our priest.

"For we do not have a high priest who is unable to sympathize with our weaknesses, but we have one who in every respect has been tested as we are, yet without sin. Let us therefore approach the throne of grace with boldness, so that we may receive mercy and find grace to help in time of need (vv. 15,16)."

Lord Jesus, thank you that you understand everything about us and everything about this life. You know what we are going through this day and every day. You are our merciful Priest. We draw near to you, confident that you will help to enter into a new level of trust and rest. Alleluia!

Sunday, January 14, 2007 Baptism of the Lord
Isaiah 62, 1-5
Jerusalem the Lord's Bride

"For Zion's sake I will not keep silent, and for Jerusalem's sake I will not rest, until her vindication shines out like the dawn, and her salvation like a burning torch. The nations shall see your vindication, and all the kings your glory; and you shall be called by a new name that the mouth of the LORD will give. You shall be a crown of beauty in the hand of the LORD, and a royal diadem in the hand of your God. You shall no more be termed Forsaken, and your land shall no more be termed Desolate; but you shall be called My Delight Is in Her, and your land Married; for the LORD delights in you, and your land shall be married. For as a young man marries a young woman, so shall your builder marry you, and as the bridegroom rejoices over the bride, so shall your God rejoice over you (vv. 1-5)."

What kind of bridegroom would just stand by and allow his beloved to suffer injustice? Would he remain silent while his beloved was mistreated, afflicted, forsaken, or forgotten by others?

The Lord rises up on behalf of Jerusalem! The Lord promises vindication, honor, and victory for his bride.

Lord Jesus, you delight in us and rejoice in us. You loved us to death. You shed your blood to wash away our sins. You made us pure and holy in your sight. We are clothed in dazzling bridal white and crowned with sparkling jewels. We belong to you. Let us learn to see ourselves as you see us. Alleluia!

Monday, January 15, 2007
Hebrews 5, 1-10
Jesus, Compassionate High Priest

Within the framework of his vocation, Jesus grew. Jesus was truly human. Jesus was truly God.

"In the days of his flesh, Jesus offered up prayers and supplications, with loud cries and tears, to the one who was able to save him from death, and he was heard because of his reverent submission. Although he was a Son, he learned obedience through what he suffered; and having been made perfect, he became the source of eternal salvation for all who obey him, having been designated by God a high priest ... (vv. 7-10)."

Jesus is truly God's beloved Son. Jesus is truly our Priest.

While on this earth, Jesus prayed. Jesus wept. Jesus suffered. Jesus even learned to obey because of his sufferings.

Wasn't Jesus perfect? Why did he have to learn to obey?

Jesus went through the temptation to disobey God, because he knew that we would go through the temptation to disobey God.

He was, remember, completely human like us except that he did not sin (Hebrews 4, 15). He understands us completely. He understands why WE feel the way we feel and why we are so frustrated.

Lord Jesus, when we struggle with obedience, thank you that you are with us to strengthen us. Let us offer our willingness to obey God in every detail of our lives. Thank you for interceding for us. Thank you that the Holy Spirit is here to guide us. Alleluia!

> Tuesday, January 16, 2007
> Hebrews 6, 10-20
> Exhortation to Spiritual Renewal; God's Promise Immutable

This winter, especially, I have felt like hibernating! There is definitely a sense of being sluggish, a quality the writer to the Hebrews says to shun.

When we're tired and we've waited a long time, there is a tendency to become sluggish, weary, and even despondent. Is God ever going to show up?

In this reading, we are reminded to trust the promises of God. God is God!

What God promises will happen. God is worthy of our complete trust.

"We have this hope, a sure and steadfast anchor of the soul, a hope that enters the inner shrine behind the curtain, where Jesus, a forerunner on our behalf, has entered, having become a high priest forever … (vv. 19,20)."

Lord Jesus, thank you for being our compassionate Priest. Thank you for interceding for us. Strengthen us to think, to speak and to act in confidence, because our confidence is in you. Let us live today in the glorious sunlight of your love. Alleluia!

> Wednesday, January 17, 2007 St. Anthony
> Hebrews 7, 1-3,15-17
> Melchizedek, a Type of Christ

Abraham, returning from his mission to rescue his nephew Lot (Genesis 14, 14-20), was met by the mysterious Melchizedek. Melchizedek was king of peace and priest of God.

Jesus will come in glory as King. He will come as the royal Messiah who will bring peace. Jesus is already here as our High Priest before God.

Lord Jesus, thank you that you are our peace. You alone are the King you can bring peace to us and to our world. Thank you that you are our Priest. You are the only one who understands us perfectly. You know exactly how to intercede for us before the throne of God. Lift our spirits to confide in you as our Priest and to worship you as our King. Alleluia!

Thursday, January 18, 2007
Hebrews 7, 25 - 8, 6
Melchizedek, a Type of Christ; Heavenly Priesthood of Jesus

Jesus, our Priest, is always interceding for us. His priesthood is a permanent priesthood. "Consequently he is able for all time to save those who approach God through him, since he always lives to make intercession for them (v. 25)."

Lord Jesus, you offered yourself as a pure, innocent Lamb for our sins. As our brother and as our Priest, you know exactly how to pray for us and for those we love. You are exalted at the right of God. You live in us and we live in you. We praise you and trust you as we live this mystery. Alleluia!

Friday, January 19, 2007
Hebrews 8, 6-13
Heavenly Priesthood of Jesus; Old and New Covenants

New! All new.

A new covenant. A new priesthood.

The old covenant was written on stone. The new covenant is written on our hearts and is in our minds.

The Lord promised, "… I will put my laws in their minds, and write them on their hearts, and I will be their God, and they shall be my people (v. 10b)."

All will know God. ALL!

"And they shall not teach one another or say to each other, 'Know the Lord,' for they shall all know me, from the least of them to the greatest. For I will be merciful toward their iniquities, and I will remember their sins no more (vv. 11-12)."

Lord Jesus, thank you that the Holy Spirit is teaching us how to live in the "new" and in the "now." Alleluia!

Saturday, January 20, 2007 Sts. Fabian and Sebastian
Hebrews 9, 2-3,11-14
The Worship of the First Covenant; Sacrifice of Jesus

On our behalf! Jesus entered the sanctuary on our behalf. He was not there to offer to God the blood of animals.

Jesus, our high priest, offered his own blood for our cleansing. The sacrifice of Jesus, the Lamb of God, was perfect and complete.

Jesus, our high priest, offered himself to "... purify our conscience from dead works to worship the living God (v. 14b)!"

Lord Jesus, thank you for helping us to stop trying to do idiotic things which we think will please God. As the Lamb of God, you offered yourself as the one, perfect Sacrifice on our behalf. Because of your sacrifice, we are cleansed. In you, we are complete. We are free to live and to serve you. Alleluia!

Sunday, January 21, 2007 Third Sunday in Ordinary Time
Nehemiah 8, 2-4,5-6,8-10
Ezra Reads the Law

Ezra was priest and scribe. He stood and gave God's word to God's people.

This was a very long reading. Ezra read God's law "... facing the square before the Water Gate from early morning until midday, in the presence of the men and the women and those who could understand; and ears of all the people were attentive to the book of the law (v. 3)."

Liturgical posture police did not have to be present. The spirit of God moved on the people.

The people rose to their feet to hear God's laws proclaimed. They raised their hands.

In agreement, they exclaimed "Amen." They bowed before God. They lay prostrate before God. They wept.

This was meant to be a holy day and a happy day. The people were instructed not to weep or to mourn, but rather to feast!

"Go your way, eat the fat and drink sweet wine and send portions of them to those for whom nothing is prepared, for this day is holy to our LORD; and do not be grieved, for the joy of the LORD is your strength (vv. 10-11)."

Lord Jesus, we rejoice in you! You have given us yourself. We are free to live gladly and boldly, with joy and strength. Alleluia!

Monday, January 22, 2007 St. Vincent
Hebrews 9, 15,24-28
Sacrifice of Jesus

Jesus will return shining in glory! We will see him.

Jesus, as the Lamb of God, slain for us, entered into the holiest place of all. He entered into heaven, to appear before God on our behalf.

"For Christ did not enter a sanctuary made by human hands, a mere copy of the true one, but he entered into heaven itself, now to appear in the presence of God on our behalf. And just as it is appointed for mortals to die once, and after that the judgment, so Christ, having been offered once to bear the sins of many, will appear a second time, not to deal with sin, but to save those who are eagerly waiting for him (vv. 24, 27-28)."

Because of this transaction in heaven, we are forgiven and free. Jesus did it all.

Lord Jesus, thank you that you will come in glory for us. We are waiting for you with such longing. Help us to live now in the freedom and wholeness you died to give us. Alleluia!

Tuesday, January 23, 2007
Hebrews 10, 1-10
One Sacrifice instead of Many

Holy! We are made holy by the will of God. The will of God is our sanctification, our holiness (1Thessalonians 4, 3).

"And it is by God's will that we have been sanctified through the offering of the body of Jesus Christ once for all (v. 10)."

Jesus came to do the will of God. Jesus was the only Lamb who could accomplish this mission.

Lord Jesus, you came to do your Father's will. Thank you for your cleansing Blood. We pray for your will to be accomplished in our lives. Alleluia!

Wednesday, January 24, 2007 St. Francis of Sales
Hebrews 10, 11-18
One Sacrifice instead of Many

Instead of offering ineffective sacrifices over and over, Jesus offered one sacrifice. He offered HIMSELF! He offered himself completely for God's purposes.

Jesus was perfect Priest and perfect Lamb of sacrifice. He freely offered himself as sacrifice for us.

We who have benefited from this sacrifice of Jesus, the Christ, have been made perfect forever. Forever?

How can that be? Obviously, we do not always act perfectly.

It is crucial that we yield daily to the work of the Holy Spirit dwelling within us. Positionally, however, we are in Jesus and Jesus is perfect. We may ask for and receive forgiveness.

God has even forgotten our sins. God is God and God can do that.

Lord Jesus, enough already! How can we begin to grasp these realities which have both heavenly and earthly ramifications? In the midst of these wonders, we adore you and praise you and thank you. Alleluia!

Thursday, January 25, 2007 Conversion of St. Paul
Acts 9, 1-22
Saul's Conversion; Saul's Baptism; Saul Preaches in Damascus

Light! Saul was not changed until light from heaven surrounded him. He heard the voice of Jesus.

Jesus! Saul was given the realization that when he injured Christians, he was, in fact. persecuting Jesus himself.

Jesus instructed Saul to arise and to go into Damascus. It was in Damascus that Saul would be told what to do. For three days, he could not see. Neither did he eat or drink.

What do we do when we pray for conversion in others? Sometimes we try to shine a little flashlight of our own invention on the intended convert. Sometimes we spout Bible verses at them.

Do we play or do we pray? It may be that we are trying to play God, instead of praying that God will enter that person's life in the way that is best.

In Saul's case, the Lord instructed Ananias, a disciple in Damascus, to minister to Paul. It was the Lord himself who told Ananias that Saul was specifically chosen for a particular mission of evangelism that would involve great suffering.

Ananias treated Saul with gentleness and respect. He addressed Saul as "brother." Saul, no longer blinded, was baptized and began to regain his strength.

Saul, now filled with the Holy Spirit, began to proclaim Jesus as the Messiah, God's Son, in the synagogues of Damascus. The people were quite naturally astonished.

Lord Jesus, forgive us when we try to force belief in ways that are subtle or not so subtle. Let us learn to be like Ananias who, although frightened, obeyed your instructions to minister to Saul. Let us respect others as we pray for you to reach them. Alleluia!

Friday, January 26, 2007 Sts. Timothy and Titus
Titus 1, 1-5
Greeting; Titus in Crete

Paul referred to himself as God's slave and Jesus' apostle. Paul referred to Titus as his own child in the Christian faith. Paul relayed words of grace and words of peace to Titus.

Titus was on a mission on the island of Crete. He was charged with the serious responsibility of assigning presbyters for the church.

This is a pastoral letter that Paul was sending to Titus. The pastoral relationship between the two was healthy and open. This was crucial before Titus begins this work in Crete which will affect the church.

Lord Jesus, we pray that all church relationships are set in order. You know who is to serve where and in what capacity. You are our Shepherd and our Great High Priest. Let your voice be heard and obeyed. Alleluia!

Saturday, January 27, 2007 St. Angela Merici
Hebrews 11, 1-2, 8-19
Faith of the Ancients

"Now faith is the substance of things hoped for, the evidence of things not seen (v. 1 KJV)."

We may be in a foreign land dwelling temporarily in a tent, but, if God has called us to that place, we may rejoice! The best place to dwell is in the center of God's will.

Once on this journey to the heavenly Jerusalem, we have to practice looking forward. Although the way becomes puzzling and obstacles seem insurmountable, we are not alone. God will pull off the "impossible"!

We may be as sterile in our current level of faith as Sarah was in her body. Still, she somehow trusted that God could create life in her. God can breathe new life and new hope into us, also.

We may be as radical in our trust as was Abraham. Without full understanding, he still trusted God and ventured forth in faith.

"By faith Abraham obeyed when he was called to set out for a place that he was to receive as an inheritance; and he set out, not knowing where he was going (v. 8)."

Having finally received the promised Isaac, Abraham still trusted that God, by whose will Isaac had been conceived and was born, could bring Isaac back to life.

Lord Jesus, sometimes it seems that all the Isaac-laughter has faded from our lives. We seem stuck and sterile, hopeless and heart-weary. Breathe fresh new life into us. We trust in you. Let us arise, push back the flap of our tent and walk into a bright new day. Alleluia!

Sunday, January 28, 2007 Fourth Sunday in Ordinary Time
Jeremiah 1, 4-5, 17-19
Call of Jeremiah

Too old. Too young.

Abraham was too old and Jeremiah was too young. So they thought.

Not so!. When God calls, age goes.

Reservations and hesitations fly out the window. GOD calls.

There will be opposition. There will be struggle. God will prevail.

God said to Jeremiah, "And I for my part have made you today a fortified city, an iron pillar, and a bronze wall, against the whole land – against the kings of Judah, its priests, and the people of the land. They will fight against you; but they shall not prevail against you, for I am with you, says the LORD, to deliver you (vv. 18,19)."

Lord Jesus, thank you for making us strong and confident to live out our vocation before you. Deliver us from all fears and from all foes. Be glorified in us today. Alleluia!

Monday, January 29, 2007
Hebrews 11, 32-40
Faith of the Ancients

Do you want a little resurrection or a great big resurrection? Let's choose both.

The heroes of the Hebrew scriptures lived up to the faith they knew. They lived out the faith they knew. They were amazing in their righteous, radical trust in the living God.

Yet, because of the time in which they lived, they did not receive all that God had ready for them. In a sense, they were waiting for us.

Truly, the world in which they lived so bravely was unworthy of them. Sometimes I think that we, too, are unworthy of them. We thank God for them and ask to become worthy of their example.

Lord Jesus, thank you that we will experience resurrection! You are our crucified and risen Redeemer. Let the hopes that you planted within us come back to life. Let us live today in the sure knowledge of the great resurrection awaiting us as well as the heroes of old. Alleluia!

Tuesday, January 30, 2007
Hebrews 12, 1-4
God our Father

"Therefore, since we are surrounded by so great a cloud of witnesses, let us also lay aside every weight and the sin that clings so closely, and let us run with perseverance the race that is set before us, looking to Jesus the pioneer and perfecter of our faith, who for the sake of the joy that was before him endured the cross, disregarding its shame, and has taken his seat at the right hand of the throne of God (vv. 1,2)."

Not just up there, but all around! The holy ones who have gone before us are called witnesses. They encircle us like a cloud.

Just think! Abraham. Sarah. David. The prophets. The martyrs.

We are not alone. We are surrounded by these friends. As we run this earthly race, they are cheering for us and praying for us.

As the Scottish runner, Eric Liddell, threw back his head and ran joyfully across the finish line at the 1924 Olympics, so we run joyfully across the finish line of life into the waiting arms of Jesus.

Jesus knew how to run this race on earth. He knew what it was like to be spoken against, to be opposed on all sides, and to endure crucifixion.

Lord Jesus, thank you for those who surround us to cheer us on as we continue our earthly assignment. Thank you for giving us new strength and hope. Alleluia!

Wednesday, January 31, 2007 St. John Bosco
Hebrews 12, 4-7,11-15
God our Father; Penalties of Disobedience

God is not so much our coach as our Father. A coach imposes various disciplines to train for winning an earthly competition.

God, our compassionate, loving Father (Abba) sees much farther ahead. God is training us for eternity.

We would not be able to endure the shining brightness of eternity if we were still darkened by our sins. Day by day, we are being disciplined and trained for eternal glory.

"Endure trials for the sake of discipline. God is treating you as children; for what child is there whom a parent does not discipline (v. 7)." Unlike earthly parents who may not know how to discipline with love, our heavenly Father knows exactly how to discipline us with love.

Lord Jesus, sometimes we get so exhausted and discouraged. Thank you for strengthening us to walk, with joyful obedience, in the path assigned to us today. Alleluia!

> Thursday, February 1, 2007
> Hebrews 12, 18-19, 21-24
> Penalties of Disobedience

Don't be afraid! We're not approaching a wild, fearsome, unknown message from an unknowable deity.

"But you have come to Mount Zion and to the city of the living God, the heavenly Jerusalem, and to innumerable angels in festal gathering ... and to God the judge of all ... and to Jesus, the mediator of a new covenant ... (vv. 22-24)."

Home! We're going Home. Mount. Zion. Jerusalem, the heavenly city. Angels. Our loving God, who alone knows how to judge. Jesus, our Redeemer and mediator.

The old is over. The new is here.

Lord Jesus, let us practice what we believe. Let us live in the glad reality of the heavenly Jerusalem. Let us rest in the arms of our loving Father God, our own Abba. Thank you for taking us by the hand and leading us Home. Alleluia!

> Friday, February 2, 2007 The Presentation of the Lord
> Malachi 3, 1-4
> The Messenger of the Covenant

The Lord will come to the temple! A most comforting passage.

I was reminded of the hymn, "The King Will Come." Indeed.

Yes, the Lord will come suddenly. The Lord will come to purify and to refine the priests so that appropriate sacrifices may be offered.

Lord Jesus, help us not to be frightened, but to rejoice! Let us trustingly yield to your purifying process in our lives. Let us be ready to acclaim you when you come again in glory! Alleluia!

> Saturday, February 3, 2007 St. Blaise, St. Ansgar
> Hebrews 13, 15-17, 20-21
> Final Exhortation, Blessing, Greetings

God, who raised Jesus from the dead, has promised to provide all that is good for us. We respond in praise and trust. We are eager to share with others and to obey those in leadership.

Lord Jesus, thank you that you are our Good Shepherd. Thank you that you will accomplish your plans for us. Thank you for strengthening us to continue to praise you and to trust you as you lead us Home. Alleluia!

Sunday, February 4, 2007 Fifth Sunday in Ordinary Time
Isaiah 6, 1-2a,3-8
Call of Isaiah

This is a compressed call. Isaiah, in the temple, was called to prophetic ministry.

Isaiah saw the Lord! The LORD!

He saw the Lord exalted and on a throne. The seraphs around the throne called one to another, " 'Holy, holy, holy is the LORD of hosts; the whole earth is full of his glory (v. 3)."

Isaiah did not initially "see" himself as he really was. He was dazzled by and consumed with the revelation of the holiness of God.

It was then that he comprehended the depth of his own sinfulness and realized the impurity of his speech. He experienced desolation when he saw himself as he was.

He lamented, "Woe is me! I am lost, for I am a man of unclean lips, yet my eyes have seen the King, the LORD of hosts (v. 5)."

The Lord immediately sent a seraph to Isaiah to purify him. In an instant, Isaiah's iniquity was removed and his sin was removed.

Isaiah was now a clean vessel through whom the Lord could speak. The seraph reassured him, "… your guilt has departed and your sin is blotted out (v. 7)."

The process of cleansing and purification usually takes a lifetime. We have glimpse of the majestic, holy God. We have glimpses of ourselves.

If we are wise, we will not waste time lamenting our sinfulness. We will quickly throw ourselves on the mercy of God. We will acknowledge that we need for God to cleanse us. We will avail ourselves of the graces in the powerful healing sacrament of reconciliation. We will be clean and we will be free to follow God's call on our lives.

Lord Jesus, thank you that you do not give up on us. You gently call us to continue to follow you and to trust you for the results. Let us rejoice! You have trusted us to be your followers and you have sent us out into the world. Alleluia!

> Monday, February 5, 2007 St. Agatha
> Genesis 1, 1-19
> First Story of Creation

First the evening and then the morning. The day began with the evening. Light followed.

It is good to read again this passage from Genesis. In the midst of chaos, God spoke. God spoke and creation followed.

Lord Jesus, help us remember in the evening that morning will follow. Out of seeming chaos, your creation will follow. Alleluia!

> Tuesday, February 6, 2007 St. Paul Miki and Companions
> Genesis 1, 20 - 2, 4
> First Story of Creation

Life and health abound! Birds. Sea creatures. Land creatures.

And then God created human beings. God created us male and female. In the image of God we were created and instructed to multiply.

We were given authority over the living creatures. We were given plants for our food. God, pleased with creation, pronounced a special blessing on the seventh day, a holy day of rest.

Lord Jesus, thank you that we are made in God's own image. Let us honor and respect ourselves and others. Let us tend carefully the creation entrusted to our care. Alleluia!

> Wednesday, February 7, 2007
> Genesis 2, 4-9,15-17
> Second Story of Creation

God is in the gardening business! God knows how to plant us and where to place us.

Our garden is where God plants us and our place in the garden is where God places us. It is here that we are to live and to thrive and to serve.

Lord Jesus, sometimes we become restless and long to be planted in another garden or in another part of your vineyard. Thank you for the

Holy Spirit who continues to teach us to trust in you. Let us trust that we are currently planted and placed where we are meant to be for this season. Let us carefully adhere to the boundaries and the limitations of this place. Let us flourish within this garden and yield readily to you if you decide to plant us in another place. Alleluia!

> Thursday, February 8, 2007
> Genesis 2, 18-25
> Second Story of Creation

The man and the woman were meant to be partners in life. Their unity was God's idea.

From the rib of the man, God formed the woman. It was the Lord God who designed her and built her to be a woman.

Lord Jesus, please build me up and breathe new strength into me. Let me fulfill your assignment for my life. Alleluia!

> Friday, February 9, 2007
> Genesis 3, 1-8
> The Fall of Man

The woman saw, but her eyes were not really open. She saw the attractive aspects of the forbidden fruit, but not the hidden implications of consuming it.

After the woman and the man had eaten the fruit, their eyes were open. Their innocence was lost. They began to try to hide from the loving God who had called their lives into existence.

Lord Jesus, thank you that you came to restore what was lost through the decisions of our ancestors. Thank you for the cleansing power of your Blood on the Cross. Thank you for the cleansing waters of our baptism. Let us live today in the joy, purity, and strength you long for us to enjoy. Alleluia!

> Saturday, February 10, 2007 St. Scholastica
> Genesis 3, 9-24
> The Fall of Man

It would be heartbreaking to read this passage without the knowledge we have another tree, the Cross of Christ. The way is never blocked to this tree, this life-giving tree, the Cross.

Jesus came and undid the damage, damage of cosmic proportions, instigated by Adam and Eve. Their decisions affected the lives of all who followed them.

Our decisions are also crucial. Our decision about Jesus will affect, in one way or another, the lives of others.

Lord Jesus, thank you for entering this messy picture, painted by our lives of disobedience, disordered desires, and disastrous decisions. Thank you for living for us. Thank you for showing us how to live, in trusting obedience, to our loving God. Thank you for dying for us and rising again. Thank you for freeing us to choose life. Alleluia!

Sunday, February 11, 2007 Sixth Sunday in Ordinary Time
Jeremiah 17, 5-8
True Wisdom

"Thus says the LORD: Cursed are those who trust in mere mortals and make mere flesh their strength, whose hearts turn away from the LORD. They shall be like a shrub in the desert, and shall not see when relief comes. They shall live in the parched places of the wilderness, in an uninhabited salt land. Blessed are those who trust in the LORD, whose trust is the LORD. They shall be like a tree planted by the water, sending out its roots by the stream. It shall not fear when heat comes, and its leaves shall stay green; in the year of drought it is not anxious, and it does not cease to bear fruit."

It is the Lord in whom we trust and hope. The Lord is our reference.

If we have misplaced our hope in other human beings, we are not wise. We will fail them. They will fail us. They cannot be our reference.

Lord Jesus, let us be like the tree stretching forth its roots to the waters in the nearby stream. Let us draw our true life from you. Alleluia

Monday, February 12, 2007
Genesis 4, 1-15,25
Cain and Abel; Descendants of Cain and Seth

Resentment and disappointment! These monsters can take over and cause great harm to ourselves and to others.

In the case of Cain, these emotions, common to us all, were freely indulged. They led to the murder of his brother, Abel. Cain was a marked man, condemned to wander the earth without the joy of living in God's presence.

Lord Jesus, let us learn to acknowledge our wild emotions, bring them to you. and ask you to help us. When we have expressed our emotions in wrong ways, forgive us. Thank you for healing the hurts which activate our emotions. Forgiven and freed, let us joyfully continue our earthly pilgrimage. We are marked. We are marked with the sign of the Cross. We live now and forever in your presence. Alleluia!

> Tuesday, February 13, 2007
> Genesis 6, 5-8; 7, 1-5
> Warning of the Flood; Preparation for the Flood

Grief! Regret!

Grieved by the wickedness of the very people lovingly created in God's own image, God, even God, acknowledged grief.

Noah, however, did not fit the mold of the other people of his time. Noah was a just man and God looked with favor upon him. God lovingly made provision for the protection of Noah and his family as the time of flood approached.

Lord Jesus, we run into the ark of your Body, the Church, as the "flood" approaches. Thank you for all the gifts you have given us. Let us live in humility and gratitude before you. We pray for mercy for all. We look to you for our protection. Alleluia!

> Wednesday, February 14, 2007   Sts. Cyril and Methodius
> Genesis 8, 6-13
> The Great Flood

Into the ark. Flood! Out of the ark

Noah built the ark in obedience to God's warning and God's instructions. Noah took his family into the ark for safety. Noah, his family, and the animals were all protected throughout the time of the flood.

Noah and his family emerged from the ark only when God directed. The time had come to walk on dry ground and to begin a new life.

Noah constructed an altar to the Lord. The Lord God had faithfully spared his life and the life of his family.

Lord Jesus, thank you for the safety in the ark of your Church. The gates of hell cannot destroy your Church. We are safe with you. Thank you that, in time, we will emerge from the ark into a new life in the heavenly Jerusalem. We will see you clearly. Alleluia!

Thursday, February 15, 2007
Genesis 9, 1-13
Covenant with Noah

Noah's family emerged safely from the ark. Then they were commissioned to fill the earth.

We emerge from the ark of the Church. We are commissioned to preach the Gospel to every creature.

Lord Jesus, thank you that we are made in God's own image. We are held accountable to treat every other person with respect. Thank you for the beautiful, sparkling rainbow to remind us of the covenant between God and all the earth. Alleluia!

Friday, February 16, 2007
Genesis 11, 1-9
The Tower of Babel

Whose name is of primary importance to us? Are we, like the people who built the Tower of Babel, seeking to promote ourselves? Or is our passion to magnify the name of the Lord our God?

Lord Jesus, let us live to exalt you and to lift up your name. Clarify the confusion caused by selfish ambition. Simplify us in your service. Alleluia!

Saturday, February 17, 2007   Seven Servite Founders
Hebrews 11, 1-7
Faith of the Ancients

Noah did not understand, but still he proceeded, with reverence, to construct an ark in the desert. Did this make sense to others? No.

Noah was convinced that God had told him to do this seemingly outrageous thing. Although Noah was mocked and scorned, he persisted in obeying God. As a result, Noah, with his family, survived the flood.

We take others with us, whether we want to or not. Our relationship with God is not merely personal. We are always affecting others by the way we relate to God.

Lord Jesus, when we do not fully understand, we still follow you. We trust you to direct us, to redirect us when necessary, and to bring us safely Home. Alleluia!

Sunday, February 18, 2007
Seventh Sunday in Ordinary Time
1 Samuel 26, 2,7-9,12-13,22-23
Saul's Life Again Spared; Saul Admits His Guilt

David was radical in honoring the King. King Saul may have been crazy and mean, but he was still the King.

David knew better than to mess with the one who had anointed by God to serve as King. "The LORD forbid that I should raise my hand against the LORD's anointed … (1 Samuel 26, 11a)."

Lord Jesus, you know how to reward us when we trust you and do the right thing. As we cry out to you for mercy, so let us also be merciful to all. Alleluia!

Monday, February 19, 2007
Sirach 1, 1-10
Praise of Wisdom

Wisdom originates from the Lord. It is the Lord who generously bestows wisdom upon us.

The Lord's wisdom may surprise us! The ways and the methods the Lord uses in our lives may baffle us. The Lord's ways are so far above our ways (Isaiah 55, 8-9). The Holy Spirit will teach us how to express the wisdom of the Lord (1 Corinthians 12, 8).

Lord Jesus, we lift our weary, puzzled hearts and minds to you. Thank you for the Holy Spirit who gives us wisdom to live today. Alleluia!

Tuesday, February 20, 2007
Sirach 2, 1-11
Duties toward God

It is a duty, a joyful, demanding duty, to learn to trust God. It's not something that we "sorta" try to do.

It is something we LEARN to do. We learn to trust God in order to live, to love, and to serve.

God doesn't need wishy-washy whiners. God longs for us to be radical in our trust. We will not be disappointed as we step out in trust.

After all, God is GOD. God wins!

Lord Jesus, we reach out to you, knowing you will lead us victoriously through all the trials in our life of discipleship. Thank you for the rewards promised to us as we boldly place our trust in you. We smile and we rejoice as we face the future. Alleluia!

Wednesday, February 21, 2007 Ash Wednesday, Year C
Joel 2, 12-18
The Day of the Lord; Blessings for God's People

The Scottish poet, William Dunbar, said "... please thy Maker and be merry ...."

On this first day of Lent, this glorious time of approaching spring, we are allowed to be merry!

Yes, we mourn because we have grieved the Lord by our lack of trust, etc. etc. Yes, we weep and fast and pray and give. Still, we rejoice as we trust in God's mercy.

Lord Jesus, let us look to you and see your face in a new way this Lent. Let us trust you to guide us gently as we face ourselves and our sins. You are greater than our sins. You loved us and died for us. Our sins are gone. Extract us from the dreary round of endless self-analysis and self-reproach. Let us confess our sins and receive your forgiveness. Let us learn, this Lent, to love ourselves. We cannot love others in a healthy way unless we can love ourselves. Thank you for the amazing grace and glory in the sacrament of reconciliation. Thank you for the joy of receiving your Body and Blood in Holy Communion. Let us indeed be merry this Lent!

Thursday, February 22, 2007 Chair of St. Peter
1 Peter 5, 1-4
Advice to Presbyters

Peter writes as a concerned shepherd to other concerned shepherds. Peter writes as one deeply aware of his own failings and his own flaws. Only Jesus, the Good Shepherd, the Head of the Church, is without sin, without flaws, without failings.

Lord Jesus, let all earthly shepherds tend your flock with humility and gentleness. Thank you for your example of total surrender and relinquishment to your loving Abba.

Friday, February 23, 2007 St. Polycarp
Isaiah 58, 1-9
True Fasting

"Is this not the fast that I choose: to loose the bonds of injustice, to undo the thongs of the yoke, to let the oppressed go free, and to break every yoke? Is it not to share your bread with the hungry, and to bring the homeless poor into your house; when you see the naked, to cover them, and not to hide yourself from your own kin? Then your light shall break forth like the dawn, and your healing shall spring up quickly; your vindicator shall go before you, the glory of the LORD shall be your rear guard. Then you shall call, and the LORD will answer; you shall cry for help, and he will say, Here I am (vv. 6-9)."

Fasting is not to be a maudlin way of self-exaltation. Fasting is for others!

We're called to share our resources with others. We're called to break out of our comfort zone and to intervene to set others free.

Then the Lord steps in and sets US free! The Lord hears our cries and vindicates us.

Lord Jesus, thank you for healing us as we reach out to others. You are our nourishment. You are our reward. Let us experience true freedom this Lent.

Saturday, February 24, 2007 Lenten Weekday
Isaiah 8, 9-14
True Fasting

Regardless of what others around us are doing, we have a particular path to walk before God. If we follow the Lord's specific instructions, great joy awaits us.

What are we to do? Refrain from speaking and acting in ways displeasing to the Lord. Feed the hungry. Intervene on behalf of the suffering. Honor the sabbath.

What does the Lord promise? The Lord promises us light in the midst of darkness. The Lord promises to guide us. We will have plenty. Our strength will be renewed. We will be like a parched garden refreshed with cool water. We will even be like a bubbling spring! Since we have been instruments of restoration, the Lord will tenderly rebuild for us what seemed long lost.

Lord Jesus, we delight in you and thank you for all these glorious promises. Purify our hearts, our thoughts, and our words. Let us think and speak with gentleness and kindness. Direct our actions to be blessings for others. You will lift us to heights we never dreamed of seeing in this life.

Sunday, February 25, 2007 First Sunday in Lent, Year C
Deuteronomy 26, 4-10
Thanksgiving for the Harvest

"Sound the text." That is what I decided to do after first reading this passage silently. When I was in the seminary, our homiletics professor said to read aloud the text as one of the steps in preparing a homily.

Aloud! The words came alive as I read aloud these amazing words.

The first of the best! With joyful gratitude, the Israelites gave God their offering of thanksgiving.

They knew what it was like to have changes of fortune. From one, they had become many. They became strong. They became a nation.

Facing terrible treatment and oppression, they cried to the Lord for deliverance. God, the Almighty, heard them and led them out of Egypt, the land of their bitterness, into a sweet land of honey and milk.

"When the LORD restored the fortunes of Zion, we were like those who dream. Then our mouth was filled with laughter, and our tongue with shouts of joy … (Psalm 126, 1-2a)."

What could they give back to the Lord? Hearts filled with gratitude and hands filled with the very best of the harvest of their land.

Lord Jesus, how can we thank you for dying for us to take us out of the bitter land of living for ourselves into the sweet land of living for you? We offer ourselves to you this Lent. Thank you for continuing to purify and us and to heal us. Thank you for transforming us this Lent.

Monday, February 26, 2007 Lenten Weekday
Leviticus 19, 1-2,11-18
Various Rules of Conduct

HOLY! Our heart attitude and our conduct are to be holy. God is holy and commands us to be holy.

We need God's purity and holiness within us in order to exercise discernment. We are told not to be swayed either by the weakness or the strength of others, but to judge with God's own wisdom!

We are not to cherish hatred and resentment in our hearts. We may need to speak out on a particular matter and to confront another person, but we are not to sin.

Lord Jesus, thank you for transforming our hearts this Lent. Thank you for teaching us to exercise your gentleness, strength, and wisdom as we relate to others.

>Tuesday, February 27, 2007 Lenten Weekday
>Isaiah 55, 10-11
>An Invitation to Grace

"For as the rain and the snow come down from heaven, and do not return there until they have watered the earth, making it bring forth and sprout, giving seed to the sower and bread to the eater, so shall my word be that goes out from my mouth; it shall not return to me empty, but is shall accomplish that which I purpose, and succeed in the thing for which I sent it (Isaiah 55, 10-11)."

This is a deeply comforting and reassuring passage. Just as the snow and the rain are sent on a mission to the earth, so the word of God goes forth. The snow and the rain water the earth. The word of God accomplishes the purposes of God.

I think of this passage in conjunction with another passage in Isaiah. The exhausted prophet seems to have travailed to no avail and yet the prophet's reward is with God. "… I said, 'I have labored in vain, I have spent my strength for nothing and vanity; yet surely my cause is with the LORD, and my reward with my God (Isaiah 49, 4).'"

Lord Jesus, let me know and trust that my life has not been in vain. Even when I'm exhausted and discouraged, let me believe with all my heart that your purpose for my life is being fulfilled and will continue to be fulfilled.

>Wednesday, February 28, 2007 Lenten Weekday
>Jonah 3, 1-10
>Conversion of Ninevah

Go and tell! Leave the results with God.

Jonah answered God's second call to go to Ninevah and to speak God's message. Jonah had traveled only part of the way through the huge city, dutifully delivering the solemn message from God.

Surprise! The people who lived in Ninevah actually believed what God was telling them through the reluctant prophet, Jonah. They made a decision to get serious with God.

The king, too! He extended the penitence and the fasting even to the animals. The people and the animals were all to put on sackcloth and to call to God. Moo! Meow! Baa! The people repented and God relented.

Lord Jesus, thank you that we don't have to understand everything fully in order to step out and follow you. Let us, this day, boldly go where you lead us to go and do what you guide us to do.

Thursday, March 1, 2007 Lenten Weekday
Esther C 12, 14-16,23-25
Prayer of Esther

MERCY! Queen Esther threw herself and her people entirely on the mercy of God. She reminded God of his past faithfulness to her ancestors, the people of Israel.

For herself, she prayed for courage and for the appropriate words as she went to meet the king. She asked God to save her people and to help her. Truly, she felt alone in this crisis.

Lord Jesus, thank you that, in everyday matters, as well as in matters of life and death, we may cry out to you. Let us not live in a state of perpetual crisis, cranking up our adrenaline when it is not necessary. Help us to form the habit this Lent of quiet trust. We are not alone. You are with us.

Friday, March 2, 2007 Lenten Weekday
Ezekiel 18, 21-28
Personal Responsibility

When we turn to the Lord, w are received with love and mercy. This reminds us of the parable of the father, who runs to meet his erring son, and brushes aside any protestation of guilt on the son's part (Luke 15, 20-22).

Lord Jesus, this is a scary passage when we read about intentional sin and intentional turning away from virtue. Let us examine ourselves this Lent, honestly bringing to you those areas of our lives where we are full of stubbornness and self-will. Let us ask for your mercy, go to the sacrament of reconciliation, receive your forgiveness, and proceed on our journey to Easter.

Saturday, March 3, 2007 St. Katharine Drexel
Deuteronomy 26, 16-19
The Covenant

Today! Today! Today!

Listening to God and walking in God's way is for today. Everyday!

We are called to observe God's decrees wholeheartedly. God is in charge of our destiny. God desires our trusting cooperation.

Lord Jesus, thank you that you showed us how to listen to God and how to walk with God every step of the way. Let us live this day with a fresh commitment to listen to you and to obey you.

Sunday, March 4, 2007 Second Sunday in Lent
Genesis 15, 5-12
The Covenant with Abram

HONESTY! Abram (who will later be called Abraham) lamented to God that even God's gifts weren't that great if Abram continued to be childless (Genesis 15, 2). Abram did not hesitate to pour out his troubles to God.

God did not rebuke Abram for his honesty. Instead, Abram was told to gaze up at the sky and try to count all the stars. That's how many descendants would eventually come from this one old man, Abram.

Abram, still childless, believed! He believed and trusted the Lord even before the fulfillment of the promise/

Lord Jesus, we grow so weary in waiting. We grow weary of nay sayers. We just grow weary. Refresh us this Lent to believe again, to trust again, and to live boldly, knowing that all of God's promises to us will be gloriously fulfilled.

Monday, March 5, 2007 Lenten Weekday
Daniel 9, 4-10
Gabriel and the Seventy Weeks

Yearning to understand Scripture, Daniel turned to God in prayer. His prayers were joined to fasting and to other signs of penitence (Daniel 9, 2-3).

Do we pray and seek God over our reading of Scripture? If we don't understand what we're reading, do we ask the Holy Spirit for guidance?

Daniel realized, after spending time in Scripture study and prayer, that he was summoned to serious intercession on behalf of his ancestors who had sinned against God. He prayed, first acknowledging the greatness and the mercy of God.

Daniel prayed "we" prayers, not "they" prayers. He was part of the nation of Israel and so shared in his nation's sins against God.

Lord Jesus, thank you for our privilege and our responsibility to link ourselves with others as we pray. We cannot live in isolation. We ask for renewal and redirection for ourselves and for all for whom we pray. Let us learn to be attentive to your message to us through others.

Tuesday, March 6, 2007 Lenten Weekday
Isaiah 1, 10,16-20
Isaiah's Sinfulness

"Wash yourselves; make yourselves clean; remove the evil of your doings from before my eyes; cease to do evil, learn to do good; seek justice, rescue the oppressed, defend the orphan, plead for the widow (vv. 16,17)."

"Come now, and let us reason together, saith the LORD: though your sins be as scarlet, they shall be as white as snow; though they be red like crimson, they shall be as wool (v. 18 KJV)."

The Lord calls us to purity and to power. Purity of heart results in powerful service.

Lord Jesus, let us stop being so concerned about defending ourselves and caring so much about the opinions of others. You will defend us! Let us reach out to defend those who have no one to defend them. Thank you for purifying us this Lent.

Wednesday, March 7, 2007 Sts. Perpetua and Felicity
Jeremiah 18, 18-20
Another Prayer for Vengeance

The lot of the prophet is to suffer for fidelity to God. Either live for God and suffer for it or else live a life of constant compromise.

Jeremiah interceded for his adversaries. He cried out to God on their behalf.

What was their response? They plotted against him. They wanted to see him destroyed. They wanted to use his own words against him.

Lord Jesus, when we try to live for you we will suffer. You understand this perfectly. You were both human and divine. In your humanity, you suffered as we suffer. Strengthen us this Lent to live for you and trust you to take care of us. You are sovereign. You are in charge of our destiny.

Thursday, March 8, 2007 St. John of the Cross
Jeremiah 17, 5-10
True Wisdom

"Thus says the LORD: Cursed are they who trust in mere mortals (v. 5a)."

The Lord tells us through the suffering prophet, Jeremiah, that we are actually cursed if we are so stupid as to put our ultimate trust in other people. We're like a bush in the desert that will never bloom.

On the other hand, if we trust and hope in the Lord, we will blossom and bear fruit because we are planted by living waters.

"Blessed are those who trust in the LORD, whose trust is the LORD. They shall be like a tree planted by water, sending out its roots by the stream. It shall not fear when heat comes, and its leaves shall stay green; in the year of drought it is not anxious, and it does not cease to bear fruit (vv. 7-8)."

The Lord understands the human heart. "The heart is devious above all else; it is perverse – who can understand it? I the LORD test the mind and search the heart, to give to all according to their ways, according to the fruit of their doings (vv. 9,10)."

Lord Jesus, you alone understand my heart. Let me trust in you and yield to your testing this Lent. Let me bear fruit for you beside the still waters.

Friday, March 9, 2007 Lenten Weekday
Genesis 37, 3-4,12-13,17-28
Joseph Sold into Egypt

Dream? Can you still dream in the pit?

If you have been betrayed, can you still dream? If others are jealous of you, can you still trust God and believe in the dream God has placed within you?

Joseph dreamed. He dreamed the dream of God.

Although Joseph was in for a long period of suffering, God's dreams for Joseph would eventually come to pass in a most amazing way.

Lord Jesus, refresh the dreams that seem to have died within us. Remind us that whatever dreams you dream in us and for us will indeed come to pass.

Saturday, March 10, 2007 Lenten Weekday
Micah 7, 14-15,18-20
Condemnation and Prayer

Jesus, my Good Shepherd, is leading me into a secluded place this Lent. This Lent, I will dwell apart with my Shepherd.

My strong, loving God removes my guilt as well as forgives my sins and hurls them into the sea. They are gone. I am free.

Lord Jesus, in the midst of the outer noise, let me learn to dwell apart with you this Lent. Let to reach out to others as you direct. Let me recognize the signs of your tender love.

Sunday, March 11, 2007 Third Sunday in Lent
Exodus 3, 1-8,13-15
The Burning Bush; The Call of Moses

Baptism! The Israelites were baptized into Moses (1 Corinthians 10, 2).

Baptism! As Christians, we are baptized into Christ (Romans 6, 3; Galatians, 3, 27).

God told Moses at the burning bush not to come any closer. Moses was instructed to remove his sandals because he was on holy ground.

God now tells us to come very, very close. God became as close as possible to us.

God became a human being, one of us. Jesus.

God knew very well the trials, afflictions, and suffering of his people in Egypt. God came to rescue his people from that land of oppression and to lead them to a new land, a land of sweetness, of honey and milk.

God knows very well the trials we are suffering. Jesus is here to be with us and to deliver us.

Lord Jesus, thank you that we are already in the land of milk and honey because of what you have done for us. You are the Holy One, yet you call us to come close to you. We run to you this Lent and ask you to help us to understand more clearly what you died to give us. Thank you for holding us close to your heart and healing whatever is hurting us in our heart. You are close. You are here with us.

Monday, March 12, 2007 Lenten Weekday
2 Kings 5, 1-15
Cure of Naaman

Healing comes in God's ways and through God's messengers. If we long for healing enough, we won't be fussy about God's curious methods.

A little girl! The seemingly insignificant little servant girl was God's instrument to get Naaman, the army commander, to Elisha, the prophet of God.

Naaman, in spite of his position and his power, was a very sick man. Sick and stubborn!

Washing seven times in the Jordan River was not exactly Naaman's idea of how he should be healed. His servants politely reasoned with him.

So down to the river he went. Plunging into the river, in obedience to God's word through Elisha, Naaman was gloriously healed of his leprosy.

Lord Jesus, I too can be stubborn when I am sick. Please forgive me and help me. Thank you for healing me the way you know is best. I trust in you.

Tuesday, March 13, 2007 Lenten Weekday
Daniel 3, 25,34-43
The Fiery Furnace

Stand up! You may be in a fiery trial, but you can still pray.

You can still praise God. You can still remind God of his covenant, his mercy, and his promises. You can still entreat God to deliver you.

Lord Jesus, thank you that you are standing with us in our trials. You understand us and you still love us even when our trials are a result of our own sins. Have mercy on us and deliver us in a wonderful way. Let our lives bring glory to you.

Wednesday, March 14, 2007 Lenten Weekday
Deuteronomy 4, 1,5-9
Advantages of Fidelity

Our response to the commands of the Lord is an evidence of our intelligence. We are wise to observe what the Lord is telling us to do or not to do. We are to follow the Lord closely and to teach our children the ways of the Lord.

Lord Jesus, we can't just do our own thing and not have others affected. Thank you for your gentle patience with us even when we are in sin. Thank you for revealing our sin to us when we are able to bear the truth. Thank you for forgiving us and leading us on to the next step in your will for us. Help us to trust you and step out in loving obedience. You will bless us and all those around us. You are calling us to life, to a life of joy and fulfillment.

Thursday, March 15, 2007 Lenten Weekday
Jeremiah 7, 23-28
Abuses in Worship

Hard words were given by the Lord to the prophet Jeremiah to be spoken at the gate of the temple. The Lord was warning his people that they could not hide behind the externals of worship if they were defying the Lord in matters of conduct.

The people had turned away from the Lord and were ignoring the warnings of the prophets sent from the Lord. At one point, Jeremiah was instructed not even to intercede for these rebellious people anymore (Jeremiah 7, 16).

Lord Jesus, forgive us when, in ways subtle or not so subtle, we turn from you. You know us through and through. You know how we reason as we do and why we act as we do. Purify us this Lent and let us see ourselves as you wish us to see ourselves. Let us repent and cooperate with the action of the Holy Spirit within our hearts.

> Friday, March 16, 2007 Lenten Weekday
> Hosea 14, 2-10
> Sincere Conversion

"Take words with you and return to the LORD; say to him, Take away all our guilt; accept that which is good, and we will offer the fruit of our lips (vv. 2-3)."

Poor, exhausted, sinful Israel is being invited to return to the Lord for forgiveness and restoration. The Lord will be like gentle, soft dew to Israel. Israel will blossom and flourish!

"They shall again live beneath my shadow, and they shall flourish like a garden; they shall blossom like the vine, their fragrance shall be like the wine of Lebanon (v. 7)."

Lord Jesus, we become exhausted when we pursue our own ways. Let us return in silence to you this Lent. Forgive us and restore us. Let us blossom forth into a new, deeper, and more trusting relationship with you.

> Saturday, March 17, 2007 St. Patrick
> Hosea 6, 1-6
> Insincere Conversion

" ' Come, let us return to the LORD; for it is he who has torn, and he will heal us; he has struck down, and he will bind us up. Let us know, let us press on to know the LORD; his appearing is as sure as the dawn; he will come to us like the showers, like the spring rain that waters the earth (vv. 1,3).' "

We are revived and restored in order to live in the Lord's presence. The Lord will come to us. The Lord is already with us. The Lord will come like the fragrant rain of spring.

Lord Jesus, you desire love and not pretentious sacrifices. You long for us to long for you.

Sunday, March 18, 2007 Fourth Sunday in Lent
Joshua 5, 9,10-12
Rites at Gilgal

Manna! The manna was there when the Israelites needed it for nourishment in the wilderness.

When they were camping on the Jericho plains, they celebrated the feast of Passover. The next day, they ate of the grain which came from the land of Canaan.

Now, there was no more need for manna. The Lord was providing for them in a different way.

Lord Jesus, let us not become fixated on any one method or any one way in which you come to us. You are the Lord! Thank you for removing the reproach which was against us. You know how to come to us in the way we most need. We are always in need of you. Let us look to you and recognize you this Lent.

Monday, March 19, 2007 St. Joseph
2 Samuel 7, 4-5,12-14,16
David's Concern for the Ark; The Lord's Promises

David's sincere concern and desire was to build a place suitable for housing the ark of the covenant. However, it was to be David's heir, not David himself, who would build a dwelling place for the name of God.

God's concern is for us! God longs to come and to dwell within us. God wants to take up residence within us.

Lord Jesus, thank you that you are living within us. You know how we feel. You know us through and through. You understand how frustrating it is to live in this imperfect world. Remind us that you will show us how to live as we currently inhabit these earthly dwellings of flesh. You are leading us to our eternal dwelling.

Tuesday, March 20, 2007 Lenten Weekday
Ezekiel 47, 1-9,12
The New Stream

Can my life be fruitful where I am currently living? Sometimes I get tired of those "bloom where you're planted" people.

In a vision, the priest and prophet Ezekiel saw the temple and the water flowing from the temple. Wherever the water flowed from the temple, life resulted. This was a beautiful vision infused with hope for restoration for God's people.

Frankly, it seems hard to be fruitful where I am. There has been constant construction noise in this neighborhood for years. Tear down. Rebuild. Rebuild some more. Do another change, Update. Change this. Rebuild that. Concrete mixers. Dump trucks. Jackhammers. Taco trucks. Portable toilets. I long for peace and quiet.

Lord Jesus, thank you that the Holy Spirit is within me, flowing with life. Help me to be fruitful in the midst of this noise. You are the source of my life. Thank you for your patience and your loving understanding.

Wednesday, March 21, 2007 Lenten Weekday
Isaiah 49, 8-15
The Liberation and Restoration of Israel

Right now! It's right now that the Lord is acting in our lives whether we realize it or not.

It's right now that the Lord is answering us. It's right how that the Lord is helping us to endure and to wait.

It's right now that the Lord is guiding us by springs of fresh water. It's right now that the Lord is making a way for us through all the obstacles.

'Sing for joy, O heavens, and exult, O earth; break forth, O mountains, into singing! For the LORD has comforted his people, and will have compassion on his suffering ones (v. 13)."

Lord Jesus, thank you that you have not forgotten us, although we may feel weary and discouraged. We may even think that nothing is happening. You have not abandoned us. You are acting at this very moment on our behalf. Help us to trust you and to be patient until the full manifestation of your intervention. You delight in calling us to come out of our darkness to venture forth into your glorious light and life.

Thursday, March 22, 2007 Lenten Weekday
Exodus 32, 7-14
The Golden Calf

After the people and Aaron, the priest, who should have known better, worshipped a golden calf of their own design, the Lord blew up! The Lord was about to wipe them out because of this horrendous sin. Then Moses interceded for the people.

Moses reminded the Lord that these were not Moses' people, but that they were the Lord's own people. These were the very people who had been led out of Egyptian slavery by the Lord's amazing power. Moses then referred to Abraham, Isaac, and Jacob (Israel) and to the promises made to them for the future.

Lord Jesus, thank you that you are the Great High Priest who never leads us astray. You lead us in straight, though sometimes difficult, paths, to our true Home. Forgive us when we make any kind of idol. Forgive us when we have divided loyalties and choose our own way. Thank you for all who intercede for us.

Friday, March 23, 2007 St. Torino
Wisdom 2, 1,12-22
The Wicked Reject Immorality and Justice Alike

Is our thinking right? What are we thinking? Does it matter?

The wicked perceive that the just are thought censors. The just are different.

It's hard for the wicked even to see the just. Their mere existence is a silent reproach to the evil intent of the wicked.

The wicked may plot and may even seem to succeed in silencing the just. However, ultimate power and ultimate justice is in God's hands. God has ways of rewarding innocence, purity, and holiness.

Lord Jesus, we ask you to purify our thoughts as well as our words and our deeds. Let us place all our trust in you. You are just and you are merciful.

Saturday, March 24, 2007 Lenten Weekday
Jeremiah 11, 18-20
The Plot Against Jeremiah

The prophet, Jeremiah, like an innocent lamb, did not immediately realize that his enemies were busy plotting to destroy him. The suffering prophet placed his trust in God. What else could he do?

"But I was like a gentle lamb led to the slaughter. And I did not know that it was against me that they devised schemes .... But you, O LORD of hosts, who judge righteously, who try the heart and the mind, let me see your retribution upon them, for to you I have committed my cause (vv. 19a,20)."

Lord Jesus, so often it seems that evil triumphs and that the just are destroyed and left in the dust. Let us see, this Lent. that you have a larger perspective. You alone are the Lord. It seemed that you were defeated on the Cross. You died and yet you rose triumphant over death. We place our trust in you. You will raise us to new life.

Sunday, March 25, 2007 Fifth Sunday in Lent
Isaiah 43, 16-21
Promises of Redemption and Restoration

God, the all-wise, all powerful, and all-loving God, instructs us not to dwell on the past. God has something new in mind! Who are we to argue with God?

Even though our lives may currently resemble a parched desert, God has a promise for us. God is promising us water and a way through this wilderness.

"Behold, I will do a new thing; now it shall spring forth; shall ye not know it? I will even make a way in the wilderness, and rivers in the desert (v. 19 KJV).

Lord Jesus, forgive me when I really don't believe these promises. Forgive me for brooding over the past. Thank you for pouring fresh energy into me today to see you at work in my life in a new way.

Monday, March 26, 2007 The Annunciation of Our Lord
Isaiah 7, 10-14; 8, 10
Birth of Immanuel

"Therefore the Lord himself shall give you a sign; "Behold, a virgin shall conceive, and bear a son, and shall call his name Immanuel (Isaiah 7, 14 KJV)."

JESUS is the greatest sign! Immanuel. God is right here with us.

What could be greater? Who could be greater?

Lord Jesus, let your life within us be a sign. Let us live as signs of God's wondrous grace.

Tuesday, March 27, 2007 Lenten Weekday
Numbers 21, 4-9
The Bronze Serpent

To me, complaining is a serious sin. I'm always surprised when others don't think that complaining is such a big deal.

It is a big deal. Look at the Israelites wandering around in the wilderness after God had miraculously delivered them out of their terrible suffering in Egypt.

God even provided honey-flavored manna for their nourishment. At first, the people were in awe and wonder over God's provision (Exodus 16).

Later, however, they began to complain about the manna. God was not pleased and sent snakes to bite them. Some of the people even died.

Voilà! They were enlightened. Complaining about God's groceries was definitely not a good thing,

They whined to Moses about this matter. Poor old Moses interceded for God's children. They were behaving like brats, but they were still God's kids.

The Lord told Moses to fashion a serpent made of bronze and to mount this odd creation upon a pole. Anyone who had been bitten by a serpent was to look up at the bronze serpent and live!

Lord Jesus, I've complained about so many things. Forgive me. Today, I look up to you. You were mounted upon the Cross. I look to you and live. I look to you and say thank you. I look to you as my Savior and Friend. Thank you for your provision for my life. Thank you for leading me Home.

Wednesday, March 28, 2007 Lenten Weekday
Daniel 3, 14-20,91-92,95
The Fiery Furnace

The Church needs people like Daniel and his friends who will not worship the modern equivalents of the golden calf. These three men could not be moved by the rage or the threats of the misguided king.

For refusing to obey the unrighteous demand of the king, the three who were thrown into the furnace of fire were actually serving the king. By witnessing the power of Almighty God on behalf of the three brave men, King Nebuchadnezzar came to belief in this amazing God.

A new math. Three were thrown into the furnace, but four were clearly seen by the king!

Lord Jesus, you are with us in whatever furnace we find ourselves today. Thank you for helping us to stand firm in our trust in you. Let us refuse compromise with convenience or capitulation to forces contrary to your holiness. We are placed here to fulfill your purposes. Thank you for your presence and your power. Let our trust in you us shine forth.

Thursday, March 29, 2007 Lenten Weekday
Jeremiah 20, 10-13
Jeremiah's Interior Crisis

Do you ever wish that you had never been born? Jeremiah did.

The mighty prophet Jeremiah even cursed the day he was born (Jeremiah 20, 14). He had had it!

Why? His suffering had become intolerable.

Jeremiah, however, in the midst of intense personal suffering, was still aware of the Lord's presence. Even though he was aware that his fidelity to God's call had caused him great personal suffering (Jeremiah 20, 7-9), he still clung to God. Jeremiah's cause was safely committed to God.

Lord Jesus, thank you that we can be completely honest with you and pour out our hearts before you. Thank you that we may also sing to you and praise you in the midst of our anguish. We trust you, our crucified and risen Redeemer. Thank you that you will bring about our resurrection and our restoration.

Friday, March 30, 2007 Lenten Weekday
Genesis 17, 3-9
Covenant of Circumcision

Age! What is it to God?

Abram was a mere lad of seventy-five when the Lord told him to leave his homeland and take off for a new land (Genesis 12, 1-4).

After years and years of waiting and waiting for the fulfillment of the Lord's promises, Abram, at the age of ninety-nine, had another significant encounter with the Lord. The Lord again reassured Abram that he would be the father of many nations.

In this encounter, the Lord changed the awestruck Abram's name to Abraham. Abraham and his future descendants were charged with keeping the covenant with the Lord.

"Hoping against hope, he [Abraham] believed that he would become 'the father of many nations' …. No distrust made him waver concerning the promise of God, but he grew strong in his faith as he gave glory to God, being fully convinced that God was able to do what he had promised (Romans 4, 18a,20,21)."

Lord Jesus, help us to remember Abraham when we grow weary of waiting. Your ways and your timing are beyond our comprehension. Let us praise you and trust you. You are our heart's deepest desire. You renew us in your love and we delight in you.

Saturday, March 31, 2007 Lenten Weekday
Ezekiel 37, 21-28
The Two Sticks

This unity of the people of Israel, represented by the joining of the two sticks into one, is symbolic of the unity for which we yearn, pray, and work. This is what Jesus prayed for before he died, that his followers would be one (John 17, 11).

Only God can take what was broken and divided and bring wholeness. God can cleanse, renew, and restore.

Lord Jesus, you are our Shepherd and Messiah. You are the Lamb of God who died for us all. Let us continue to seek for unity amongst your followers. Let us prepare to greet you when you come in glory as our triumphant King!

Sunday, April 1, 2007 Palm Sunday of the Lord's Passion
Isaiah 50, 4-7
Salvation Only through the Lord's Servant

The Lord's Servant had been carefully trained to speak words of encouragement. The Lord's Servant was prepared to suffer in order to fulfill the plan of salvation. Jesus, God's beloved Son, was the Servant who suffered and died for us.

Lord Jesus, you set your face unflinchingly to meet your agony and death. You knew that your ultimate fate was in the hands of God. We look to you this last week of Lent and ask for your help. Let us learn to think and to speak words to lift those who are cast down by this hard life. Let us bravely continue to trust in you. You are our innocent Lamb and our wise Shepherd, leading us Home. We long for our lives to glorify you.

Monday, April 2, 2007 Monday of Holy Week
Isaiah 42, 1-7
The Servant of the Lord

"Here is my servant, whom I uphold, my chosen, in whom my soul delights; I have put my spirit upon him; he will bring forth justice to the nations. He will not cry or lift up his voice, or make it heard in the street; a bruised reed he will not break, and a dimly burning wick he will not quench; he will faithfully bring forth justice (Isaiah 42, 1-3)."

Silence. The Lord's chosen servant does not need to shout.

The Lord's servant is gentle. The Lord will not allow those who are suffering and vulnerable to be stifled or overcome. Justice will be established.

This week, as the remodeling construction noise rages on both sides of our house, I need to learn to be silent. City Hall cannot, or will not, solve these problems of seemingly endless construction in these formerly peaceful, quiet neighborhoods. I entrust this unbearable situation, which has gone on for years, to the Lord. Perhaps we will have to move away.

Lord Jesus, you are gentle in your strength and often silent as you work on our behalf. During this Holy Week, let us breathe and live for you. Let your light shine in us to free others.

Tuesday, April 3, 2007 Tuesday of Holy Week
Isaiah 49, 1-6
The Servant of the Lord

While we are hidden and concealed, the Lord has not forgotten us. We are being prepared and polished for the Lord's service. "... in the shadow of his hand he hid me; he made me a polished arrow, in his quiver he hid me away .... (Isaiah 49, 2bc)."

This service may or may not be noticed by others. What matters is that it is noticed by the Lord.

We may grow weary and discouraged. We may think that our work has been in vain.

"But I said, 'I have labored in vain, I have spent my strength for nothing ... yet surely my cause is with the LORD, and my reward with my God (Isaiah 49, 3b-4).'" The Lord, who is continually giving us new strength, will reward us.

Lord Jesus, your plan for us is greater than we realize. When we are discouraged with ourselves, help us to remember that you are smiling upon us with complete understanding and unconditional love. Let us learn to rest in you. Refresh us and gently lead us into the next assignment you have waiting for us.

Wednesday, April 4, 2007 Wednesday of Holy Week
Isaiah 50, 4-9
Salvation Only through the Lord's Servant

The Lord's servant focus is on the Lord, not on personal suffering. The Lord's servant is treated shamefully, but knows that the Lord is in charge and will bring vindication.

The Lord's servant does not speak in self-defense, but rather to encourage others. Each new day brings an opportunity to listen to the Lord.

Lord Jesus, forgive us when we mistreat you. We say that we believe in you, but we don't act as if we really trust you. We open our mouths eagerly to defend ourselves, rather than trusting you to defend us. Forgive us for all the ways we have wounded you. Let us keep silence before you this Holy Week and listen.

> Thursday, April 5, 2007 Holy Thursday
> Exodus 12, 1-8,11-14
> The Passover Ritual Prescribed

Forget January! Abib is the month that the Lord said was to be of first importance in the Jewish calendar.

Abib! This was the time in the spring when Passover was to be celebrated.

Jesus is our Passover Lamb. In baptism, we are signed with the sign of the cross of Christ. We are marked as Christ's own forever.

The Jewish people fleeing Egypt were to consume the Passover meal standing, sandal-clad, staffs in hand, and ready to go!

When we receive Jesus, our Lamb, in Holy Communion, we also are to be ready to go! Where will the Lord send us today?

Lord Jesus, you are our Great High Priest and our Prophet who constantly speak God's word to us. You are the Word of God! You will come again as our risen and glorious King. When will you come? Abib? Another time? Let us live for you, wait for you, and keep the feast with rejoicing.

> Friday, April 6, 2007 Good Friday
> Isaiah 52, 13 - 53, 12
> Suffering and Triumph of the Servant of the Lord

Jesus knew what it meant to be avoided, misunderstood, rejected, and defiled. He knew. He knows.

He was" … despised and rejected … a man of sorrows, and acquainted with grief: and we hid as it were our faces from him; he was despised, and we esteemed him not. Surely he hath borne our griefs, and carried our sorrows …. All we like sheep have gone astray … and the LORD hath laid on him the iniquity of us all (Isaiah 53, 3,4a,6 KJV)."

Jesus knew what it meant to suffer for the sins of others. He knew. He knows.

Jesus knew what it meant to be considered defeated and to be pronounced dead. He knew. He knows.

Jesus knew what it meant to give his life for others. He knew. He knows.

Lord Jesus, you offered yourself for others. You offered yourself for us. You know how to lead us from suffering to triumph. You traveled the path of suffering, but you did not stay there forever. Many will be amazed when you come in glory. Let us trust you to lead us from our temporary suffering into joy that will endure forever.

Saturday, April 7, 2007 Easter Vigil
Genesis 1,1 - 2, 2
First Story of Creation

From out of chaos and darkness, God called forth light! God called forth the sea, the stars, the plants, and all the creatures. God called us forth. God called you forth! God called me forth! God called all of creation good.

Lord Jesus, you are the living Word through whom God spoke. Speak to us today as our Risen Lord. We are here on a mission which we do not fully understand. Let us know that we have been called forth and that we are loved. Alleluia!

Sunday, April 8, 2007 The Resurrection of the Lord, Year C
Acts 10, 34,37-43
Peter's Speech

God "... anointed Jesus of Nazareth with the Holy Spirit and with power; ... he went about doing good and healing all who were oppressed by the devil, for God was with him. We are witnesses to all that he did both in Judea and Jerusalem. They put him to death by hanging him on a tree; but God raised him on the third day and allowed him to appear, not to all the people but to us who were chosen by God as witnesses, and who ate and drank with him after he rose from the dead. He commanded us to preach to the people and to testify that he is the one ordained by God as judge of the living and the dead (vv. 38-42)."

Anointed with the Holy Spirit and with the power of Almighty God, Jesus moved about his home turf of Judea. He did so many good things. He healed every single one who was experiencing oppression.

How was he treated? He was killed.

What did God do? God raised Jesus from the dead.

What did Jesus do then? Jesus told his followers to go and tell others about him.

"All the prophets testify about him that everyone who believes in him receives forgiveness of sins through his name (Acts 10, 43)."

Lord Jesus, God has appointed you to be judge of all who have ever lived. You promise that when we trust you, our sins are forgiven. Help us truly to believe this and to live in Easter joy and light. Thank you for living for us, dying for us, and living with us and in us forever. Let us live joyfully, knowing that we are living for you and for your glory. Alleluia!

Monday, April 9, 2007 Easter Monday
Acts 2, 4,22-33
Peter's Speech at Pentecost

Peter! Peter's mouth had, at last, been redeemed and released.

Peter, always ready to pop off with the most extraordinary statements, was at last flowing in the vocation which Jesus had foreseen for him that morning after breakfast by the Sea of Tiberius (John 21).

Peter, following the resurrected and ascended Jesus, was feeding the lambs. Peter was proclaiming Jesus.

Free! Peter, his soul now healed by the forgiveness of Jesus, was free at last to live out his vocation.

With wisdom and eloquence infused by the Holy Spirit, Peter quoted the prophet Joel and the psalmist and prophet, King David. Peter was learning how to feed the lambs of Jesus the food they needed.

Lord Jesus, thank you that you have freed us to live for you. Let us speak of you today in ways that will feed your lambs. Alleluia!

Tuesday, April 10, 2007 Easter Tuesday
Acts 2, 36-41
Peter's Speech at Pentecost

When we are convicted by the Holy Spirit of our sins, what do we do? The people in Jerusalem who heard Peter speak were pierced within their hearts. They knew that their sins were the reason for the crucifixion of Jesus.

Peter told them to repent and to be baptized. Then the glorious gift of the Holy Spirit would be theirs.

Lord Jesus, thank you that we may always come to you with our sins. You are eager to forgive us and to cleanse us. Thank you for the sacrament of reconciliation and for the joyful assurance of your forgiveness. Filled with the Holy Spirit, let us enjoy this beautiful day in Easter. Alleluia!

Wednesday, April 11, 2007 Easter Wednesday
Acts 3, 1-10
Cure of the Crippled Beggar

From the gate of the temple in Jerusalem into the very temple itself. The crippled man had been unable to get beyond the door, or the gate.

It may have been called the Beautiful Gate, but it was still only the gate. He was stuck, it seemed, and completely dependent upon others.

Three o'clock in the afternoon! Something was about to change.

John and Peter arrived at the temple for the time of prayer. They did not give alms to the man. Instead of a few coins, which he did not even have, Peter offered, instead, a whole new life.

When Peter took the man's right hand and began to lift him up, the power of God entered into the man. His feet and his ankle bones became strong!

Walking on his own, indeed leaping, and praising God, he entered the temple with Peter and John! A new life was about to begin. All the people were astonished.

Lord Jesus, help us not to ignore people on the edges, by the gates of life. Let us ask you what we are to do for them. If we ourselves are the ones by the gate and unable to enter, thank you for sending someone to help us arise. Let us enter the temple, walking and leaping, to praise you. Alleluia!

Thursday, April 12, 2007 Easter Thursday
Acts 3, 11-26
Peter's Speech

Peter spoke to the people soon after the healing of the crippled beggar at the Beautiful Gate of the Temple. Peter used this amazing healing as an opportunity to glorify the crucified and risen Jesus! It was because of trust in Jesus that the crippled man was now enjoying strength and health.

Peter referred to the patriarchs and to the prophets as he spoke with the people. The prophets had told over and over of the coming of the Messiah who would suffer and die.

Peter called his hearers his brothers and assured them that they and their leaders had acted in ignorance by crucifying Jesus. They were now invited to repentance and renewal.

Peter reminded his hearers that they, the Jewish people, were children of the covenant, God's covenant with Abraham. For the Jews first and foremost, collectively and individually, Jesus was sent.

Lord Jesus, let us be alert for opportunities today in which to speak of you and to glorify you. Fill us with respect and love for those to whom we speak. Alleluia!

Friday, April 13, 2007
Acts 4, 1-12
Peter's Speech; Before the Sanhedrin

Here come the big guys in the religious establishment. While Peter and John were still engaged in telling the people about Jesus, the church leaders stepped in for a showdown. They had opposed Jesus, so, of course, they would oppose the followers of Jesus.

Here they were, the high priest and other leaders and elders. Peter and John, who had been held captive, were now summoned before this group of leaders, the Sanhedrin.

Again, Peter glorified the crucified and risen Lord Jesus Christ. Again, he confronted the leaders with their role in crucifying Jesus. Peter referred to Jesus as the stone rejected, now the cornerstone (Isaiah 28, 16). Salvation comes only through Jesus.

"This Jesus is 'the stone rejected by you, the builders; it has become the cornerstone.' There is salvation in no one else, for there is no other name under heaven ... by which we must be saved (vv. 11-12)."

Lord Jesus, wherever we speak of you, let us speak words that will glorify you and lead our listeners to trust in you. Alleluia!

Saturday, April 14, 2007 Easter Saturday
Acts 4, 13-21
Before the Sanhedrin

Holy boldness! Peter and John amazed the learned leaders who presumed to sit in judgment on them, the apostles of Christ.

Peter and John were plain, simple fishermen, right? Yes, but they had been with Jesus.

The result of their prayers was standing right there for all to see. The man who had been crippled from birth was now strong and well! He was a living example of the power of the name of Jesus.

Now, what on earth could these poor frightened, threatened, insecure leaders do? Bluffing, like the cowards they were, they forbade the apostles to speak in the name of Jesus.

No way! For Peter and John, it was impossible not to speak of what they had seen for themselves and heard for themselves.

" 'Whether it is right in God's sight to listen to you rather than to God, you must judge; for we cannot keep from speaking about what we have seen and heard (vv. 19-20).' "

Lord Jesus, thank you for inviting us be your companions and to learn to spend quiet time with you. Thank you that we will come to know you for ourselves. Thank you that we will become increasingly confident as we live and speak for you. Alleluia!

> Sunday, April 15, 2007 Second Sunday in Easter
> Divine Mercy Sunday
> Acts 5, 12-16
> Signs and Wonders of the Apostles

The people around Jerusalem brought their sick in mind and body to the apostles. ALL, not merely some, but ALL were cured.

Jesus told us very clearly that the works that he did we were to do also. Do we really believe this?

"Very truly, I tell you, the one who believes in me will also do the works that I do and, in fact, will do greater works than these, because I am going to the Father (John 14, 12)."

Lord Jesus, thank you for the Holy Spirit who teaches to live and speak and pray in powerful ways. Thank you that you will work through us today. Alleluia!

> Monday, April 16, 2007
> Acts 4, 23-31
> Prayer of the Community

Boldness! With a radical trust in the power of the name of Jesus, the disciples rode out this particular storm of opposition and continued to speak God's word with boldness.

Sometimes boldness is confused with arrogance. Boldness is based on confidence in God. Arrogance is based on a misguided confidence in oneself.

The whole community prayed with boldness. They were all filled with the Holy Spirit. All spoke boldly.

Lord Jesus, let us individually and as a faith community trust boldly in you. Let us live and speak with increasing confidence in you. Alleluia!

> Tuesday, April 17, 2007
> Acts 4, 32-37
> Prayer of the Community

Unity! The unity of the Christian community led to their powerful witness to the resurrected Jesus. They were one in heart and mind.

Sometimes it's easy to share property and possessions, yet next to impossible to share recognition. We sometimes so crave approval and recognition for ourselves that we behave in ways that are unbecoming to followers of the Lord Jesus.

Relax! There's plenty to go around.

We don't have to brag or to namedrop. We are secure in our risen Lord. The Lord sees our hearts and our motives. The Lord knows how and when to reward us.

Lord Jesus, let us learn to be like Barnabas and to be generous in our giving to others. Let us joyfully give consolation and encouragement as well as material offerings. Alleluia!

> Wednesday, April 18, 2007
> Acts 5, 17-26
> Trial before the Sanhedrin

Vindication! Thrown into a public jail by the jealous high priest and Sadducees, the apostles were soon to be publicly vindicated.

An angel of the Lord came at night to open the prison doors, release them, and instruct them to go to the temple. In that particular place, the temple, they were to tell the people about the Christian life.

Lord Jesus, thank you for releasing us in your time to go to the place you assign and to tell others about you! Let us live in the joy and freedom you died and rose again to give us. Alleluia!

> Thursday, April 19, 2007
> Acts 5, 27-33
> The Trial before the Sanhedrin

The apostles had witnessed the resurrected Jesus for themselves. The hostile religious leaders had not.

Even if they had, they probably would have explained it away somehow. Their minds were darkened and their hearts were hardened against Jesus.

The apostles knew that they had to witness to the resurrection of Jesus. They had to proclaim once again that God had sent Jesus as Savior. The opportunity to repent and to receive forgiveness was still there.

Lord Jesus, let us be witnesses to you, but realize that we cannot force belief. We pray that the Holy Spirit will strengthen us to continue to trust you and to bear witness to you. We pray that the Holy Spirit will speak through us to others and that many will come to you. We give ourselves to you and pray that you will be glorified in us today. Alleluia!

Friday, April 20, 2007
Acts 5, 34-42
The Trial before the Sanhedrin

A respected Pharisee, Gamaliel, one of their own in the Sanhedrin, offered wise counsel in the matter regarding the apostles of Jesus. If the apostles were saying and doing these extraordinary things on their own, their movement would eventually cease. If, on the other hand, the apostles were actually sent from God on a mission, their message could not be destroyed.

" 'So in the present case, I tell you ... if this plan or this undertaking is of human origin, it will fail; but if it is from God, you will not be able to overthrow them – in that case you may even be found fighting against God (vv. 38-39).' "

Although tortured for their proclamation of the crucified and risen Christ, the apostles actually rejoiced! They did not cease telling others about the Lord Jesus Christ, both at home and in the temple.

Lord Jesus, let us trust you and continue to bear witness to you. Let us witness to you as you direct us. Let us witness in silence, in word, and with actions. Alleluia!

Saturday, April 21, 2007
Acts 6, 1-7
The Need for Assistants

Years ago, I was visiting an Episcopal clergy friend who was in the hospital labor room prior to the birth of her first son. We were chatting about ministry gifts.

Laughingly, she said she was glad I was there instead of a young clergyman we knew who was gifted in music ministry and youth ministry. We also agreed that strumming a guitar and singing were not my gifts!

Fulfillment. We are fulfilled, no longer frustrated, and those around us are blessed when we are fulfilling the ministry for which we are called.

The apostles knew their ministry was to pray and to serve as ministers of the word. Others were selected for other necessary work.

What happened? Lo and behold, God's word spread and there were more and more disciples. Even Jewish priests were becoming attentive to the faith.

Lord Jesus, thank you that you will open doors for us to fulfill the ministry to which you have called us. Let us rejoice in you. Alleluia!

Sunday, April 22, 2007 Third Sunday in Easter
Acts 5, 27-32,40-41
Trial before the Sanhedrin

The high priest before whom the apostles stood would one day stand before the Lord Jesus Christ. Jesus is the only one who is qualified to judge us and to judge others.

The apostles were treated with consummate cruelty. What else could be expected? The same group who had crucified Jesus would not be likely to be well-disposed towards the followers of Jesus.

We have only so much energy. We have only so much time. Our time on this earth is brief, no matter how long we live.

Let us trust Jesus. Let us follow Jesus as well as we know how to follow him. He died and rose again. So will we.

Lord Jesus, let us not get sidetracked by injustice. You know how to sort everything out and how to fulfill your plans. Let us trust in your love, justice, and mercy. Alleluia!

Monday, April 23, 2007 St. George, St. Adalbert
Acts 6, 8-15
Accusation before the Sanhedrin

Yes! It's happening again. No wonder this passage seems so familiar.

What happened to Jesus, the Son of God? He was filled with the power and life of God. He was hated by the religious authorities and was crucified.

Here was Stephen, a newly minted deacon in the early Christian church. What was he like?

"Stephen, full of grace and power, did great wonders and signs among the people (v. 8)." He was filled with the power of the Holy Spirit and with the grace of God. Stephen spoke with wisdom and worked signs and wonders among the people.

He was set up. He was lied about.

Stephen, like Jesus, was brought before the Sanhedrin. False witnesses popped up, quite willing to lie about him and his ministry.

Stephen! His face was radiant.

"And all who sat in the council looked intently at him, and they saw that his face was like the face of an angel (v. 15)."

Lord Jesus, thank you for filling us with grace, wisdom, and power this day. Let us speak and act as you direct. Let us look upon you and shine for you. Alleluia!

Tuesday, April 24, 2007 St. Fidelus
Acts 7, 51 - 8, 1
Conclusion; Stephen's Martyrdom

Stephen may have had the face of an angel (Acts 6, 15), but he also had the heart, mind, and mouth of a true prophet. Stephen boldly spoke the truth! He told it like it was.

The members of the Sanhedrin who were sitting in judgment on him were doing just what their ancestors had done. Their ancestors persecuted the prophets, the very ones sent by God to speak the words of God.

Stephen was already living on another level, another plane, God's plane. Before Stephen was murdered by his accusers, he saw the open heavens. He saw Jesus at God's right hand. Jesus, his Lord, was there to receive him.

Lord Jesus, you will us receive us, also. Before you call us to leave this earth, let us truly learn to live for you. Let us be bold and joyful as we proclaim you as the Risen Lord. Alleluia!

Wednesday, April 25, 2007 St. Mark
1 Peter 5, 5-14
Advice to the Community

What kind of designer clothes or discount store clothes do you wear? What does the label inside say?

St. Peter tells us to be clothed in humility. All of us can afford this kind of clothing.

We are to humble ourselves willingly under our loving and powerful God. God knows when it is the right time to exalt us. That is not our concern.

Indeed, we are to hand over to God all our concerns, all that we worry and fret about in this short life. God is caring for us, truly God is caring for us, more that we understand.

We are to be realistic and attentive. We do have an opponent out to destroy us. The devil is like a lion, always on the prowl, seeking our destruction.

We are to be strong in the strength of the Lord, however, We are strong and steadfast as we resist the devil. We are not alone in our struggle. Christians all over the world are also suffering for their witness to the Lord.

Praise God! The God who calls us will also strengthen us and restore us after we have suffered.

Lord Jesus, thank you for being with us each step of our journey through this world. Let us not be fixated on suffering. Suffering is temporary. Let us focus, instead, on you. You are eternal and we will live with you forever and ever. Alleluia!

Thursday, April 26, 2007
Acts 8, 26-40
Philip and the Ethiopian

The way that leads through the desert may be the way that will blossom for us in unexpected ways. That's the way it was for Philip.

Step by step, the adventure unfolded. First, Philip was instructed simply to go south on the road from Jerusalem that led to Gaza.

Then, the Holy Spirit told Philip to run to the Ethiopian in the chariot. The Ethiopian, puzzled by the passage he was reading from Isaiah, invited Philip to join him and to explain this prophetic passage. Philip explained that the prophecy referred to Jesus!

The Ethiopian then requested baptism. As soon as Philip had baptized him, the Holy Spirit took Philip off another mission.

Lord Jesus, our days, like this day in Philip's life, are also filled with opportunities to proclaim you. Let us be attentive to you and willing to speak and to act as you direct. Alleluia!

Friday, April 27, 2007
Acts 9, 1-20
Saul's Conversion; Saul's Baptism; Saul Preaches in Jerusalem

All of this seems to happen so fast. A dramatic conversion!

Baptism. A redirected life and ministry.

Saul was already serving God, or so he thought. In his mistaken zeal, he was persecuting Christians.

Saul's zeal was overpowered only by an intervention of the One who is Truth (John 14, 6). Jesus! Only Jesus could get through to Saul.

Saul had to see Jesus for himself. He has to realize who Jesus really was. He had to understand that he was persecuting Jesus when he persecuted the Church.

Once Saul truly saw Jesus, everything else began to change. He submitted to the ministry of one of Jesus' disciples, Ananias.

Ananias prayed for Saul to see and to be filled with the Holy Spirit. Saul was baptized. He saw. This time, he saw correctly.

Lord Jesus, thank you that you will intervene in our lives and in the lives of those for whom we pray. You alone know the best way to reveal yourself. You alone know how to remove spiritual blindness in us and in those for whom we pray. Let us see you as you really are. Let those for whom we pray see you. Alleluia!

>Saturday, April 28, 2007 St. Peter Chanel, St. Louis de Montfort
>Acts 9, 31-42
>The Church at Peace; Peter Heals Aeneas at Lydda;
>Peter Restores Tabitha to Life

After a time of turbulence and persecution, the Lord granted the church a time of peace. This was a time when the power of God was evident. This was a time when the church increased in numbers.

Peter announced to Aeneas, who had been in a state of paralysis for eight long years, that Jesus was now healing him. Aeneas immediately arose!

All the people in that area of Lydda and Sharon saw Aeneas. They came to believe in Jesus.

Peter, alone, knelt and prayed over the body of a woman named Tabitha. She was a disciple who had lived in Joppa and had faithfully toiled on behalf of others and had given alms.

Peter told this dead woman to arise. Tabitha, whose name meant "gazelle," was restored to life! Many in Joppa came to believe in Jesus.

Whether we feel we are living in a state of paralysis or whether we feel we are living without hope and purpose, Jesus can come and heal us. Jesus can send someone to us who will help us to arise and live.

Lord Jesus, thank you that you will bring us back to life. Let us be used also to bring others back to life. Let many come to believe in you through our prayers and our active trust in you. Alleluia!

>Sunday, April 29, 2007 Fourth Sunday of Easter
>Acts 13, 14,43-52
>Paul's Arrival at Antioch in Pisidia;
>Paul's Address in the Synagogue; Address to the Gentiles

Paul and Barnabas did things in God's order. They ministered first of all to God's beloved people, the Jews.

Because of the jealousy and violence of some of the Jewish people at this particular time, Paul and Barnabas spoke bluntly to them and then turned to the Gentiles. The Gentiles were full of delight and were eager to receive the Lord's word.

Again, some of the Jewish leaders were filled with jealousy and persecuted Paul and Barnabas. They even threw them out of that area.

Rather than lamenting this treatment, the apostles responded in another way. They simply moved on to another place, Iconium.

Lord Jesus, let us move with love and with grace to the next place where you call us to minister. Just because you call us to minister in a certain place at a certain time does not mean that it will be easy. We reach out in love and service as we are able and then leave all the results with you. Remove from our feet and from our hearts the dust of the memories of the past. Thank you for the joy you have in store for us. Alleluia!

Monday, April 30, 2007 St. Pius V
Acts 11, 1-18
The Baptism of the Gentiles Explained

Jesus, the Good Shepherd, is calling to us all. One day, there will indeed be one flock with one Shepherd (John 10, 16).

Peter was led by God to understand that the Gentiles, as well as the Jews, could repent and receive both baptism in water and baptism in the Holy Spirit. God does not show partiality (Acts 10, 34).

Therefore, neither could Peter show partiality! God is able to cleanse us all, whether we are Jewish or Gentile.

Lord Jesus, show us the subtle and not so subtle ways we show partiality. Let us repent and learn to reach out to all. Lead us and all your sheep, wherever they are, into one flock. Thank you for being our loving and strong Shepherd. Alleluia!

Tuesday, May 1, 2007 St. Joseph the Worker
Acts 11, 19-26
The Church at Antioch

The Lord was with those who were reaching out to the so-called outsiders. These missionaries to the Gentiles had fled because of persecution and now they were seeing people come to the Lord.

When Barnabas came from Jerusalem to Antioch to check things out, he was filled with joy at what he saw. He encouraged the new believers to stay close to the Lord.

Barnabas then went to Tarsus, brought Saul (Paul) out of seclusion and took him back to Antioch. Barnabas and Paul were with the believes in Antioch for an entire year.

Antioch! Antioch, the place where the oppressed, persecuted believers had fled and proclaimed Jesus, became the very place where the disciples were first referred to as "Christians."

Christians! The dividing walls were coming down.

Lord Jesus, let us not dwell on our past hardships in your service, but instead let us proclaim you where we are today. Let us invite others to trust you and encourage them to begin to share their faith. Alleluia!

Wednesday, May 2, 2007 St. Athanasius
Acts 12, 24-13,5
Herod's Death; Mission of Barnabas and Saul;
First Mission Begins to Cyprus

Worship, pray, fast, and then see what the Holy Spirit will do! This is not a formula. This is a way of life.

The time had come for Barnabas and Saul (Paul) to be sent out for a special work for the Lord. They were to sail to Cyprus and to preach the word of God in the synagogues.

Lord Jesus, we may or may not be sailing to Cyprus today, but we ask that we continue to serve you, to pray, and to fast. Thank you that you will show us how we are to live and how we are to serve you. Alleluia!

Thursday, May 3, 2007 Sts. Philip and James
1 Corinthians 15, 1-8
The Gospel Teaching; Results of Denial

"Now I would remind you ... of the good news that I proclaimed to you, which you in turn received, in which also you stand, through which also you are being saved, if you hold firmly to the message that I proclaimed to you – unless you have come to believe in vain. For I handed on to you as of first importance what I in turn had received: that Christ died for our sins in accordance with the scriptures, and that he was buried, and that he was raised on the third day in accordance with the scriptures ... (vv. 1-4)."

Saved and being saved. We are still in the process of salvation. We are living in and living out the glorious gospel.

As a relay runner, in a sense, Paul passed on the message, the tradition, he himself had received. Christ died for us. He was buried in a tomb and rose again! He appeared to Peter, to the other apostles, to hundreds of others, to James and to Paul.

Lord Jesus, thank you for dying for us and for rising for us. Let us rejoice in our salvation. Let us hand on to others this message that you are alive and that you are making us whole. Alleluia!

> Friday, May 4, 2007
> Acts 13, 26-33
> Paul's Address in the Synagogue

Paul speaks of Jesus in a context his hearers can understand. After a rapid run through salvation history, Paul speaks of Jesus as the fulfillment of all the prophecies in the Hebrew scriptures.

The great news is that there has been fulfillment of the prophecies. Jesus died. God raised Jesus from the dead. Jesus is alive!

Lord Jesus, you are alive today. You long to live more fully in us this very day. Come Lord Jesus and let your resurrection life flow into us and through us. We eagerly await the fulfillment of the promise that you will come again in glory. Alleluia!

> Saturday, May 5, 2007
> Acts 13, 44-52
> Address to the Gentiles

Speaking the truth, even speaking the truth in love, is no guarantee that the truth will be well-received. Jesus experienced this. The apostles experienced this. We will experience this.

If those to whom we offer the Gospel reject the Gospel, there will be others who are starving for the Gospel. We continue to proclaim the Gospel without looking back.

Lord Jesus, your followers simply shook the dust off their feet and continued on their way. They did not appear to lament the rejection of some of the jealous, abusive people in any particular place. They were filled with joy as they headed to their next assignment. Let us also be filled with the Holy Spirit and with joy as we live for you today. Alleluia!

> Sunday, May 6, 2007 Fifth Sunday of Easter
> Acts 14, 21-27
> Paul and Barnabas at Lystra; End of the First Mission

In Iconium, also, the apostles found some who believed and others who did not believe and were toxic to their ministry. The city was divided (Acts 14, 1-4).

That's what the truth always does. Not all welcome light and truth. Not all welcome the Gospel or those who proclaim the Gospel.

Moving on to Lystra, the apostles encounterd a man who had been crippled from birth. Jesus healed this man! The people went wild and tried to worship Paul and Barnabas.

This unhealthy adulation was quickly followed by those who stoned Paul and threw him out of town. Never a dull moment when Jesus is involved. Off to a new place, Derbe!

Paul and Barnabas, after all these adventures in ministry, then returned to Lystra, Iconium, and Antioch. They went to encourage the believers and to remind them that following Jesus was not going to be easy. They appointed leaders for the churches, prayed, fasted, committed them to the Lord, and then continued their journey.

Lord Jesus, let us keep moving as you lead us and as you open new doors before us. You are in charge! You love us and you have a place for us to serve you. Alleluia!

> Monday, May 7, 2007
> Acts 14, 5-18
> Paul and Barnabas at Iconium; Paul and Barnabas at Lystra

The apostles were attacked both verbally and physically, yet continued to proclaim the Gospel. They did not allow fear to intimidate them or to stop them. Neither would the apostles accept praise and adulation which belonged to God alone.

Lord Jesus, help us to stay on course with your purpose for our lives. Thank you for your presence with us and within us. Heal us and strengthen us to continue to spend time in your presence and to serve others as you instruct us. Alleluia!

Tuesday, May 8, 2007
Acts 14, 19-28
Paul and Barnabas at Lystra; End of the First Mission

Paul and Barnabas returned to places where they had previously ministered. After the tremendous rejection and mistreatment in certain places, they were returning to those very places.

Although very much living and ministering in the world, they had to live on another level. They had to learn to live above their circumstances.

In those places to which they were returning, there were good memories as well as bad memories. There were people there who had joyfully accepted the Gospel that Paul and Barnabas had sacrificially proclaimed to them.

For their sake, for the sake of the new believers in Jesus, Paul and Barnabas returned. For their sake, Paul and Barnabas returned and appointed leaders for their churches.

They "…strengthened the souls of the disciples and encouraged them to continue in the faith, saying, 'It is through many persecutions that we must enter the kingdom of God (v. 22)."

Lord Jesus, when we have suffered in a certain place, we may shrink from returning to that place. Thank you for healing our memories of what happened in that place. Thank you for strengthening us to follow you wherever you call us to serve you. If you call us to return, you will give us grace and strength to minister your love. Alleluia!

Wednesday, May 9, 2007
Acts 15, 1-6
Council of Jerusalem

The eighth day! In Jewish law (Leviticus 12, 3), a baby boy was circumcised on his eighth day after birth. This was the law.

Jesus came and perfectly fulfilled and completed the law (Matthew 5, 17). It is a new day.

There is also a new circumcision. Paul later referred to interior circumcision, the invisible circumcision of the heart, accomplished not by law, but by the Holy Spirit (Romans 2, 29).

Lord Jesus, some of your followers still fuss over what is necessary for salvation. Councils and committees still abound. Thank you that you are the Head of the Church. You, the Word of God incarnate, have the final word. Let us learn to live in the new day. Let us live out your Easter victory. Alleluia!

Thursday, May 10, 2007 Bl. Damian of Molokai
Acts 15, 7-21
Council of Jerusalem

Grace! Peter tells the disputing church leaders in Jerusalem that is through the grace of Jesus that we are all saved, whether or not we are Jewish.

It is the sheer, essential amazing grace of the Lord. This grace is free.

God sees into our hearts, knows our hearts, and chooses to make no distinction among us. The grace of God is able to cleanse us all.

It was hard for the Pharisees, even the Pharisees who had come to believe in Jesus, to understand this incredible grace. They still wanted to perform outer rituals and to keep the law of Moses.

It's also hard for many others to grasp the liberating concept of grace. How can grace to free?

Many have tried so hard and so long to seek God's favor by their own efforts. How can grace be free?

Lord Jesus, thank you for this wonderful, life-giving gift of your grace. Open our hearts, so wounded by this hard life, to receive your gift and to live in the freedom of serving you as you desire to be served. Alleluia!

Friday, May 11, 2007
Acts 15, 22-31
Letter of the Apostles

Those at the council came to agreement, with the help of the Jerusalem church leader, James (Acts 15, 13-19). They composed a letter, to be personally delivered by Barnabas, Paul, and two others. By both the written and the spoken word, the new non-Jewish believers would be reassured that circumcision was not necessary in order to follow Jesus.

Lord Jesus, when the leaders agreed, the people were freed! They were free to follow you in their new life of grace. Thank you for all who lead your flock. Let there be unity of heart and mind among the leaders. Let us all experience and manifest joy and strength as we proclaim you as our Risen Lord. Alleluia!

Saturday, May 12, 2007 St. Nereus and Achilleus, St. Pancras
Acts 16, 1-10
Paul in Lycaonia: Timothy; Through Asia Minor

Sometimes we are blocked from doing what we believe to be God's will. It is very puzzling and very frustrating.

There are many factors involved. There are matters of timing. The free will of others also is involved. God is still in control.

Even the great St. Paul experienced this difficult form of guidance in his own ministry. Paul and his traveling companions were not allowed to preach in two different areas. Clearly, a closed door!

Then, a door was opened to preach in Macedonia. Paul, Timothy, and the others set off on their new assignment.

Lord Jesus, help us to continue to trust you and to know that you have good reasons when doors of ministry are closed. Help us to live, serve, and wait with joyful trust until you open the next door for us. Alleluia!

Sunday, May 13, 2007 Sixth Sunday of Easter
Acts 15, 1-2,22-29
Council of Jerusalem; Letter of the Apostles

Presumably you have heard about disagreement within the church? I was a political science major in college before even thinking of going to seminary. Trust me, there are no politics like church politics!

The elders and apostles in Jerusalem were able to overcome their internal disagreements in order to reach out in loving, pastoral concern to the confused new Christian believers in Antioch. In their letter, they referred to themselves as brothers and wrote to the Christians in Antioch, calling them brothers also.

They spoke and wrote the truth about what had gone wrong. They acknowledged that those who had spread confusion had not been authorized to do so. With care for Christ's flock uppermost in their minds and hearts, the leaders set out to correct the errors.

Lord Jesus, let us continue to learn from the Council of Jerusalem. Let obedience to your will and loving concern for your flock be the motivation of all decisions. YOU are Head of the Church. Alleluia!

Monday, May 14, 2007 St. Matthias
Acts 1, 15-17,20-26
The Choice of Judas' Successor

In a way, Matthias, without knowing it, was a secret apostle. He had been a disciple of Jesus all along. He just didn't know that he would, one day, be among the Twelve.

Lord Jesus, we continue to follow you without knowing exactly where you will lead us. Let us be content where we are today and trust you, knowing that you are lovingly leading us to the right place. Alleluia!

Tuesday, May 15, 2007 St. Isidore
Acts 16, 22-34
Imprisonment at Philippi; Deliverance from Prison

From your place of solitude and suffering, you may lead many to light and to freedom. This difficult time in your life matters. This time in your life affects others.

Paul and Silas had been lied about and then mercilessly beaten. At the dark hour of midnight, they were awake in their prison cell, praying and praising God.

Earthquake! There was a literal earthquake.

The prison shook, the doors were flung open, and the chains of the prisoners were suddenly loosed. The distraught jailor, about to kill himself, was restrained and reassured by Paul.

Witnessing such great deliverance, such amazing power of God to save his people, the jailor cried out to Paul. He asked Paul what he had do in order to be saved.

BELIEVE! Paul told the jailor that if he believed in Jesus, not only he, but also his whole household would be saved.

There was a big party that night. The jailor and those in his household put their faith in God and were all baptized. A joyful meal of celebration followed.

Lord Jesus, when we have suffered and are in what seems like a prison cell, we think it will last forever. Help us to trust you by continuing to praise you. Thank you for delivering us and for bringing others to faith in you as they see your power in our lives. Alleluia!

> Wednesday, May 16, 2007
> Acts 17, 15,22 - 18, 1
> Paul in Beroea; Paul's Speech at the Areopagus; Paul in Corinth

The people in Athens were trying to reach God as well as they knew. Paul wisely addressed them with respect and understanding.

"Then Paul stood before the Areopagus and said, 'Athenians, I see how extremely religious you are in every way. For as I went through the city and looked carefully at the objects of your worship, I found among them an altar with the inscription, 'To an unknown god.' What therefore you worship as unknown, this I proclaim to you. The God who made the world and everything in it, he who is Lord of heaven and earth, does not live in shrines made by human hands, nor is he served by human hands, as though he needed anything, since he himself gives to all mortals life and breath and all things. From one ancestor he made all nations to inhabit the whole earth, and he allotted the times of their existence and the boundaries of the places where they would live, so that they would search for God and perhaps grope for him and find him – though indeed he is not far from each of us. For 'In him we live and move and have our being'; as even some of your own poets have said, 'For we too are his offspring (vv. 22-28).'"

Paul comprehended some of their unwholesome fears and sought to lead them to wholesome reverence of God. He led them to understand that our loving God is very close to all of us, requires repentance of all of us, and will judge us all of us.

Lord Jesus, God raised you from the dead and appointed you to be our merciful judge. Thank you for leading us into true repentance, freedom, worship and service. Alleluia!

> Thursday, May 17, 2007
> Acts 18, 1-8
> Paul in Corinth

Connections. Divine connections!

Open doors. Closed doors. God was clearly at work in all the circumstances of Paul's life.

The tentmakers, Aquila and Priscilla, had been ordered to leave Rome, along with all the other Jews. In Corinth, Paul, also a tentmaker, found a home with them.

When it became clear that the Jews were not receptive to Paul's message, he knew it was time to go to the Gentiles with the Gospel. This time, Paul stayed with Titus Justus, who happened to live right next door to a synagogue.

Surprise! The official of the synagogue, Crispus, came to believe in the Lord Jesus. Crispus' whole household and many other Corinthians believed in the Lord Jesus and were baptized.

Lord Jesus, thank you for strengthening us to proclaim you wherever you place us. Thank you for open doors and also for closed doors. Thank you for protecting us and for providing for us in every way. Alleluia!

Friday, May 18, 2007 St. John I
Acts 18, 9-18
Accusations before Gallio

Paul must have been very frightened. "One night the Lord said to Paul in a vision, 'Do not be afraid, but speak and do not be silent; for I am with you, and no one will lay a hand on you to harm you, for there are many in this city who are my people (vv. 9,10)."

When life has seemed too hard for too long, the normal tendency is to withdraw. There is indeed a time for solitude and reflection. There is also a time for activity and for speaking.

Even after the uproar involving the tribunal, Paul remained in Corinth. This time, before Paul could utter a word, Gallio, the proconsul, spoke up and addressed those who were against Paul.

The time came, however, to leave Corinth. Paul sailed away to a new assignment, accompanied by Priscilla and Aquila.

Lord Jesus, thank you for your presence with us at all times. In our times of fear and apprehension, thank you that you are with us to strengthen us. Thank you for giving us the grace to keep silent at some times and the courage to speak out boldly at other times. Alleluia!

Saturday, May 19, 2007
Acts 18, 23-28
Return to Syria Antioch; Apollos

Having received strength from the Lord, the apostle Paul then offered the Lord's strength to the disciples. Paul's travels were mercifully peaceful and orderly this time.

Then, the learned and fascinating scholar of the Hebrew scriptures, Apollos, appeared on the scene in Ephesus. Apollos spoke out eloquently and taught others about Jesus, the Messiah, as well as he could. Priscilla and Aquila further instructed Apollos in his understanding of Jesus.

Lord Jesus, help us to continue to speak out, continue to study, to learn, and to welcome instruction from those better qualified than we are, those who are more advanced in understanding the Christian life. Thank you for instructing us through others. Alleluia!

Sunday, May 20, 2007   Ascension of the Lord
Acts 1, 1-11
The Promise of the Spirit; The Ascension of Jesus

Trumpets and triumph! We may not hear a blare of trumpets (Psalm 47, 6), but we still rejoice in our Lord's victory.

Mission accomplished! Back Home to his loving, proud Abba.

Jesus, who suffered, LIVES! Jesus, who ascended, lives with us and within us.

The Holy Spirit whispers and shouts. The Holy Spirit encourages us to continue our work here on earth.

At the right time, we, too will rejoice, when our mission is complete. We will rejoice when Jesus comes in glory.

Lord Jesus, thank you for the Father's promise of the Holy Spirit. Open us to receive the promise and the power of the Holy Spirit. Thank you for the Holy Spirit who teaches us to wait with joy and with expectancy. Let us yield to the person and the power of the Holy Spirit and witness to you until you return. Alleluia!

Monday, May 21, 2007;
St. Christopher Magellanes and Companions
Acts 19, 1-6
Paul in Ephesus

Listen! Even the great apostle Paul learned to speak AFTER prayerful listening to the Holy Spirit. He asked some of the Ephesian disciples whether they had received the Holy Spirit.

The Holy Spirit? These particular disciples admitted honestly that they had not even heard about the Holy Spirit!

Paul continued to ask them questions to determine where they were, spiritually. Then they were baptized, received the Holy Spirit, and began to speak forth in other languages and in prophecy.

Interestingly, this was a group of twelve. Paul then spent three months in the synagogue, speaking of God's kingdom.

Lord Jesus, thank you for helping us to learn to listen to the Holy Spirit when we speak with others. Let us learn to ask questions with respect and then to listen. Let us learn to discern the true needs of those with whom we speak. Let us respond with love and wisdom. Let us say what will lead others closer to you. We trust you to take what we say and interpret our words to the minds and hearts of our hearers. Alleluia!

Tuesday, May 22, 2007 St. Rita of Cascia
Acts 20, 17-27
Paul's Farewell Speech at Miletus

Paul spoke with blunt honesty as well as with love to the presbyters of the church at Miletus. He made it clear that he had done his part.

Paul had humbly and faithfully proclaimed the Gospel, in the midst of all his suffering. He had taught the necessity of repentance and of trusting Jesus.

As for himself, he was concerned only with joyfully completing the ministry entrusted to him by Jesus. Paul was well aware that even more suffering lay ahead for him as he traveled to Jerusalem.

Lord Jesus, just as Paul told the church leaders that he had proclaimed the kingdom of God and that he was no longer responsible for them, let us also learn to draw the lines of responsibility. We are responsible to you for living out, as well as we are able, the ministry to which you have called us. We are not responsible for the reactions and the decisions of others. Let us be at peace, trusting that, after we are gone, you are still at work in the lives of those among whom we labored. Alleluia!

>   Wednesday, May 23, 2007
>   Acts 20, 28-38
>   Paul's Farewell Speech at Miletus

"Keep watch over yourselves and over all the flock, of which the Holy Spirit has made you overseers, to shepherd the church of God that he obtained with the blood of his own Son (v. 28)."

Paul admonished the leaders of the church at Miletus to keep guard over themselves as well as over the flock entrusted by the Holy Spirit to their care. Over the course of the three years Paul had spent in Melitus, he had wept with great concern over the Lord's flock. He had worked to support himself and those with him during this time.

We are all completely dependent upon the Lord and it is wise to remind ourselves of this truth. Then, and only then, are we fit to serve others in the Lord's flock.

Wolves are inevitable, as are false shepherds. Constant vigilance is required. However, Jesus, the Good and Great Shepherd, will deal with all who hurt his lambs.

Lord Jesus, teach us to trust you completely with ourselves and with all your flock, wherever they may be scattered. You gave yourself completely to us. We give ourselves completely to you. Alleluia!

>   Thursday, May 24, 2007
>   Acts 22, 30; 23, 1-6
>   Paul before the Sanhedrin

Jesus once told the scribes and Pharisees that they were like tombs, white on the outside, yet filled with death (Matthew 23, 27). Hmmm!

Paul, before the council sitting in judgment on him, called Ananias, the high priest, a wall that had been whitened. That was because Ananias had told one of his assistants to sock Paul on the mouth. Aren't church meetings fun?!

Upon being told that Ananias was the high priest, Paul acknowledged that he did not know that. It was forbidden to curse a ruler (Exodus 22, 27).

However, it was not forbidden to state one's own identity. Paul identified himself as a Pharisee, as one who believed in resurrection.

Riot! There was a big outcry.

The Pharisees believed in the resurrection and the Sadducees did not. They began to argue with each other. Finally, Paul was removed by the civil authorities for his own safety.

Lord Jesus, you came to Paul after this incident to cheer him on and to encourage him as he testified to you. Help us to speak with courtesy and with courage as we live for you and bear witness to you today. Alleluia!

Friday, May 25, 2007 St. Gregory VII, St. Bede,
St. Mary Magdalene de Pazzi
Acts 25, 13-21
Paul before King Agrippa

Paul, a real hot potato, was being passed from ruler to ruler. He was in the midst of church authorities and also civil authorities. He was caught up in dynamics beyond his control.

Lord Jesus, when we are caught up in the issues of others and the rivalries of others, let us stay in peace. Only you can sort out all of these many concerns. You love all involved and you will do what is best for all. Help us to stay in peace, knowing that you are in control. Alleluia!

Saturday, May 26, 2007
Acts 28, 16-20, 30-31
Arrival in Rome; Testimony to Jews in Rome

Although under house arrest in Rome, Paul still had some freedom. People came to him, in his home.

Living there for two years at his own expense, Paul proclaimed Jesus and taught about God's kingdom. Some believed. Some did not believe. Paul still proclaimed Jesus.

Lord Jesus, we may feel stifled or cramped when we can't venture out into the world at will. Thank you for Paul's example of serving you wherever we are. You are Israel's hope, You are our hope. You raise us from the dead to new life. From wherever we are, let us boldly proclaim you today. Alleluia!

Sunday, May 27, 2007 Pentecost, Year C
Acts 2, 1-11
The Coming of the Spirit

The Holy Spirit descended upon all. All were filled with the Holy Spirit.

All spoke in other languages, declaring the greatness of God. ALL!

Come, Holy Spirit. Breathe new life into all of us today. Alleluia!

Monday, May 28, 2007
Sirach 17, 20-24
Appeal for a Return to God

The Lord welcomes us back. We don't have to pretend to be perfect. The Lord who loves us as we are is the only one who can transform us.

Lord Jesus, we return to you as our Good Shepherd. Thank you for your understanding and your compassion for us. You know why we think the way we think, feel the way we feel, and act the way we act. Help us to turn to you and to turn away from whatever displeases or grieves you. Thank you that the Holy Spirit is at work within us helping us to repent as well as to confess. We thank you and praise you for your mercy. Alleluia!

Tuesday, May 29, 2007
Sirach 35, 1-12
The Worship of God

We are to give generously and joyfully, knowing that we can never out-give God. We are to be aware that God looks upon the spirit of the giver, not merely the pocketbook.

Lord Jesus, you gave yourself both cheerfully and tearfully to God Most High. You knew that there would be a great harvest from your willing sacrifice. Let us give ourselves, tears and all, into the hands of our loving Father to be poured out for others. Come, Holy Spirit. Fill us and send us forth. Alleluia!

JANIS WALKER   FIRST READING

Wednesday, May 30, 2007
Sirach 36, 1,4-5,10-17
A Prayer for God's People

This is a prayer for God's prophecies to be fulfilled. It is a cry for help!

It is a cry for mercy for Israel and for Jerusalem. It is a prayer for the glory of God to fill the temple.

Lord Jesus, we too cry to God for all the ancient promises and prophecies to be fulfilled. Thank you, Holy Spirit, for filling us, filling the Church, and filling the whole earth with your glory. Help us to be joyful as we travel to the heavenly Jerusalem. Alleluia!

Thursday, May 31, 2007
Visitation of the Blessed Virgin Mary
Zephaniah 3, 14-18
Reproach and Promise for Jerusalem

There is the Lord's part and there is our part. Even though God has removed our reproach, we still cry out for help as we begin to manifest our trust in the Lord.

We decide to live in joy! We sing and we even shout for joy.

We reject fear. We choose not to give in to discouragement.

The Lord our God is right here with us. The Lord is our strong Savior.

The Lord rejoices over us! The Lord's love brings us renewal. The Lord even sings over us.

Lord Jesus, thank you for helping us as we learn to live in gladness and exultation. This summer, let us practice resting quietly in your love. Thank you that you will fulfill all your promises to us. Alleluia!

Friday, June 1, 2007 St. Justin
Sirach 44, 1,9-13
Praise of Israel's Great Ancestors

It is gloriously possible to be great. We may not be famous in the worldly sense, but it is possible for us to live great lives for God and for others.

Lord Jesus, thank you that you never forget us or forsake us. Thank you for your faithful care of us and our families. Alleluia!

Saturday, June 2, 2007 Sts. Marcillinus and Peter
Sirach 51, 12-20
Epilogue and Canticles

When we seek wisdom, beautiful, blossoming wisdom, we are seeking the Lord Jesus Christ. Jesus truly embodies and truly is God's wisdom (1 Corinthians 1, 24).

Lord Jesus, we cannot seek wisdom without seeking you. Come, Holy Spirit, the promise of our Father. Thank you, blessed Trinity, for taking up residence within us and filling us. Let us work with wisdom and joy in your vineyard today. Alleluia!

Sunday, June 3, 2007 Trinity Sunday
Proverbs 8, 22-31
The Discourse of Wisdom

Wisdom was created by God. Wisdom is poured out to play upon the earth!

We may think of wisdom as weighty, imponderable, or unbearably dull, but that is not God's view. Wisdom is God's delight!

Lord Jesus, let us seek to enter the joyful, playful dance of wisdom. It is never too late to receive wisdom so generously poured forth. Alleluia!

Monday, June 4, 2007
Tobit 1, 3; 2, 1-8
His Virtues: Courage in Burying the Dead

Tobit had a passionate zeal for the serving the Lord, in spite of any personal consequences. He reached out to the poor and buried the dead.

Lord Jesus, help us to continue serving you, even when we are misunderstood. You alone are able to discern the hidden motives of the heart. Let us live joyfully before you and continue to reach out to others as you lead us. Let us be honest before you and before others when we are the ones in need of help. Alleluia!

Tuesday, June 5, 2007 St. Boniface
Tobit 2, 9-14
Tobit's Blindness

Tobit, during the four years of his blindness, was cared for by his nephew. Anna, Tobit's wife, was working as a weaver during this time.

Poor Tobit. In his illness, he seemed to be getting angry and suspicious without cause.

Lord Jesus, help us when we are not able to live as we would like to live. Thank you for those you send to help us. Help us to trust you with ourselves, with those around us, and with our difficult circumstances. Thank you for leading us triumphantly through this time. Alleluia!

Wednesday, June 6, 2007 St. Norbert
Tobit 3, 1-11,16-17
Tobit's Blindness; Tobit's Prayer for Death;
Sarah Falsely Accused; Sarah's Prayer for Death;
An Answer to Prayer

The plot is thickening! Poor Tobit, already suffering blindness, was further tormented by his wife's harsh words.

Tobit wept. He acknowledged God's justice and mercy. Then he prayed to die.

Poor Sarah, already suffering from loss, is now insulted by a maid. She too prays to the Lord, acknowledges God's mercy, and then prays to die (Tobit 3, 13).

Both prayers reach God. God sends the angel Raphael to bring healing to both Tobit and Sarah.

Tobit would no longer be blind. He would once again enjoy God's beautiful sunlight.

Sarah would no longer be tormented. She would, instead marry Tobiah, the son of Tobit. How wonderfully God intervened in the lives of Tobit and Sarah.

Lord Jesus, sometimes life is just too hard. We love you and we know that you are just and merciful. It's just that life is so hard. Help us to trust you. Rather than merely longing for an end to our suffering, let us trust you to bring us healing and joy. Please send an angel to help us. Alleluia!

JANIS WALKER   FIRST READING

Thursday, June 7, 2007
Tobit 6, 10-11; 7, 1,9-17; 8, 4-9
Raphael's Instructions; At the House of Raguel;
Marriage of Tobiah and Sarah; Expulsion of the Demon

The story keeps getting better and better! The angel, Raphael, is traveling incognito with young Tobiah. Tobiah and Sarah are now happily married.

A new life is beginning for Sarah and Tobiah. Sarah's father is quite naturally worried about the past, however.

Tobiah obeyed Raphael's instructions and the evil entitiy which had troubled Sarah was expelled. The young couple began their married life with prayers for God's mercy and deliverance. How wonderfully God worked in the lives of Tobiah, Sarah and their familes.

Lord Jesus, thank you for sending us help from heaven this very day. Raise our drooping spirits and refresh us with new hope. Thank you for delivering us from all evil and giving us a new life. Alleluia!

Friday, June 8, 2007
Tobit 11, 5-17
Homeward Journey; Sight Restored

God's tenderness and bounty overflowed upon Tobiah's parents. Anna, sitting beside her blind husband, Tobit, and waiting for Tobiah to return, was ready to settle for death. She had wanted only to see her son again and now he was home safely.

God had other ideas. The family's afflictions of illness and poverty were to be turned into health and prosperity.

Tobiah followed Raphael's instructions and applied a rather unusual medicine to his father Tobit's eyes. By following Raphael's instructions, his young wife, Sarah, had been freed. What would happen this time?

Tobit saw again! First of all, he saw his son.

Tobit walked without assistance to greet Sarah, his new daughter-in-law. Before all the people, Tobit told how God had healed him.

Lord Jesus, thank you for giving us hope today. Let us dwell in despondency no more. You have countless ways to heal us. You have innumerable angels ready to do your bidding. Send us the help we need today. Let us give you all the glory and tell all of your intervention on our behalf. Alleluia!

> Saturday, June 9, 2007 St. Ephrem
> Tobit 12, 1,5-15,20
> Raphael's Wages; Exhortation; Raphael's Identity

Because they were righteous. Tobit and Tobiah wanted to pay Raphael, whom they believed to be Azariah, a fellow Israelite, for all his work. After all, Raphael had accompanied Tobiah on his journey and had advised Tobiah what to do in order for Tobit and Sarah to be healed.

Raphael instructed Tobit and Tobiah to give God the praise and the glory. He told the two men that, although it was good to pray and to fast, it was even better to give alms with a right spirit.

Surprise! Raphael revealed his own identity.

He was an angel, who had heard the prayers of both Tobit and Sarah. He had given the prayers to the Lord. The Lord then sent Raphael both to test and to heal Tobit and Sarah.

Lord Jesus, how often are angels sent to us and we fail to recognize them? Let us live in righteousness, as did Tobit. Let us trust you and praise you. You have wondrous ways to be with us in our trials, to deliver us, and to bring us joy. Alleluia!

> Sunday, June 10, 2007 Most Holy Body and Blood of Christ
> Genesis 14, 18-20
> The Four Kings

Abram returned victorious! The battles were over and his nephew, Lot, had been rescued from his captors.

The mysterious Melchizedek, both king and priest, gave Abram bread, wine, and a blessing. Abram, in turn, gave to Melchizedek one tenth of all he had.

Lord Jesus, thank you for this early story which prepares us for your saving work on our behalf. We thank you for giving yourself to us, for giving us your Body and Blood. We give ourselves to you and ask for you to bless us as we live for you in this starving world. Alleluia!

JANIS WALKER — FIRST READING

> Monday, June 11, 2007 St. Barnabas
> Acts 11, 21-26; 13, 1-3
> The Church at Antioch; Mission of Barnabas and Paul

Barnabas lived up to his name as one who brings encouragement. The Jerusalem church chose Barnabas to go and see what was happening in the Antioch church. In Antioch, there were Cyrenians and Cypriots who were reaching out to those who were not Jewish and telling them all about Jesus.

Barnabas could identify with this particular ministry situation. Although Jewish (a Levite), he had been born a Cypriot. Living up to his name, he was a source of encouragement to those in the Antioch church.

Barnabas also saw this situation as an opportunity to involve Saul (Paul) in the ministry at Antioch. After a year of active ministry in Antioch, Barnabas and Paul were commissioned by the Holy Spirit for another mission.

Lord Jesus, thank you for helping us to live up our names as Christians in the place where we are today. Let us rejoice in you and be a source of encouragement to all around us. Let us be flexible, willing to involve others in our ministry, and willing to remain where we are or to go elsewhere as the Holy Spirit chooses. Alleluia!

> Tuesday, June 12, 2007
> 2 Corinthians 1, 18-22
> Paul's Sincerity and Consistency

God anoints us, seals us, and gives us our security in Christ. Then we are free to tell others that God's "yes" is found in Jesus. Jesus is the great Amen of God.

Lord Jesus, let our lives sing forth that you are the answer to our deepest longings. You are our Amen. Alleluia!

> Wednesday, June 13, 2007 St. Anthony of Padua
> 2 Corinthians 3, 4-11
> Ministers of a New Covenant; Contrast with the Old Covenant

Filters. Some of us live lives filtered through fear.

As Christians, however, we are free to live our lives filtered through our Lord Jesus Christ. God looks at us lovingly through the filter of Jesus, his beloved Son.

We don't have to struggle for approval and recognition. God has qualified us. We have nothing to prove. We are free to be ministers of life.

Lord Jesus, let us live this glorious life you have made it possible for us to live. Thank you for being our filter. Alleluia!

Thursday, June 14, 2007
2 Corinthians 3, 15 - 4, 1,3-6
Contrast with the Old Covenant; Integrity in the Ministry

When we turn to Jesus, whatever veils our understanding of God is removed. We see clearly.

"Now the Lord is the Spirit, and where the Spirit of the Lord is, there is freedom. And all of us, with unveiled faces, seeing the glory of the Lord as though reflected in a mirror, are being transformed into the same image from one degree of glory to another; for this comes from the Lord, the Spirit (vv. 17,18)."

We learn to gaze upon the Lord's glory and we are transformed. We are free to proclaim the Lord and to serve others.

At a wedding, after the veil is removed from the bride's face, the bridegroom and the bride see one another clearly. They kiss and begin their new life. They are one.

Lord Jesus, you are our Bridegroom. Lift the veil from our hearts. Let us, your Bride, your Church, see you clearly. Let us learn to love others as you love us. Alleluia!

Friday, June 15, 2007   Sacred Heart of Jesus
Ezekiel 34, 11-16
Parable of the Shepherds

"For thus says the LORD GOD: I myself will search for my sheep, and will seek them out. As shepherds seek out their flocks when they are among their scattered sheep, so I will seek out my sheep. I will rescue them from all the places to which they have been scattered on a day of clouds and thick darkness. I will bring them out ... and will bring them into their own land; and I will feed them on the mountains of Israel .... I myself will be the shepherd of the sheep, and I will make them lie down, says the LORD GOD. I will seek the lost, and I will bring back the strayed, and I will bind up the injured, and I will strengthen the weak ... (vv. 11-13a,15-16a)."

A true shepherd's instinct is to care for the sheep. A true shepherd rescues, leads, gathers, retrieves, and pastures the flock into green meadows. There the sheep may rest while their shepherd heals them.

Lord Jesus, let us rest in your care this summer. You are our Good Shepherd. You know how to care for us. Alleluia!

Saturday, June 16, 2007 Immaculate Heart of Mary
2 Corinthians 5, 14-21
The Ministry of Reconciliation

I long to know and to live these verses. For decades, they have been in my mind. On one level, I believe them. On a deeper level, I still cannot grasp them.

How can we ever grasp God's love? How can it be that Jesus took into himself all the sins of all people of all times? All!

Then, when Jesus died, our sins died. Jesus died for us all so that we are free to live for him.

This is beyond arbitration, mediation, or negotiation. This is radical reconciliation. We are reconciled to GOD. God loves us.

We are miraculously made new. "So if anyone is in Christ, there is a new creation: everything old has passed away; see, everything has become new (v. 17)!"

Now we are to go out into the world and be God's agents of reconciliation. This is our ministry.

Lord Jesus, sometimes I still don't get it. Please help me to take a step of trust and begin bravely to live the ministry of reconciliation. Alleluia!

Sunday, June 17, 2007 Eleventh Sunday in Ordinary Time
2 Samuel 12, 7-10,13
David's Punishment; David's Repentance

David was the mighty king of Israel. God had chosen David, when he was a young shepherd lad, to be the future king. God had rescued David from his troubled predecessor, King Saul, who had tried to kill David.

David was now the king! He had everything.

Except Bathsheba. So he sent for her.

After learning that Bathsheba was pregnant, King David arranged for Bathsheba's husband, Uriah, to be killed in battle to cover up the fact that Bathsheba was pregnant by none other than the king. (2 Samuel 11).

God sent the prophet Nathan to confront King David. Nathan was charged with informing King David of God's displeasure and of the consequences in store for the king.

King David, by his flagrant action, had despised the God who had saved him from Saul, blessed him beyond belief, and elevated him to be king. King David would experience evil and suffering from within his own household from this time forward. The king had sinned in secret, but God would deal with him publicly.

Lord Jesus, we are not in the high position that King David was and yet we too have sinned against you in so many ways. We think and say and do things in secret and yet you see. You know. You know our hearts. Have mercy upon us. Forgive us. Purify our hearts, our words, and our actions. Let us remember that you are the Lord. You are in control. Let us obey you because you love us and gave your life for us. Thank you that you continue to give us your life. Alleluia!

Monday, June 18, 2007
2 Corinthians 6, 1-10
The Experience of the Ministry

Paul made it clear that Christian ministry involves great suffering as well as great responsibility. In spite of the unrealistic expectations heaped upon them, ministers of the Gospel are charged with living in integrity, truth, and righteousness. They are to rejoice always in the Lord.

Lord Jesus, we may see the outer glitz, the mitres and the microphones, of some ministries, yet not see the suffering behind the scenes. We do not see the long years of preparation, the misunderstanding, the rejection, or the humiliation of those who serve you. Let us be faithful to be all that you have called us to be. Let us be faithful to do, to the extent that we are able, all that you have called us to do. Let us rejoice always in the privilege of serving you. Alleluia!

Tuesday, June 19, 2007 St. Romuald
2 Corinthians 8, 1-9
Generosity in Giving

The right order. The right recipe. The right example.

The right order. Before jumping into any ministry or any good cause, we need to give ourselves first to the Lord and to our spiritual leaders. We are thus fully yielded to God's will and God's way.

The right recipe. The Macedonians had a great recipe for giving. Their joy was combined with their poverty! The result was an amazing generosity.

Jesus is our example in how to give. Jesus chose to become poor, for our sake, so that we might share in his riches.

Lord Jesus, we are always rich in your love and in all the resources at your disposal. Let our joy overflow today as we give ourselves to you and to others. Alleluia!

Wednesday, June 20, 2007
2 Corinthians 9, 6-11
God's Indescribable Gift

It has been said that God is not a God of subtraction or even a God of addition. God is a God of multiplication!

How we sow determines how we will later reap. God is longing for us to sow with trust, hope, and joy.

Lord Jesus, sometimes we are afraid to give. We think we won't have enough for ourselves or our families. We may give, but out of a joyless sense of duty. We may even resent giving to others, if they are unappreciative or if they don't deserve our gifts. Strip away from our minds and our hearts all the distorted ways we have looked at the matter of giving. Thank you for giving yourself completely to us. We trust you today as we learn to give ourselves to you. Let us bravely and boldly sow seeds for an abundant harvest. Alleluia!

Thursday, June 21, 2007 St. Aloysius Gonzaga
2 Corinthians 11, 1-11
Preaching without Charge

With deep humility, Paul had poured himself out in sacrificial ministry to the Corinthians and they still didn't seem to get it. They had a long way to go in the matter of maturity and discernment.

They were ready to go off onto tangents and to follow imposters. Paul loved them so much, and yet he was frustrated and exasperated.

Lord Jesus, when we pour ourselves out in your service, and then we are met with spiritual brats, help us to continue to trust you. We are here for your purposes. You love your lambs and your sheep. You are in control. Let us continue faithfully to serve you, knowing that this difficult assignment is not forever. You will reward us for our labor in this place. Alleluia!

Friday, June 22, 2007 St. Paulinus
Sts. John Fisher and Thomas More
2 Corinthians 11, 18,21-30
Paul's Boast: His Labors; Paul's Boast: His Weakness

The outer sufferings of Paul were terrible. He suffered on the land and on the sea. He suffered imprisonment, torture, shipwrecks, hunger, thirst, etc. All for the sake of the Gospel. All for Jesus.

The inner sufferings of Paul were also terrible. Paul suffered for the Church, the Body of Christ.

How often he must have reminded himself that this was the flock of Jesus, the Good Shepherd. The flock belonged to the Lord.

Paul agonized over the Church. He worked and prayed for the well-being of the new followers of Christ. He yearned for their spiritual maturity.

Lord Jesus, thank you that Paul was even willing to boast of his weakness. Let us trust you with all our suffering, the suffering in our lives which everyone sees and the suffering which you alone see. Our suffering is temporary. Our relationship with you is eternal Our life with you is eternal. Thank you for your presence in the midst of our weakness and in the midst of our suffering. Alleluia!

Saturday, June 23, 2007
2 Corinthians 12, 1-10
Paul's Boast; His Weakness

The apostle Paul was intimately acquainted with suffering and eventually came to terms with this aspect of his ministry. "Therefore I am content with weaknesses, insults, hardships, persecutions, and calamities for the sake of Christ; for whenever I am weak, then I am strong (v. 10)."

All the suffering of Paul was eventually distilled and filtered through Christ. For the sake of the Lord Jesus Christ, Paul learned to be content and to be at peace in the midst of his personal suffering.

It did not mean that his suffering wasn't real. It did not mean that his suffering wasn't terrible.

It meant that Christ was free to shine through Paul. Paul had learned, at last, that when he was most aware of his weakness, the strength of Christ was most operative through him.

Lord Jesus, whether we realize it or not, you are actively at work within us when we are aware of our complete dependence upon you. Let your light shine in us and through us today. Alleluia!

Sunday, June 24, 2007
The Nativity of St. John the Baptist
Isaiah 49, 1-6
The Servant of the Lord

"The Lord called me before I was born, while I was in my mother's womb he named me. He made my mouth like a sharp sword, in the shadow of his hand he hid me; he made me a polished arrow, in his quiver he hid me away (vv. 1b-2)."

The Lord calls us and then the Lord conceals us. When the Lord calls us into a particular ministry, that is only the beginning.

The Lord conceals us as we are being trained for his glory and for his purpose. This can be very confusing and very frustrating. We may even think the Lord has forgotten us.

As Oswald Chambers said, "God gives us a vision, then he takes us down to the valley to batter us into the shape of the vision, and it is in the valley that so many of us faint and give way. Every vision will be made real if we will have patience (the selection for July 6, My Utmost for His Highest by Oswald Chambers, Dodd, Mead & Company, 1935)."

We may think that all our work has been futile. Isaiah lamented, "I have labored in vain, I have spent my strength for nothing ... yet surely my cause is with the LORD, and my reward with my God (v. 3b-4)."

God has not forgotten us. Our reward is with God.

We have suffered enough to know that our strength comes from God alone. God will now use us as instruments of restoration.

Lord Jesus, thank you that you call us to be a light in this world. You long for all to know of your power to heal us and to make us whole. Shine through us we live out your call. Alleluia!

Monday, June 25, 2007
Genesis 12, 1-9
Abram's Call and Migration

GO! Get out of here and go. Get a life out "there."

God spoke and Abram (who would be given the name "Abraham") went. He was seventy-five years old.

As Abram traveled, he built altars to the Lord. He called upon the Lord. He kept moving.

Lord Jesus, we start out and then we stop. We falter. We wonder. We wait. We stagnate. Call us again! Let us hear you and go. Thank you that you will lead us to the place you have prepared for us. Alleluia!

Tuesday, June 26, 2007
Genesis 13, 2,15-18
Abram and Lot Part

It is not possible to outdo God when it comes to generosity. Abram willingly allowed his nephew, Lot, to choose which part of the land he wanted.

Lot chose what appeared to be the better land, the area near Sodom. The inhabitants of Sodom, however, were very wicked.

The Lord then told Abram to gaze at his own land and to be aware of its vastness. The Lord promised countless descendants to this childless old man.

The Lord told Abram to start walking around his land. So off he went and built yet another altar to the Lord.

Lord Jesus, let us never fear being generous. Let us not worry that others will take advantage of our generosity. You have countless ways to reward us. Let us walk about today, with a spirit of adventure, in the vastness of your kingdom. Alleluia!

Wednesday, June 27, 2007 St. Cyril of Alexandria
Genesis 15, 1-2,17-18
The Covenant with Abram

After Abram had rescued Lot, who had been kidnapped (Genesis 14, 11-16), the Lord came again to Abram. The Lord promised Abram a great reward.

Abram lamented his childlessness and asked what good this reward would be without any descendants. The Lord made a covenant with Abram, again assuring him that he would have many descendants.

Lord Jesus, when we grow weary of waiting, come to us again and reassure us of your presence and of your promise. Let us be brave and adventurous as we live in joyful expectation of what you will do. Alleluia!

> Thursday, June 28, 2007 St. Irenaeus
> Genesis 16, 1-12,15-16
> Birth of Ishmael

Ishmael! This is what happens when we get tired of waiting for God and take matters in our own hands. When we decide to be God's little helpers and try to make God's vision for our lives come true all by ourselves, chaos erupts!

There will be misunderstanding, blaming, running away, and then the tragic results of our ego-driven disobedience. God is still merciful, but will keep us waiting until the time is truly right.

Lord Jesus, help us not to give up and try to make things happen on our own. Help us to wait until your moment to act, no matter how long the wait. Thank you for closing doors for us as well as for opening doors. Alleluia!

> Friday, June 29, 2007 Sts. Peter and Paul
> Acts 12, 1-11
> Herod's Persecution of Christians

Nothing can keep the Lord from acting in our lives. Peter, in prison, was doubly chained and guarded by four soldiers, even when he slept. No problem.

The church was praying fervently for Peter. The prayers were heard and answered in wonderful ways.

The Lord's angel simply woke Peter and led him out of the prison. Even the gates of the prison opened automatically for them to leave!

Lord Jesus, thank you for the light which shone in Peter's prison. Thank you for the wonderful way Peter was rescued. When we grow weary of praying, help us to remember that our prayers will indeed be answered in the very best way. Obstacles which would not budge for decades melt away. Doors which were slammed in our faces will be held open for us. Alleluia!

> Saturday, June 30, 2007 First Martyrs of Rome
> Genesis 18, 1-15
> Abraham's Visitors

When we grow accustomed to sorrow, we may think that we will not have joy ever again. We are used to a certain form of dull, listless living devoid of positive expectations.

Then God shows up and tells us something totally preposterous! It's so crazy that we may even laugh in God's face.

We would like to believe, but we are afraid. We've been disappointed so many times.

After all the waiting, the time came for Abraham and his Sarah to have their own child. God visited Abraham and Sarah right there in their own home. God promised that the child would arrive in one year.

Lord Jesus, we ask you to visit us today. Heal us. Help us. Bring us back to life. Thank you for gently opening our withered hearts to new life and to love. Alleluia!

> Sunday, July 1, 2007 Thirteenth Sunday in Ordinary Time
> 1 Kings 19, 16,19-21
> Flight to Egypt; Call of Elisha

A new assignment. A new king. A new prophet.

The Lord gave poor, depressed Elijah new direction for his life. The mighty prophet, although he had just seen the Lord act in amazing ways, was just wiped out.

He desperately need to rest. After a period of rest, he was ready to hear what the Lord had in store for him now.

Elijah was to anoint Jehu as Israel's king. Then, he was anoint Elisha be his successor. Elijah placed his own cloak over Elisha.

Lord Jesus, thank you for placing the mantle of your anointing over us. Let us trust you with our own lives and with the lives of those we love. Let us arise and follow you. Alleluia!

Monday, July 2, 2007
Genesis 18, 16-33
Abraham's Intercession for Sodom

Abraham did his part. He persisted in asking God to spare the city of Sodom if there were only ten people there who were innocent.

As events transpired (Genesis 19), only Lot and his family were saved. The inhabitants had behaved in unspeakably wicked ways. God considered their sin to be grievous. God's limit had been reached.

Abraham inquired about the justice of God. Abraham asked, "Shall not the Judge of all the earth do right (Genesis 18, 25c KJV)?"

God, although infinite in mercy and compassion, was and is the ultimate Judge. Sodom was destroyed.

God has given all judgment to Jesus (John 5, 22). We will all stand before God's judgment seat of the Lord Jesus Christ (Romans 14, 10).

Lord Jesus, thank you that you are our loving intercessor as well as our judge. Help us to do our part to cooperate with you as you intercede for us today. Thank you for the privilege of interceding for others. Alleluia!

Tuesday, July 3, 2007 St. Thomas
Ephesians 2, 19-22
Generosity of God's Plan

"So then you are no longer strangers or aliens, but you are citizens with the saints and also members of the household of God, built upon the foundation of the apostles and prophets, with Christ Jesus himself as the cornerstone (vv. 19-20)."

You count. You're in! You're in the right place. You're in God's own household. You're right there with the saints.

The household of God has a strong foundation of prophets and apostles. Jesus is the cornerstone.

Jesus holds us all together. We are in a safe place where we can grow up as we are being formed. How amazing that we are the place where God dwells.

Lord Jesus, thank you that we may rest secure. Our security is in you. You have promised never to leave us or to forsake us. We are not wandering about as orphans. You are our strong, loving Brother helping us and leading us Home. Alleluia!

Wednesday, July 4, 2007
Genesis 21, 5,8-20
Birth of Isaac

At last! When Abraham was one hundred years old, Isaac was born. The promise of the Lord to Sarah and Abraham had been faithfully fulfilled. There was great rejoicing.

There was also Hagar and Ishmael. What about them? They were living reminders of the consequences of trying to hurry up the work of God.

God, ever merciful, provided for both Hagar and her son, Ishmael. God even promised to make a nation of Ishmael.

Lord Jesus, help us to wait, to work, and to trust you to fulfill your promise at the right time. Thank you for your compassion on all who wait and upon all whose lives are affected by those who do not wait well. Thank you for your love and care for all of us. Alleluia!

Thursday, July 5, 2007 St. Anthony Zaccaria
Genesis 22, 1-19
The Testing of Abraham

Testing? Hasn't poor old Abraham been tested enough already? After all, he had long ago taken off and left his comfort zone in order to follow the Lord.

This is a deeper test. Will Abraham, now that the promised Isaac is here, still put the Lord first?

YES! Abraham was prepared even to lose Isaac rather than to disobey the Lord.

"The angel of the LORD called to Abraham a second time from heaven, and said, 'By myself I have sworn, says the LORD: Because you have done this, and have not withheld your son, your only son, I will indeed bless you, and I will make your offspring as numerous as the stars of heaven and as the sand that is on the seashore ... because you have obeyed my voice (vv. 15-17,18b).'"

Because of Abraham's obedience and his radical trust in the Lord, the Lord, not to be outdone, blessed Abraham even more. The old man, tested almost beyond endurance, was promised countless descendants.

All of his descendants would experience special blessing because of Abraham's willingness to obey the Lord at all costs.

Lord Jesus, I feel pretty shabby compared to Abraham. I don't want to sacrifice anything. Forgive me. Heal any distorted ideas I still have about you and your love for me. Free me to follow you and be willing to lose everything rather than to distrust you, dishonor you, or disobey you. Alleluia!

> Friday, July 6, 2007 St. Maria Goretti
> Genesis 23, 1-4,19; 24, 1-8,65-67
> Purchase of a Burial Place; Isaac and Rebekah

The princess. Sarah!

Sarah, the princess, died. It was the Lord who had changed her name from Sarai to Sarah, which means "princess" (Genesis 17, 15).

"God said to Abraham, 'As for Sarah your wife, you shall no longer call her Sarai, but Sarah shall be her name. I will bless her, and moreover I will give you a son by her. I will bless her, and she shall give rise to nations; kings of peoples shall come from her.' Then Abraham fell on his face and laughed, and said to himself, 'Can a child be born to a man who is a hundred years old? Can Sarah, who is ninety years old, bear a child (Genesis 17, 15-17)?"

The short answer. YES!

It was the Lord who had chosen Sarah to be the mother of Isaac. It was fitting that Sarah be buried with honor.

The Lord was watching over Sarah's son, Isaac, after she was gone. Abraham gave specific instructions that Isaac was to marry a good Jewish girl.

Rebekah! Beautiful Rebekah became Isaac's wife.

Lord Jesus, help your "princesses" to wait patiently for the birth of their "Isaacs." Thank you for taking care of our "Isaacs" after we leave this life to go Home. Alleluia!

Saturday, July 7, 2007
Genesis 27, 1-5,15-29
Jacob's Deception

The blessing! Isaac, who had favored his son Esau, the older of the twins, was now being deceived by his son, Jacob. Tragically, his mother, Rebekah, had planned this deception and Jacob consented.

The seeds of bitterness over the behavior of Esau were sprouting. Esau had shown contempt for his birthright, preferring a hot bowl of savory lentil stew, instead.

Also, Esau had married a Hittite woman. This was a source of great displeasure to both Isaac and Rebekah.

Jacob, although not the first-born, was given his father's blessing. This was the solemn, beautiful, powerful blessing of Jacob, as he was dying.

Lord Jesus, thank you for continually pouring your blessing upon us. We don't have to struggle, to compete, or to connive to receive your blessing. We are free to thank you by obeying you and serving others in truth and with humility. Alleluia!

Sunday, July 8, 2007 Fourteenth Sunday in Ordinary Time
Isaiah 66, 10-14
Mother Zion

Stop mourning over Jerusalem. Instead, rejoice!

"As a mother comforts her child, so I will comfort you; you shall be comforted in Jerusalem (v. 13)." Jerusalem.

Jerusalem will be powerful and prosperous. Nourishment and consolation will again flow from Jerusalem.

Lord Jesus, thank you that we will rejoice in the heavenly Jerusalem. Your saving power will at last be fully manifested in your servants. Alleluia!

Monday, July 9, 2007
Genesis 28, 10-22
Jacob's Dream at Bethel

Fleeing from Esau, his outraged brother, Jacob camped one night at a shrine. As he slept with a stone for a pillow, the Lord appeared to him. The Lord assured Jacob of his presence, his protection, and the fulfillment of his promises.

Jacob, upon awakening, realized that he had been in the presence of the living God. " ' Surely the LORD is in this place – and I did not know it (v. 16)!' "

Jacob poured oil on the stone and named the shrine Bethel. He vowed to give a tenth of all he had to God.

Lord Jesus, thank you that you are with us at all times. Thank you for the times when we experience your presence in special ways. Thank you for the times when we feel nothing. You are with us and that's all that matters. Alleluia!

> Tuesday, July 10, 2007
> Genesis 32, 23-33
> Struggle with the Angel

En route to appease his furious brother Esau, Jacob had to contend with a heavenly being appearing to him in human form. That was a pivotal night in Jacob's life.

Until dawn, Jacob struggled with the angel, At last, the angel yielded to Jacob's fierce demand to be blessed.

The blessing! Jacob was big into getting blessings.

The angel changed Jacob's name. Israel!

Israel was to be the name of the feisty man who had dared to fight with God's angel. Before the dawn came, Jacob named that place Peniel. At Peniel, he had encountered God in a way that would alter his life forever.

Lord Jesus, you came to earth so we could see God face to face. You are the Lord and yet you desire us to be bold in coming to you. We are safe with you. You will not reject us. As we are en route to heaven, teach us what it means to wrestle with you in prayer. You want to take us

to a new level of trust in our relationship with you. Let us not be afraid, but launch out today into this new realm of prayer. Alleluia!

Wednesday, July 11, 2007 St. Benedict
Genesis 41, 55-57; 42, 5-7,17-24
Pharaoh's Dream; The Brothers' First Journey to Egypt

Joseph, who had been cooped up in a desert cistern and then cooped up in Pharaoh's prison, was now the one who was opening the cities of Egypt and distributing grain during the famine. He was living out the interpretation of Pharaoh's unusual dream (Genesis 41, 1-32).

Joseph's brothers, who had mocked his dreams and tried to kill him, now traveled from Canaan to Egypt to kneel before him and to beg for bread. Joseph, who loved his brothers, must have remembered other dreams, his own prophetic dreams of old which had now come true (Genesis 37, 5-11). Overcome with emotion, he wept.

Lord Jesus, your word to us will come true, no matter how long we have been cooped up in various pits. Let us trust you and do your will during what seems to be a time of captivity. Let us not waste this time of enclosure. We are enclosed within your will. You will lead us out, at the right time, to open your blessings to others. Alleluia!

Thursday, July 12, 2007
Genesis 44, 18-21,23-29; 45, 1-15
Final Test; The Truth Revealed

"Then Joseph could no longer control himself before all those who stood by him, and he cried out, 'Send everyone away from me.' So no one stayed with him when Joseph made himself known to his brothers. And he wept so loudly that the Egyptians heard it, and the household of Pharaoh heard it. Joseph said to his brothers, 'I am Joseph. I am your brother, Joseph whom you sold into Egypt. And now do not be distressed or angry with yourselves, because you sold me here; for God sent me before you to preserve life. So it was not you who sent me here, but God ... (Genesis 45, 1-4b,5,8a)."

Joseph wept as he revealed his identity to his astonished brothers. The annoying little pipsqueak of a brother, who had dreamed unusual dreams, was now in charge of their very lives. Knowing their guilt, the brothers were, of course, very frightened.

Joseph wept over his brothers. He even told them not to worry about what they had done to him.

Joseph now had the larger picture, the broader perspective. Joseph could now see that it was God who had permitted it all. God was going to use Joseph to save the lives of many people, including the members of his own family.

Lord Jesus, when we rail against circumstances and feel victimized, let us remember that you are still in charge. Let us trust you to bring good out of these difficult times. Thank you for giving us a larger perspective and using us to be a blessing for others. Alleluia!

Friday, July 13, 2007 St. Henry
Genesis 46, 1-7, 28-30
Migration to Egypt

The elderly Jacob had one more journey to accomplish. The Lord told him to take all his family and migrate to Egypt.

It was in Goshen that Jacob was reunited with his beloved son, Joseph. Joseph was not lost after all!

Peace had come at last to the old man. Joseph, his son, was alive.

Lord Jesus, it's so hard to watch old people suffer, especially when they suffer because of family misunderstandings. Help us to learn to honor the elderly instead of avoiding them. Let us treat them with respect and affection as they make their last journey. Alleluia!

Saturday, July 14, 2007 Blessed Kateri Tekakwitha
Genesis 49, 29-32; 50, 15-26
Farewell and Death; Plea for Forgiveness; Death of Joseph

With their aged father Jacob buried, Joseph's brothers, to save their own skin, said that Jacob had charged them to entreat Joseph to forgive them for their cruel treatment. Again, Joseph wept.

"Joseph wept when they [his brothers] spoke to him. Then his brothers also wept, fell down before him, and said, 'We are here as your slaves.' But Joseph said to them, 'Do not be afraid! Am I in the place of God? Even though you intended to do harm to me, God intended it for good … (Genesis 50, 17,18)."

Joseph was clearly in a new place in his relationship with God and with his family. He acknowledged that his brothers had intended evil against him, but that God had another plan.

God had eventually worked it all out for good. Before he died, Joseph reassured his brothers that God would continue to care for them.

Lord Jesus, thank you for reworking and reweaving what has happened to us in the past. Thank you for the good that is coming forth and will continue to come forth! We give you thanks and praise for our future. Alleluia!

Sunday, July 15, 2007 Fifteenth Sunday in Ordinary Time
Deuteronomy 30, 10-14
Mercy for the Repentant; God's Commands Clear

God's commands are near and clear. They are written in the depths of our hearts.

Lord Jesus, thank you for helping us to say yes to you and thus to say yes to ourselves. Help us when we are afraid to obey, fearing loss. You are not trying to deprive us of anything that is good for us. Let us speak out and live out your beautiful plan for our lives. Alleluia!

Monday, July 16, 2007 Our Lady of Mount Carmel
Exodus 1, 8-14,22
The Oppression; Command to the Midwives

Tyrants cannot abide freedom. They are terrified of all who obey God. Tyrants, such as Pharaoh, become frantic when their power is threatened.

The people of God continued to survive even in their captivity in Egypt. The brave Hebrew midwives defied Pharaoh by refusing to kill the newborn Hebrew boys. God honored the midwives for protecting the babies.

Lord Jesus, we need spiritual midwives today. We need people who will assist the doomed to live and to fulfill your purpose for their lives. Thank you for sending us spiritual midwives to bring to birth your plans. Alleluia!

Tuesday, July 17, 2007
Exodus 2, 1-15
Birth and Adoption of Moses; Moses' Flight to Midian

The mother. The sister. The daughter. God used these three women to save Moses, who would save the Israelites.

Moses' mother must have prayed as she carefully placed her beautiful, three month old baby boy into his little ark on the river bank. Moses' sister carefully watched over her little baby brother.

Pharaoh's daughter had a heart of compassion for the crying infant. She arranged for his care and later adopted him, in spite of her father's hatred of the Israelites and his directives to kill the male infants at birth.

Lord Jesus, thank you for these three brave women who protected Moses and his ultimate vocation. Thank you for all who seek to protect life. Let vocations otherwise doomed be spared and protected in order to fulfill your will. Alleluia!

Wednesday, July 18, 2007 St. Camillus de Lellis
Exodus 3, 1-6,9-12
The Burning Bush; The Call of Moses

Horeb. Horeb was the mountain where Moses, the shepherd who had led the flock belonging to his father-in-law over the desert, saw the bush ablaze with the fiery presence of God.

Horeb. Horeb would be the mountain where Moses and God's people would worship God after Moses had led them out of their slavery in Egypt.

Instead of shepherding the sheep of his father-in-law, the Midianite priest named Jethro, Moses would shepherd the sheep belonging to Almighty God. These people belonged to God and God had chosen Moses to lead them to freedom.

The time had come. God was calling on Moses to act. Ready or not, Moses was God's choice for this vocation.

Lord Jesus, you are our Good Shepherd and our Great High Priest. Thank you for leading us through the deserts of today to the mountain where we will worship you in freedom. Alleluia!

Thursday, July 19, 2007
Exodus 3, 13-20
The Call of Moses

A journey from a land of misery to a new land of sweetness, a land of honey and milk. That was the journey that God had planned for the Israelites.

God knew this would not be a journey readily endorsed by the cruel king of Egypt. It would take God's awesome power to force the king to release God's people.

Nevertheless, this was the journey that had to be made in order for God's people to live in freedom and abundance. Moses, in spite of his awareness of his own inadequacy, was assured of God's presence for this mission.

Lord Jesus, we are on a journey whether we realize it or not. Since our baptism, you have called us and led us to continue to travel the road which leads back to you. Free us from the shackles we choose for the sake of cowardice or comfort. Forgive us and free us to travel with joyful hearts on this holy ground. Alleluia!

Friday, July 20, 2007
Exodus 11, 10 - 12, 14
Tenth Plague; The Death of the Firstborn;
The Passover Ritual Prescribed

Eat and run! The time had come for the Israelites to get out of Egypt.

After the Passover meal, the Israelites were to hasten out of Egypt. God was about to execute a terrible judgment.

The blood of the Passover lamb would be a sign that God, as he judged the Egyptians, would pass over his own people. They would be spared.

Lord Jesus, thank you that you are our Passover Lamb. You have made it possible for God not only to pass over our sins, but actually to dissolve them in your Precious Blood. Let us rejoice as we continue to celebrate this feast. Alleluia!

Saturday, July 21, 2007 St. Lawrence of Brindisi
Exodus 12, 37-42
Departure from Egypt

The Lord was keeping vigil. The Lord was watching over his people. The Lord was doing what was necessary to bring his beloved people into freedom.

We become exhausted when we think we are the only ones responsible. We seem to work and worry and wait to no avail.

"... I have labored in vain, I have spent my strength for nothing ... yet surely my cause is with the LORD, and my reward with my God (Isaiah 49, 3-4)."

The Lord is watching over us. The Lord is watching out for us. Let us trust the Lord, obey the Lord, and see a mighty deliverance.

Lord Jesus, your ways are mysterious. We wonder why you do things in strange and wonderful ways. Quiet our agitated spirits. Let us learn to wait for you, keep vigil for you, and discern your voice. Let us hasten to follow you, perhaps on very short notice, when you call us. Alleluia!

Sunday, July 22, 2007 Sixteenth Sunday in Ordinary Time
Genesis 18, 1-10
Abraham's Visitors

The Lord came to Abraham's tent home one hot day. Abraham was simply sitting by a tree right outside his tent.

The Lord comes to us wherever we are. We are being sought out by our loving Lord.

The Lord is coming to give us a gift. Being in the Lord's presence is the greatest gift.

The Lord is coming to give us a message. We don't have to be afraid. The Lord has good in store for us.

Lord Jesus, let us be eager to serve all who come to us today. Thank you for the gift of your presence. Alleluia!

Monday, July 23, 2007 St. Bridget of Sweden
Exodus 14, 5-18
Toward the Red Sea; Crossing of the Red Sea

Approaching freedom, the Israelites panicked! Slavery in Egypt, terrible though it had been, was at least familiar. They saw death in the parched desert as their only option.

No! Moses had heard from the Lord and knew what to say to the terrified people.

They were instructed not to give in to fear. They were to stay the course and watch God win the victory for them.

Lord Jesus, sometimes we see our options in very limited ways. We give in to complaining, fear, and ultimately unbelief. Thank you for strengthening us today to learn to stand still, to thank you in advance for your deliverance, and then to march forward in the triumph you have won for us. Alleluia!

> Tuesday, July 24, 2007
> Exodus 14, 21 - 15, 1
> Crossing of the Red Sea; Destruction of the Sinners

The Lord knows how to deal with our opponents. We don't need to worry about that. A mere glance from the Lord caused the furious Egyptians to panic.

Our responsibility is to follow the Lord through our own Red Sea. The turbulent waters will part. We are safe!

Lord Jesus, we sing your praise for delivering us from sin. We sing your praise for leading us into a new land. Alleluia!

> Wednesday, July 25, 2007
> 2 Corinthians 4, 7-15
> The Paradox of the Ministry

"We are afflicted in every way, but not crushed; perplexed, but not driven to despair; persecuted, but not forsaken, struck down, but not destroyed; always carrying in the body the death of Jesus, so that the life of Jesus may also be made visible in our bodies … because we know that the one who raised the Lord Jesus will raise us also with Jesus, and will bring us with you into his presence (vv. 8-10,14)."

The same power that raised Jesus from the dead is flowing through us. It is crucial remember this when we experience suffering in our ministry.

Although we carry the death of Jesus within us, we also carry his life within us. We will experience the resurrection of our bodies and live forever with Jesus, our Lord.

Lord Jesus, you were sent to earth to accomplish the plan of your loving Father. Help us to remember that we are here on earth to fulfill your purposes. Let us rejoice, even in the midst of all our suffering, knowing that you have already won the victory for us. Thank you that your life flowing through us today! Alleluia!

Thursday, July 26, 2007 Sts. Joachim and Anne
Exodus 19, 1-2,9-11,16-20
Arrival in Sinai; The Great Epiphany

A cloud! The Lord chose to appear to Moses within a cloud. The Israelites were learning to respect and to trust Moses as well as the Lord.

With lightening, thunder, cloud, smoke, and trumpet blasts, the Lord spoke with Moses. The people kept their distance.

Lord Jesus, thank you that we may speak with you at any time. We do not have to keep our distance. You are with us at all times. Let us today confide in you all our concerns. Let your light shine in us and through us. Alleluia!

Friday, July 27, 2007
Exodus 20, 1-17
The Ten Commandments

Power! With great power, Lord rescued the Israelites out of slavery in Egypt and led them into the promised land. The Lord, to protect them in their new land, instructed them how to live.

Lord Jesus, thank you that you came to show, as well as to tell. You showed us how to live. Let our lives show forth your love and your power. Alleluia!

Saturday, July 28, 2007
Exodus 24, 3-8
Ratification of the Covenant

Moses " ... rose early in the morning, and built an altar at the foot of the mountain, and set up twelve pillars, corresponding to the twelve tribes of Israel (v. 4b)

The altar! The altar at the base of Mount Sinai was supported by twelve pillars. All the twelve tribes of Israel were acknowledged as part of the covenant.

Lord Jesus, thank you for the twelve tribes of Israel, the twelve apostles, and all your faithful ones who serve you in the Church. Thank you for the altar where we receive your Body and Blood. Thank you for your steadfast love as you continue to give yourself to us. Thank you that one day we will feast with you at another table, a table in heaven, at your wedding supper, the supper of the Lamb. Alleluia!

Sunday, July 29, 2007 Seventeenth Sunday Ordinary Time
Genesis 18, 20-32
Abraham Intercedes for Sodom

When we are feeling desperate about the state of our country and the state of the world, we do well to remember Abraham. Abraham boldly questioned God.

Abraham approached God and asked, "... will you indeed sweep away the righteous with the wicked? Far be it from you to do such a thing, to slay the righteous with the wicked, so that the righteous fare as the wicked! Far be that from you! Shall not the Judge of all the earth do what is just (vv. 23-25)?"

Abraham zeroed in on God, specifically the justice of God. How on earth could God, the Supreme Justice of the universe, not act out of justice?

Lord Jesus, we give up too easily. You long for us to pray with compassion, boldness, and persistence. Let us come boldly to you and pray, as you lead us, for the world. Let your kingdom come and let your glorious will be done right here on earth. Alleluia!

Monday, July 30, 2007 St. Peter Chrysologus
Exodus 32, 15-24, 30-34
The Golden Calf; The Atonement

An inappropriate response to what seems to be a delay on God's part may lead to great sin. It is a sign of presumption and of lack of trust in God.

The people of Israel grew tired of waiting for Moses to return from the mountain. Moses was meeting with GOD!

Why couldn't they wait? Why can't we wait?

Instead, the Israelites committed idolatry. One sin led to another. Aaron, the priest, instead of leading the people to continue to trust God and to wait, spinelessly yielded to their pressure (Exodus 32, 1-6).

The result? A golden calf. When confronted by Moses, Aaron blamed the people.

What a mess! Moses minced no words as he confronted the people with their sin.

Nevertheless, Moses pleaded with God to forgive them. Moses even offered to be removed from God's book if that was necessary to save the people.

Lord Jesus, forgive us when we commit idolatry and then blame others. Thank you for having made atonement for us. Let us learn to trust you and to wait. You are never late. You will never disappoint us. Alleluia!

> Tuesday, July 31, 2007 St. Ignatius Loyola
> Exodus 33, 7-11; 34, 5-9,28
> Moses' Intimacy with God; Renewal of the Tablets;
> Radiance of Moses' Face

The people stayed at a distance while Moses was in God's presence. The Lord spoke with Moses in a direct way.

The covenant was renewed. God's compassion was greater than the people's sin.

Lord Jesus, thank you that we may come and speak with you at any time. You are with us always. You invite us to speak with you as our friend. Thank you for your tender love and mercy. Let us learn to trust in you and in your faithfulness. Alleluia!

> Wednesday, August 1, 2007 St. Alphonsus Liguori
> Exodus 34, 29-35
> Radiance of Moses' Face

Knowledge that Moses had been in close, personal contact with God produced great awe in the Israelites. The very face of Moses had become shining and radiant from having been in God's presence. Moses was unaware of this, but others were very much aware of it.

When we pray and seek God, we are transformed, whether we realize it or not. We are transformed whether others realize it or not. All that matters is that God shines forth into our world!

Lord Jesus, you are the light of the world. You even told us that we are the light of the world. Heal us as you shine forth in us and purify us of all darkness. Heal others as you shine forth through us. All glory to you, Lord Jesus Christ. Alleluia!

Thursday, August 2, 2007 St. Eusebius of Vercelli
Exodus 40, 16-21,34-38
Erection of the Dwelling; God's Presence in the Dwelling

Jesus promised to send the Holy Spirit to be with us and to be within us, to teach us and to guide us (John 14, 16,17,28; John 16, 12). This means that it is possible for GOD to dwell within us!

We are learning to listen to the Holy Spirit. We are learning to think, to speak, and to act as the Holy Spirit directs us.

We may initially think that it was easier for the Israelites. After all, all they had to do was to observe the tent where God's presence dwelt. When the cloud over the tent moved, they moved. If the cloud did not move, they stayed put.

Through the cloud, signifying God's presence by day, and the fire, signifying God's presence by night, the Israelites were guided. All the people saw the cloud. All the people saw the fire. God was guiding each person in each and every part of the journey.

Lord Jesus, thank you for the presence of the Holy Spirit to be with us and to be within us to lead us. Let us grow today in our ability to discern the voice of the Holy Spirit and then to move accordingly. Alleluia!

Friday, August 3, 2007
Leviticus 23, 1,4-11,15-16,21
Passover; Pentecost; The Day of Atonement

The Lord commanded celebration! The Israelites were to stop their work, assemble as a community, and celebrate the feasts of Passover, Unleavened Bread, and Pentecost.

The Lord also commanded the Israelites to observe, with great solemnity, the Day of Atonement. They were to stop their ordinary work, to practice self-denial, and to make an offering to the Lord.

Lord Jesus, thank you that there is a time for feasting and a time for fasting. Let us learn to practice self-denial and to fast as you direct us. Let us also learn to celebrate. Thank you that we, as your followers, may look forward with great joy to the marriage supper of the Lamb. Alleluia!

Saturday, August 4, 2007 St. John Vianney
Leviticus 25, 1,8-17
The Sabbatical Year; The Jubilee Year

Sabbatical. Jubilee!

These very words lift our weary spirits. Rest! Even the land itself was to rest during the sabbatical year.

We may not be able to have a sabbatical year in the traditional sense, but we are still able to have a sabbatical once a week. The sabbath is a gift for us to enjoy. Jesus even told us that the sabbath was made for us.

The blare of the trumpet on the Day of Atonement during the year of jubilee announced liberty for all. Not one year out of fifty, but every moment of every day we may celebrate our liberty in the Lord. We revere the Lord and deal honorably with all.

Lord Jesus, we come to you for our sabbatical. We are tired. You are our sabbatical. We come to you for our jubilee. You offer us true freedom. You have set us free from all slavery. We are free to live, to love, and to serve. Thank you for our sabbatical. Thank you for our jubilee. Alleluia!

Sunday, August 5, 2007 Eighteenth Sunday Ordinary Time
Ecclesiastes 1, 2; 2, 21-23
Vanity of Toil without Profit; To Others the Profit

This passage would be a real downer without the light of Christ. The writer laments the futility of it all. Work hard. Others get your stuff. Bummer. Life is the pits.

The writer clearly believes in God and in serving God, but does not yet have a complete understanding of the mercy and justice of God. The parable of the workers in the vineyard, told by Jesus, sheds light on the dilemma of the obvious inequalities and injustices we all see in this life (Matthew 20, 1-16).

Lord Jesus, even now we sometimes get discouraged and maybe even fall into despair. We work hard and everything seems to fall apart. Injustice is everywhere. Life is a mess. Today, during our sabbath, thank you for reminding us that you have conquered all the stuff that bothers us. You lived for God. You died for us. You rose again so that we could live in triumph. Let us breathe in the fresh air of Easter. Let us live today in the light of your victory over life and over death. Glory to you! Alleluia!

Monday, August 6, 2007 Transfiguration of the Lord
Daniel 7, 9-10,13-14
Vision of the Four Beasts

Daniel, in a dream, was given a glimpse into the heavenly realm. The throne of God. The Everlasting God, clothed in dazzling white!

Blazing purity. Countless worshippers before the throne of God.

Clouds! Then, in the clouds, another, the One we call Jesus!

Not only Son of God, but also, even more wonderfully and mysteriously, the Son of Man. God granted to Jesus sovereignty over all.

Lord Jesus, we have no idea who you really are. We know you as the baby in Bethlehem, the teacher, the healer, the suffering servant of God, and the crucified and risen Christ. You are truly our representative before God. We did not elect you. Rather, God chose you to represent us. Give us a glimpse today into your heavenly realm. Let us live today knowing that you long to lead us into a deeper understanding of this realm, our true Home. Alleluia!

Tuesday, August 7, 2007 St. Sixtus and Companions;
St. Cajetan
Numbers 12, 1-13
Jealousy of Aaron and Miriam

God knows how to deal with those who rebel against those in leadership. GOD chose Moses. Moses was not perfect, but he was still God's choice to lead the Israelites out of Egypt.

Aaron and Miriam, Moses' siblings, each had important ministries to fulfill. Aaron was called to priestly ministry (Exodus 28, 1). Miriam's was called to prophetic ministry (Exodus 16, 20).

Moses himself was incredibly humble. He did not have an exalted opinion about his own importance. After all, he was reluctant to answer God's call in the first place, according to Exodus 3 and Exodus 4.

God did not and does not tolerate rebellion against legitimate authority. God alone knows the best place for us in the vineyard, the best way to promote us, and, if necessary, the best way to vindicate us.

Lord Jesus, let us be content to serve you in the way you know is best. Lead us into the work you have for us to do. Let us rejoice in our relationship with you. Alleluia!

Wednesday, August 8, 2007 St. Dominic
Numbers 13, 1-2,25; 14, 1,26-29,34-35
The Twelve Scouts; Their Return; The Lord's Sentence

Die in the desert or enter the promised land?! How could the Israelites even hesitate?

They had seen their mighty God in action. They had Moses and other leaders to guide them.

So, what happened? Fear. Doubt. Unbelief. Lack of trust in God. Complaining.

Only two of the twelve who were sent on the reconnaissance mission brought back an accurate account. Caleb and Joshua reported to Moses and to the whole community about their exploration of the new land.

The land of honey and milk also had great big grapes. However, the people did seem ferocious and the towns were large and heavily protected. Still, Caleb and Joshua recommended taking the land.

The nay sayers won the battle, but lost the land. By their doom saying, they kept themselves and the people out of the very land the Lord had promised.

The Lord basically said, "OK, have it your way. Just die in the desert." The Lord had had enough of their complaining.

Lord Jesus, you are with us and you want us to disregard the giants and enter boldly into the land of your promise. You are with us. We acknowledge our fear, but we choose not to follow our fear. We follow you into this new realm of trust. Who knows where you will lead us! We are ready for a new adventure with you. Alleluia!

Thursday, August 9, 2007 St. Teresa Benedicta of the Cross
(Edith Stein)
Numbers 20, 1-13
Death of Miriam; Water Famine at Kadish;
Sin of Moses and Aaron

Moses and Aaron didn't even bother initially to try to respond to the people's griping about the lack of water. Instead, wisely, Moses and Aaron went immediately to the Lord. They lay prostrate before the Lord.

It was the Lord who had called them to this task of leadership. Only the Lord could direct them. They understood that. So far, so good.

The Lord told Moses to gather the people. Moses and Aaron were to tell the rock to yield water for the thirsty people and animals.

Instead, Moses spoke with anger to the people. He disobeyed God. Instead of speaking to the rock and trusting God to release the water, he whacked the rock twice with his staff.

Water did indeed flow form the rock for the benefit of the people and their animals. However, Moses did not do God's work God's way.

Because Moses and Aaron did not behave in a way that manifested the holiness of God, God told them that they would not lead the people into the land.

Just because we are called to a certain work, we still can't take matters into our own hands. We are called to holiness. We are called to strict obedience.

Lord Jesus, you call us to behave in a way that honors you. Having fits of temper does not honor you. Forgive us when we act out of our human exasperation. Help us to be still and ask you how to respond. Help us to think, to speak, and to act according to your plan. Alleluia!

Friday, August 10, 2007 St. Lawrence of Rome
2 Corinthians 9, 6-10
God's Indescribable Gift

It's OK. It's OK to give with the hope of being blessed. We don't have to feel super-spiritual in order to give.

God does look at our heart, but God also looks at our hands. Do we give?

Do we give, knowing that God loves us? Do we know that God is debtor to no one?

Lord Jesus, even if we have little to give, let us give with a joyful heart, knowing that we will be cared for and extravagantly rewarded by our wealthy Father in heaven. Alleluia!

Saturday, August 11, 2007 St. Clare
Deuteronomy 6, 4-13
The Great Commandment; Fidelity in Prosperity

What the Lord requires is to be put first. The Lord is to be first in our minds, in our hearts, and on our lips.

We are free to enjoy the gifts of the Lord. The Lord generously gave the Israelites the houses, cities, cisterns, vineyards and olive trees of their new land.

Enjoy! But don't forget the Lord who made it all possible. Don't forget the Lord who delivered you from slavery. Serve the Lord. Worship the Lord.

Lord Jesus, when we learn how to worship, we will know how to serve. Teach us today how to begin to live out our gratitude. Alleluia!

Sunday, August 12, 2007 Nineteenth Sunday in Ordinary Time
Wisdom 18, 6-9
Fifth Example: Death of the Egyptian Firstborn;
The Israelites are Spared

Wait! The Lord's people had to wait.

They had to wait until the Lord's time came to render justice. They had to trust and to wait until they were rescued and their enemies were destroyed.

Lord Jesus, when we wait in secret for you to act, give us courage. Let us live sacrificial lives of trust, knowing that you are sovereign. Alleluia!

Monday, August 13, 2007 Sts. Pontian and Hippolytus
Deuteronomy 10, 12-22
The Lord's Majesty

"So now, O Israel, what does the LORD your God require of you? Only to fear the LORD your God, to walk in all his ways, to love him, to serve the LORD your God with all your heart and with all your soul, and to keep the commandments of the LORD your God and his decrees that I am commanding you today, for your own well-being (vv. 12-14)."

From the heights of the heavens to the tiniest of microorganisms, all belong to God. Angels and ants. Stars, sun, and moon. Truly, as the old hymn proclaims, "This Is My Father's World."

We are free to contemplate our mighty God and the beautiful world made by God. We are free to respond in love and service.

We learn a little at a time to love and to serve. Caring for widows, orphans, and aliens is important to God and therefore important to us.

Lord Jesus, thank you for leaving the glory of heaven to come to us. You are our example in loving and serving. You lived the truth and spoke the truth. You ministered as your heavenly Father directed you. Let us listen to the Holy Spirit and go forth to love and to serve today. Alleluia!

> Tuesday, August 14, 2007 St. Maximilian Kolbe
> Deuteronomy 31, 1-8
> The Lord's Leadership; Calling of Joshua

Take courage! The Lord is with us and goes before us. Therefore, we are to be courageous.

Moses declared to the people, " 'I am now one hundred twenty years old. I am no longer able to get about …. The LORD your God himself will cross over before you (vv. 2,3a).' "

Moses, at an advanced age, was preparing the people for his departure. He would not be there to cross the Jordan into the promised land. Joshua had been chosen for that task.

Before all the Israelites, Moses commissioned Joshua to lead the people. He reminded Joshua that the Lord would be with him and would go before him.

Lord Jesus, thank you that you are with us and that you go before us. You will not fail us. Help us to march bravely and confidently through this day with its joys and its trials. Thank you for the day when we will cross Jordan and be Home. Alleluia!

> Wednesday, August 15, 2007
> The Assumption of the Blessed Virgin Mary
> Revelation 11, 19; 12, 1-6,10
> The Two Witnesses; The Woman and the Dragon

Amidst all the drama of this passage, a quiet reassurance reigns. God is in charge. God reigns.

Years ago, I asked my young son, Christopher, who was fascinated by the book of the Revelation, "Well, what do you think this book is all about? What does it mean?" Christopher answered quietly, "It's very simple. It means, 'God wins.'"

Lord Jesus Christ, we do not have to go into an apocalyptic angst or become theological pretzels trying to figure out this book. You are the victor! We rest in your victory and trust in you. Alleluia!

> Thursday, August 16, 2007 St. Stephen of Hungary
> Joshua 3, 7-11,13-17
> Preparations for Crossing the Jordan; The Crossing Begun

The priests waited until everyone had crossed the Jordan. They went before the people, carrying the ark of the Lord's covenant.

When the soles of the priests' feet touched the Jordan River, the water stopped flowing. Standing still on dry land, the priests waited until all the people had crossed into their new land.

Lord Jesus, thank you that you are our Great High Priest. You went before us and you wait for us. You wait for us to realize that you made it possible for us to cross over into a new life. Thank you for the waters of our baptism. You are calling us to live today in the freedom you died to give us. Alleluia!

> Friday, August 17, 2007
> Joshua 24, 1-13
> Reminder of the Divine Goodness

Through Joshua, God gave all the people of Israel a history lesson, a summary of divine guidance, provision, and protection. Over and over, God delivered the people. God provided a land filled with vineyards and olive trees. How good God was and still is!

Lord Jesus, when we feel frightened and out of control, thank you for reminding us that you are in control. We place our trust in you to continue to guide us Home. Alleluia!

> Saturday, August 18, 2007
> Joshua 24, 14-29
> Renewal of the Divine Goodness;
> Renewal of the Covenant; Death of Joshua

Joshua, Moses' successor, continued to address the people about their relationship with the Lord. They were challenged to serve the Lord wholeheartedly.

If the people chose not to serve the Lord, then they should decide about the object of their worship. Joshua and his own household were firmly committed to serving the Lord. As he affirmed, "… as for me and my household, we will serve the LORD (v. 15)."

The people also solemnly vowed to serve the Lord. With a book of statutes and a stone as a silent witness, a covenant was made.

Lord Jesus, thank you for helping us when we knowingly or unknowingly serve other gods, gods of convenience, lust, or power. Forgive us. We return to you to cleanse us and to heal us. Thank you that you forgive us. Thank you for the gift of the sacrament of reconciliation. Let us trust you with all our needs and desires and serve you with all our hearts. Alleluia!

Sunday, August 19, 2007 Twentieth Sunday in Ordinary Time
Jeremiah 38, 4-6,8-10
Jeremiah in the Muddy Cistern

Speak the truth and get thrown into the mud. That's what happened to the prophet, Jeremiah, who dared to speak forth God's word. The fearful king allowed his underlings to mistreat God's prophet.

An Ethiopian, Ebed-melech, in the palace hierarchy, came to Jeremiah's aid. He told the king about the prophet's plight. The king then authorized Jeremiah's release.

Lord Jesus, thank you that you are higher in authority than anyone on earth. You know the times when we have spoken the truth and then suffered. You know how and when to release us and to vindicate us. Let us not fear those who are driven by fear. Let us rejoice in You! You lead us, by grace, into freedom. Alleluia!

Monday, August 20, 2007 St. Bernard
Judges 2, 11-19
Infidelities of the Israelites

This generation of Israelites did not truly understand, for themselves, what the Lord had done for their ancestors. The Lord had delivered their ancestors out of slavery in Egypt. The Lord had provided a land of promise.

This generation of Israelites, in effect, abandoned the Lord and served pagan gods. The Lord allowed disasters to befall them.

Then the judges provided by the Lord would deliver the people. However, the people persisted in refusing to follow the judges.

On and on it went. There was no real change of heart.

Lord Jesus, thank you that you allow us, both individually and as a people, to learn of our need of your saving power. Help us to be quick to acknowledge our sins, to receive forgiveness, and to continue to serve you. Alleluia!

> Tuesday, August 21, 2007 St. Pius X
> Judges 6, 11-24
> The Call of Gideon

Gideon, who did not exactly have a Ph.D. in self-esteem, was going about his chores when the Lord's angelic messenger came to him. Gideon, who saw himself as a basic wimp from not the best family, was nevertheless chosen by the Lord God to rescue Israel.

Gideon, of all people! God seems to enjoy calling the most unlikely people for the most amazing missions.

"… God chose what is foolish in the world to shame the wise; God chose what is weak in the world to shame the strong; God chose what is low and despised in the world, things that are not, to reduce to nothing things that are, so that no one might boast in the presence of God (1 Corinthians 1, 27,28)."

The Lord began by reassuring Gideon of his presence. The Lord even called Gideon "…thou mighty man of valour (Judges 6, 12 KJV)."

Gideon basically answered, "Yeah, well, if the Lord is with us, why are we abandoned to these Midianite meanies who make our lives so miserable?" The old question we all ask: "Why?"

Israel had committed idolatry, that's why, in this case. But the Lord did not bring up that indelicate truth at this time.

The Lord told Gideon to go in the strength that he currently had to rescue Israel from the Midianites. Gideon didn't think a lot of his own strength, but that's what the Lord said to do. The Lord reassured Gideon of his presence.

Gideon decided to ask for extra reassurance that all this was really from the Lord. The Lord put up with this and did as Gideon requested.

When, at last, Gideon was convinced that he was hearing from the Lord, he became alarmed. He realized that he had actually been in the presence of an angel.

Graciously, the Lord gave to Gideon the gift of peace. "Peace be unto thee; fear not: thou shalt not die (Judges 6, 23 KJV)." Gideon constructed an altar which referred to the Lord as Jehovah-Shalom which means "The Lord is peace."

Lord Jesus, some of us still struggle with feelings of deep inferiority. We do not see ourselves as you see us. We find it hard to believe that you care for us and that you have a special work for us. You call us to humility, but not to self-loathing. You want us to love and accept ourselves. You know how to help us. You see us and you know all about us. You can use as we are right now to accomplish a particular work. We thank you and we are excited about serving you. You know what you're doing with our lives. You see us as mighty champions! Alleluia!

Wednesday, August 22, 2007 Queenship of Mary
Judges 9, 6-15
Gideon's Son Abimelech

Who me? Give up anything in order to serve others? Bummer!

The olive tree would have to relinquish its golden oil. The fig tree would have to give up its sweetness. The vine would have to give up its grapes which offer cheer.

Why? Why give anything up?

Do we bargain with God? Do we fear that, if we do give anything up for God's service, that we will suffer or lack anything?

Abimelech became king, yes, but in the wrong way. He killed all but one of his many brothers in order to promote himself.

The survivor, Jothan, challenged all of Israel about their selection of king. Then, Jothan, having delivered this cryptic message, departed.

There is a price to be paid, a sacrifice to offer, for the privilege of leadership. The three trees in Jothan's story knew what would be required for the task of leadership. Their very essence would be required.

Lord Jesus, we want to keep everything and then serve you in our own way. Help us today to release into your hands the oil, the figs, and the grapes. Let us give up to you whatever holds us back from being given over completely to your service. We give you the very essence of our being to transform and to use in your service. Alleluia!

> Thursday, August 23, 2007 St. Rose of Lima
> Judges 11, 29-39
> Jepthah's Vow

STUPID! What a stupid vow Jepthah made.

I know we are not living in that ancient culture, but to vow to offer another human being as a sacrifice to God?! How barbaric. How utterly stupid.

Yes, the Lord did give Israel's enemies, the Ammonites, into Jepthah's hands. Yes, Jepthah did fulfill his rash vow to sacrifice as a burnt offering the first person who met him from the battle. This person was his own daughter, his only child.

Lord Jesus, thank you for healing our distorted views of God. Our attempts to bargain with God reveal the pathetic state of our spiritual lives. You came to show us what God is really like. Let us learn from you how to serve God with intelligent reverence. Let us learn from you how to serve others. Alleluia!

> Friday, August 24, 2007 St. Bartholomew
> Revelation 21, 9-14
> The New Jerusalem

"Then one the seven angels ... said to me, "Come, I will show you the bride, the wife of the Lamb (v. 9)."

Holy. Radiant. A pure bride. This is the way the Church will be.

Lord Jesus, you are the Lamb of God. The Church is your bride. Thank you that you are our bridegroom, our true Love. Let us live in the purity you died to give us. Alleluia!

> Saturday, August 25, 2007 St. Louis' St. Joseph Calasanz
> Ruth 2, 1-3,8-11; 4, 13-17
> The Meeting; Boaz Marries Ruth

A divine connection! This was a matchmaking service straight from heaven.

It all came out of a tragedy. The tragedy of Naomi's widowhood and the loss of her sons was followed by the amazing graces given by God to Ruth, Naomi's loyal daughter-in-law.

Ruth! An outsider, a foreigner. And yet, Ruth, in her own grief, was the one to stay with Naomi.

Ruth was humble. She was content to glean wherever she could. This just happened to be in Bethlehem, in the barley field of Boaz.

All sorts of good things began to happen. Boaz knew of Ruth's devotion to Naomi, his kinswoman. Boaz was committed to caring for Ruth and protecting her.

This beautiful book closes with the marriage of Ruth and Boaz and the birth of their son. The neighbor women, rejoicing with Naomi, named this baby Obed. Obed was the future grandfather of King David.

Lord Jesus, some stories do have happy endings and even happier new beginnings. Help us to expect divine connections today. Alleluia!

Sunday, August 26, 2007 Twenty-first Sunday in Ordinary Time
Isaiah 66, 18-21
Gathering of the Nations

This is not only a big picture. This is a huge picture!

God is so much bigger than we can imagine. God chooses people who would never be chosen otherwise. That way God receives all the glory!

Lord Jesus, we long for the heavenly Jerusalem. We long for the time when your kingdom will indeed come on this earth. Thank you for purifying us to be vessels to glorify you and to display your holiness. Alleluia!

Monday, August 27, 2007 St. Monica
1 Thessalonians 1, 1-5,8-10
Greeting; Thanksgiving for their Faith

Conversion! The Christians of Thessalonica turned from the worship of idols to the worship of the true God. Their belief was then translated into active service of the Lord.

Their belief was shown forth in their endurance and in their work. Their active faith was known everywhere.

Lord Jesus, thank you that we have the privilege of not only trusting in you but also the privilege of serving you. Show us how to love you by serving others today. Strengthen our hope in you and in the coming of your kingdom on earth. Forgive us, cleanse us, and purify us of anything that holds us back from serving you. Alleluia!

> Tuesday, August 28, 2007 St. Augustine
> 1 Thessalonians 2, 1-8
> Paul's Ministry Among Them

Paul was remarkably honest and transparent as he articulated his way of ministry. Although Paul and his ministry colleagues had suffered abusive treatment in another location, they were still willing to proclaim the Gospel in Thessalonica.

Paul and his companions knew that God had trusted them with speaking forth the Gospel. They were seeking to please God, who alone is able to discern the workings of the human heart.

The ministry attitude of Paul and his companions was one of humility, not one of haughtiness. They did not try to pull rank because of their status as apostles.

With gentleness and affection, they shared themselves as they proclaimed the Gospel. They were truly authentic.

Lord Jesus, thank you for purifying us so that we may be transparent carriers and transmitters of the Gospel. Prune us of all that is unbecoming to ministers of the Gospel. Let us not fear sharing ourselves with others. Alleluia!

> Wednesday, August 29, 2007 Martyrdom of St. John the Baptist
> 1 Thessalonians 2, 9-13
> Paul's Ministry Among Them; Further Thanksgiving

Paul reminded himself and the Thessalonians of all the efforts he and his companions had expended in ministry. He assured the Christians at Thessalonica that God's word was at work in them.

Lord Jesus, thank you that it's OK to acknowledge our hard work. Thank you that it is not responsibility to produce belief in others. It is our responsibility to live and proclaim the Gospel. Thank you that the Holy Spirit is at work in those among whom we work and for whom we pray. Alleluia!

Thursday, August 30, 2007
1 Thessalonians 3, 7-13
Paul's Recent Travel Plans; Concluding Thanksgiving and Prayer

"Is it well with the child (2 Kings 4, 26 KJV)?" That was the question the prophet Elisha posed to the Shunammite woman.

That is always the question burning in the heart of every loving parent, no matter the age of the child. Is it well with the child? Is it well with the children?

Paul was a truly loving father in Christ to the new Christians in Thessalonica. He loved them. He prayed for them. He yearned over them. He was almost a father-hen! In the midst of his own suffering, he was always concerned for them.

Paul was reassured that these new Christians were steadfast in their faith. They were still growing their faith. For his part, Paul remained constant in prayer for them and prayed to be able to see them again.

Lord Jesus, let us continue to trust and to be confident that you are working in the lives of those for whom we pray. We love them, but you love them even more. You know them better than we do and you know what is best for them. Let us do our part to pray, to love, and to serve. Let us then release them to you and rejoice in you. Alleluia!

Friday, August 31, 2007
1 Thessalonians 4, 1-8
General Exhortations; Holiness in Sexual Conduct

God's will is our holiness in all aspects of our lives. That was God's will for the Christians at Thessalonica and it is God's will for us.

Lord Jesus, thank you for the gift of the Holy Spirit to dwell within us. Let us learn to live in the joyful holiness to which we are called. Alleluia!

Saturday, September 1, 2007
1 Thessalonians 4, 9-11
Mutual Charity

Tranquility! Attending to your own business. Working with your own hands. Being independent in a healthy way. Paul's prescription for the Christians in the city of Thessalonica sounds like good medicine for us, too.

Lord Jesus, we are not tranquil when we are storming around trying to be in charge of everything. We are not in charge. You are. Teach us to live in love and simplicity. Alleluia!

Sunday, September 2, 2007
Twenty-second Sunday in Ordinary Time
Sirach 3, 17-18,20,28-29
Humility; Alms for the Poor

Lord Jesus, thank you for the Holy Spirit who is teaching us live in simplicity and humility. Help us not to try to figure everything out, but to relinquish all into your hands. Let us be attentive to you and merciful to others. Alleluia!

Monday, September 3, 2007 St. Gregory the Great
1 Thessalonians 4, 13-18
Hope for the Christian Departed

Perspective! We may get so caught up in the joys and sorrows of everyday life that we forget that all of this is temporary.

We are here on earth for such a short time. Earth is not our true home.

In this passage of Paul's letter to the Christians at Thessalonica, we have a glimpse into the heavenly realm. This amazing picture is complete with an archangels's voice, a blare of God's trumpet, and the actual descending of the Lord Jesus from heaven!

Those who died in Christ are rising first! Then, the believers still on earth are rising to meet them in the clouds. Can you imagine that meeting?

Lord Jesus, we do believe and trust that, just as you died and rose again, so will we. Everything is going to happen in the proper order and at just the right time. Let us live this day in fidelity to our present tasks and in joyful anticipation of your coming in glory. Alleluia!

Tuesday, September 4, 2007
1 Thessalonians 5, 1-6,9-11
Vigilance

Paul is encouraging the Christians in the city of Thessalonica to live in the light and to encourage one another. This is the way we are meant to live, also.

Live in the light of Christ! We are to live in a state of preparedness to meet the Lord at any time.

There are no guarantees in this world. There is a guarantee, however, of the Lord's constant presence with us. Whether or not we feel the Lord's presence does not matter so much. We may be sure that the Lord is with us, loving us, forgiving us, protecting us, and guiding us.

Let us remember to encourage one another! It is not so much the words we speak, but who we are. Yes. it's good to speak words of encouragement to each other, but it's even better to show forth our trust in the Lord by our lives.

Lord Jesus, it's so easy to get scared. This is a scary world. So many things are completely out of our control. Thank you that you are in control. Help us today to walk in the light of your love and goodness. Alleluia!

Wednesday, September 5, 2007 Blessed Teresa of Calcutta
Colossians 1, 1-8
Greetings; Thanksgiving

The Gospel bears fruit! The Gospel bears fruit in all the world. The Gospel is bearing fruit in you and in me, whether we realize it or not.

When we live for God, it is easy to become terribly discouraged. We see such need in the world. We realize our own inability to do very much. We are acutely aware of our own failings.

With the example of Blessed Mother Teresa, let us bravely do what we can. We are truly God's instruments of mercy.

Lord Jesus, thank you that you are at work in us and in the lives of all for whom we pray. Encourage us today and give us fresh hope and courage. Let us be gentle with ourselves and with others. Alleluia!

Thursday, September 6, 2007
Colossians 1, 9-14
Prayer for Continued Progress

Paul prayed that the Christians in the city of Colossae would truly know God's will. We pray this for ourselves, also.

What is God's will? God's will is for us to be sanctified, to be holy, to be pure (1 Thessalonians 4, 3). God's priority is our purity.

When we are pure, God's power may flow freely through us to others. Provision has already been made for our purity.

God, our loving heavenly Father, has removed us from the realm of darkness and planted us in the realm of Jesus, our Redeemer. This is a place of life and light.

Everyday, we are growing stronger as we grow in our knowledge of God. We are learning each day to live in a way that honors God. When we sin, we quickly acknowledge our sin, ask for and receive God's forgiveness, and then continue to love and to serve.

Lord Jesus, let us live this day with our chief desire being to please you. Thank you that you delight in us and you long to lead us closer to you. Alleluia!

Friday, September 7, 2007
Colossians 1, 15-20
His Person and Work

Identity. Vocation.

Who is Christ? What is his work?

His identity. GOD. He is God. He is a true image of God, an image we may see and understand. The invisible God became visible in Jesus. He shows us what God is like. We see what God is like when we read the Gospels.

A vocation of creation. Everything in heaven and on earth was created through Jesus and for Jesus. Everything is held together in Jesus.

A vocation of leadership. Jesus is the leader of the Church. Jesus is the Head of the Church.

An identity and a vocation of manifesting the reality of the unseen God. Total abandonment to the plan of God.

Lord Jesus, the list could go on forever as we sing the praises of who you are and what you are doing. Let us see you today in Scriptures, sacraments, and in any of the countless ways in which you may choose to reveal yourself to us. Alleluia!

Saturday, September 8, 2007 Nativity of the Blessed Virgin Mary
Romans 8, 28-30
God's Indomitable Love in Christ

We are called by God. God, knowing all about us, made the decision to call us be like Jesus.

It is God who justifies us. It is God who will glorify us.

Everything we are going through will work out for our good. We may rest in God and trust in God.

We trust God and thank God before we can see the answer. The young Virgin Mary trusted God before she saw the manifestation of God's promise to her.

Lord Jesus, it is not easy to see how you can turn everything into good for us. That is what you promised. We trust you and thank you in advance. Alleluia!

Sunday, September 9, 2007
Twenty-third Sunday in Ordinary Time
Wisdom 9, 13-18
Solomon's Prayer

Lord Jesus, thank you for gift of the Holy Spirit. Thank you that we may ask for and receive wisdom. We are living here on earth in these little tent-bodies. We grow weary and frightened and are unsure of our path. Thank you for guiding us in the path that is the wisest for us. Alleluia!

Monday, September 10, 2007
Colossians 1, 24 - 2, 3
Christ in Us

"I am now rejoicing in my sufferings for your sake, and in my flesh I am completing what is lacking in Christ's afflictions for the sake of his body, that is, the church. I became its servant according to God's commission that was given to me for you, to make the word of God fully known (vv. 24-25)."

Paul's struggles and sufferings were on behalf of others, the Christians in Colossae. He realized that his life and ministry were not for his own ego inflation.

Paul lived and suffered for others. He even came to rejoice in his suffering fro the church.

With tender, loving concern, Paul labored for the spiritual growth of others, even those he had never personally met. He longed for their spiritual maturity.

We cannot change others. That is the work of the Holy Spirit. We can, however, pray for others and offer our sufferings on their behalf.

Lord Jesus, thank you that we are complete in you. The fact that you live in us is our hope and glory. Sometimes it takes us a long time to realize this. Help us to learn to intercede for others and then to leave the results in your hands. Let us live this day in the joy of knowing you. Alleluia!

>Tuesday, September 11, 2007
>Colossians 2, 6-15
>Christ in Us; General Admonitions

Rooted in Christ. Built upon Christ. Walking in Christ. Firmly established in the Christian faith.

All of God dwells in Christ. ALL. As Christians, we share in God's fullness.

When we were baptized, we died and were buried with Christ. When we were baptized, we were also raised with Christ.

How? What does that mean?

God raised Jesus from the dead. God will also raise us from the dead.

Lord Jesus, thank you that God brought us to life with you and in you. It is gloriously possible to live this new life even as we struggle to grasp its wonder. You made this possible for us by your death. You died for us even when we had no clue what you were doing. Thank you that our transgressions are not only forgiven, but also that they are completely gone! All that would have been held against us was nailed to the cross. You took it all with you to the cross. You died and rose. We are in you. We are now free to live for you. Alleluia!

Wednesday, September 12, 2007 Holy Name of Mary
Colossians 3, 1-11
Mystical Death and Resurrection; Renunciation of Vice

A new place! In Christ, we are living in a new place. A place above.

Yes, I know we're still on earth, living in our bodies. There are problems, illnesses, bills to pay, carpets to clean, and so on.

Our real life, however, is transcendent. Our real life is in Christ and with Christ.

It is inappropriate to indulge in speech or behavior that is unworthy of our life in Christ. It does not honor Our Lord when we give way to fits of anger, obscene language, slander, lying, etc.

We are called to purity. Thank God that we may ask for and receive forgiveness and cleansing.

Lord Jesus, we rejoice that we are in a new place! Let us live to honor you on earth, knowing that our real life is safely enclosed in our relationship with you. At the right time, you will return for us and we will be with you in realms of glory. Alleluia!

Thursday, September 13, 2007 St. John Chrysostom
Colossians 3, 12-17
Mystical Death and Resurrection

Tucked away in the latter part of this passage is a key word. GRATITUDE!

True gratitude, in the depths of our hearts, will change us. When we are grateful, we long to rejoice.

It is then that we may be compassionate, forgiving, and forbearing, with greater ease. Having just experienced the forgiving love of God, we are quick to give this gift to others. Our gratitude impels us to do this.

Peace. We are gently guided by God's peace. We are beginning to discern how God is leading us.

Lord Jesus, we long for your word to live freely in us. You have showered your love and mercy on us in such amazing ways. We sing your praise and now shower your mercy on others. Let your peace truly reign in us today as we continue to be grateful. Alleluia!

Friday, September 14, 2007 Exaltation of the Holy Cross
Numbers 21, 4-9
The Bronze Serpent

Exhaustion sometimes leads to complaining. The Israelites, tired of the long journey in the desert, complained against God and God's servant, Moses.

For some of the Israelites, this actually led to death. To God, complaining is a serious offence.

God was fed up with their whining and sent snakes to bite them. As soon as people started dying, the others had a wake-up call.

They went to Moses and acknowledged their sin of complaining. Moses, servant of God, interceded for them.

The Lord mercifully provided a remarkable way for those who had been bitten by snakes to be healed. A bronze saraph, a poisonous serpent, was to be made and mounted on a pole. Even a person who had already been bitten would recover by looking at this bronze serpent.

Lord Jesus, thank you for forgiving us for complaining when we become exhausted. You were lifted high on the Cross to take away all of our sins and offenses. We exalt you. We exalt your Cross. We look upon you and know that we will live forever. Thank you for the strength and energy to live for you and to glorify you today. Alleluia!

Saturday, September 15, 2007 Our Lady of Sorrows
1 Timothy 1, 15-17
Gratitude for God's Mercy

Jesus came on a rescue mission! He came from heaven to earth to rescue those who needed him most.

Paul recognized his own deep need of the saving mercy of God working through Jesus. Paul even considered himself more in need than anyone else of God's saving power

Lord Jesus, thank you for coming to rescue us, especially when we don't even know we need help. We were stuck and you came to pull us out of the pit. You cleansed us and made us strong and secure in you. Glory to you, Lord Jesus Christ. Alleluia!

JANIS WALKER FIRST READING

Sunday, September 16, 2007
Twenty-fourth Sunday in Ordinary Time
Exodus 32, 7-11,13-14
The Golden Calf

Moses had a habit of defending others. As a much younger man, he took matters in his own hands when he killed an Egyptian who was mistreating a Hebrew slave (Exodus 2, 11). He also intervened on behalf of the daughters of a Midianite priest who were trying to draw water for their father's flock (Exodus 2, 16-17).

In this reading, Moses is interceding for the Israelites who have committed unspeakable idolatry. Moses reminded the Lord that these erring ones are still the Lord's own people. Moses also reminded the Lord of the promises the Lord had made long ago to Abraham, Isaac, and Jacob (Israel).

Lord Jesus, just as you have mercy on us, we ask your mercy for others. Help us to continue to offer mercy to others, aware of our own constant need of your forgiveness and mercy. Alleluia!

Monday, September 17, 2007 St. Robert Bellarmine
1 Timothy 2, 1-8
Prayer and Conduct

"First of all, then, I urge that supplications, prayers, intercessions, and thanksgivings be made for everyone, for kings and all who are in high positions, so that we may lead a quiet and peaceable life in all godliness and dignity. This is right and is acceptable in the sight of God our Savior,

who desires everyone to be saved and to come to the knowledge of truth (vv. 1-4)."

The will of God. Mysterious? Yes. Unclear? No.

It is God's will for all to be rescued, saved, and made whole. It is God's will for all to come to know the truth.

Sainte Thérèse of Lisieux, a doctor of the Church, stated that she only searched for the TRUTH!

The apostle Paul called for prayer that all lead a life of tranquility. He asked that the prayer be made without anger and arguments.

Lord Jesus, thank you for the Holy Spirit who teaches us how to live and to pray in accordance with God's will. Help us not to be afraid of God's will, but to know that God truly knows what is best. Let us live joyfully this day and embrace God's loving plan for us. Alleluia!

> Tuesday, September 18, 2007
> 1 Timothy 3, 1-13
> Qualifications of Various Ministers

Integrity! All ministers of God are called to be people of personal integrity as well as people of personal faith.

Those who supervise and oversee the household of God, the church, must know how to oversee and manage their children and their own households. They are not to love money. They are to exercise self-control in all personal habits.

The deacons are also to be people of dignity, as well as people of faith in Christ. They are not to be greedy. They are to be faithful to God in all matters. They too must know how to manage their children and their households.

Lord Jesus, thank you for all who serve as ministers in your household, your Church. Let us continue to pray that your household, your Church will live according to your plan. Alleluia!

> Wednesday, September 19, 2007 St. Januarius
> 1 Timothy 3, 14-16
> The Mystery of Our Religion

Christians live in God's household, the Church. This is a real household, a living household, since it's the household of our God and God is alive!

This household, the Church, is the foundation and the pillar of truth. Jesus is the cornerstone of the whole house which is built upon the foundation of the prophets and the apostles (Ephesians 2, 19-20).

You count! You belong!

You are in there with Jesus, the apostles, the prophets, the saints, and the martyrs. Talk about being in the "in" crowd. You and I are living in God's own household. We are not alone.

Lord Jesus, thank you that you came to us in human flesh. The Holy Spirit vindicated you. Angels saw you and worshipped you. You were proclaimed to both Jews and Gentiles. We believe in you and we believe in ourselves as part of your household. Let us live out our calling to follow you as we await your return in glory. Alleluia!

> Thursday, September 20, 2007 St. Andrew Kim Taegon,
> St. Paul Chong Hasang and Companions
> 1 Timothy 4, 12-16
> Counsel to Timothy

Auto-pilot? We are to attend to ourselves personally as well as to our ministry.

It is easy to attend to our outer work and to think that we ourselves are on auto-pilot. We're not!

We are our own greatest mission field. The Holy Spirit is our teacher and the one with whom we cooperate. Our thought lives and our outer lives are to be pure.

Our faith will then be credible. Our love will then be believable.

We are not to disregard or to neglect what we have been given. We don't need to envy the gifts of others. We are to value ourselves and to value the gifts which God has given to us.

Lord Jesus, please forgive us for wasting gifts, time, and energy. Thank you for filling us with hope and joy as well as with faith and love. Let us live for you today and trust that you are using our lives for your glory. Alleluia!

> Friday, September 21, 2007 St. Matthew
> Ephesians 4, 1-7,11-13
> Unity in the Body; Diversity of Gifts

Household! Living out our vocation begins with humility and is accompanied by gentleness and patience. All these qualities are essential if we are to learn to put up with each other and to love each other in this household of ours, the Church.

Group travel! We are all very different and yet we are one in Christ. We live out our baptism in different ways, serving the same Lord. We are traveling as a group to full maturity. We need each other.

Lord Jesus, thank you that others have been putting up with us and have been patient and loving with us. Help us to believe that what we have to offer is needed in your household, the church. Help us to be tender in heart and gentle in speech today, remembering that you are very patient with us. Alleluia!

> Saturday, September 22, 2007
> 1 Timothy 6, 13-16
> Exhortations to Timothy

"In the presence of God, who gives life to all things, and of Christ Jesus … I charge you to keep the commandment without spot or blemish until the manifestation of our Lord Jesus Christ … (vv. 13,14)."

Timothy was charged to live always cognizant of the reality of the Lord's return in glory. He was to be completely committed to the Lord Jesus Christ.

Lord Jesus, let us think, speak, and live this day in the light of eternity. Help us to be faithful to our appointed tasks, remembering that you are with us at every moment. Let your light shine within us, healing us, and helping us to continue to live in this present world while rejoicing in the reality of the world to come. Alleluia!

> Sunday, September 23, 2007
> Twenty-fifth Sunday in Ordinary Time
> Amos 8, 4-7
> Against Greed

The Lord does not forget anything that is done to harm the poor and those in need. The Lord does not forget the malice, the greed, or the trickery.

Perhaps you are not materially poor, but you are humble and poor in spirit. Perhaps you have been tricked and trampled on by others.

The Lord does not forget how you were treated. The Lord knows and remembers.

Lord Jesus, it's hard to live on earth. So many people are ruled by pride. So many people seek only power for themselves. They think too much of money. When we are weary of the wickedness around us, let us remember that it was that way, too, when you walked this earth. Let us continually ask forgiveness for our sins and then joyfully, radically live for you. We trust you to redeem all our suffering. Alleluia!

Monday, September 24, 2007
Ezra 1, 1-6
The Decree of Cyrus

Exile is over! God's people are given freedom to return to Jerusalem.

They are given the means with which to build God's house. Restoration at last!

Lord Jesus, thank you that one day our exile on earth will be over. We will worship you in the heavenly Jerusalem. Let us be patient during this last part of our exile. Let us be faithful and joyfully expectant. Alleluia!

Tuesday, September 25, 2007
Ezra 6, 7-8,12,14-20
The Decree of Darius; The Passover

The words of the prophets were crucial in the rebuilding of the temple in Jerusalem. King Darius had authorized the building of the temple and provided material for the builders.

The words of the prophets, however, provided the spiritual underpinnings of the work. The prophets were speaking forth God's words of encouragement. With these words resounding in their hearts, the builders progressed wonderfully in their work.

"And the elders of the Jews builded, and they prospered through the prophesying of Haggai the prophet and Zechariah .... And they builded and finished it according to the commandment of the God of Israel ... (Ezra 6, 14 KJV)."

The temple was joyfully dedicated. The priests and the Levites again served God in the temple in Jerusalem. The Passover was celebrated with joy.

Lord Jesus, let us realize the power of our words. Let us learn to support ourselves and others with words of cheerful encouragement. Thank you for rebuilding us and filling us with joy. Alleluia!

Wednesday, September 26, 2007 Sts. Cosmas and Damian
Ezra 9, 5-9
Ezra's Exhortation

In the midst his anguished intercession for the Israelites, Ezra recalled the Lord's goodness and mercy. Ezra himself had gathered exiled Israelites to return to Jerusalem (Ezra 7, 27-28).

Even after experiencing the amazing love and provision of the Lord, the people, the priests, and the Levites had sinned by contracting mixed marriages (Ezra 9, 1-2). Their apostasy was appalling.

With deep humility, Ezra, priest and scholar of the law, interceded for the people. Ezra prayed "we" prayers, not "they" prayers, identifying himself with the sin and guilt of the people. The example of his prayer touched the hearts of the people and led them to repentance (Ezra 10, 1-4).

Lord Jesus, there is always hope when we acknowledge our sin and cry out to you for mercy. Let us run to you and receive your forgiveness. Let us then mourn, fast, and intercede for others who also need your mercy. Alleluia!

Thursday, September 27, 2007 St. Vincent de Paul
Haggai 1, 1-8
Exhortation to Rebuild the Temple of the Lord

A prophet spoke and the governor and high priest listened. The prophet, Haggai, spoke the Lord's message to Judah's governor, Zerubbabel, and to Joshua, the high priest.

The Lord was calling and challenging the people of Israel to consider their selfish ways. They were to put first the building of the temple of God.

Lord Jesus, you have spoken to us many times, through others, to put us first. Sometimes we understood that it was really you speaking and other times we did not understand or did not want to accept the message. Forgive us. Forgive our selfishness, procrastination, and fear. Let us start afresh today and do the work you have called us to do. Alleluia!

Friday, September 28, 2007 St. Wenceslaus
Haggai 2, 1-9
Future Glory of the New Temple

Courage! Work!

We need both. The Lord is with us.

Lord Jesus, thank you for filling us with peace as we trust in you and do our work. Be glorified in us today. Alleluia!

Saturday, September 29, 2007
Michael, Gabriel, and Raphael, Archangels
Daniel 7, 9-10,13-14
Vision of the Four Beasts

Brightness of glistening snow! Flames of fire!

Daniel can only give us partial descriptions of his vision. GOD! The everlasting God. How can one describe God?

Jesus! Jesus appeared in Daniel's vision. Jesus, human like us, and yet truly God.

Jesus came from heaven to earth. God gave to Jesus, Son of God and Son of Man, all glory and all dominion.

Lord Jesus, we worship you as Son of God and Son of Man. You know all about us. You know what it is like to live on earth. You are with us every step of the way. You are our Brother, our God, our King. Come in glory, Lord Jesus Christ. Alleluia!

Sunday, September 30, 2007
Twenty-sixth Sunday in Ordinary Time
Amos 6, 1a,4-7
Third Woe

The Lord chose Amos, a shepherd who lived near Bethlehem, to speak forth strong words of condemnations to the leaders of Zion. These rulers did not know how to rule themselves, much less others. They gave themselves over to lives of self-indulgence, not caring for others.

These leaders were not serving God. They appeared to be addicted to serving their own desires. The Lord confronted them for their complacency, and condemned them to exile.

Lord Jesus, when we choose self-indulgence over surrender to you, we condemn ourselves to exile. Let us learn to worship you in humility. Let us enjoy the good things you give us, but not live for them. We are here for your purposes. Alleluia!

Monday, October 1, 2007 St. Thérèse of Lisieux
Zechariah 8, 1-8
In the Days of the Messiah

"Thus says the LORD of hosts: Old men and old women shall again sit in the streets of Jerusalem, each with staff in hand because of their great age. And the streets of the city shall be full of boys and girls playing in its streets. Thus says the LORD GOD of hosts: Even though it seems impossible to the remnant of this people in these days, should it also seem impossible to me, says the LORD of hosts (vv. 4-6)?"

Jerusalem! To dwell in the city on the holy mountain. The city of Jerusalem. Jerusalem, the faithful city.

Peace. Old men and women sitting safely in the city streets. Children playing safely in the streets. The streets and squares of Jerusalem. Peace

Security. God is there. There is no need to fear. God dwells within Jerusalem. Safety.

Lord Jesus Christ, thank you for the heavenly Jerusalem where we are bound. Help us not be so frightened here on our earthly pilgrimage. You are with us, leading us Home. Alleluia!

Tuesday, October 2, 2007 The Guardian Angels
Zechariah 8, 20-23
In the Days of the Messiah

Humility will replace haughtiness. Many will come, in humility, to Jerusalem, because it is clear that God favors this city (Zechariah 8, 15).

Instead of coming in haughtiness to seek to destroy Jerusalem, they will come in humility to seek God in Jerusalem. God's presence with the Jewish people will be obvious to all.

In God's mysterious providence, those who are not Jews may share fully in the promises of God. In Christ, we are one, regardless of our ancestry, race, gender, or state in life (Galatians 3, 28).

Lord Jesus, thank you for making us one in you. Thank you for the time when we will all worship you as our royal Messiah in Jerusalem. Alleluia!

Wednesday, October 3, 2007
Nehemiah 2, 1-8
Appointment by the King

Pray first. Speak later.

It worked for the practical prophet, Nehemiah, cupbearer to King Artaxerxes. Nehemiah prayed before approaching the king.

The king not only granted Nehemiah's original request to return to Jerusalem, but also his request for materials necessary for rebuilding the temple. God was clearly granting Nehemiah favor with the king.

Lord Jesus, thank you that Nehemiah was granted the ability to fulfill his holy vocation of rebuilding the temple in Jerusalem. Please grant to all in your Church the ability to fulfill the vocations to which they are called. Alleluia!

Thursday, October 4, 2007 St. Francis of Assisi
Nehemiah 8, 1-12
Ezra Reads the Law

"For there shall be a sowing of peace; the vine shall yield its fruit, the ground shall give its produce, and the skies shall give their dew; and I will cause the remnant of this people to possess all these things (v. 12)."

To God be all the glory! God had worked in the heart of the king to allow Nehemiah to return to Jerusalem to rebuild the temple It was God who helped the people to complete this project (Nehemiah 6, 16).

Ezra, priest and scholar, read aloud from the law of Moses to the assembled people at the Water Gate, southeast of the temple. This law was God's prescription for the people.

The people not only listened with great attention, but they also took the words to heart and wept. Ezra assured them that this was a day that was both holy and joyful!

They were to rejoice in the Lord. Therein lay their strength. They were to enjoy a feast and share with others.

Lord Jesus, thank you for the Holy Spirit who teaches us to listen attentively to your prescription for us. You are our strength. You bring us healing. We rejoice in you. Alleluia!

Friday, October 5, 2007
Baruch 1, 15-22
Confession of Guilt

"WE!" This was a group confession. The people and their leaders, the kings, prophets, and priests had all sinned by disregarding the Lord's instructions.

They prayed, with fasting and weeping before sending offerings to Jerusalem (Baruch 1, 5-7).They acknowledged the justice of God before praying for God's mercy and help.

Lord Jesus, we need your forgiveness for disregarding your words to us. You alone are perfectly just. Have mercy on us and forgive us. Let us truly put you first in our lives. Alleluia!

Saturday, October 6, 2007 St. Bruno,
Blessed Marie-Rose Durocher
Baruch 4, 5-12,27-29
God's Promises Recalled

Even in the midst of the Israelites' apostasy and subsequent exile, there was hope! Even in the midst of Jerusalem's mourning, there was hope.

Although God was just in allowing the Israelites to reap the consequences of their betrayal and idolatry, God was also merciful. God's children were told not to live in a state of fear, but were invited, instead, to seek God. God had joy in store for them!

Lord Jesus, sometimes we just get stuck. We choose to sin, not thinking that there will be consequences. We give in to fear, no longer believing in joy. Lift us today out of this quagmire of selfish confusion. Let us seek you first and follow you. You are full of concern and mercy for us. Thank you for leading us again to joy. Alleluia!

Sunday, October 7, 2007
Twenty-seventh Sunday in Ordinary Time
Habakkuk 1, 2-3; 2, 2-4
The Prophet's Complaint and Its Answer

"O LORD, how long shall I cry for help ....? Why do you make me see wrong-doing and look at trouble. Destruction and violence are before me; strife and contentions arise. (vv. 2-3)."

The vision! What is the vision?

Where did it go? Is it lost? Have you forgotten?

In the midst of the prophet Habakkuk's laments over present trials, the Lord reminded him of the vision. The Lord instructed him to write the vision down on tablets.

Just because the vision had not yet come to fulfillment did not mean that it was not going to be fulfilled. Timing!

"I will stand at my watchpost, and station myself on the rampart; I will keep watch to see what he will say to me, and what he will answer concerning my complaint. Then the LORD answered me and said: Write the vision; make it plain on tablets, so that a runner may read it. For there is still a vision for the appointed time; it speaks of the end, and does not lie. If it seems to tarry, wait for it; it will surely come, it will not delay (2, 1-3)."

The vision will indeed be fulfilled. Live, wait, and trust.

Lord Jesus, sometimes we think we don't even have a vision for our lives. You have a vision of us and a vision for us. You call us to trust you, to live, as well as we are able, the vocation entrusted to us. You will triumph in our lives. Your vision of us and your vision for us will be fulfilled. Let us take courage and learn to live in expectant trust. Alleluia!

Monday, October 8, 2007
Jonah 1, 1 - 2, 2,11
The First Mission; Psalm of Thanksgiving

An evangelist in spite of himself! Even before arriving in Nineveh, Jonah, in spite of himself, was being used by God as an evangelist.

After Jonah, the unwilling prophet, was thrown into the sea, the sea became calm. The amazed people on board the ship were in awe of the Lord!

What about Jonah? His mission to Nineveh was merely delayed, not cancelled. Instead of going to Nineveh as the Lord had told, him, he had tried to go in the opposite direction to Tarshish.

Bad idea. Very bad idea.

He went from the city of Joppa to a ship and from the ship into the depths of the sea. From the sea he went into the huge fish. That did it!

From the interior of the fish, he cried out to the Lord for deliverance and promised to fulfill his vow to the Lord (Jonah 1, 9). He was then deposited on the shore.

Lord Jesus, thank you that you manage to use us even when we are afraid and unwilling to make a total commitment to you. You alone know why we are so afraid. Thank you for guiding us, in whatever way is necessary, to obey you. For our sake and for the sake of others, let us honor you by our trust and our obedience today. Alleluia!

Tuesday, October 9, 2007 St. Denis and Companions;
St. John Leonardi
Jonah 3, 1-10
Conversion of Ninevah

Whodathunkit? Disobedient prophet tries to run away from the Lord, actually goes in the opposite direction, gets thrown into the sea, swallowed by a really big fish, and then decides, after all, to obey the Lord.

The Lord had not given up on Jonah. Again, the Lord told Jonah to go to the big city of Ninevah and tell the people that Nineveh would be wiped out in forty days.

Jonah obeyed and the people actually believed God's message spoken through this unlikely prophet, They humbled themselves and fasted.

Their king even sat in the midst of ashes. He ordered that the animals as well as the people should fast. Nothing to eat. Nothing to drink. Every single person was to stop doing evil. They were to cry out to God. The king was hoping that God would forgive them all.

God indeed decided not to destroy the big city. God took note of the people's actions. They not only prayed, but they also fasted. They humbled themselves and forsook evil.

Lord Jesus, help us to show by our actions and not merely by our words that we take you seriously. Let us honor you by our actions of obedience today. Alleluia!

Wednesday, October 10, 2007
Jonah 4, 1-10
Jonah's Anger; God's Reproof

Worms! Winds!

God can send worms and winds, if necessary, to speak to us. A worm was God's instrument to destroy the large, leafy gourd plant which had been God's provision for the pouting prophet, Jonah.

It was important to Jonah, apparently, to be vindictive. He did not rejoice because God spared the lives of the huge city of Nineveh.

Jonah was so angry that he wanted to die. All because God mercifully spared the city of Nineveh.

Oh yes, the cattle. God also cared about the cattle of Nineveh. After all, they had been forced to fast along with all the people!

Lord Jesus, we too pout and whine. Help us to grow up! You have been so gentle and compassionate with us. You hear us when we cry to you. Let us learn to be gentle and compassionate with others who also need your mercy. Alleluia!

Thursday, October 11, 2007
Malachi 3, 13-20
The Messenger of the Covenant

An excellent passage to absorb when we feel drained and dispirited! It was written over four hundred years before the birth of Christ.

This was a time when priests were not living up to their holy calling. The people had not kept the faith, deciding it just wasn't worth it to try to serve God.

The Lord, however, was all the while tenderly attentive to his beloved people. He knew those who truly trusted him.

The Lord would act at the right time with compassion for his own. The Lord would bring justice.

Lord Jesus, shine on us today and bring us healing. Let us not give in to our weariness. Let us wait for you in joy. Alleluia!

Friday, October 12, 2007
Joel 1, 13-15; 2, 1-2
Call to Penance; The Day of the Lord

Four hundred years before the birth of Christ, the prophet Joel was sounding the alarm! The priests were called to weep, to manifest contrition, and to call for an assembly in the Lord's house. The "day" of the Lord was approaching.

Lord Jesus, the trumpet will blare again. You will return in glory. Let us seek forgiveness for our own personal sins and for the sins of others. Thank you for privilege of interceding for others. Thank you for those who have, unknown to us, interceded for us. Gather us in and help us to trust in your mercy. Alleluia!

Saturday, October 13, 2007
Joel 4, 12-21
Judgment upon the Nations; Salvation for God's Elect

Now! The time has come for God to deal with the nations which caused suffering and distress for Israel. No one, no one touches God's chosen people without facing the judgment of God.

This should give us great peace and great courage. We are one in Christ, no longer concerned with whether we are Jews, Gentiles, slaves, free, male or female (Galatians 3, 28). We share in all the promises to Israel.

God will bring restoration to Israel. Jerusalem, once trampled. underfoot by heathen, will shine in purity and holiness.

Lord Jesus, thank you that you are with us in the valley and on the mountain. You are always with us. We need not fear valleys, earthquakes, darkness, or decisions. We will live in safety in the heavenly Jerusalem. Alleluia!

Sunday, October 14, 2007
Twenty-eighth Sunday in Ordinary Time
2 Kings 5, 14-17
Cure of Naaman

Would you rather be ticked off or transformed? Would you rather insist that God act according to your expectation or are you open to a miracle because God chooses to act in a very creative, unusual way?

When the commander of the king's army, Naaman, who was afflicted with leprosy, was told by the prophet, Elisha, to wash in the Jordan River seven times, he balked

Here was a chance to be healed and yet Naaman fussed at God's methods which included the bold faith of a little servant girl (2 Kings 5, 1-5).

When Naaman finally yielded to Elisha's instructions, he was indeed cleansed. No more leprosy! He had a new understanding of God.

Lord Jesus, thank you that we may confess our sins and be continuously cleansed (1 John 1, 9). Let us be open today to hearing you speak to us through others. Thank you for the gift of the healing sacrament of reconciliation. Let us be open to being healed in any way you choose. Alleluia!

Monday, October 15, 2007 St. Teresa of Avila
Romans 1, 1-7
Greetings

Called! You are called to Jesus. You belong to Jesus.

Called! You are called to holiness. The same Spirit who raised Jesus from the dead lives in you (Romans 8, 11) and is calling you to holiness.

Called! You are called to serve the crucified and risen Lord Jesus Christ. You are called to serve in a particular way in the particular place to which you are sent.

Lord Jesus, thank you that we are called to be with you. Thank you that we belong to you and that you are caring for us. Thank you that we are called to live in purity. Thank you that we are called to live in the power of the Holy Spirit as we bear witness to you today in this place. Alleluia!

> Tuesday, October 16, 2007 St. Hedwig,
> St. Margaret Mary Alacoque
> Romans 1, 16-25
> God's Power for Salvation; Punishment of Idolaters

The Gospel is for available for everyone! It is God's way of bringing about the salvation of everyone who chooses to trust. God will gladly give us the gift of trust.

When we trust God, even when we are just beginning to trust God, God sees us in a new way. God actually sees us as righteous!

Then we start to live out our fledgling faith. We trust God and begin to live in the light of God's truth. God is very tender and patient with us.

Lord Jesus, thank you for the beauty of creation. Let us enjoy creation and yet not deify creation. Help us to continue, day after day, to trust you, to worship you, and to live in light and truth. Alleluia!

> Wednesday, October 17, 2007 St. Ignatius of Antioch
> Romans 2, 1-11
> God's Just Judgment

God is not partial! If God is not partial, who are we to pass judgment on others?

We only observe the actions of others. We are not capable of looking into their hearts and discerning their motives. That is God's business, not ours.

Lord Jesus, forgive us when we are quick to judge and to condemn others. When their actions have harmed us, help us to forgive them. You will make up to us the harm they have caused. You alone know what is best to do. Thank you for pouring out your gracious kindness on all of us, longing to bring all to repentance. Alleluia!

> Thursday, October 18, 2007 St. Luke
> 2 Timothy 4, 10-17
> Paul's Loneliness

Friend! Jesus is the friend who will always stand by us. The great apostle Paul knew this from first hand experience.

At a time when Paul needed support, he was deserted by others. The Lord was with him, however, and gave him the courage to complete his work of proclaiming the Gospel.

Lord Jesus, we trust you to deal with all who cause harm to us. Let us concentrate on you and on faithfully fulfilling the assignment you have entrusted to us. Alleluia!

Friday, October 19, 2007 St. John de Brebeuf;
St. Isaac Jogues and Companions
Romans 4, 1-8
Abraham Justified by Faith

Choose! You can believe God or you can believe your circumstances.

Abraham had this choice. So do we.

What was the big deal about Abraham? The big deal was that, in the face of seemingly impossible circumstances, Abraham dug in his heels and still trusted God.

God had made Abraham quite a promise. God promised this ninety-nine year old man that he would have numerous descendants (Genesis 15, 1-6).

Even more "impossible" was that his elderly wife, Sarah, would be the mother (Genesis 17, 15,16)! Abraham quite simply trusted God to fulfill this promise.

Faith! This was not just faith in what Abraham wanted, but faith in GOD!

Because of Abraham's trust, God considered Abraham righteous. Abraham was in good standing with God.

Lord Jesus, Abraham believed in spite of all evidence to the contrary. Help us to honor you with our firm belief and trust. You are in charge of our lives and you will make sure that your will for us is fulfilled. Alleluia!

Saturday, October 20, 2007 St. Paul of the Cross
Romans 4, 13,16-18
Inheritance through Faith

"For the promise that he would inherit the world did not come to Abraham or to his descendants through the law but through the righteousness of faith. If it is the adherents of the law who are to be the heirs, faith is null and void and the promise is void. For the law brings wrath; but where there is no law, neither is there violation. For this reason it depends on faith, in order that the promise may rest on grace and be guaranteed to all his descendants, not only to the adherents of the law but also to those who share the faith of Abraham (for he is the father of all of us, as it is written, 'I have made you the father of many nations') – in the presence of God in whom he believed who gives life to the dead and calls into existence the things that do not exist. Hoping against hope, he believed that he would become the 'father of many nations .... (vv. 13-18a)."

To God be all the glory! God made a promise to Abraham and Abraham believed God.

We pray for the faith of Abraham. We pray to believe God.

God does not play favorites. The same God who made the "impossible" become a reality for Abraham will also move in our lives in a powerful way.

From nothingness, God brings forth life. God creates anew!

Abraham? He kept believing, trusting, and hoping. He believed God. He trusted God. He hoped in God.

Lord Jesus, thank you for the gift of faith. Help us to stay firm in our trust in you. You are bringing to birth new life in us and new life through us. Alleluia!

Sunday, October 21, 2007
Twenty-ninth Sunday in Ordinary Time
Exodus 17, 8-13
Battle of Amalek

We need help! Even Moses needed help.

As long as Moses stood at the top of the mountain with God's staff in his hand, Israel, under Joshua's leadership, won the battle with the Amalekites.

Eventually, Moses had to sit down and to let Aaron and Hur help him. Moses' hands, with the staff, were still raised high, but it was Aaron and Hur who were supporting him and holding up his hands. Israel won the battle!

Lord Jesus, let us be ready to help others as they serve the Lord. Let us accept help from others when we, too, grow weary. Thank you that you are with us to strengthen us. Alleluia!

Monday, October 22, 2007
Romans 4, 20-25
Inheritance through Faith

Abraham, although his own circumstances looked hopeless, grew strong and powerful because of his trust in God. So can we!

"No distrust made him waver concerning the promise of God, but he grew strong in his faith as he gave glory to God, being fully convinced that God was able to do what he had promised (vv. 20-21)."

Abraham gave God all the glory. So can we!

We can be strong in the Lord, whatever our current circumstances. Our circumstances are only temporary. God is eternal.

Abraham was confident in God. We, too, can be strong and confident when we place our entire lives in God's hands. Others may call this arrogance, but God knows otherwise.

Lord Jesus, thank you for Abraham's example. He kept on trusting and he was empowered to live. Let us live this day, not in faithless fear, but in the strength of the Holy Spirit. We trust that your will is being accomplished in us and through us. You lived, died, and rose again for us. You are victorious over all. Alleluia!

Tuesday, October 23, 2007 St. John of Capistrano
Romans 5, 12,15,17-19,20-21
Humanity's Sin through Adam; Grace and Life through Christ

Wake up! You're not under condemnation any more. You have been acquitted.

Because of Adam's sin, you and I were under condemnation. Infected with Adam's sin, we were spiritually dead.

"Therefore just as one man's trespass led to condemnation for all, so one man's act of righteousness leads to justification and life for all (v. 18)."

Because of Christ's action on our behalf, we are alive! We are not just alive and breathing. We are alive in the spirit.

Lord Jesus, you live within us and you long to bring life to our world. You choose to do this through us. Let us rejoice and live out this day, knowing that you call us not to crawl through this life but to live victoriously. Alleluia!

Wednesday, October 24, 2007 St. Anthony Mary Claret
Romans 6, 12-18
Freedom from Sin; Life in God

Are we driven? We can frantically drive ourselves to serve ourselves or we can be led by the Holy Spirit to follow God and to serve God. We can be determined to have our own way or we can be committed to living freely in God's way for God's purposes.

Only the Holy Spirit can give us the power to live completely for God. The Holy Spirit is able to prune our thoughts and to cleanse our motives. The Holy Spirit is able to purify us and to fill us with the power to live for God.

Lord Jesus, thank you for giving us the paradigm shift we need in order to live in a new way. You gave yourself entirely for the purposes of your heavenly Father, your Abba. You are with us, you are protecting us, and you are leading us in paths of righteousness. Alleluia!

Thursday, October 25, 2007
Romans 6, 19-23
Freedom from Sin; Life in God

Show up! Sign up!

Show up for God. Sign up for righteousness and holiness.

In the sacrament of Holy Baptism, we are already signed up. We are signed with the sign of the Cross. We belong to Jesus forever and ever.

However, when we merely live for ourselves and don't care about others, all we receive is shame. This kind of living is really a kind of death. "For the wages of sin is death, but the free gift of God is eternal life in Jesus Christ our Lord (v. 23)."

However, if we choose to live out our baptism, we live in a different way. We live as those who know that they have already entered into life everlasting.

Life "here" and life "there." It is of one essence.

Lord Jesus, thank you that we may come to you, confess our sins, and receive your forgiveness. Thank you for the sacrament of reconciliation and for the healing that is available in this sacrament. Thank you that we are free to live for you! Alleluia!

Friday, October 26, 2007
Romans 7, 18-25
Sin and Death

As long as we are living in these earthly bodies, these little "tents," we will struggle and we will be tempted. The battle has already been won, praise God! Jesus won the battle for us and Jesus lives in us.

Lord Jesus, thank you that this struggle will not last forever. Right now, though, we're still on earth, and we still struggle. Let us remember that you are with us and that you hold the key to victory in every situation. Thank you that the Holy Spirit is giving us the wisdom and the strength we need for today. Alleluia!

Saturday, October 27, 2007
Romans 8, 1-11
The Flesh and the Spirit

"There is now no condemnation for those who are in Christ Jesus, For the law of the Spirit of life in Christ Jesus has set you free from the law of sin and death (vv. 1-2)."

There is a new you! Under the old law of Moses, all were condemned. In Christ, however, you and I are not condemned. We are free.

We are free from the old sin and death cycle. We are free to live under the guidance of the Holy Spirit and to enjoy peace.

God made all this possible by sending Jesus to live on earth. Jesus gathered up all our sins into himself.

God then condemned these sins and Jesus died. When Jesus died, all our sins died.

The Holy Spirit raised Jesus to life. The same Holy Spirit makes it possible for us to live a holy life and to experience resurrection after our earthly bodies die.

Lord Jesus, sometimes we forget we are free and we act as if we are condemned. Thank you that we may confess our sins, receive your forgiveness, and continue to a holy life of joy and freedom. Alleluia!

Sunday, October 28, 2007 Thirtieth Sunday in Ordinary Time
Sirach 35, 12-14,16-18
True Worship of God

This is a deeply reassuring passage for those of us who get discouraged and wonder if God even hears our prayers or whether God will ever do anything to help us.

God's very heart has been moved and even pierced by our sorrows. God will secure justice for us.

Lord Jesus, you lived on this earth and you know how hard it is for us to live here. You reached out in tenderness and compassion to heal. You became indignant when you observed how people were being hurt by some of the religious leaders. You will take care of all our concerns. Thank you for your mercy and your justice. Alleluia!

Monday, October 29, 2007
Romans 8, 12-17
The Flesh and the Spirit; Children of God through Adoption

We become afraid when we forget who we are and whose we are. We are God's children. We belong to God.

We are learning to be led by the Holy Spirit, rather than merely caving in to our own cravings. "For all who are led by the Spirit of God are children of God (v. 14)." The Holy Spirit strengthens us and reassures us of our true identity.

The Lord Jesus Christ is our brother. We are heirs of God along with Jesus.

Jesus suffered. We suffer.

Jesus is now glorified. We, too, will be glorified.

Lord Jesus, please help us when we are afraid. You know the root of all of our fears. Thank you that we are safe in your care. We trust you. Alleluia!

Tuesday, October 30, 2007
Romans 8, 18-25
Destiny of Glory

"I consider that the sufferings of this present time are not worth comparing with the glory about to be revealed to us. For the creation waits with eager longing for the revealing of the children of God (vv. 18-19)."

We are called to live with courage as we await the final unfolding of God's plans. God has glorious plans for us and for all of creation. We are learning to be stouthearted in our hope, because our hope is in God.

All of creation will be freed. All creation will rejoice when we are fully revealed as God's children!

Lord Jesus, we still don't fully comprehend our identity as God's children. Let us be patient with ourselves and live in eager anticipation of our future glory. Alleluia!

Wednesday, October 31, 2007
Romans 8, 26-30
Destiny of Glory; God's Indomitable Love in Christ

We may breathe a sigh of relief as we read this passage. Sometimes we become so preoccupied with trying to measure our own spiritual temperature that we forget that God is in control!

We may worry about the right way to pray. We are free to relax!

The Holy Spirit lives within us. The Holy Spirit, knowing all about us, knows how to intercede for us.

Although all things are definitely not good, God is still in control. God is good and will make everything work out for our good.

"We know that all things work together for good for those who love God, who are called according to his purpose (v. 28)."

Long ago, God chose us and called us. God is the one who puts us in right standing. God justifies us. God is shaping us and conforming us to the image of Christ. God will even glorify us!

Lord Jesus, thank you for the Holy Spirit who teaches us how to relax and to be willing to trust. This is hard when we have been hurt by life. Thank you for the work of the Holy Spirit on our behalf. We trust you with ourselves and we trust you for all for whom we pray. Alleluia!

> Thursday, November 1, 2007 All Saints
> Revelation 7, 2-4,9-14
> The 144,000 Sealed; Triumph of the Elect

We are lifted into the heavenly realm for a preview of true worship. A multitude clothed in white, palm branches in hand, before God's throne, surrounded by angels!

They had been through great suffering and were now in God's presence. Prostrate before God, they praised and worshipped constantly.

The Lamb of God, their Good Shepherd, was there to care for them. There would be no more weeping. Fountains of fresh water flowed to refresh them.

Lord Jesus, thank you for your blood which cleanses us and erases our sins. Thank you that we are signed with the sign of the cross. We are marked as yours. Thank you for those in heaven who are at this moment interceding for us. Thank you for giving us courage to continue to bear witness to you. Alleluia!

> Friday, November 2, 2007 All Souls
> Wisdom 3, 1-9
> The Hidden Counsels of God

The book of Wisdom, written about a hundred years before the birth of Christ, was written to encourage those who were suffering and enduring oppression. The writer gave assurance that those who had died were safely in God's hands.

We too may be assured that God will tenderly care for those who have died. God will honor those who have trusted in him. They will shine!

Lord Jesus, thank you for your mercy for all of us. Thank you that you are tenderly watching over us today. You are our Good Shepherd and you are leading us Home. Alleluia!

Saturday, November 3, 2007 St. Martin de Porres
Romans 11, 1-2,11-12,25-29
The Remnant of Israel; The Gentiles' Salvation;
God's Irrevocable Call

"So that you may not claim to be wiser than you are, brothers and sisters, I want you to understand this mystery: a hardening has come upon part of Israel, until the full number of the Gentiles has come in. And so all Israel will be saved …. (vv. 25,26a)." ALL!

God's beloved people, Israel, will all be saved. ALL!

This is God's promise (Romans 11, 26)! God called Abraham and all the patriarchs. God's call was and is irrevocable.

Lord Jesus, thank you that we may share in the rich heritage of the patriarchs, prophets, apostles, and martyrs. Help us to be brave and faithful today in the call you have given us to follow you. Alleluia!

Sunday, November 4, 2007 Thirty-first Sunday in Ordinary Time
Wisdom 11, 22 - 12, 2
Digression on God's Mercy

God's mercy is truly over all his creation. With consummate care and with infinite attention to every detail, God delighted in creating the universe. The sea and the land, the plants and the animals, and you and me. God yearns over his creation and continues to breathe life into us all.

Lord Jesus, thank you for you tender care for us. You were in the beginning with God and you participated in creation. Help us to be increasingly sensitive to the Holy Spirit's creative work in us and through us. Let us quickly repent and ask forgiveness of you and of others when we have sinned. Thank you for your arms of mercy open to receive us. Alleluia!

Monday, November 5, 2007
Romans 11, 29-36
God's Irrevocable Call; Triumph of God's Mercy

How can so much good come from so much evil? How can God's mercy triumph over the rebellion and disobedience of mortals?

God's ways are not for us to fathom. We muse and we marvel. We wonder and we worship.

"O the depth of the riches and wisdom and knowledge of God! How unsearchable are his judgments and how inscrutable his ways (v. 3)!"

Lord Jesus, let us never take for granted the price you paid for our disobedience to God. You humbled yourself on our behalf and died for us. Let us thank you always for your death and for your life. Thank you for the Holy Spirit who makes it possible for us to receive your awesome mercy and to extend your mercy to others. Alleluia!

Tuesday, November 6, 2007
Romans 12, 5-16
Many Parts in One Body; Mutual Love

As Christians, we are all part of the Body of Christ, the Church. We need each other.

You are important. What you have to offer is important.

I am important. What I have to offer is important.

We are not to tolerate evil. We are to despise evil.

It is evil to deceive others. We deceive others when we do not live and speak the truth.

We are learning to bless those who hurt us, knowing that we are called to bless. God will take care of us.

We are learning to rejoice with others and to weep with others. We are secure in the Lord and are able to rejoice with others. Their success does not threaten us.

We are able to weep with others because the Lord has allowed us to be with them in their agony. We are learning to trust the Lord in a deeper way.

Lord Jesus, help us to be real. Help us to live and to speak the truth. You will take care of us and all that concerns us. Alleluia!

Wednesday, November 7, 2007
Romans 13, 8-10
Love Fulfills the Law

We may always act in love, regardless of our feelings. In the previous passage, Paul wrote of paying one's dues. We are under obligation to pay taxes, tolls, respect, and honor to others.

If we love God by loving others, we have already fulfilled our obligations. The Holy Spirit continually leads us to act in unselfish love.

This love must also be extended to ourselves. We are to care wisely for ourselves as well as for those around us.

Lord Jesus, bring our actions of love under your wise sovereignty. Show us how to love ourselves and how to love others. Let us love you by obeying your instructions. Alleluia!

Thursday, November 8, 2007
Romans 14, 7-12
To Live and Die for Christ

In order to have my own way, I have sometimes made choices knowing full well that others could be offended. Does that mean I have to be a doormat? No, but I do have to grow in my understanding of how to live the Christian life.

Jesus prayed for unity of his Body, the Church (John 17, 20-21). It would be because of this unity, this unselfish love of Christians one for another, that the world would believe that Jesus was actually sent from God.

The Lord Jesus Christ is the Lord of us all, living or dead. All of us are alive in the eyes of God (Luke 20, 38).

We are not qualified to judge another or to disdain another. Each of us will stand before God and give an account of ourselves alone.

Lord Jesus, help us not to be frightened, but to be actively in pursuit of pleasing you by loving others. Let us learn to discern your will and to treat others with your love. Alleluia!

Friday, November 9, 2007 Dedication of the Lateran Basilica
Ezekiel 47, 1-2, 8-9, 12
The Wonderful Stream

In the vision of the priest and prophet Ezekiel, wherever the water from the Temple flowed, life became possible. The sea water became fresh. Life flowed from the Temple.

Lord Jesus, thank you for letting your life flow from our lives. Let our lives bear fruit for others. Alleluia!

Saturday, November 10, 2007 St. Leo
Romans 16, 3-9,16,22-27
Paul's Greeting; Greetings from Corinth; Doxology

Many had ministered along with Paul. Paul was eager to acknowledge these men and women and to express his gratitude for their sacrifices and for their ministry.

Paul concluded his letter by glorifying God! God alone was able to give strength to the Christians in Rome and to give strength to us also.

We may or may not be acknowledged publicly for our work for the Lord. Regardless of recognition, the ministry entrusted to us is essential for the proper functioning of the Body of Christ, the Church.

Lord Jesus, thank you for the sweet ways you encourage us, especially when our ministry is hidden. You see us and you smile upon us. Thank you for strengthening us to continue to live the vocation to which you have called us. Alleluia!

Sunday, November 11, 2007
Thirty-second Sunday in Ordinary Time
2 Maccabees 7, 1-2,9-14
Martyrdom of a Mother and Her Sons

Martyrs of today, as well as martyrs of old, are given the courage and strength they need to obey God. They know their true life is with God.

Lord Jesus, strengthen us to bear witness to you in our daily life. Thank you for the Holy Spirit's gift of wisdom as we speak and act in your name. Alleluia!

Monday, November 12, 2007 St. Josaphat
Wisdom 1, 1-7
Exhortation to Justice, the Key of Life

Yielding to the gentle voice of the Holy Spirit will lead us into lives which manifest the holiness and the justice of God. We will abhor deceit of any kind and learn to speak the truth and live the truth.

Lord Jesus, thank you for both the power and the sensitivity of the Holy Spirit. Let us nor grieve or wound the gentle Holy Spirit by our thoughts, our words, or our actions. Let us yield ourselves in joyful trust to the Holy Spirit's guidance. Alleluia!

> Tuesday, November 13, 2007 St. Frances Xavier Cabrini
> Wisdom 2, 23 - 3, 9
> The Wicked Reject Immorality and Justice Alike;
> The Hidden Counsels of God

All those pious people who glibly say that death is just a part of life are wrong, according to Scripture. Death was not God's original idea, but was the result of the choice to sin (Romans 5, 12).

God promises that death will be ultimately be destroyed (Isaiah 25, 8). St. Paul referred to death as an enemy, an enemy which would be destroyed (1 Corinthians 15, 26).

When Jesus entered the picture, he changed everything. By going through what we all fear, death, and emerging alive and triumphant, we need no longer fear death. The same power that raised Jesus from the dead is able to raise us also to new life.

We will shine! We will shine with the light of Christ now on this earth and we will live forever.

Lord Jesus Christ, comfort all who mourn and grieve. Help us to live our lives in the sure knowledge and in firm joy that we are secure in you and with you. Let us trust you today and live with confidence. Alleluia!

> Wednesday, November 14, 2007
> Wisdom 6, 1-11
> Exhortation to Serve Wisdom

God is very concerned with how those in power exercise their authority. They are subject to the strict scrutiny of God.

What those in power are to do is to desire to hear from God. God then promises to instruct them.

Lord Jesus, we intercede for all who are in positions of power and responsibility. Strengthen them to be humble and to ask for you to speak to them. Alleluia!

Thursday, November 15, 2007
Wisdom 7, 22 - 8, 1
Solomon Prays for Help to Speak of Wisdom;
Nature and Incomparable Dignity of Wisdom

Friends and prophets. God's friends. God's prophets.

Who can be trusted to speak for God? Who can be trusted with silence? Who can be trusted with the silence in which one is enclosed with God?

God's friends are content to be silent in God's presence. They are learning to be still and to know that God is God. God may give them words to speak to others.

Sometimes prophets know that they are speaking forth God's words. They faithfully do their best to speak what God has given them to speak.

Other times, prophets are clueless. They may puzzle others. They want most of all to be God's friends. They desire most of all to be in God's presence. The wisdom of God flows from their simple lives of purity and power.

Lord Jesus, you called your first followers first of all simply to be with you. You called them to be disciples, to learn from you before you sent them out as apostles. Let us learn to be content to be with you. You are the Lord and you will decide how we are to serve you. Alleluia!

Friday, November 16, 2007
St. Margaret of Scotland; St. Gertrude
Wisdom 13, 1-9
Digression of False Worship; The Carpenter and Wooden Idols

Source Author. God is the Source. God is the Author. Creation manifests God's glory.

Lord Jesus, let us rejoice in the beauty of creation. Let us live in joyful gratitude and worship the Creator. Alleluia!

Saturday, November 17, 2007 St. Elizabeth of Hungary
Wisdom 18, 14-16; 19, 6-9
Fifth Example: Death of the Egyptian Firstborn;
The Israelites are Spared

From the terror of the hasty Exodus from Egypt to the safe crossing of the Red Sea, the Lord was carefully guiding the Israelites. Their way was unimpeded, because of the Lord's protection.

The Red Sea gave way to a grassy flatland. The Israelites were free to roam about like horses and to frolic like lambs in a meadow!

Our way may be terrifying, but the Lord is guiding us. The Lord will either remove the obstacles before us or guide us through the obstacles to our destination.

Lord Jesus, thank you that we are sheltered in your presence as we continue our journey through this life to the place you have prepared for us. Alleluia!

Sunday, November 18, 2007
Thirty-third Sunday in Ordinary Time
Malachi 3, 19-20
The Message of the Covenant

We will be like happy little calves loosed from their stalls when our King comes for us. It will be a time of sunshine and healing.

Lord Jesus, let us learn to live in joy and hope. You are our Redeemer and our King. You will come in glory! Alleluia!

Monday, November 19, 2007
1 Maccabees 1, 10-15,41-43,54-57,62-63
Pact Between Jews and Gentiles;
Prohibition against Religion

There have always been those who compromised their faith. We have no idea what their reasons were. Only God knows.

In this particular time in Jewish history, before the birth of Christ, there was terrible suffering and persecution. There were some Israelites who abandoned their covenant with God.

The evil king ordered the desecration of the altar in the temple in Jerusalem. He ordered that those who did not cooperate with him to be searched out and killed.

Still, many Israelites refused to profane their covenant with God or to eat food that had been declared unclean. They chose death over compromise.

Lord Jesus, we still want it both ways. We want all the comforts of our culture and we want to believe that we serve you. Let us be thankful for the good things given to us and yet not be in servitude to them. We cry out to you for mercy and for forgiveness for all the ways we have offended you. Let us cleave to you and give witness to you. We pray for all to come to knowledge of you. Alleluia!

Tuesday, November 20, 2007
2 Maccabees 6, 18-31
Martyrdom of Eleazar

The ninety year old Jewish scribe, Eleazar, could have easily compromised his faith and avoided horrible suffering and death. Instead of compromise, he chose death.

He chose the honor of God over saving himself. This was a true death with dignity.

Lord Jesus, let us live for you with joy and trust. When you call us to come to you, let us die for you, knowing that you are with us and you will strengthen us to complete your plan for us. We will live with you forever and ever. Alleluia!

Wednesday, November 21, 2007
Presentation of the Blessed Virgin Mary
2 Maccabees 7, 1,20-31
Martyrdom of a Mother and Her Sons

After the executions of his six brothers, the youngest brother could have accepted the king's bribes. The young man, by compromising his faith, could have not only survived but also prospered.

No! The young man's mother, who had already endured the loss of six of her seven sons, courageously continued to place her trust in the Lord. The Lord who had given life to her sons would also give life back to them.

The young man was, of course, tortured and killed. The brave mother was then killed.

Lord Jesus, thank you for the example of this faith-filled family. Let us remember how brief our time is here on earth. Let us bear witness to you, trusting you with every moment of our life. We are safe and secure with you. Alleluia!

> Thursday, November 22, 2007 St. Cecilia
> 1 Maccabees 2, 15-29
> Pagan Worship Refused

Mattathias and his sons also suffered for their faith, refusing to accept the king's bribes of riches and temporal honor. Zealous for God's law, they abandoned their earthly possessions in the town of Modein and fled to the mountains and into the wilderness.

Lord Jesus, whether we are in the midst of the city or in the seclusion of the desert, we are still subject to temptation. We have numerous overt and subtle opportunities to compromise our faith and to promote ourselves. Let us learn to recognize these temptations for what they are. Let us then turn to you and be stouthearted in our trust! You alone are in ultimate control of our lives. We praise you, thank you, and place all our trust in you. Alleluia!

> Friday, November 23, 2007 St. Clement I,
> St. Columban, B. Miguel Pro
> 1 Maccabees 4, 36-37,52-59
> Purification of the Temple

A new altar! On the very anniversary of the desecration of the old altar, the new altar was consecrated.

Judas Maccabeus, son of Mattathias, prayed, fasted, humbled himself, and sought the Lord's guidance for the restoration of the people of Israel and the sanctuary of the temple. The Lord granted the defeat of those who had persecuted the people of Israel.

A new altar! A new beginning.

The people rejoiced with music, adoration, and praise to the Lord. The celebration, which we know as Hannukah, continued for eight days.

When there has been desolation in our lives and there is now joy, it is crucial to celebrate. The Lord has brought us through our suffering and the Lord is victorious!

Lord Jesus, thank you that you are the light in our darkness. You call us to prayer, fasting, and repentance. You also call us to celebrate! Alleluia!

Saturday, November 24, 2007
St. Andrew Dung-Lac and Companions
1 Maccabees 6, 1-13
Defeat and Death of Antiochus IV

We don't need to worry about those who fight against God's people and seem to prevail. God is still in charge and has ways to see that justice is accomplished.

While in Persia, King Antiochus was informed that the Israelites had destroyed the abomination in the temple in Jerusalem. The king, on his deathbed, remembered his evil deeds. He remembered taking the sacred vessels from the temple in Jerusalem. God's people had suffered greatly because of this king.

Lord Jesus, help us to live bravely for you. Help us to trust you to do what we cannot do. Alleluia!

Sunday, November 25, 2007   Christ the King
2 Samuel 5, 1-3
David King of Israel

When Saul was the king of Israel, it had been David, the young shepherd, who had fought for the people of Israel against their enemies. It was the Lord, who alone sees into our hearts, who had chosen David to be king (1 Samuel 16, 7). Now was the time for David to be publicly anointed as King of Israel.

There is time when ministry is silent and invisible. There is a time for seclusion. There is a time for suffering.

There is also a time when ministry is public. There is a time when God's choice, made in the mystery of God's wisdom and sovereignty, is made public.

Lord Jesus, thank you that you are our King. You left the glory of heaven to dwell in the womb of Mary, your mother. You were born in obscurity and lived a life of poverty and humility. You suffered and died for us. God raised you from the dead. Alleluia! Thank you that you will return as King. All will acknowledge you as King and will kneel before you. Alleluia!

Monday, November 26, 2007
Daniel 1, 1-6, 8-20
The Food Test

Those who honor God and seek to please God will receive honor from God (1 Samuel 2, 30). God is debtor to no one.

The young Daniel, in exile in Babylonia, declined the food and wine from the table of the king. He preferred to drink water and to eat vegetables rather than to defile himself or to dishonor God.

The Lord honored Daniel and the three other Israelites. These four young men adhered strictly to their diet of vegetables and water for ten days. At the end of that time, they appeared healthier than those who had dined at the king's table.

God had given these four young Israelites great gifts in the fields of literature and science. In addition, God had given to Daniel great discernment in the interpretation of dreams and visions.

This gift would be crucial at a later time. Even in this time of captivity, God was with Daniel and his friends and was honoring their integrity.

Lord Jesus, sometimes we feel stuck in some form of captivity or exile. Open our hearts to see the gifts you have given us right now, even if we are not where we would like to be. Let us use these gifts and honor you in every way during this difficult time. At the right time, you will lead us forth into a new life. Alleluia!

Tuesday, November 27, 2007
Daniel 2, 31-45
The King's Dream

Daniel's gift of interpretation of dreams was about to be used! King Nebuchadnezzar, greatly troubled by a dream, had sought, in vain, to have the dream interpreted. In his frustration, he had ordered that all his supposedly wise advisors, unable to explain the dream, be killed.

Daniel, being among those considered wise, was, of course pretty nervous about this decree. He exercised great prudence as he sought to save the lives of his Israelite friends, his own life, and the lives of the king's advisors who had been unable to interpret the dream

Daniel notified his friends to pray and to seek God's mercy. God revealed to Daniel the meaning of the dream and Daniel immediately thanked God (Daniel 2, 17-23). It is crucial always to give God the glory!

Daniel gave glory to God even before he revealed to the king the meaning of the dream. Daniel made it clear that, although the king's advisors (magicians, astrologers, and others) were unable to interpret the dream, God was quite able to give the meaning of the dream. The awestruck king, realizing that God had indeed given Daniel the gift of interpretation of dreams, promoted Daniel to a high position.

The dream? In brief, although earthly kingdoms would be destroyed, the kingdom of God would endure forever.

Lord Jesus, we worship you as our King. Let your kingdom come in us and let your will be done in us today and forever. Alleluia!

Wednesday, November 28, 2007
Daniel 5, 1-6,13-14,16-17,23-28
The Writing on the Wall

King Belshazzar was about to be confronted by God! The king had thrown a big bash, had had too much to drink, and then allowed the guests to drink from the vessels which had been stolen from the temple in Jerusalem.

The guests not only drank from these vessels, intended for use in the temple, but they also worshipped idols made of gold and silver. Bad idea.

The king freaked out and panicked when he saw a hand writing mysterious words on the wall. In his terror, he called for his astrologers and others who were, of course, unable to interpret the message.

Daniel, however, could and would interpret the message written on the wall. Disdaining the king's bribes, Daniel spoke the hard truth to the king. Daniel reminded the king that the previous king, Nebuchadnezzar (Belshazzar's father), had become proud and was, as a result, severely humbled by God.

King Belshazzar had apparently not learned from his father's experience. Throwing a party with vessels designated for use in the temple and then worshipping idols did not please God.

As the message on the wall indicated, the king had indeed been weighed on God's scales and was to experience the loss of the kingdom. He would also experience, that very night, the loss of his life.

Lord Jesus, let us continually acknowledge your sovereignty in our lives. Our idolatry may not be as blatant as that of the Babylonian king, but there is always the possibility that we veer from worship of God to worship of self. Thank you for the presence of the Holy Spirit to confront us, to convict us, and to correct us. Let us ask for mercy and forgiveness and then continue to worship you and obey you as our King. Alleluia!

Thursday, November 29, 2007
Daniel 6, 12-28
In the Lions' Den

Motivated by jealousy, the other two supervisors in King Darius' kingdom decided to find a clever way to get rid of Daniel. They perceived Daniel, a holy man, as a threat to their own ambitions.

How do you trap those who are so dedicated to God? Easy. Lie about them and then cast them into a den of lions to be devoured.

Daniel was accustomed to placing God first, no matter what. He continued to pray to God, irrespective of the decree that prayer was now to be directed solely to the king.

God indeed closed the mouths of the lions. Daniel was not hurt at all. The other supervisors, however, were then cast into the den of lions and were destroyed.

"Then King Darius wrote to all peoples and nations of every language throughout the whole world: 'May you have abundant prosperity! I make a decree, that in all my royal dominion people should tremble and fear before the God of Daniel: for he is the living God enduring forever. His kingdom shall never be destroyed, and his dominion has no end. He delivers and rescues, he works signs and wonders in heaven and on earth; for he has saved Daniel from the power of the lions.' So this Daniel prospered during the reign of Darius and the reign of Cyrus the Persian (vv. 25-28)."

Lord Jesus, thank you for Daniel's example of steadfast determination to honor God. Whether we are in or out of our equivalent of a den of lions, let us trust in you and serve you. You will not allow the motives of others to stop your plan for us. Alleluia!

Friday, November 30, 2007 St. Andrew
Romans 10, 9-18
Righteousness Based on Faith

Heart. Mouth.

St. Paul tells us, "… if you confess with your lips that Jesus is Lord and believe in your heart that God raised him from the dead, you will be saved. For one believes with the heart and so is justified, and one confesses with the mouth and so is saved. The scripture says, 'No one who believes in him will be put to shame.' For there is no distinction between Jew and Greek; the same Lord is Lord of all and is generous to all who call on him. For 'Everyone who calls on the name of the Lord shall be saved (vv. 9-13).'"

Only the Holy Spirit can bring our heart and our mouth into agreement. Our wholeness and our salvation are evidenced by this agreement.

If we believe in our heart that Jesus has risen from the dead, we will, in some way, speak forth this knowledge. Our words and our lives will manifest this quiet knowledge which rests in our heart.

Everyone! Everyone, whether Jewish or Gentile, who calls out to Jesus will be made whole and will experience salvation.

Home at last! Jesus takes us by the hand, enters our heart in the Person of the Holy Spirit, and leads us home at last to God, our loving Father.

How thankful we are for those who proclaim this extraordinary news. They help us to trust God We need their voices.

"And how are they to proclaim him unless they are sent? As it is written, 'How beautiful are the feet of those who bring good news (v. 10)!'"

Lord Jesus, sometimes our heart is so wounded that, although we believe, we have become silent. Restore us and remind us that the same power of the Holy Spirit that raised you from the dead is now living in us. Let us speak again the message you call us to speak. Alleluia!

Saturday, December 1, 2007
Daniel 7, 15-27
Vision of the Four Beasts

Daniel understood that his spirit was clothed within his flesh. He was terribly shaken and terrified in his spirit as he was given visions of what was to come.

However, before he was given the frightening vision, he was granted an even more important vision. Jesus! Daniel saw Jesus as Son of Man, coming in clouds and receiving total authority from God (Daniel 7, 13-14).

Daniel, in his vision, saw that there would be not only great suffering in store for God's holy people but also that there would be a great victory. The Most High God was victorious!.

Lord Jesus, you are victorious over suffering and death. You will come in great glory. Come soon, Lord Jesus, as our King. We worship you! Alleluia!

Sunday, December 2, 2007 First Sunday of Advent, Year A
Isaiah 2, 1-5
Zion, the Messianic Capital

"In days to come the mountain of the LORD's house shall be established as the highest of the mountains, and shall be raised above the hills; all the nations shall stream to it. Many peoples shall come and say, 'Come, let us go up to the mountain of the LORD, to the house of the God of Jacob; that he may teach us his ways and that we may walk in his paths.' For out of Zion shall go forth instruction, and word of the LORD from Jerusalem (vv. 2,3)."

Jerusalem! Jerusalem is the real capital hill! The temple. God's house.

Let us go to our God in prayer this Advent. Let us ask God to teach us. Let us accept God's rule.

Lord Jesus, you are the holy Anointed One. You are the royal Messiah. Let us truly live for you this Advent. Let us live in peace with you, with ourselves, and with others. Alleluia!

Monday, December 3, 2007 St. Francis Xavier
Isaiah 4, 2-6
The Messianic Branch

We continue to pray for the peace of Jerusalem (Psalm 122, 6) as we await the full revelation of Jesus as our royal Messiah. There will be a manifestation of life and holiness beyond our current ability to comprehend. The Lord's glory will be manifest in Jerusalem.

"On that day the branch of the LORD shall be beautiful and glorious ... (v. 2)."

Lord Jesus, you are the branch from the remnant stump of King David's dynasty. You are the divine Vine and we are your branches. Let your life and holiness flow through us this Advent as we await your coming in glory. Alleluia!

Tuesday, December 4, 2007 St. John of Damascus
Isaiah 11, 1-10
The Rule of Immanuel; Union of Ephraim and Judah

The revelation of God blossomed forth in Jesus of Nazareth. The Holy Spirit reigned freely in Jesus.

When Jesus reigns as the royal Messiah, we will at last know peace. All creatures will dwell in safety. All will know the Lord.

Lord Jesus, shine forth in us today! We long for your coming in glory. We long for your reign upon earth. Rule and reign in us today. Alleluia!

Wednesday, December 5, 2007 Advent Weekday
Isaiah 25, 6-10
The Divine Vindicator

"On this mountain the LORD of hosts will make for all peoples a feast of rich food, a feast of well-aged wines, of rich foods filled with marrow, of well-aged wines strained clear. And he will destroy on this mountain the shroud that is cast over all peoples, the sheet that is spread over all nations; he will swallow up death forever. Then the LORD GOD will wipe away the tears from all faces …. It will be said on that day, Lo this is our God, we have waited for him, so that he might save us. This is the LORD for whom we have waited; let us be glad and rejoice in his salvation. For the hand of the LORD will rest on this mountain (vv. 6-10a)."

Our path through life may seem impossible and yet, as our loving, strong Shepherd leads us, our path will become smooth. We will be able to continue along the path we called to tread.

Lord Jesus, we look to you to make right what is currently still not right. We trust you and praise you! Alleluia!

Thursday, December 6, 2007 St. Nicholas
Isaiah 26, 1-6
The Divine Vindicator

Walls for protection. Gates for celebration!

We are enclosed, even is difficult times, for our protection. The Lord is caring for us in the best way.

The Lord is always victorious! We share in the Lord's victory and will one day enter through the victors' gates. "Open to me the gates of righteousness: I will go into them and I will praise the LORD …. (Psalm 118, 19 KJV)."

Lord Jesus, thank you for the walls which puzzle us and frustrate us. Help us to see that these walls are here for our protection. Thank you for the victory you have gained for us. Thank you for the time when the gates will open and we will enter and praise you forever. Alleluia!

> Friday, December 7, 2007 St. Ambrose
> Isaiah 29, 17-24
> Redemption

Time! When God's time comes for restoration and redemption, it will be glorious!

It will be beyond anything we could have imagined. God's thoughts and God's ways are always higher than our thoughts and our ways (Isaiah 5, 9).

There will be no need to fear tyrants. They will no longer trouble us.

The Lord of mercy and compassion is also the Lord of justice and judgment. The Lord knows how to teach all of us what we still need to learn. We will understand one day what we struggle to understand now.

Lord Jesus, thank you that the Holy Spirit knows how to rewire our spiritual, mental, and emotional circuits. Thank you for the joyful transformation that awaits us as we continue to be honest with you and trust you. Alleluia!

> Saturday, December 8, 2007 Immaculate Conception
> Genesis 3, 9-15,20
> The Fall of Man

Fixation. Focus.

Adam and Eve were fixated on fear and blame. The Blessed Virgin Mary was focused on God.

Lord Jesus, thank you for entering our world and overcoming it. Thank you that we are now free to follow you. Alleluia!

> Sunday, December 9, 2007 Second Sunday of Advent
> Isaiah 11, 1-10
> The Rule of Immanuel; Union of Ephraim and Judah

God is with us. Immanuel. Jesus!

How will Jesus, the royal Messiah, rule when he comes in glory? How did Jesus live when he walked the earth? He lived in complete loving obedience to God, his Father. He was led by the Holy Spirit.

When he returns as our King, Jesus will rule with wisdom and justice. There will at last be peace because he is our peace.

Lord Jesus, your reign among us will be powerful and unhindered when you return in glory. All will acknowledge you and honor you. Let us honor you today by our loving obedience and trust. Alleluia!

Monday, December 10, 2007 Advent Weekday
Isaiah 35, 1-10
Israel's Deliverance

"The wilderness and the dry land shall be glad, the desert shall rejoice and blossom; like the crocus it shall blossom abundantly and rejoice with joy and singing (vv. 1,2a)."

Bloom! The dry and parched desert will bloom.

Those who have lived dry and parched lives of suffering will also bloom. They will bloom into new strength with the coming of their saving God.

The blind will see. The deaf will hear. The lame will be able to jump for joy. The silent will be able to sing at last.

In this desert which blooms, there is a highway for those who are redeemed. On this way of holiness, they will make their journey to Zion.

"And the ransomed of the LORD shall return, and come to Zion with singing; everlasting joy shall be upon their heads; they shall obtain joy and gladness, and sorrow and sighing shall flee away (v. 10)."

Lord Jesus, thank you for strengthening us to make our journey bravely in this world of suffering. Let us live lives of holiness as we travel, knowing that we will live in joy forever. Alleluia!

Tuesday, December 11, 2007 St. Damasus I
Isaiah 40, 1-11
Promise of Salvation

No matter what "desert" we are in, we may prepare a way for the Lord to enter our situation. The mighty God who comes with power to save us is also as tender as a shepherd enfolding his lambs in his arms, feeding them, and caring for the lambs' mothers.

"He shall feed his flock like a shepherd; he will gather the lambs in his arms, and carry them in his bosom, and gently lead the mother sheep (v. 11)."

Lord Jesus, show us how to prepare for you this Advent. You are God's Word made flesh. You will return in glory and splendor. Today, Lord Jesus, hold us in your strong, tender shepherd's arms all the lambs and their mothers who need your care. Alleluia!

Wednesday, December 12, 2007 Our Lady of Guadalupe
Zechariah 2, 14-17
The New Jerusalem

Suffering Jerusalem is addressed tenderly as "daughter" and is invited to rejoice and to sing! Jerusalem is the Lord's beloved, the Lord's chosen.

It is dangerous to hurt Jerusalem. The mighty Lord encircles Jerusalem (Zechariah 2, 9). Jerusalem is the apple of the Lord's eye (Zechariah 2, 12).

Lord Jesus, we wait in adoration and in silence for you. Come. Lord Jesus. Alleluia!

Thursday, December 13, 2007 St. Lucy
Isaiah 41, 13-20
The Liberation of Israel

"For I, the LORD your God, hold your right hand; it is I who say to you, 'Do not fear, I will help you (v 13).'"

The Lord promises to help us and to make us new. The Lord will never forsake us. The Lord will perform wonders!

Lord Jesus, come into the desert of our lives and let your springs of life-giving water burst forth. You are the Lord with whom nothing is impossible. Alleluia!

Friday, December 14, 2007 St. John of the Cross
Isaiah 48, 17-19
Exhortation to the Exiles

"Thus says the LORD, your Redeemer, the Holy One of Israel: I am the LORD your God, who teaches you for your own good, who leads you in the way you should go (v. 17)."

The Lord promises us individual guidance. The Lord will tell us what we are to do.

Lord Jesus, help us to obey you and to believe you love us and know what is best for us and for those we love. When we choose our own way and disobey you, forgive us and please continue to lead us. Thank you for strengthening us to entrust ourselves completely to you and to obey you with all our heart. Alleluia!

Saturday, December 15, 2007 Advent Weekday
Sirach 48, 1-4,9-11
Elijah and Elisha

The mighty prophet Elijah, sensitive soul that he was, was held within the capsule of God's grace. He lived and ministered in a time of great wickedness. Evil, sinfulness, and idolatry were rampant.

In this difficult time, Elijah came and spoke forth God's message. He informed King Ahaz of an upcoming drought (1 Kings 17, 1). He prayed to the Lord and a widow's dead son returned to life (1 Kings 17, 19-21). Elijah also prayed to the Lord and the fire of the Lord descended (1 Kings 17, 36-38)!

Before his difficult and dramatic public ministry, Elijah was enclosed with the Lord by the stream of Cherith. There, by the brook, the Lord met all his needs.

Lord Jesus, let us learn to be still and quiet with you this Advent. Thank you that we are encapsulated in your grace as we live and speak for you. Alleluia!

Sunday, December 16, 2007 Third Sunday in Advent
Isaiah 35, 1-6, 10
Israel's Deliverance

Future! This glorious prophecy reassures us that there will be a glorious future for God's people.

Living in the here and now is very difficult. We become discouraged and even fearful.

We are told, however, not to fear! We are to stay strong.

God is here for us." Say to them that are of a fearful heart, Be strong, fear not: behold, your God will come … and save you (Isaiah 35, 4 KJV)."

Lord Jesus, thank you for ransoming us and redeeming us. Thank you for infusing us with new strength as we continue our pilgrimage to the heavenly Jerusalem, where our future is one of joy. Alleluia!

Monday, December 17, 2007 Late Advent Weekday
Genesis 49, 2,8-10
Jacob's Testament

God's timing! Mysterious.

God's ways. Even more mysterious. Judah was the son of Jacob and the unloved Leah (Genesis 29, 35).

How could the patriarch Jacob have truly understood what he was speaking forth to his son, Judah? "The scepter shall not depart from Judah .. (KJV)."

Generation after generation would go by. At last there would appear King David, from the tribe of Judah.

Generation after generation would go by. At last there would appear Jesus!

Generation after generation. Jesus will return as King. The scepter is his forever.

Lord Jesus, you came to us as infant. You will return as King, as the royal Messiah. All will worship you then. Let us worship you now with faces and hearts uplifted, waiting in joy for your return and for your reign. Alleluia!

Tuesday, December 18, 2007 Late Advent Weekday
Jeremiah 23, 5-8
Messianic Reign

One day, the dark days of exile will be over! God's flock will enjoy safety and freedom in the sunlit meadows of Israel.

The King will come. The King, the true King, the King who is wise and just, will reign.

Lord Jesus, as these long, dark days of winter Advent continue, let us remember that you are always with us and you are our Light and our Salvation. You are our Good Shepherd, leading us through our own exile into your bright sunlit meadows. Alleluia!

Wednesday, December 19, 2007 Late Advent Weekday
Judges 13, 2-7
The Birth of Samson

Deliverance! The Lord was planning to deliver the people of Israel from the Philistines.

It was because the Israelites had grievously offended the Lord that they were in this predicament. Still, the merciful Lord was planning to deliver them.

Samson was chosen, before his birth, to be consecrated to the Lord. Samson was to begin the process of delivering the people of Israel.

It was to an obscure, childless woman (we aren't even told her name) that the Lord's angel came to deliver this extraordinary message. She was to become the mother of a man consecrated to the Lord's service for life. She was instructed to abstain from alcohol and to eat nothing unclean. She was the chosen vessel to bear this chosen child.

Lord Jesus, you came to deliver us and yet we still seem to dwell in bondage. Let us not grow weary this Advent. Come to us and deliver us from despair. Let us live in the wonder and freedom you came to give us. Nothing is impossible with you! Alleluia!

Thursday, December 20, 2007 Late Advent Weekday
Isaiah 7, 10-14
Birth of Immanuel

Again! The Lord was trying again to get a message across to King Ahab of Judah.

The Lord had previously spoken to the king through the words of the prophet Isaiah, instructing the king to remain peaceful and fearless (Isaiah 7, 4). Judah was faced at that time with serious threats of invasion.

The Lord continued to speak to the king through the prophet Isaiah. The king was invited to be bold and to ask the Lord for a sign!

Whether or not Ahaz asked for a sign, the Lord was still sending a sign, born of a virgin. Immanuel! The ultimate sign.

Lord Jesus, over and over you speak to us through Scripture, through sacraments, and through others. Forgive us when we shrink back from accepting the message you are giving us. You are with us at this very moment and we have nothing to fear. Let us trust that you are redeeming our past and preparing us to receive anew your message of love. You are truly with us. Alleluia!

Friday, December 21, 2007 St. Peter Canisius
Song of Songs 2, 8-14
A Tryst in the Spring

In the midst of winter, in the final days of Advent, life and love rush forth! This beautiful passage from the Song of Songs breathes the promise of spring into our waiting hearts.

Vines! A dove's song. A fig tree. Fragrant blooms.

Jesus! Our Lover, Jesus, is here.

Lord Jesus, your love for us is so hard for us to comprehend. We hurt you when we doubt your love. Forgive us. Thank you, Father in heaven, for sending your Beloved Son to us. Thank you, gentle and powerful Holy Spirit for filling us with light and love as we wait.

Saturday, December 22, 2007 Late Advent Weekday
1 Samuel 1, 24-28
Samuel is Offered to God

In between. This was an in between time for Hannah, the mother of Samuel. Her time of sorrow was over. Samuel, the child for whom she had prayed, was here.

Faithfully fulfilling her promise to the Lord, Hannah took Samuel to the temple to be trained for the Lord's service. She entrusted her little son to the Lord and departed. She did not know what lay ahead of her.

Hannah, rejoicing in the Lord's gift of Samuel, rejoiced even more in the Lord! The Lord who had given her Samuel had great joy in store for her. For this woman who had known great suffering, the Lord gave three more sons and two daughters (1 Samuel 2, 21).

Lord Jesus, we give ourselves and our loved ones to you. In all the times of our lives, we rejoice in you. Alleluia!

Sunday, December 23, 2007 Fourth Sunday of Advent
Isaiah 7, 10-14
Birth of Immanuel

Ask! The Lord told King Ahaz to ask for a sign.

Jesus told us ask (Matthew 7, 7; Luke 11, 9). Jesus said that everyone who asks will receive (Matthew 7, 8; Luke 11, 10). We are told to ask in the name of Jesus in order that our "… joy may be full. (John 16, 24 KJV)."

The Lord loves us and will not give us what would harm us. If we ask unwisely, we will still receive. We will receive what the Lord knows we need and what will be for our good.

Lord Jesus, you are the Sign that completes our joy. You are Immanuel. You are God with us. Alleluia!

Monday, December 24, 2007 Late Advent Weekday
2 Samuel 7, 1-5,8-12,14,16
David's Concern for the Ark; The Lord's Promises

God chooses the ways in which we are to serve. David, a shepherd boy, was chosen by God to be the future king.

David, as king, greatly desired to build a house for God. However, the building of a house (temple) for God would be accomplished during the reign of King David's son, King Solomon.

Lord Jesus, thank you that you are with us as you were with David in the grassy meadows filled with grazing sheep. You are our Good Shepherd. You are the Shepherd of shepherds. This last day of Advent, let us trust you that you are leading us into the pastures where we are to serve you. Let us be faithful to you in our present assignment and trust you for the future. Alleluia!

Tuesday, December 25, 2007 The Nativity of the Lord, Year A
Isaiah 52, 7-10
Let Zion Rejoice

Beautiful! "How beautiful upon the mountains are the feet of the messenger who announces peace, who brings good news, who announces salvation, who says to Zion, 'Your God reigns (v. 7).'"

Did you ever see Mother Teresa's feet? I once saw, in a book, a black and white photo of her feet. These poor old, sandal-clad feet were beautiful in God's service! She brought joyful tidings to our dark world,

This Christmas Day, we may sing! Our God has come to us!

Jesus is here to restore us, to comfort us, and to redeem us. We too may bring joy to the world.

Lord Jesus, we give you our feet, our hearts, our hands, our entire being into your wise and tender care. You came to be with us. We worship you and trust you. Alleluia!

Wednesday, December 26, 2007 St. Stephen
Acts 6, 8-10; 7, 54-59
Accusation against Stephen

Crib. Cross.

From his crib to his Cross, Jesus, guided by the Holy Spirit, was living out the will of his Father.

Stephen, the first Christian martyr, was also guided. Stephen, filled with the power of the Holy Spirit, was clearly guided by the Holy Spirit as he spoke with boldness to his accusers.

Before he was martyred, Stephen saw into heaven. He saw Jesus! He spoke with Jesus. Jesus was there to receive the spirit of his faithful follower.

Lord Jesus, thank you for being with us as we follow you. You know we are far from perfect. We falter and we compromise. Sometimes we don't even speak the truth to ourselves, because it is so painful. You love us even in our flawed condition. Give us hope and trust that we will finish our course on earth and that you will be there, smiling, to welcome us Home. Alleluia!

Thursday, December 27, 2007 St. John
1 John 1, 1-4
The Word of Life

The spoken Word became the visible Word! The first disciples and apostles actually saw Jesus.

We too "see" Jesus as we read the accounts of his earliest followers. They were flawed and so are we. Yet, they saw Jesus. They followed Jesus.

We are included in their company and in their fellowship. What better company could we keep?

Their fellowship was with the Son of God and Son of Mary, Jesus. The apostles wrote to us for their own sake as well as for ours. They knew that their joy would be full because they had faithfully told us about Jesus.

Lord Jesus, speak your own words of life into our lives. Let your life become increasingly visible in our lives. Let us remember we are in good company, in the very best company. We are with you and with all who love you and are trying to follow you. Alleluia!

Friday, December 28, 2007 Holy Innocents
1 John 1, 5 - 2, 2
God is Light; Christ and His Commandments

Cleansed! Not only forgiven, but also cleansed. The blood of Christ has cleansed us from all our sins. We are free to walk in God's pure and holy light.

Lord Jesus, thank you that you are our Advocate with God. You paid the price for our sins and for the sins of everyone! Let us rejoice in you and live with joy this beautiful new day. Alleluia!

Saturday, December 29, 2007 St. Thomas Becket
1 John 2, 3-11
Christ and His Commandments; The New Commandment

The darkness of this world, so overwhelming, is not permanent. The light of Christ shines forth and is victorious!

Lord Jesus, thank you that you have conquered all darkness within us and within our poor, sin-wracked world. You are our Redeemer and you know how to take all darkness and to transform it into light. Let us learn to keep your commandment to love. Let us live with courage this new day. Let us be patient with ourselves as your love grows stronger and stronger within us. Alleluia!

>Sunday, December 30, 2007 The Holy Family
>Sirach 3, 2-6,12-14
>Duties toward Parents

Honor. Honor. Honor.

Even as we grow older and our parents grow older, we are to honor them. Yes, they made mistakes. We are still to honor them.

If they are no longer on earth, we may still honor them. We may still speak well of them. They were human and therefore fallible. Still, they gave us life!

Lord Jesus, help us to be careful how we speak of our parents. Let us treat them with tenderness. Let us honor their memory. Alleluia!

>Monday, December 31, 2007 St. Sylvester 1
>1 John 2, 18-21
>Antichrists

Jesus will return to us in glory! Jesus will return as the royal Messiah to reign.

Lord Jesus, thank you for your protection as we live and wait for you. Thank you for the Holy Spirit's gift of discernment. Thank you for the anointing which we have been given. Let us walk in your strength and joy this day. Alleluia!

>Tuesday, January 1, 2008 Mary, Mother of God
>Numbers 6, 22-27
>The Priestly Blessing

" 'The LORD bless you and keep you; the LORD make his face to shine upon you, and be gracious to you; the LORD lift up his countenance upon you, and give you peace (vv. 24-26).' "

Our year begins with God's blessing. God is indeed speaking good words over us.

God is blessing us and keeping us. God is smiling upon us and looking upon us with kindness. God is giving us peace.

Lord Jesus, you are our Great High Priest. We thank you and receive your blessing today. Let us live in the strength of your blessing this day and all the days of this year. Alleluia!

Wednesday, January 2, 2007 St. Basil the Great'
St. Gregory Nazianzen
1 John 2, 22-28
Antichrists; Life from God's Anointing' Children of God

Alignment! This year I want my life to be more closely aligned to Christ.

How do I do this? I don't. It's already been done. A done deal.

Remain. Stay put. All I have to do is to remain in my safe and secure relationship with Jesus and with God the Father.

How? That's the work of the Holy Spirit. The Holy Spirit is teaching me how to remain.

Lord Jesus, I've struggled and struggled and yet you've made it so easy. Help me this new year to learn to relax into your arms and to remain in your love. I want to learn to live in your heart. Thank you that the gentle Holy Spirit is my Teacher, who will bring my life into correct alignment. Alleluia!

Thursday, January 3, 2008 Most Holy Name of Jesus
1 John 2, 29 - 3, 6
Children of God; Avoiding Sin

Right now! We are God's beloved children right now. We don't have to struggle to prove anything. We are who God says we are. We are safe and secure in our identity.

This gets better and better! There is even an exciting element of mystery. God has not yet revealed what we will become in the future.

All we are told is that we will somehow be like God. We will see God as God really is. Our misconceptions will vanish.

Hope! Since this amazing hope has been given to us by God, let us seek to live lives of purity.

Lord Jesus, thank you that you came to take away our sins. We could not do this for ourselves, so you came to earth and did it for us. Let us truly believe that we are God's children. That makes you our big brother. Thank you for watching out for us and leading us safely Home to our loving Father. Alleluia!

> Friday, January 4, 2008 St. Elizabeth Ann Seton
> 1 John 3, 7-10
> Avoiding Sin

Jesus! Jesus came to undo and destroy the devil's works. Jesus lived and spoke the truth. If we are living the truth, we will experience light (John 3, 21).

As God's children, we share in God's nature. We have the Holy Spirit within us, giving us the power to love and to act in righteousness.

Lord Jesus, help us to remember who we are. We are God's children. We live in light. Let our identity as God's children of light be manifest today by our actions of love. Alleluia!

> Saturday, January 5, 2008 St. John Neumann
> 1 John 3, 11-21
> Avoiding Sin; Confidence before God

Love and life. Hatred and death.

Jesus gave his life for us. We are now free to live our lives for others.

We are learning to love ourselves and to reach out in love to others. We are living out our identity as God's beloved children.

Lord Jesus, thank you for freeing us. Let us not focus so much on our failings, but on YOU! Let us learn to receive forgiveness and then to live with boldness and confidence. Alleluia!

> Sunday, January 6, 2008 Epiphany of the Lord
> Isaiah 60, 1-6
> Glory of the New Zion

"Arise, shine; for your light has come, and the glory of the LORD has risen upon you (v. 1)."

Light! It's time to get up, ready or not. God's glory is shining upon you. Bounteous gifts are being delivered to you.

Lord Jesus, thank you that you are here with us! We are radiant as we gaze upon you. Let your light fill us this day and this year. Alleluia!

Monday, January 7, 2008 St. Raymond of Penafort
1 John 3, 22 - 4, 6
Confidence before God; Testing the Spirits

You're a winner! The Holy Spirit living in you is eternal. The Holy Spirit is bigger and stronger than the deceptive spirits that are loose in this temporary world.

You're already a winner! Jesus came in the flesh and won the victory for you.

Hooray! Let's live this day as the winners we truly are. Life cannot defeat us. Death cannot defeat us. Jesus lived, died, and rose again for us.

Lord Jesus, let us stand up straight and tall today. Let us shine with joy. We are winners because of you. Let us trust you and love others. Alleluia!

Tuesday, January 8, 2008
1 John 4, 7-10
God's Love and the Christian Life

Lord Jesus, thank you for the Holy Spirit who teaches me to receive, to receive, to receive your love for me. Let your love so fill me that I have plenty of your love to give away to others. Alleluia!

Wednesday, January 9, 2008
1 John 4, 11-18
God's Love and Christian Life

God's Spirit is in us! As believers in the Lord Jesus Christ. God has given us the gift of the mighty Holy Spirit

We are learning to think, to love, and to act as God thinks, loves and acts. "For who hath known the mind of the Lord ....? But we have the mind of Christ (1 Corinthians 2, 16 KJV)."

Lord Jesus, thank you for removing unhealthy fear from us. Thank you that the powerful Holy Spirit lives within us, filling us with love. Alleluia!

Thursday, January 10, 2008
1 John 4, 19 - 5, 4
God's Love and Christian Life; Faith is Victory over the World

As God's children, we are overcoming the world! The victorious Holy Spirit lives in us and works through us.

God loves us. We are freed to love God and to offer God's love to others.

Lord Jesus, let us learn to see ourselves as you see us. You see us as victors! Alleluia!

Friday, January 11, 2008
1 John 5, 5-13
Faith is Victory over the World

We are victorious over this world because of our trust in Jesus. Everlasting life is found in Jesus, the Son of God. God testifies on behalf of Jesus.

After Jesus was baptized in the waters of the Jordan River, the Holy Spirit descended upon him in the form of a dove. From heaven, God the Father spoke, affirming that Jesus was his beloved Son, with whom he was very pleased. God was testifying on behalf of Jesus.

After Jesus died on the Cross, a soldier pierced his side. From the wounded side of the crucified Christ flowed water and blood. God was testifying on behalf of Jesus.

Lord Jesus, we have our true life in you. This life in you will last forever and ever. Let us trust you and trust also the testimony placed within our hearts by the Holy Spirit. You are ours and we are yours forever. Alleluia!

Saturday, January 12, 2008
1 John 5, 14-21
Prayer for Sinners

Safe. We are in Jesus. We are safe.

We are God's children. God is protecting us.

Lord Jesus, thank you for the Holy Spirit's gift of discernment as we pray. Thank you for the privilege of interceding for others. Let us be cautious and yet carefree as we live today. You are with us and we are safe. Alleluia!

> Sunday, January 13, 2008 Baptism of the Lord
> Isaiah 42, 1-4,6-7
> The Servant of the Lord

"Here is my servant, whom I uphold, my chosen, in whom my soul delights; I have put my spirit upon him; he will bring forth justice to the nations. He will not cry or lift up his voice, or make it heard in the street; a bruised reed he will not break, and a dimly burning wick he will not quench; he will faithfully bring forth justice (vv. 1-3)."

The chosen servant. The one through whom God delights to work.

What is this chosen servant like? Proud? Haughty?

No. The chosen servant is not a self-promoter. The chosen servant works passionately for justice, yet without a big fuss.

The chosen servant is gentle with others. The chosen servant is the one through whom God opens the eyes of the blind, sets the prisoners free at last, brings those in various dungeons of despair into light.

Lord Jesus, you are the ultimate example of God's chosen servant. Help us to be like you. Let us care deeply and work passionately for justice. Let us be gentle with ourselves as well as with others. Alleluia!

> Monday, January 14, 2008
> 1 Samuel 1, 1-8
> Elkanah and his Family at Shiloh

This reading sets the stage for the explosive scene in the following reading. So much drama!

Basically, the childless Hannah seemed stuck. Yes, she was married to Elkanah, who truly loved her. The Lord, however, allowed Hannah to remain without a child. How puzzling.

Hannah was also stuck with suffering the taunts of that pest, Peninnah, also married to Elkanah. Peninnah, who had children, constantly reminded Hannah of Hannah's childless condition.

The annual pilgrimage from Ramah, in the Ephraim hills, to the temple in Shiloh must have been lots of fun. Peninnah was being a pain, as usual. Hannah was weeping and refusing to eat. Not exactly a Disney cruise! How could this continue?

Lord Jesus, when we seem stuck in intolerable circumstances, thank you for being with us and telling us what to do. No matter how set the stage seems, everything can change when you enter the scene. Let us not lose heart. Alleluia!

> Tuesday, January 15, 2008
> 1 Samuel 1, 9-20
> Hannah's Prayer; Hannah Bears a Son

One day in the temple in Shiloh, Hannah had had enough! Enough of being taunted and reproached. Even enough of tender concern. Enough, period.

Hannah went directly to God. After all, God was the only one who could help her. Only God could give her a child.

So what if Eli, the priest, thought she was drunk. She was used to being misunderstood.

Hannah stood her ground. She prayed and prayed. She wept and wept.

The Lord was there. The Lord heard Hannah.

Hannah promised the Lord that if she bore a son, she would give him into the Lord's service. This child would be dedicated totally to the Lord.

After pouring out her sorrow to the Lord, she left the temple in peace. Even Eli, the priest, spoke to her with kindness and understanding.

Hannah did bear a son. She named him Samuel. Samuel would learn to be a great prophet and judge in Israel.

Lord Jesus, we are so foolish to forget to cry out to you when we are in unbearable circumstances. Thank you that you are present with us. You are listening to the cry of our heart. Thank you for bringing new life out of our present trials. Alleluia!

Wednesday, January 16, 2008
1 Samuel 3, 1-10,19-20
Revelation to Samuel; Samuel Acknowledged as Prophet

The Lord delights to work patiently with us, wherever we are spiritually. Young Samuel was no exception.

It took a while for Samuel to realize that it was truly the Lord calling him. It even took a while for the elderly priest, Eli, to realize that the Lord was calling Samuel directly.

Listen! Samuel was learning to listen to the Lord. The Lord trusted Samuel to speak forth the Lord's message.

Samuel matured and was acknowledged as a true prophet of the Lord. Since everything Samuel said came true, all of Israel listened to him.

Lord Jesus, thank you for your patience with us. No matter our age, you still speak to us. Let us continue to discipline ourselves to make time to be silent in your presence and listen to you. Alleluia!

Thursday, January 17, 2008 St. Anthony
1 Samuel 4, 1-11
Defeat of the Israelites; Loss of the Ark

Don't just ask God the question. Wait!

Wait for God to answer. Don't take matters into your own hands. God does not like that.

The Israelites were defeated by their enemies, the Philistines. Four thousand died. The leaders of Israel asked why the Lord had allowed their defeat.

Instead of waiting on the Lord for direction, they decided to remove the ark of the covenant from the temple in Shiloh and to take it with them into the next battle. They thought that would insure their victory.

No dice. God was not playing their game.

The Israelites lost the battle to the Philistines. Thirty thousand died. They lost the ark as well to the Philistines. Eli's two sons, who had blasphemed the Lord (1 Samuel 3, 13) died.

Lord Jesus, let us learn to wait in your presence and listen to you. You honor those who honor you with their time and their trust. Alleluia!

> Friday, January 18, 2008
> 1 Samuel 8, 4-7,10-22
> Request for a King; God Grants the Request;
> The Rights of a King; Persistent Demand

"Therefore." It has been said that when we see the word "therefore" in Scripture, we should find out what it's there for.

In this case, the people asked for a king because the sons of the holy prophet, Samuel, were not like their father. They were judges who did not judge wisely. They were corrupt. How tragic.

The people knew that Samuel was old and would soon be gone. What would they do, since right now they seemed stuck with these two bad judges?

Instead of waiting for God's provision, the people told Samuel that his sons were not like him. Therefore, they wanted a king as judge over them.

Even after Samuel warned them of the potentially harsh treatment they would receive at the hands of a king, the people still insisted. They were in for a big dose of consequences.

Samuel, as always, took the matter to the Lord in prayer. The Lord assured his faithful servant, Samuel, that the people were not rejecting him personally. They were rejecting having God as their king.

Samuel had done his best to follow the Lord. His sons had not turned out well. The people of Israel were not trusting the Lord to be their ruler. How tragic.

Lord Jesus, help us to continue to trust you and to pray, especially when everything seems hopeless. Everything seemed hopeless when you died on the cross and yet death did not win. You won! You rose from the dead. You will win in our lives, also. You will triumph and we too will triumph. Alleluia!

Saturday, January 19, 2008
1 Samuel 9, 1-4,17-19; 10, 1
Persistent Demand; The Lost Asses;
Samuel's Revelation about Saul; Saul's Anointing

The Lord loved his people so much that he was preparing a way to rescue them from the Philistines. Since the people had insisted on a king, the Lord would give them a king.

Was young, tall and handsome Saul ready to be king? Probably not.

Donkeys. All he was concerned about at that time was fulfilling his father's directions to go out into the countryside and find some lost donkeys.

The Lord had something bigger for Saul than finding donkeys. The Lord was about to entrust Israel into Saul's care.

The Lord had already told his faithful servant, the elderly prophet Samuel, to anoint Saul as the one who would govern Israel. Saul was anointed to save the Lord's people from their enemies.

What about the lost donkeys? Samuel assured Saul that they had been found.

Lord Jesus, thank you that you are always watching out for us. No matter how often we have failed you, you are still caring for us and preparing a good future for us. Raise our vision to be open to the future work for which you are preparing us. Alleluia!

Sunday, January 20, 2008 Second Sunday in Ordinary Time
Israel 49, 3,5-6
The Servant of the Lord

Concealed. Revealed.

Initially, the servant of the Lord is hidden and concealed. Called from the womb into the Lord's service, the servant is concealed for a time.

Timing. There is a time to be concealed and a time to be revealed.

At the right time, the Lord's servant is revealed for the Lord's purposes. Light! Restoration! Salvation!

Lord Jesus, let us be content to be concealed for your purposes. Let us also be brave to be revealed for your purposes. Alleluia!

Monday, January 21, 2008 St. Agnes
1 Samuel 15, 16-23
Saul Is Reproved

Pride. Partial obedience, otherwise known as disobedience. A big ego waiting to be indulged. Compromise.

King Saul had fallen into the sin of yielding to the temptations faced by all leaders. He was confronted by the holy prophet, Samuel, who, of course, spoke the truth to him.

Samuel reminded Saul that the Lord had anointed Saul as king and had commissioned Saul for a particular work. Saul had hedged. He had not completed the work the Lord had given him to do. Then, of course, he had tried to defend and to justify his actions.

Samuel confronted Saul with Saul's sins of disobedience, divination, and presumption. Since Saul had chosen to reject the Lord's commands, the Lord now rejected Saul as king.

Lord Jesus, help us to be willing to face the truth about ourselves. Let us not become defensive when we are confronted. Let us ask you and ask others for forgiveness. Let us receive forgiveness and then continue to serve you as you direct. Alleluia!

Tuesday, January 22, 2008 St. Vincent
1 Samuel 16, 1-13
Samuel Sent to Bethlehem

A new mission! The Lord told Samuel to stop grieving over the rejected Saul.

"And the LORD said unto Samuel, How long wilt thou mourn for Saul, seeing I have rejected him from reigning over Israel? fill thine horn with oil, and go, I will send thee to Jesse the Bethlehemite; for I have provided me a king among his sons (1 Samuel 16, 1 KJV)."

There was a new mission for Samuel. He was to go to Bethlehem and anoint Saul's successor as king. The Lord promised to reveal to Samuel the identity of the future king.

After meeting the seven sons of Jesse, Samuel still had not met the future king. Who was he? The Lord told Samuel not to try to judge by outer appearance. The Lord had different criteria. The Lord alone saw into the heart.

Almost as an afterthought, Jesse acknowledged to Samuel that he still had one more son. This son, the youngest, was out tending the sheep. Samuel sent for this son.

David! The Lord told Samuel that this handsome, ruddy young shepherd lad, David, was to be king. After Samuel anointed David, the Holy Spirit came upon David with power and might.

Lord Jesus, thank you for sending us on a new mission. Let us not grieve over the past. Let us be ready for the new assignment you have for us. Alleuia!

> Wednesday, January 23, 2008
> 1 Samuel 17, 32-33,37,40-51
> David Fights Goliath; Preparation for the Encounter;
> David's Victory

David offered himself for the king's service. David offered to fight the huge Philistine, Goliath. King Saul was dubious, given David's youth and inexperience.

David did have experience, however. As a shepherd, he had learned how to defend his sheep. With his own simple weapons of staff, sling, and stones, David hastened to defeat the Philistine, Goliath. Goliath would no longer insult Israel.

David did have a secret weapon. His secret weapon was his complete trust and assurance in the power of the Lord. David knew the power of acting in the name of the Lord.

"Then said David to the Philistine, Thou comest to me with a sword, and with a spear, and with a shield: but I come to thee in the name of the Lord of hosts, the god of the armies of Israel, whom thou hast defied (1 Samuel 17, 45 KJV)." David knew that the battle belonged to the Lord.

Lord Jesus, we offer ourselves into your service. You are our Shepherd and our King. Let us learn to trust in your power. Thank you that you have already won the battle we are now facing. Alleuia!

Thursday, January 24, 2008 St. Francis de Sales
1 Samuel 18, 6-9, 19, 1-7
Saul's Jealousy; Persecution of David;

King Saul's son, Jonathan, intervened on behalf of David. Saul, jealous of David's acclaim after the slaying of Goliath, was planning to kill David.

Jonathan, with respect and gentleness, spoke the truth to his father, King Saul. Jonathan reminded Saul that David had bravely served the king. As a result of Jonathan's intervention, David's life was spared.

Lord Jesus, thank you that you came to earth to intervene on our behalf. Let us be brave and intervene on behalf of those who have no one to defend them and whose reputations and lives are at stake. Alleluia!

Friday, January 25, 2008 Conversion of St. Paul
Acts 22, 3-16
Paul's Defense before the Jerusalem Jews.

Paul was a Jew! Paul first of all identified himself as a Jew among Jews.

He identified himself with their zeal for God and for the honor of God. When he persecuted the followers of Jesus, Paul truly thought he was serving God.

Only the light of God could penetrate into the darkness of Paul's thinking. Quickly, Paul began to see in another way. He learned for himself who Jesus really was.

Ananias, a disciple of the Lord Jesus, who was highly regarded by the Jewish community in Damascus, ministered to Paul at this crucial time. Paul had been blinded by the light he had experienced. Ananias ministered to Paul with great respect.

Ananias laid his hands on Paul (Acts 9, 17) and Paul received his sight again. Ananias told Paul that Paul would now be a witness to Jesus. Paul was then baptized. His new life had begun.

Lord Jesus, this all seemed to happen so fast and yet you knew Paul would one day come to faith in you. Let us learn to identify ourselves with all who believe in you. Let us wait with respect for others for your coming in glory! Alleluia!

Saturday, January 26, 2008 Sts. Timothy and Titus
2 Timothy 1, 1-8
Greeting; Thanksgiving; The Gifts Timothy Has Received

Rekindle! Timothy was reminded to rekindle the gift God had given to him.

Yes, his grandmother Lois and his mother Eunice were women of true faith. Timothy, however, was charged with tending the gift of God entrusted to him.

Paul charged Timothy to be strong and to exercise self-control. Timothy was not only to bear witness to the Lord, but also to suffer for the Gospel.

Lord Jesus, thank you that the Holy Spirit daily strengthens us to serve you, whether we are in a time of tranquility or in a time of turmoil. Thank you for the faith of all who went before us. Thank you for the gift of faith we are given to live this day well. Alleluia!

Sunday, January 27, 2008 Third Sunday of Ordinary Time
Isaiah 8, 23 - 9, 3
The Prince of Peace

The time of darkness was over! The light of God was now shining.

It was a time of rejoicing. The burden had been lifted.

In the eighth century before Christ, the prophet spoke forth God's words of comfort to his suffering people. They were to be redeemed.

Lord Jesus, our Redeemer, you are shining forth for all to see. Thank you for shining forth in us today. Alleluia!

Monday, January 28, 2008 St. Thomas Aquinas
2 Samuel 5, 1-7,10
David King of Israel; Capture of Zion

David! The Lord chose David. The Lord prepared David.

The Lord provided for David. The Lord caused David to triumph over opposition.

David, the shepherd boy, was now David, King of Israel. Because of the Lord's presence with him, David was becoming more and more powerful.

Lord Jesus, you call us to follow you. You are our Good Shepherd. You are our King who will come again in glory. Thank you for your protection and for your sovereignty in our lives. Thank you that your presence with us makes us powerful. Thank you for the glorious future you have prepared for us. Alleluia!

Tuesday, January 29, 2008
2 Samuel 6, 12-15,17-19
The Ark Brought to Jerusalem

Joy! Dancing!

There is a time for joy! There is a time for dancing! King David freely rejoiced and danced before the Lord when the ark of the covenant was returned safely to Jerusalem.

After offerings were made to the Lord, King David shared his joy with the people. Every man and woman was given gifts to take home.

Lord Jesus, when life is hard, we forget that there will come a time when we will rejoice again. Our circumstances are always changing, but your love is constant. Help us to rejoice even now because you are with us. Alleluia!

Wednesday, January 30, 2008
2 Samuel 7, 4-17
David's Concern for the Ark; The Lord's Promises

It is the Lord who is in charge! The Lord is in charge of us.

The Lord is in charge of our family and friends. The Lord is in charge of our vocation.

Although David desired to build a house for the Lord, the Lord had other plans. It would be David's son, Solomon, who would build this house.

The Lord reminded David of David's past as a shepherd lad. The Lord specifically chose David to lead Israel. This was the work entrusted to David.

Lord Jesus, we entrust ourselves and all for whom we pray into your care. You are our loving Father and you truly know what is best for us. Alleluia!

Thursday, January 31, 2008 St. John Bosco
2 Samuel 7, 18-19,24-29
King David's Prayer

David sat in the Lord's presence and simply talked with the Lord. The prophet Nathan had just related to King David the promises of the Lord to David and to his descendants. Overwhelmed by the magnitude of these promises, David sought the Lord.

Silence. We need time to be silent in the presence of the Lord. We also need time to speak in the Lord's presence.

Time. We need time to take in the Lord's love for us and the Lord's power on our behalf. David found courage to pray and to ask the Lord to bring to fulfillment the promises to him and his family.

Lord Jesus, thank you for inviting us simply to sit in your presence and talk with you. You love us. You have all the power in the universe to act on our behalf. Thank you for all that you have already done on our behalf. Thank you for all the wonderful promises that you will faithfully fulfill for us at the best time. We rest in your presence. We rest in your love. Alleluia!

Friday, February 1, 2008
2 Samuel 11, 1-10
David's Sin

David openly sinned and then tried to cover his sin, first by trying to have Uriah, his armor-bearer, claim responsibility. That scheme having failed, David arranged for Uriah to be killed in battle.

David. The shepherd boy called by God to be king. David.

Lord Jesus, we stand aghast at David's sin. Yet we have sinned in many ways and then tried to blame others. We are without excuse. Forgive us. Cleanse us. Restore us. Let us walk with you in a new way. We now know ourselves in a new way. We also know that your grace is greater than our sins. You will never us let us go. Alleluia!

Saturday, February 2, 2008 The Presentation of the Lord
Malachi 3, 1-4
The Messenger of the Covenant

First the priests! Into the refiner's fire for the purpose of purification.

When we pray for the Lord to come, we are playing with fire. We are praying for fire.

The Lord is indeed coming! The Lord is holy.

Purified priests will lead in a new way. Purified priests will care for the Lord's flock with integrity.

Lord Jesus, thank you for coming to us in gentle ways. You also come to us in frightening ways. You are preparing us to live with you in glory. Let us welcome, with humility and trust, your ways of purifying us. We trust in your mercy. Alleluia!

Sunday, February 3, 2008 Fourth Sunday in Ordinary Time
Zephaniah 2, 3; 3, 12-13
The Day of the Lord: A Day of Judgment

In the late seventh century B.C., the Lord gave a serious, even frightening, message for the prophet Zephaniah to announce. The Lord would confront and would judge all wrongdoers, regardless of their status.

The Lord, however, would care tenderly for the humble. The humble would be sheltered.

Lord Jesus, teach us to be silent in your presence. Teach us to speak the truth and to live with integrity. Thank you that you will care for us. Alleluia!

Monday, February 4, 2008
2 Samuel 15, 13-14,30; 16, 5-13
David Flees Jerusalem; David and Shimei

Tragedy. Humiliation. Flight from Jerusalem.

How tragic to see King David running away from his own son, Absolom, who was scheming to become king himself. David wept copiously and continuously as he fled Jerusalem.

Shimei, from the family of King Saul, David's predecessor, threw dirt and stones at King David, cursing him bitterly. David accepted this abuse in humility and refused to retaliate.

Why? Why was all this happening to King David? How had David come to dishonor the Lord and to seek, at all costs, to have his own way?

This was the tragic unfolding of the Lord's words to David after David, in order to have Bathsheba, ordered that Uriah, Bathsheba's husband, be placed in the front lines of the battle and then abandoned. Uriah was then killed by sword in battle.

The Lord then told David that the sword would not depart from his own home and that evil would come upon him from within his own home. This would happen because David had, by his actions, despised the Lord (2 Samuel 12, 9-12).

Lord Jesus, thank you for your tender mercy. Thank you for forgiving us. Thank you for helping us to bear with humility the consequences of our sins. Thank you for interceding for us as our Great High Priest. Let us seek to honor you at all times and to trust you to give us what you know is best for us. Alleluia!

Tuesday, February 5, 2008 St. Agatha
2 Samuel 18, 9-10,14,24-25,30 - 19, 3
Death of Absolom; David Told of Absolom's Death
Joab Reproaches David

Weeping. Mourning.

David's son, Absolom, was dead. Absolom had been brutally killed by David's own general and by other military officers.

"And the king was much moved, and went up to the chamber over the gate, and wept: and as he went, thus he said, O my son Absolom, my son, my son Absolom! would God I had died for thee, O Absolom, my son, my son (2 Samuel 18, 33 KJV)!"

Lord Jesus, you are with us when we weep. You are with us when we mourn. Lead us gently through these times of weeping and mourning. Thank you for reassuring us that you love us and you love those for whom we mourn. Alleluia!

Wednesday, February 6, 2008 Ash Wednesday, Year A
Joel 2, 12-18
The Day of the Lord; Blessings for God's People

Return. Return. Return.

We are called to return wholeheartedly to the Lord. The Lord is gracious and merciful. The Lord cares tenderly for us.

Lord Jesus, let us turn again to you with all our hearts. Forgive us when we are so consumed with faithless fears that we fail to trust. you. Let us turn to you for healing this Lent. Heal us and help us to know how gracious and full of mercy you are. Let us feast on your mercy this Lent. You are full of tender concern for us. Let us offer mercy and compassion to others.

Thursday, February 7, 2008 Thursday after Ash Wednesday
Deuteronomy 30, 15-20
The Choice before Israel

Moses was summarizing the choice which lay before the people of Israel. At this point, they had not yet crossed the Jordan River into the Promised Land.

God's commands are not all that mysterious. They are already within our hearts. They only await carrying out into action. "But the word is very nigh unto thee, in thy mouth, and in thy heart, that thou mayest do it (Deuteronomy 30, 14 KJV)."

Choice! The choices is between life and death. Life includes all that is good. Death, of course, includes doom.

Life involves fidelity to the Lord. Death is the result of refusing to listen to the Lord and choosing, instead to chase after other "gods."

Moses urged the people of Israel to choose life. Life for themselves and life for their descendants.

Lord Jesus, we choose life when we choose you. We choose death when we choose to persist, stubbornly, in choosing our own way. Lead us gently this Lent to the level of trust we need in order to say "yes" with all our heart to you and to life.

Friday, February 8, 2008
St. Jerome Emiliani, St. Josephine Bakhita
Isaiah 58, 1-9
True Fasting

God will answer us speedily when we fast in God's way. Light, healing, and vindication await us!

Caring for the oppressed, sharing what we have with those in need, and refusing to speak with malice exemplify the kind of fast that God desires. Are we willing to fast in this way?

Lord Jesus, help us to fast your way this Lent. Cleanse our hearts and fill our hearts with compassion. Let our words and our actions be filled with your love, Open us to receive light, healing, and vindication.

Saturday, February 9, 2008 Saturday after Ash Wednesday
Isaiah 58, 9-14
True Fasting

When our strength is renewed and we are like a garden which has been freshly watered, we will be able to do the particular work of restoration to which we are called. The Holy Spirit, even as we are being healed, is springing up within us!

The Lord will continue to guide us as we refuse to speak with malice of others. This is very important. Even if what we have to say is true, we are commanded not to speak with malice.

The Lord guides us as we give freely of our own resources to others. We will give, not with a dreary sense of duty, but with joy.

Rest. Sabbath rest. We will learn, at last, the true meaning of sabbath rest.

Lord Jesus, as I recover from surgery, help me to continue to learn to be still in your presence. You are in charge. I am not. Breathe new life into me. Let me be gentle with myself and with others as I learn to trust you and to delight in you this Lent.

Sunday, February 10, 2008 First Sunday of Lent, Year A
Genesis 2, 7-9; 3, 1-7
Second Story of Creation; The Fall of Man

When we lament the tragic state of the world, we cannot blame God. We remember God's original intent.

Life! God breathed life into us. We were given a beautiful garden in which to dwell in safety and delight.

All this was lost when Eve entered into dialogue with the devil. All this was lost when Adam agreed to partake of what God had forbidden.

The innocence of Adam and Eve was lost. Not even their pathetic attempt to hide from God by wearing fig leaves could overcome the consequences, to themselves and to us, of what they had done.

Lord Jesus, you came to us! You restored, by the complete offering of your life, what we lost when our first ancestors sinned. We don't need to hide. We don't need to fashion fig leaves anymore. Come, Holy Spirit, breathe new, fresh life into us this Lent. Remind us of the pure waters of our Baptism. Heavenly Father, thank you for accepting the sacrifice of your beloved Son, Jesus, the Lamb of God. Thank you that our relationship with you has been completely restored. Let us delight this Lent, this springtime, in the garden of your love.

Monday, February 11, 2008 Our Lady of Lourdes
Leviticus 19, 1-2,11-18
Various Rules of Conduct

Perhaps all politicians would benefit from following this passage! The Lord, through Moses, was instructing the entire Israelite community on interpersonal relationships.

Interestingly enough, the people were instructed not to be partial to the poor and weak and nor to defer to the rich and powerful. God's standard is one of strict impartiality in judgment.

Holiness! The entire community was summoned to holiness! They were all called to be holy in thought, word, and deed. There was to be no holding onto hatred. No grudges. No slander.

Lord Jesus, we know we are to love others as we love ourselves. Sometimes we don't love ourselves. This Lent, purify us in our ways of thinking about ourselves and others. Prune our words about ourselves and others. Direct all our actions. Let us grow in holiness this Lent.

Tuesday, February 12, 2008 Lenten Weekday
Isaiah 55, 10-11
An Invitation to Grace

"For as the rain and the snow come down from heaven, and do not return there until they have watered the earth, making it bring forth and sprout, giving seed to the sower and bread to the eater, so shall my word be that goes out of my mouth; it shall not return to me empty, but it shall accomplish that which I purpose.(Isaiah 55, 10-11)."

I love this bold passage! It gives us great courage when we have to wait a long time for God's promises to be fulfilled.

Rain. Snow. The snow and the rain come down.

Seeds. The seeds spring up and grow into grain to nourish us and to nourish others.

Once, for fun, our son, Christopher, planted an avocado seed in our back garden. The tree grew and grew, but never produced avocados.

Surprise! Over fifteen years later, the tree was laden with avocados!

God's word also goes forth and will most definitely produce tangible results. The plan of God will definitely blossom into reality.

Many will marvel. All will be nourished.

Lord Jesus, no matter how casually or how intentionally a seed is sown, there will be results. Teach us how to sow seeds in our thought lives that will produce words of wisdom and acts of mercy. Speak your word to us and over us. Let your word take root within us and let us know that your word will become manifest to all.

Wednesday, February 13, 2008 Lenten Weekday
Jonah 3, 1-10
Conversion of Ninevah

Who would have thought that the words of the reluctant prophet Jonah would have that much power? Bingo! It wasn't Jonah's words so much as it was Jonah's obedience.

When Jonah finally obeyed God and went to Ninevah to proclaim God's message, the result was the conversion of Ninevah. Ninevah was

an enormous city. God cared about all the people and all the animals of Ninevah.

Just what did Jonah say? He simply said what God told him to say. In forty days, Ninevah would be destroyed.

God's power was in the prophet's proclamation. The people actually believed Jonah. They actually repented. God mercifully spared the city of Ninevah, animals included.

Lord Jesus, we may not think our words matter. They do matter. They matter to you. They matter to others. Let us be bold today to speak the words you give us to speak. Simple though these words seem, they will fulfill your purpose, whether or not we even know it.

Thursday, February 14, 2008 Sts. Cyril and Methodius
Esther C, 12, 14-16,23-25 or 4, 17
Prayer of Esther

We are actually cursed, injured, and harmed if we place our ultimate trust in other people (Jeremiah 17, 5). We are blessed and happy when we trust and hope in the Lord (Jeremiah 17, 7).

Queen Esther, the devout Jewish wife of a Persian king, is a glorious example of one who completely trusted in the Lord. She threw herself completely upon the mercy of the Lord.

Esther knew that only God could save her and the other Jews in the kingdom from extermination. She knew that God was the true king. God alone was the ruler of all.

Lord Jesus, when we are in desperate circumstances, let us remember that you are in charge. You are our Lord and God. You are our Good Shepherd and you will lead us through these difficult circumstances. You are able to accomplish for us what we are unable to do on our own. Thank you for the people you send to help us. We are grateful for the assistance of others, but we know that you alone are Lord. We place our trust in you.

Friday, February 15, 2008 Lenten Weekday
Ezekiel 18, 21-28
Personal Responsibility

Every person's life belongs to the Lord (Ezekiel 18, 4). The Lord rejoices when we turn from evil. The Lord wants us to live.

Lord Jesus, we turn to you with all that we don't understand. Help us to follow you and to trust you with what is mysterious. Thank you for the privilege of interceding for all to turn to you and to live.

Saturday, February 16, 2008 Lenten Weekday
Deuteronomy 26, 16-19
The Covenant

Today! Today, we are making an agreement with the Lord. We are listening to the Lord, acknowledging the Lord's sovereignty, and agreeing to live the Lord's way.

Today! Today, the Lord is making an agreement with us. We belong to the Lord and the Lord is caring for us.

Lord Jesus, thank you that you came to fulfill all that we could not fulfill. Let us live today, knowing that we are securely in your care. We belong to you.

Sunday, February 17, 2009 Second Sunday in Lent
Genesis 12, 1-4
Abram's Call and Migration

At the tender age of seventy-five, Abram went forth into a new life. The Lord summoned Abram to go forth into the unknown. With the word of the Lord to guide him, Abram obeyed and left his old life.

Lord Jesus, thank you for the example of Abraham, formerly called Abram. Help us to know it is never too late to begin again. Each day, you summon us to follow you and to go forth into new realms. Let us view this day with a spirit of adventure!

Monday, February 18, 2008 Lenten Weekday
Daniel 9, 4-10
Gabriel and the Seventy Weeks

"I prayed to the LORD my God and made confession, saying, 'Ah, Lord, great and awesome God, keeping covenant and steadfast love with those who love you and keep your commandments, we have sinned and done wrong, acted wickedly and rebelled, turning aside from your commandments and ordinances (vv. 4-5).'"

Daniel's prayer for himself and for his people began and ended in humility. Daniel, in order to understand a particular prophecy of Jeremiah, sought the Lord in deep humility. His prayer was accompanied with fasting and other evidences of penitence (Daniel 9, 2-3).

Daniel consistently prayed in the plural. "WE." Whether or not Daniel had personally participated in the sins of the people, he prayed in unity with them.

Daniel linked himself with their sins of rebellion against the Lord. He prayed, "We have sinned, and have committed iniquity, and have done wickedly, and have rebelled, even by departing from thy precepts and from thy judgments (Daniel 9, 5 KJV)."

Daniel began and ended his prayer by appealing to the Lord's majesty and the Lord's mercy. The Lord of fidelity and justice was also the Lord of forgiveness and tender compassion.

Lord Jesus, we are filled with shame when we recall our sins. Help us, this Lent, to surrender our lives to you. Let us cease judging others and instead pray for them. Let us extend the mercy to others that we long for you to extend to us.

Tuesday, February 19, 2008 Lenten Weekday
Isaiah 1, 10,16-20
Israel's Sinfulness

Interior. Exterior.

The Lord is asking for an interior conversion. An interior conversion will result in exterior deeds of mercy.

There is an old saying that you can give without loving, but you cannot love without giving. This is true even of God. God loved us and gave us Jesus (John 3, 16).

Learning to do good is a process. We learn by seeking justice for those with no one to stand up for them, with no one to fight their battles.

We learn by obeying the promptings of the Holy Spirit in every aspect of our life. We acknowledge that God is in charge.

Lord Jesus, when we sacrifice in obedience to you, you always reward us. Let us not fear loss or suffering. Let us honor you with our trust. You are debtor to no one. We will experience a new strength and a new power which come only from trusting, radical obedience.

Wednesday, February 20, 2008 Lenten Weekday
Jeremiah 18, 18-20
Another Prayer for Vengeance

God sent the prophet Jeremiah to proclaim repentance to those who were intent on committing apostasy. The people had no intention of repenting. It was easier for them to shoot the messenger, to extinguish the flame of Jeremiah's blazing mission of truth-telling.

Jeremiah, in anguish, cried out to God. He reminded God that he, Jeremiah, had interceded for these stubborn, recalcitrant people who were plotting against him, who were repaying good with evil.

Lord Jesus, if we truly follow you and if we truly live and speak for you, we will suffer. Our words will be twisted and deliberately misunderstood. Like Jeremiah, we will be slandered. Let us not fall into a victim mentality. Let us remain faithful to you. We belong to you and you know how and when to vindicate us. We are safe in your heart and in your hands.

Thursday, February 21, 2008 St. Peter Damien
Jeremiah 17, 5-10
True Wisdom

A dry, thorny bush in the desert wasteland. A green fruit-bearing tree planted by streams of fresh water.

Jeremiah compares the person who places trust in human beings to the dry bush in the wilderness. A person like this is actually cursed.

On the other hand, the person whose hope in placed in the Lord will blossom! This person whose security is in the Lord will be happy and blessed, even in the midst of trials.

The human heart is so convoluted that only the Lord is able to probe it and to understand its mysteries. Only the Lord is qualified to make correct judgments in matters of the human heart.

Lord Jesus, it's easy for us to become frightened. This world is a scary place. Help us to cling to you, trusting in you to lead us day by day. Heal our hearts and let us learn to rest this Lent beside your life-giving streams.

Friday, February 22, 2008 Chair of St. Peter, Apostle
1 Peter 5, 1-4
Advice to the Presbyters

"Now as an elder myself and a witness of the sufferings of Christ, as well as one who shares in the sufferings of Christ, as well as one who shares in the glory to be revealed, I exhort the elders among you to tend the flock of God that is in your charge, exercising the oversight, not under compulsion but willingly, as God would have you do it … (vv. 1-2)."

Tend the flock! Christian leaders are to care for God's flock.

There will always be leaders who care more for themselves than for the flock entrusted to their care. Instead of tending God's flock, they tend their own egos and their own reputations.

These leaders have strayed from the Good Shepherd. They have forgotten that the flock is not theirs. The flock belongs to the Lord.

Lord Jesus, thank you for sending wise, loving, and strong shepherds to care for your flock. Thank you for sending shepherds who know their own weaknesses and their own need for your mercy. Thank you for healing the lambs who have been starved and wounded by shepherds who have betrayed your trust. Lord Jesus, you are the Head of the Church. Thank you for setting your household, the Church, in order.

Saturday, February 23, 2008 St. Polycarp
Micah 7, 14-15,18-20
Condemnation and Prayer

Lord Jesus, this Lent, let us quietly dwell apart with you. You are our loving Shepherd and you know how and where to feed us. Thank you for forgiving our sins and removing our guilt. We rest in you.

Sunday, February 24, 2008 Third Sunday of Lent
Exodus 17, 3-7
Water from the Rock

Instead of becoming defensive or argumentative in dealing with those pesky, complaining Israelites, Moses cried to the Lord! The Israelites had accused Moses of leading them into the desert for the express purpose of dying of thirst.

Moses poured out his frustration to the Lord and asked for the Lord's guidance. The Lord answered in a specific way and gave Moses a plan of action.

Moses only needed what he already had on hand, a simple rod. The Lord promised to be with Moses as Moses, with other Israelite leaders nearby, struck the rock and water gushed from the rock.

Lord Jesus, sometimes we forget to come first to you. We pour out our problems to others. They are only human and may not be able to help us. You are human too, but you are also God! Let us turn first to you. Let us pour out our weariness, our frustration, and all our concerns to you. Let us learn to listen to you for your answer. Thank you that you will guide us. Thank you that you are our Good Shepherd.

Monday, February 25, 2008 Lenten Weekday
2 Kings 5, 1-15
Cure of Naaman

A little girl! A young Israelite slave girl spoke the truth and Naaman, a mighty military commander, was healed of leprosy.

It didn't happen all at once. It didn't happen until Naaman did what the girl had said to do, to go to the prophet, Elisha.

Instead of going to Elisha, Namaan went to the king of Aram. The king said he would send a letter to the king of Israel. The king of Israel promptly went ballistic over the whole matter.

The prophet Elisha sent word to Namaan, instructing him to go and wash himself in the Jordan River. Seven times. Then Namaan would be cleansed.

Naaman stubbornly refused. He had his own ideas of how he should be healed.

Eventually, Naaman did as the prophet Elisha had instructed him. Lo and behold, he was cleansed of his leprosy. He acknowledged that the God of Israel was the only true God. "Behold, now I know that there is no God in all the earth, but in Israel ... (2 Kings 5, 15b KJV)."

Lord Jesus, how difficult we make it for ourselves and for others when we insist of our own way. Everything becomes tormented and convoluted. This Lent, we relinquish ourselves, stubborn pride and all, into your wise hands. Have mercy on us. Forgive us. Heal us. Let us live for you. Let us be attentive to the "little," seemingly insignificant people who cross our path. They may be trying to get your message across to us.

Tuesday, February 26, 2008 Lenten Weekday
Daniel 3, 25,34-43
The Fiery Furnace

Stand up! Even in the midst of the fiery furnace, the three Israelite prisoners of conscience stood up and praised the Lord.

Azarariah, one of the captives, stood and prayed. He interceded for all the Israelites. He asked for deliverance for himself and his two friends who had refused to compromise their faith.

Lord Jesus, thank you for helping us not to give up our trust in you when we are in the midst of fiery trials. Let us stand up and sing your praise.

> Wednesday, February 27, 2008 Lenten Weekday
> Deuteronomy 4, 1,5-9
> Advantages of Fidelity; Revelation at Horeb

Enter! Enter first.

Learning to possess what the Lord has given you will follow. First, we must enter the new land into which the Lord is leading us.

This new land of milk and honey has dangers. It also has idols.

We need the Lord. We need the Lord's wisdom to confront and to overcome these obstacles in order to live as we are called by the Lord to live.

Learning to call out to the Lord and to cling closely to the Lord keeps us safe. Others will notice how close our all-powerful God is to us.

Lord Jesus, let us learn to trust you and to teach our children and our children's children, to trust you. You did not come to destroy the commandments given to Moses and the children of Israel but to fulfill them. Let us enter into a new land of milk and honey this Lent and learn how live in this new land.

> Thursday, February 28, 2008 Lenten Weekday
> Jeremiah 7, 23-28
> Abuses in Worship

There is a time to intercede for others. There is also a time not to intercede.

The Lord, at one time, instructed the prophet, Jeremiah, not to intercede for the stubborn people of Israel (Jeremiah 7, 16).

Over and over, the Lord had tried to speak to the people of Israel. They steadfastly refused to listen and to obey. Instead, they chose to commit apostasy and idolatry.

They had refused to listen to the Lord. Of course, they also refused to listen to Jeremiah, who was sent by God.

Lord Jesus, help us to be willing to listen and to acknowledge that we need to make changes in our lives. We ask you for the grace to make these changes. Instead of clinging to our excuses for not changing, let us truly repent of any way we have displeased you. Align our lives with your plan for us. You love us and long for us to live in true freedom.

Friday, February 29, 2008 Lenten Weekday
Hosea 14, 2-10
Sincere Conversion

Collapse! Our guilt causes us to collapse before God.

Blossom! Confessing our sin and trusting that we are forgiven causes us to blossom.

We will blossom like lilies. We will be as fruitful as olive trees and as fragrant as the cedars of Lebanon.

Lord Jesus, you are eager to receive us, to revive us, to forgive us, and to heal us. Let us bask in your compassion this Lent. Let us blossom and bear fruit as we walk in the path you have chosen for us.

Saturday, March 1, 2008 Lenten Weekday
Hosea 6, 1-6
Insincere Conversion

" 'Come, let us return to the LORD; for it is he who has torn, and he will heal us; he has struck down, and he will bind us up. After two days he will revive us; on the third day he will raise us up, that we may live before him. Let us know, let us press on to know the LORD; his appearing is as sure as the dawn; he will come to us like the showers, like the spring rains that water the earth (vv. 1-3).' "

Sometimes the Lord has to tear us and rend us before restoring us and raising us to a new way of living. This is painful, but necessary for our growth.

The Lord's coming is as certain as the coming of the light of dawn. Our darkness will not last forever. The Lord will come to us like the soft, gentle rain of spring.

Lord Jesus, you call us to learn to know you and to love you. When we feel torn apart, let us trust in your wisdom and your love. You will revive us and restore us.

> Sunday, March 2, 2008 Fourth Sunday of Lent
> 1 Samuel 16, 1,6-7,10-13
> Samuel Sent to Bethlehem

A new assignment! The Lord sent the prophet Samuel, who had been grieving over King Saul, to Bethlehem. In Bethlehem, the Lord would reveal to Samuel the future king of Israel.

Samuel was apparently sent by himself. No committee. No advisors. Just Samuel and the Lord.

All but one of the sons of Jesse were presented to the prophet, Samuel. No, the Lord had not chosen from among them.

Then, the youngest, David, the shepherd lad, was summoned to appear. YES!

David was God's choice to be king of Israel. Samuel, the prophet, anointed David, the future king. All of David's brothers were present.

The Holy Spirit came upon David. David was set apart and consecrated to the Lord.

Lord Jesus, how complicated leadership has become. You choose various people for various tasks. You are the Lord and you don't need endless meetings of discernment committees. Let us be open to your choice of people for leadership. Let us be open to your new assignments.

> Monday, March 3, 2008 St. Katharine Drexel
> Isaiah 65, 17-21
> The World Renewed

New! In this springtime, we are ready to release the past and to welcome the new.

One day, even the heavens will be new. The earth will also be new.

There will be happiness in Jerusalem. There will be rejoicing! No more weeping. Lives will be lived to the full in homes and vineyards.

Lord Jesus, renew us this Lent. Let us enjoy now the wonders of your creation as we anticipate the wonders of your new creation.

Tuesday, March 4, 2008 Lenten Weekday
Ezekiel 47, 1-9,12
The Wonderful Stream

Ezekiel, in the vision given to him by the Lord (Ezekiel 40, 1,2) was continually being led and guided. Over and over, Ezekiel, an exiled priest and a prophet, referred to the Lord bringing him to different parts of the temple in Jerusalem.

What Ezekiel saw in the form of vision may be of great benefit to us this Lent. Ezekiel's vision helps us to live this Lent with the promise of being refreshed and restored. We may take courage that we, too, are being led and guided through many gates into many new places.

We are God's temple right now (1 Corinthians 3, 16) and the Holy Spirit dwells in us. The Holy Spirit is continually bringing us to new places. We are brought to streams of living water. We delight in the ways the Lord refreshes us and heals us.

Lord Jesus, this Lent, lead us and bring us to you and to ourselves. Thank you for leading us beside the waters where we will find life and health.

Wednesday, March 5, 2008 Lenten Weekday
Isaiah 49, 8-19
The Liberation and Restoration of Zion

You! The liberation and restoration of you.

Me! The liberation and restoration of me.

You will be liberated. You will be restored.

I will be liberated. I will be restored.

No matter what our feelings are right now and no matter what our experience has been, the Lord promises us liberation and restoration.

The Lord is calling us out of our prison. The Lord is calling us out of darkness.

The merciful Lord is leading us to fresh meadows. The Lord is guiding us beside streams of sparkling fresh water.

The Lord is aggressively making a way for us. The Lord is cutting roads for us through the mountains of difficulties. Our way may seem impossible to us, but not to the Lord.

We are not forsaken. We are not forgotten. We may believe we have been destroyed, but the Lord is here to rebuild us.

Lord Jesus, let us arise from our prisons of darkness and believe! Let us believe that we will be liberated and restored. Let us sing your praises.

Thursday, March 6, 2008 Lenten Weekday
St. Perpetua and St. Felicity
Exodus 32, 7-14
The Golden Calf

Idols. Intercession.

We needn't roll our eyes and feel superior when we read of the Israelites worshipping a golden calf. We may have idols of a different nature.

Who made the calf? AARON!

Aaron, the priest (Exodus 32, 1-5), made the calf. Aaron listened to the people and yielded to their demands for a visible god.

Moses, on the other hand, listened to the Lord, who was thoroughly outraged over the people's idolatry. Moses then interceded for the people of Israel. The Lord listened to Moses and did not destroy the people.

Lord Jesus, forgive us when we complain and do not listen to you or trust you. Forgive us when we are like Aaron and choose to listen to others rather than to you. Let us renounce whatever constitutes idolatry in our lives. Let us listen to you, receive your forgiveness, and then intercede for others.

Friday, March 7, 2008 Lenten Weekday
Wisdom 2, 1,12-22
The Wicked Reject Immortality and Justice Alike

Holiness! There is a reward for holiness.

The pure and innocent will be rewarded. They will see God (Matthew 5, 8).

Those who live only for this life are unwise. They are not thinking correctly. They lash out in an effort to destroy those who seek to live for God.

Lord Jesus, we are aware of our own sins and yet we seek to know you and to serve you. Let us not worry if we are rejected by this passing world. Our reward is with you. We will see you and live forever in your kingdom.

Saturday, March 8, 2008 Lenten Weekday St. John of God
Jeremiah 11, 18-20
The Plot Against Jeremiah

The poor, suffering prophet Jeremiah was aware of the malice and the schemes of his enemies. He was as a lamb destined for slaughter. He entrusted himself and his cause to the Lord, the ultimate Judge of all.

Lord Jesus, thank you for protecting us this Lent. Thank you for shielding us. Thank you for strengthening us to complete the mission you have entrusted to us.

Sunday, March 9, 2008 Fifth Sunday in Lent
Ezekiel 37, 12-14
Vision of the Dry Bones

Lord Jesus, thank you for coming to me and lifting me out of my grave. Let me arise. Thank you for breathing your life into me. Thank you for filling me anew with the Holy Spirit and letting me live again. What I am doing now does not seem like living. I am so weary. Settle me in your land. I trust in your promise.

Monday, March 10, 2008 Lenten Weekday
Daniel 13, 1-9,15-17,19-30,33-62
Susannah's Virtue

The corrupt judges, who had stifled their consciences, succeeded, for a time, in destroying beautiful Susannah's reputation. A devout Jew, she was delicate, holy, and innocent.

The false accusations of these wicked men, who had sought unsuccessfully to exploit her, caused her great suffering and humiliation. They sought to save themselves and to condemn Susannah to death.

Susannah, in the midst of her weeping, gazed to heaven, trusting God completely in this ordeal. She cried out to God, who knew that the charges against her were false.

In answer to her prayer, before her execution, God moved in the spirit of Daniel. Daniel refused to allow this travesty of justice to continue.

Daniel confronted the people for allowing the corrupt judges to condemn Susannah to death without full knowledge of the facts. Under Daniel's shrewd questioning, the lies and schemes of the wicked judges were exposed. Susannah's life was spared and the wicked judges were promptly executed.

Lord Jesus, thank you that we are hidden and sheltered with you in the midst of suffering. Thank you for the eventual triumph of truth and justice. Help us to be bold to come to the defense of those who are falsely accused.

Tuesday, March 11, 2008 Lenten Weekday
Numbers 21, 4-9
The Bronze Serpent

In the wilderness of life, it is easy to complain. That's what the Israelites did when their desert journey to the land of promise had depleted their patience.

Instead of turning to God and praying for strength, they complained. Their complaints were directed to God and to Moses.

God is big and can handle our all our emotions, including our anger and frustration. We may pour out all that is in our heart to God.

The Israelites, however, did not focus on the liberation which lay ahead. They were fixated on the present difficult circumstances. They even complained about God's provision for them. They referred to God's manna as wretched.

God got fed up with this and send serpents to bite them. That strategy brought about a change of attitude!

The people then comprehended their sin against God. They begged Moses to intercede for them.

Moses fashioned a bronze serpent on a pole, as God directed. Anyone who had complained and been bitten by a serpent was instructed to gaze upon the bronze serpent. The person who did this would recover.

Lord Jesus, we complain all the time. We show our lack of trust in your goodness and in your provision when we complain. Let us be honest before you about our frustrations and let us then look at you. Let us see you lifted on the Cross. Lord, have mercy upon us. Forgive us. Thank you that you are healing us and teaching us how to live.

Wednesday, March 12, 2008 Lenten Weekday
Daniel 3, 14-20,91-92,95
The Fiery Furnace

The three Jewish men, taken captive by the Babylonian king and trained in his service, were ready to face being burned alive rather than compromise their faith in God. They steadfastly refused to bow down before the gold statue, as the king had decreed that all must do.

They informed the infuriated king that even if God did not deliver them, they still would not worship a statue. They were then hurled into a furnace of blazing fire.

The result of their trust soon was made manifest. The now perplexed king looked into the furnace and saw not only the three men, but also a fourth. All were walking about freely and were unharmed.

The amazed king blessed God and acknowledged God's power to rescue. The king then promoted the three faithful men (Daniel 3, 97).

Lord Jesus, help us to remember that you are with us in all our trials. Strengthen us to be faithful to you. Let others be aware of your presence and your power.

Thursday, March 13, 2008 Lenten Weekday
Genesis 17, 3-9
Covenant of Circumcision

As the ninety-nine year old Abram lay prostrate before God, God spoke. God changed the faithful man's name from Abram to Abraham.

God promised that Abraham would be the father of many nations. The entire land of Canaan was promised to Abraham and to his descendants.

All these wonderful promises were included in God's covenant with Abraham. Abraham's part was that he and his descendants would keep the covenant.

Lord Jesus, we come before you in humility this Lent. Let us hear your word to us and comprehend the promises you have made to us. Let us be faithful to keep the new covenant you have entrusted to us.

Friday, March 14, 2008 Lenten Weekday
Jeremiah 20, 10-13
Jeremiah's Interior Crisis

In the midst of his anguish and suffering, the prophet Jeremiah knew that the Lord was with him. It was to the Lord that Jeremiah entrusted his cause.

Although weary and worn down with the suffering inherent in his prophetic vocation, Jeremiah knew that it was crucial to praise the sovereign Lord who alone knew the inner recesses of the human heart.

Lord Jesus, let us remember that you are with us in times of suffering as well as in times of joy. Sometimes it seems that there are no times of joy, only times of suffering. Let us learn this Lent to place fidelity to you and to our vocation above our own desire for a respite from suffering. Strengthen us today to sing to you and to praise you. Thank you that you will come to us and restore us.

Saturday, March 15, 2008 Lenten Weekday
Ezekiel 37, 21-28
The Two Sticks

There are layers of fulfillment in God's promises. Whatever God has promised will be fulfilled, often in ways that baffle us and defy our understanding.

There is always more. There is always more to God's promises than we think. It is not wise to presume that a prophecy has been fulfilled when, in actuality, it has only been partially fulfilled.

The Lord God promised to gather the Israelites back into their own land. They will be delivered from apostasy and cleansed for God's glory. God will dwell with them forever.

Lord Jesus, thank you that you are our Good Shepherd. Thank you for leading us this Lent into the meadows of renewal and refreshing.

Let us rest from our weary game of second guessing. Let us worship you as our Lamb and our Shepherd.

Sunday, March 16, 2008 Palm Sunday of the Lord's Passion
Isaiah 50, 4-7
Salvation Only through the Lord's Servant

Steadfast. Although mocked and humiliated, the Lord's servant remained steadfast in trusting the Lord. The suffering, humble servant was sternly determined to honor the Lord, who would ultimately vindicate him.

Lord Jesus, you were mocked and insulted before your death on the cross. You did not retaliate in any way. You trusted your Father to vindicate you. When we feel helpless, defeated, and depleted, let us continue to be steadfast in our trust in you. Thank you for strengthening today to live in your Easter victory.

Monday, March 17, 2008 Monday in Holy Week
Isaiah 42, 1-7
The Servant of the Lord

Silence. In silence and in suffering, the Lord's servant accomplishes the purposes of the Lord.

Justice is accomplished, not by parades and protests, but by a radical reliance on the Lord and the ways of the Lord. The Lord brings about justice in a strong, powerful, yet tender way.

The Lord's servant does not bruise and crush those who are already in anguish. The Lord honors the tiniest bit of courage in those who long for vindication and deliverance.

Lord Jesus, truly your ways are not our ways. We suffer and crave immediate relief and restitution. This Holy Week, let us surrender to you and to your ways of healing us and shining your light through us.

Tuesday, March 18, 2008 Tuesday in Holy Week
Isaiah 49, 1-6
The Servant of the Lord

"... I said, 'I have labored in vain, I have spent my strength for nothing ... yet surely my cause is with the LORD, and my reward with my God ...' I am honored in the sight of the LORD, and my God has become my strength ... (vv. 3, 5)."

Reward! When we are spent and exhausted, we may forget that a glorious reward awaits us.

Recompense and reward both await us. The Lord has not forgotten us. The Lord is giving us strength right now!

Lord Jesus, you called us to follow you. Although we may be concealed and may feel alone, you see us and you are with us. Help us to continue to trust you in times when our trust is stretched to the utmost. We have not toiled or trusted you in vain.

Wednesday, March 19, 2008 Wednesday in Holy Week
Isaiah 50, 4-9
Salvation Only through the Lord's Servant

Tongue training? It's springtime and we think of spring training for athletes.

Our tongue is often the part of our being which most needs training. The Lord's servant is our example.

The Lord's servant knew how to speak to those who were weary of it all. The Lord's servant was humble in all ways. Humble, not weak.

The Lord's servant knew the nearness of the Lord. The Lord's servant would never experience final disgrace.

Lord Jesus, let us learn these last days of Lent to be silent. Let us learn to listen to you, to others. and to ourselves. Let us learn to speak according to your will. Let us trust in your saving power. Thank you for our spring training.

Thursday, March 20, 2008 Holy Thursday
Exodus 12, 1-8,11-14
The Passover Ritual Prescribed

Only after the Pharaoh of Egypt had refused over and over to release the Israelites from captivity did the Lord send the tenth plague. This plague was the death of the first-born.

The first-born, whether child or animal, would die the night of the Passover. The innocent would die because of the Pharaoh's determination to hold God's people in bondage.

The Passover meal would be eaten in readiness for flight. This would be the night when the Lord would protect his people while executing judgment upon their oppressors.

The blood of the Passover lamb on the doorposts and lintels of the homes of the Israelites would be a sign that they would not suffer the fate of their captors. They would be passed over and they would leave Egyptian captivity at last.

Lord Jesus, if we haven't heard that the war for our souls is over and that you won, let us hear it now! We are free. We may leave our prisoner of war camp and live in your freedom. You are our Passover Lamb of God. Your blood made it possible for us to be cleansed completely from the captivity of sin and to live in true freedom. Let us celebrate the Passover!

> Friday, March 21, 2008 Good Friday
> Isaiah 52, 13 - 53, 12
> Suffering and Triumph of the Servant of the Lord

The servant of the Lord was spurned by others. He was avoided by others.

He was accustomed to this kind of treatment and to infirmity. It was not his own infirmity. He was carrying OUR infirmities!

The Lord's servant surrendered knowingly and willingly to harsh treatment. He surrendered to this brutal treatment so that others might live.

Because of the voluntary suffering of the servant of the Lord, the sins of countless were taken away. There was pardon and release!

Lord Jesus, you were spurned by others. You willingly surrendered to the suffering that would set us free. You know what we feel like inside because you live inside of us. You experience our pain and suffering. You identified completely with us. You took upon yourself and within yourself all our sins, our guilt, and our suffering. The will of the Lord was gloriously accomplished in you and through you. We are free because of what you did for us. Let us live these sacred days in your light.

> Saturday, March 22, 2008 Easter Vigil
> Genesis 1, 1,26-31
> First Story of Creation

In God's image we are created, male and female. God blesses us. God multiplies us. God graciously entrusts the creatures of land, sea, and air into our care. God provides all we need.

Lord Jesus, let us comprehend with our heart that we are truly made in God's image. Let us learn to value ourselves and others. Alleluia!

Sunday, March 23, 2008 The Resurrection of the Lord, Year A
Acts 10, 34,37-43
Peter's Speech

JESUS! Peter, who once denied Jesus, now boldly proclaims Jesus!

Peter told the people how God anointed Jesus with the Holy Spirit. Anointed with the power of the Holy Spirit, Jesus then showed forth God.

What would GOD do if God was a human being? Jesus showed us exactly what God would do. Jesus reached out to do good and to heal.

Although Jesus was killed, that was not the end of the story, God raised Jesus to life. God made the decision about who would see Jesus after he had been raised from the dead. Not everyone was allowed to see the risen Jesus at that particular time.

Jesus, having lived and died as one of us, is the one who will be our judge. If we place our trust in Jesus, our sins are forgiven.

Lord Jesus, thank you for loving Peter and forgiving Peter. Even though he denied knowing you, you were not about to dismiss Peter. Thank you for not giving up on us when we deny you or betray you. Thank you for gently correcting our misconceptions about the nature of God. Thank you for forgiving us and then giving us exciting new ways to tell others about you. Alleluia!

Monday, March 24, 2008 Easter Monday
Acts 2, 14,22-33
Peter's Speech at Pentecost

Instead of running away from controversy, Peter stood and spoke. He spoke to all in Jerusalem and especially to his fellow Israelites.

Peter spoke of Jesus as the one through whom God had worked wonders. Jesus was crucified, yes, but that was not the end of the story. God raised Jesus from the dead!

Death could not keep Jesus. Jesus was in God's keeping.

From his place of honor at God's right hand, Jesus poured out the powerful Holy Spirit upon his followers. They were then let loose upon the world to continue to do the works of Jesus!

Lord Jesus, let us experience Easter joy, Easter victory, and Easter healing today. You are alive! You are with us to heal us and to send us out into the world. Let us stand and speak and live for you today. We are safe and strong in God's keeping. Alleluia!

> Tuesday, March 25, 2008 Easter Tuesday
> Acts 2, 36-41
> Peter's Speech at Pentecost

What do you do with a broken heart? That's what the Israelites asked Peter and the other apostles that day in Jerusalem.

When the Israelites truly came to realize that they had crucified the Messiah, they were devastated. Peter had spoken the truth to them about Jesus. Jesus was indeed the Lord. Jesus was the Messiah.

In anguish, they asked Peter and the apostles with him what they could do? After all, Jesus, by now had died, risen, and ascended to God.

With God, it is never too late. Never too late.

No matter what we've done, there is always a way back to God. There is always a new life ahead for us, a life infused with God's love and grace.

Peter told them to repent and to be baptized, Their sins would be forgiven and they would receive the Holy Spirit. Their new life was beginning!

Lord Jesus, thank you that there is a way back to God. YOU are the way. You are our way back to God when we sin. Thank you for forgiving us and trusting us again to follow you and to serve you. Thank you that you will heal our broken heart. Alleluia!

> Wednesday, March 26, 2008 Easter Wednesday
> Acts 3, 1-10
> Cure of a Crippled Beggar

When Peter reached down and grasped the man's hand, the man who was crippled experienced the power of God in his feet and in his ankles. Crippled from birth, he was now able to jump up, stand up, and then to walk around! Around and around the temple he went with Peter and John, walking, indeed leaping, and praising his great God who had done this marvelous deed.

Peter and John had simply gone to the temple for the regular three o'clock time of prayer. How could they have known that they would be the human vessels through whom God's power to heal flowed! An afternoon never to be forgotten. The Gate Beautiful of the temple was the gate to a new life for the crippled man.

Lord Jesus, sometimes we feel like crippled beggars at the gate of life. Other people go in and out of the gate. They are alive. They can move freely. Come to us today and take us by the hand. Let us stand up straight and praise you! Let us be sensitive to reach out to take the hand of someone who may be a silent beggar at the gate. Alleluia!

Thursday, March 27, 2008 Easter Thursday
Acts 3, 11-26
Peter's Speech

Peter used the unexpected healing of the crippled beggar as an opportunity to proclaim the risen Lord Jesus Christ. Peter and John had gone to the temple that afternoon in Jerusalem for the regular three o'clock time of prayer. Little did they know the repercussions!

The man who was healed was overjoyed, yet still clinging to Peter and John. They had been the human instruments through whom Jesus had healed him. He was at the threshold of his new life.

Peter told the amazed Israelites, who witnessed the lame man now walking about, that the God of Abraham, Isaac, and Jacob had glorified Jesus. It was because of Jesus that the lame man was now able to walk and to leap!

Peter invited his hearers to repentance and conversion. A new life was possible for them also.

Lord Jesus, let us make time to be refreshed in your presence. In your presence, we are revived and transformed. Deepen our conversion to you. Let us yield to you and trust in you. Strengthen us to stand up in your name, to speak of you, and to serve you. Alleluia!

Friday, March 28, 2008 Easter Friday
Acts 4, 1-12
Peter's Speech; Before the Sanhedrin

It still happens. As soon as the power of the risen Lord Jesus Christ is made manifest, some religious leaders become nervous and feel threatened. Who knows? Their power might actually be eclipsed by the power of God!

The apostles, Peter and John were held in custody and subjected to interrogation by the priests, scribes, and other religious leaders. These leaders had wanted to get rid of Jesus, so, of course they would want to get rid of the followers of Jesus.

The Sadducees, a group that did not believe in resurrection, were especially threatened. What if they were wrong and God really did raise people from the dead?

Peter used this occasion to proclaim Jesus as the One who had healed the crippled man. The wisdom of the Holy Spirit was manifest as Peter spoke.

Peter reminded his interrogators that they, the religious leaders, had crucified Jesus. God, in spite of the Sadducees, had raised Jesus from the dead.

It was in the powerful name of Jesus that the crippled man was healed. There is salvation only through Jesus. It was true then and it is true now.

Lord Jesus, thank you that you still save and you still heal. Let us be humble enough to receive the healing we need. Let us be courageous enough to proclaim you as the one who saves and heals. We give you all the glory! Alleluia!

Saturday, March 29, 2008 Easter Saturday
Acts 4, 13-21
Peter's Speech

At last, Peter knew himself. He knew what he had done. He knew he had denied Jesus.

However, the mercy of the Lord Jesus was far greater than Peter's sins. The mercy of the Lord is far greater than your sins. The mercy of the Lord is far greater than my sins.

Peter experienced the amazing mercy and forgiveness of Jesus. Therefore, Peter was confident and bold when he spoke of Jesus.

Lord Jesus, thank you that your mercy is greater than our sins. Thank you for breathing new life and confidence into us today. Let us live confidently for you and speak of you to others. Alleluia!

> Sunday, March 30, 2008 Second Sunday of Lent
> Divine Mercy Sunday
> Acts 2, 42-47
> Community Life

Balance! The early followers of the risen Lord Jesus Christ led a life of balance.

They learned about Jesus from the teaching of the apostles. The New Testament had not yet been written. They lived in community, broke bread in their homes, and prayed. Simple.

Lord Jesus, we need to learn how to live a simple life of balance. Let us continue to learn about you in Scripture and sacraments. Let us learn to live in peace with other Christians. Let us continue to learn to pray. Thank you for the Holy Spirit who is our teacher. Alleluia!

> Monday, March 31, 2008 The Annunciation of the Lord
> Isaiah 7, 10-14; 8, 1
> Birth of Immanuel; The Son of Isaiah

LIFE! Sometimes life come about when we don't expect it.

Life comes on God's timetable. Life comes by God's methods.

Lord Jesus, thank you that you are truly alive and that you are with us. Let us acknowledge, accept, and welcome your presence in all aspects of our lives. Let us rest in you and rejoice in you. Let us receive your word to us and let your word bear new life in us. Alleluia!

> Tuesday, April 1, 2008
> Acts 4, 32-37
> Life in Christian Community

Does my life bear witness to the fact that God raised Jesus from the dead? Does our collective life as a Christian community bear witness to the resurrected Lord? Are we united in heart and in mind?

Lord Jesus, thank you that you never give up on us. You send us encouragement in many ways. Thank you for manifesting your life within us today. Alleluia!

Wednesday, April 2, 2008 St. Francis of Paola
Acts 5, 17-26
Trial before the Sanhedrin

Jesus, before his crucifixion, went before the Sanhedrin, a council of religious leaders. The apostles were also summoned to appear before the Sanhedrin.

The authorities in this council, motivated by jealousy, seized the apostles and threw them into jail. Not a good idea. They could not block the plan of GOD!

During the nighttime, the angel of the Lord simply opened the prison and released the apostles. The angel instructed them to go to the temple and to continue telling the people about life. This was true Life, life in Christ.

Lord Jesus, thank you that we are free today to tell others about you. Let us be bold to pray, to speak of you, and to believe in your power working through us. Alleluia!

Thursday, April 3, 2008
Acts 5, 27-33
Trial before the Sanhedrin

The jealousy of the religious leaders quickly turned to fury as Peter and the apostles spoke the truth to them about Jesus. The religious leaders knew they were guilty of the blood of Jesus.

Although they had arranged for Jesus' crucifixion, they had not counted on what was to follow. Resurrection!

God not only raised Jesus from the dead, but also exalted him as Ruler and Savior! The apostles continued to obey God and to proclaim Jesus as Messiah.

Lord Jesus, when we speak of you, not everyone will welcome us or our message. Thank you that the Holy Spirit will give us wisdom as we speak. Help us to remember that we are not called to be popular and to be accepted by others. We are called to be faithful to YOU! Let us live and speak today as you instruct us. Alleluia!

JANIS WALKER — FIRST READING

Friday, April 4, 2008 St. Isidore
Acts 5, 34-42
Trial before the Sanhedrin

The apostles kept their attention on Jesus. Although the respected teacher Gamaliel intervened on their behalf and offered wise counsel to the Sanhedrin, the apostles knew that their destiny was ultimately in God's hands.

Peter and the apostles were not deterred. They rejoiced in suffering dishonor for the name of the Lord. They kept on proclaiming Jesus as Messiah in the temple and in homes.

Lord Jesus, sometimes we look to people too much. We think that people, even wise and holy people like Gamaliel, will be able to explain our vocation to others. Let us be thankful for the Gamaliels in our lives, but let us continue to obey you and to live as you call us to live. Alleluia!

Saturday, April 5, 2008 St. Vincent Ferrer
Acts 6, 1-7
The Need for Assistants

We have to be willing to serve God as GOD directs. We also have to be at peace with ourselves about the nature of our ministry.

The apostles knew what they were called to do and what they were not called to do. They delegated certain tasks to others.

Although Stephen was among the first to be designated a deacon, that is not how we remember him. We remember Stephen as an eloquent, powerful expositor of the faith and as a martyr.

Lord Jesus, when we offer ourselves for your service you may surprise us with what our service will involve. Thank you for placing us according to your plan. Alleluia!

Sunday, April 6, 2008 Third Sunday of Easter
Acts 2, 14,22-33
Peter's Speech at Pentecost

The gift of the Holy Spirit! Jesus had promised that this would happen after his ascension to his Father (Acts 1, 4-9; 2, 1-4).

Peter, filled with the power of the Holy Spirit, addressed, not only the Jews, but also all who were in Jerusalem at that pivotal time. ALL!

Peter explained how Jesus was sent to earth, bearing his Father's credentials. These credentials were clearly in the realm of the miraculous. They could only be explained by the power of the Holy Spirit working through Jesus.

Within God's mysterious economy, Jesus was given over to those who tortured and crucified him. Also within God's sovereignty, Jesus arose from the dead. Long ago, it was prophesied that death could not hold him.

Lord Jesus, thank you that the Holy Spirit will show us the path you would have us walk today. Thank you that the Holy Spirit is leading us. Thank you for expanding our understanding of how the Holy Spirit works and through whom the Holy Spirit works. You will surprise us! Alleluia!

Monday, April 7, 2008 St. John Baptist de la Salle
Acts 6, 8-15
Accusation against Stephen

Stephen was filled with the Holy Spirit! Filled with faith, he worked very great signs and wonders in the midst of the people. He spoke with great wisdom.

He was lied about and falsely accused. With the eyes of all the religious leaders in the Sanhedrin glued upon him, the face of Stephen appeared to them as the face of an angel. His mission was nearly complete.

Lord Jesus, let us not worry so much about what is said to us or about us. Let us be about your business today and live with joy and trust. Alleluia!

Tuesday, April 8, 2008
Acts 7, 51 - 8, 1
Conclusion; Stephen's Martyrdom

Stephen spoke the truth with detailed accuracy to his accusers. He was not responsible for how they would receive his words.

Victory! The Easter victory of Jesus was soon to shine through Stephen. Stephen had faithfully completed the mission assigned to him.

Lord Jesus, let us be concerned with delivering the message you have given us to deliver to those around us. Let us speak and live with truth and love. Alleluia!

Wednesday, April 9, 2008
Acts 8, 1-8
Stephen's Martyrdom; Persecution of the Church;
Philip in Samaria

Words and deeds. Preaching and results.

After Stephen's martyrdom, the followers of Jesus were scattered by intense persecution. Philip, for example, went to a city in Samaria and proclaimed Jesus as Messiah.

Philip told the people about Jesus in a way that spilled over into their lives in obvious ways. Many who were crippled in mind or body were freed.

What is in our preaching package? Do we feel we have performed our duty if we say certain words or wear a cross around our neck?

Are there evidences in our life that we belong to Jesus? Are we moved with compassion to pray for others? Do we believe our prayers matter?

Lord Jesus, let our complete lives proclaim your complete victory. Let our words, our prayers, and our actions bring wholeness to others. Let us rejoice that you are indeed working through us today! Alleluia!

Thursday, April 10, 2008
Acts 8, 26-40
Philip and the Ethiopian

Time to go! Philip's assignment in that particular city was over and he was instructed to take a journey through the desert to Gaza.

Little did Philip realize that this wilderness journey would involve both word and sacrament. Philip was simply following the lead of the Holy Spirit and doing what the Holy Spirit instructed him to do.

Clearly, the Ethiopian official, who had been worshipping in Jerusalem and was now reading the prophet Isaiah was ripe and ready to learn about Jesus. Interesting that he was reading aloud from Isaiah 53, 7-8.

"Now the passage of the scripture that he was reading was this: 'Like a sheep he was led to the slaughter, and like a lamb silent before its shearer, so he does not open his mouth. In his humiliation justice was denied him. Who can describe his generation? For his life is taken away from the earth (vv. 32-33).'"

The Holy Spirit then instructed Philip to catch up with the chariot in which the Ethiopian was traveling and to speak to the official. Beginning from the particular passage in Isaiah which the official was reading, Philip proclaimed the Gospel to the Ethiopian official.

Ready! A soon as the official learned that he had been reading a prophecy of Jesus, he desired to be baptized. Philip discerned that the Ethiopian was ready for baptism.

Immediately after the baptism, it was time for a new assignment for Philip. Immediately he was in Azotus. Holy Spirit Airlines?!

Lord Jesus, help us to learn to listen to the directions of the Holy Spirit. Let us learn to understand our part in another's faith journey. Let us then say and do what you are calling us to do. We trust you to lead us to our next assignment. Alleluia!

Friday, April 11, 2008 St. Stanislaus
Acts 9, 1-20
Saul's Conversion; Saul's Baptism;
Saul Preaches in Damascus

The Lord's mercy triumphed over Saul's crazy, misguided zeal. The Lord's provision was evident in every stage of Saul's dramatic conversion.

It took being dazzled and blinded by a light from heaven to stop Saul in his tracks. It took the voice of the risen Lord Jesus Christ to tell Saul that when he was persecuting Christians, he was personally persecuting Jesus!

Saul had to be led by the hands of his companions into the city of Damascus. Three days of darkness. Three days without food or drink.

The Lord had prepared his disciple Ananias to minister to the future apostle Paul, now still known as Saul. The Lord revealed to Ananias that Saul had been chosen for a great mission.

Ananias respectfully addressed Saul as "brother." Ananias then laid his hands on Saul who then regained his sight. Saul was filled with the Holy Spirit and was baptized.

Lord Jesus, our lives may not be the rollercoaster ride that the future St. Paul experienced. Still, we are called to continue to be your disciples and to learn from you. Thank you for sending us out on the assignments you have chosen for us. Alleluia!

Saturday, April 12, 2008
Acts 9, 31-42
The Church at Rest; Peter Heals Aeneus at Lydda;
Peter Raises Tabitha to Life

Jesus told his followers that they were to do the very things he had been doing and even greater things (John 14, 12). Peter was beginning to live out these words of Jesus.

In Lydda, Peter simply told Aeneus, a paralyzed man, that Jesus was healing him. He told Aeneus to arise and to make up his bed all by himself.

Peter was then called to a nearby town, called Joppa, where a disciple named Tabitha had died. Peter went to Joppa, put everyone else out the room, then knelt and prayed by her body.

After praying, Peter then spoke to Tabitha. He told her to arise!

Opening her eyes, she saw Peter. She, who had died, sat up, quite alive! Peter took her hand and she arose. Is that cool or what?

Lord Jesus, we may think that that was then and this is now. You have not changed. Thank you for the power in your name to bring life and wholeness. Let us be bold to pray and to trust. Let us arise! Alleluia!

Sunday, April 13, 2008 Fourth Sunday in Easter
Acts 2, 14,36-41
The Coming of the Spirit

Peter proclaimed that the crucified Jesus was truly the Lord and the Messiah. Stricken, indeed pierced, in the depths of their hearts, his hearers implored Peter and the apostles to tell them what they could do now.

Peter told them to repent. He told them to be baptized. Their sins would be forgiven and they would receive the Holy Spirit.

Lord Jesus, you continue to call us to yourself. Thank you that you continue to forgive us. Thank you for the gift of the Holy Spirit to strengthen us to live as you call us to live. Alleluia!

Monday, April 14, 2008
Acts 11, 1-18
The Baptism of the Gentiles Explained

Clean. Clean! CLEAN!

Jesus has made us clean. Jesus has made us right with God. No one can take away our relationship with the risen Lord Jesus Christ.

As Peter told the Gentiles gathered in the home of Cornelius about Jesus, the Holy Spirit descended upon them! They glorified God, spoke with other tongues, and were baptized in water (Acts 10, 44-48).

Peter confidently told the Jewish believers in Jerusalem about this experience of the Holy Spirit being poured out upon Gentiles who believed in Jesus. Peter realized that he was not to try to hinder GOD!

The Jewish believers then glorified God. They realized that all people, Jew or Gentile, could come to repentance and to faith in Jesus.

Lord Jesus, thank you for your Precious Blood poured out for us. Let us rejoice that we are cleansed and we are now pure and clean. Let us reach out in prayer and in love to all. No one is outside the reach of your mercy. Alleluia!

Tuesday, April 15, 2008
Acts 11, 19-26
The Church at Antioch

Triumph! Again, the grace of God triumphed over prejudice. Instead of proclaiming Jesus only to the Jews, some of the disciples began to tell the Greeks also.

The Lord obviously liked that a lot! Many of the Greeks believed.

Celebration! Lots of happy big Greek celebrations were in the making. Remember the film, "My Big Fat Greek Wedding?"

The church back in Jerusalem sent good, faithful Barnabas, diplomat par excellence, to Antioch to check out this Greek thing. Barnabas clearly saw God at work among the Greek Christians.

Lord Jesus, thank you for the Christians in Antioch and for the role of Barnabas. Please send more believers like Barnabas into the harvest fields of those who long for you. Let there be rejoicing as more and more come to you. Alleluia!

Wednesday, April 16, 2008
Acts 12, 24 - 13, 5
Herod's Death; Mission of Barnabas and Saul;
First Mission Begins in Cyprus

In the midst of the church of Antioch's worshipping and fasting, the Holy Spirit gave specific directions about ministry. The Holy Spirit assigned Barnabas and Saul (Paul) a specific work.

After prayer, fasting, and the laying on of hands, the two went to Seleucia. Then they sailed to Cyprus where they proclaimed Jesus in the synagogues.

Lord Jesus, let us learn to be still, to worship, to pray, to fast, and to wait. Thank you that the Holy Spirit will continue to give us instructions on what we are to do. Alleluia!

Thursday, April 17, 2008
Acts 13, 13-25
Paul's Arrival in Antioch of Pisidia; Paul's Address in the Synagogue

Paul spoke at the invitation of the leaders of the synagogue. This was the time in the service after the reading of the law and the prophets.

Paul, accepting the invitation to speak, began to address the people in the synagogue. He acknowledged both his fellow Israelites and also the other people in the synagogue who revered God.

Paul began at the beginning and spoke of God's choice of Israel. God delivered the Israelites from slavery in Egypt, led them to Canaan, provided judges, and then, a king.

From the line of King David, God brought forth a Savior for Israel. Jesus!

Jesus! John the Baptist had prepared the way for Jesus by stressing the need for repentance.

Lord Jesus, when we are asked to speak, give us the words we need to say. Let us acknowledge, with courtesy, those who have asked us to speak. Let us be faithful to speak the message you have given us to proclaim. Alleluia!

Friday, April 18, 2008
Acts 13, 26-33
Paul's Address in the Synagogue; Address to the Gentiles

Paul, in the synagogue, addressed, not only his fellow Israelites but also all who revered God. Salvation is available to all.

Although Jesus was unjustly condemned and crucified, just as the prophets had predicted, God raised him from the dead. The promise of God was fulfilled in Jesus.

Lord Jesus, when we speak to people about you, let us speak with respect. Let us trust the Holy Spirit to give us the words that will draw others to you. Alleluia!

Saturday, April 19, 2008
Acts 13, 44-52
Address to the Gentiles

Paul and Barnabas, at the invitation of the leaders of the synagogue, returned the following sabbath to speak. A huge crowd appeared and the tide rapidly turned against the apostles.

Their message was now violently rejected. It was clearly time to leave Antioch and to move to the next assignment. It was time to proclaim the message of Jesus to the Gentiles.

Shaking the dust from their feet, Paul and Barnabas departed. They were not filled with bitterness or despair. They were filled with the Holy Spirit and were joyful.

Lord Jesus, let us learn to be joyful for the privilege of living for you and speaking about you to others. Let us rejoice in you whether or not our message is accepted. Thank you for the strength of the Holy Spirit to persevere. Alleluia!

Sunday, April 20, 2008 Fifth Sunday of Easter
Acts 6, 1-7
The Need for Assistants

Complaints! Complaints within the church led to a new ministry within the church. The new ministry flourished in ways far beyond the original job description.

The word of the Lord spread and even a number of Jewish priests came to believe in Jesus. The number of disciples increased as the Twelve learned to delegate.

Complaints. We need to pay attention to complaints.

What are our own complaints about? Do we feel helpless or that a particular situation will never change?

Are we trying to do work we're not called to do? Are we frustrated by not being able to do the work we are called to do?

The Holy Spirit is here to free us to serve as we are called to serve. Because we are currently serving in one particular way does not mean that we are stuck there forever.

The Holy Spirit has exciting ways to free us. The Holy Spirit can create new ways in which we may serve.

Lord Jesus, help us when we don't know how to serve or if we are unhappy in our current ministry. You call us to be faithful. You also came that we might be joyful. Realign us and, if necessary, reassign us. Thank you, Lord. Alleluia!

Monday, April 21, 2008 St. Anselm
Acts 14, 5-18
Paul and Barnabas at Iconium; Paul and Barnabas at Lystra

Extremes! From persecution to adulation.

Paul and Barnabas had just fled Iconium where they were about to be stoned to death. In Lystra, on the other hand, after the healing of the crippled man, the apostles were about to be worshipped as gods.

Paul and Barnabas made it clear that they were human beings, not gods. They were there to proclaim the Gospel. They gave all the glory to God.

Lord Jesus, let us learn not to be deterred by either persecution or praise. Let us continue to serve you, whether or not we are treated well. You know how to bring us consolation. Let us give you all the praise and glory no matter how we are treated. Alleluia!

JANIS WALKER — FIRST READING

Tuesday, April 22, 2008
Acts 14, 19-28
Paul and Barnabas at Lystra; End of the First Mission

Mission accomplished! It wasn't easy, but it was over. It was not without great suffering, but it was accomplished by the power of the Holy Spirit.

Remember Paul's enemies from Antioch and Iconium? Well, they weren't going to give up on getting rid of Paul. They went to Lystra to try to undo the work of the apostles.

They stoned Paul and left him for dead. Surprise! He got right back up and continued his ministry.

Paul and Barnabas went right back to Iconium and Antioch. They encouraged the disciples there and reminded them that we will all suffer before entering God's kingdom. They appointed leaders in the churches and then continued their travels.

Lord Jesus, thank you for opening doors of opportunity for us to minister. Let us be faithful to you even if the mission you entrust to us involves great difficulty, misunderstanding, and suffering. You are in charge. Thank you for the joy you give us as we place our trust in you. Alleluia!

Wednesday, April 23, 2008 St. George, St. Adalbert
Acts 15, 1-6
Council of Jerusalem

More complaints! People who complain about the Second Vatican Council might not have been so jazzed about the Council of Jerusalem either

Challenges! Both councils, one in the first century and the other in the twentieth century, brought challenges to the church.

Some Pharisees, even though they had come to believe in Jesus, were still rigid rule-keepers at heart. They clung to the tradition of Moses even though they had come to believe in Jesus.

Was it really necessary to be circumcised in order to be saved? That was the question placed before the apostles and presbyters in Jerusalem.

Lord Jesus, let us be bold to ask you to set us free from anything that would hinder our following you. You are here to free us to live for you. Let us cling to you, bear witness to you, and bear fruit for you. Alleluia!

Thursday, April 24, 2008 St. Fidelis
Acts 15, 7-21
Council of Jerusalem; James on Dietary Law

Yak. Yak. Yak. Fuss. Fuss. Fuss. Argue. Argue. Argue.

SILENCE!

After all the debating at the first-century Council of Jerusalem about the new Gentile believers in Jesus, there was silence. What was the reason for the silence?

Peter had just told of his own mission to the Gentiles. Peter had observed first-hand that God made no distinctions between Jewish believers in Jesus and Gentile believers in Jesus.

The same Holy Spirit was at work and is still at work. We are all saved through trust in the Lord Jesus.

That's when it became silent in the council chambers. The Holy Spirit was clearly at work.

Stepping into this silence, the apostle James spoke. He reminded those present of the prophecies in the Hebrew scriptures that all people, including the Gentiles, would one day seek the Lord.

Lord Jesus, let us stop debating one another long enough to be silent. Let us learn to be silent and to listen to you. Thank you that you will enter the silence and you will show us your will. Alleluia!

Friday, April 25, 2008 St. Mark
1 Peter 5, 5-14
Advice to the Community

"And all of you must clothe yourselves with humility in your dealings with one another, for 'God opposes the proud, but gives grace to the humble.' Humble yourselves therefore under the mighty hand of God, so that he may exalt you in due time. Cast all your anxieties on him, for he cares for you. Discipline yourselves, keep alert. Like a roaring lion your adversary the devil prowls around, looking for someone to devour. Resist him, steadfast in your faith, for you know that your brothers and sisters in all the world are under going the same kinds of suffering. And after you have suffered a little while, the God of all grace, who has called you to his eternal glory in Christ, will himself restore, support, strengthen, and establish you. To him be the power forever and ever. Amen (vv. 5-11)."

Dress correctly! Dress to cast.

How do we dress? We are to be clothed in humility as we interact with others.

God is against the proud and haughty and is overwhelmingly merciful to the humble. God will exalt the humble.

Cast! Then we are ready to cast! We are learning to cast all our concerns on GOD, who tenderly cares for us.

We are watchful, but not fearful. We are learning to trust in God and to resist the devil. We are not alone in this. Our Christian brothers and sisters all over the world are suffering also.

This suffering will not last forever. God calls us, strengthens us, and will gloriously restore us.

Lord Jesus, let us not worry about being trampled upon in your service. When we are misunderstood and mistreated, you will eventually set the record straight. Let us continue today to humble ourselves before you, cast our concerns upon you, and joyfully follow you. Alleluia!

Saturday, April 26, 2008
Acts 16, 1-10
Paul in Lycaonia: Timothy; Through Asia Minor

Church politics and the Holy Spirit. A challenging intersection!

Politics. After all the fuss about circumcision at the Jerusalem Council, Paul still had the disciple Timothy circumcised.

Timothy's mother was a faithful Jew and his father was a Greek. It seemed best to Paul, for pastoral reasons in this particular situation, to have Timothy circumcised.

Paul and Barnabas had previously had quite a heated disagreement over the behavior of Mark (Acts 15, 36-41). As a result, the new arrangement was that Barnabas and Mark would minister together.

Barnabas and Mark sailed for Cyprus. Paul and Silas would travel together in ministry, taking Timothy with them.

These differences settled as well as possible, let the ministry continue! The missionaries traveled to various cities and the church did indeed grow stronger, both in faith and in numbers.

The Holy Spirit. The Holy Spirit, who was directing these missionary journeys, actually prevented the apostles from proclaiming Jesus in certain places, Asia and Bithynia. The apostles altered their travel plans accordingly. Paul then had a strong sense of being called by God to go to Macedonia.

Lord Jesus, help us to trust that you are at work at the intersection of church politics and the Holy Spirit. In the midst of all human imperfection and frustration, you are in charge of the Church. Thank you that the Holy Spirit will show us how and where to serve you. Alleluia!

Sunday, April 27, 2008 Sixth Sunday of Easter
Acts 8, 5-8,14-17
Philip in Samaria

Results! The crowds in Samaria paid attention to Philip's proclamation of Christ because his proclamation produced results. People were healed in mind and body.

Then the church in Jerusalem sent the apostles Peter and John to Samaria to pray for the newly baptized believers in Jesus to receive the gift of the Holy Spirit. They laid hands on them and the new Christians received the Holy Spirit.

Lord Jesus, let us learn to proclaim the Gospel as you call us and to pray for others as you call us. Thank you that there will be results in our lives and in the lives of all for whom we pray. Alleluia!

Monday, April 28, 2008 St. Peter Chanel; St. Louis de Montfort
Acts 16, 11-15
Into Europe

A sabbath prayer group by the riverside! This group was meeting outside the gates of Philippi, since there was no synagogue in the city.

Paul and his ministry companions sought out this place of prayer. They spoke with the women assembled there and proclaimed Jesus

Lydia, a merchant of costly purple fabric, was ready to hear Paul's message about Jesus. She was already a person who reverenced God. Lydia and her whole household were then baptized!

Lord Jesus, let us learn to pray in many places and to speak to the people in those places. Thank you that you will open the hearts of our listeners to hear your message. Alleluia!

Tuesday, April 29, 2008 St. Catherine of Siena
Acts 16, 22-34
Imprisonment at Philippi; Deliverance from Prison

UNFAIR! Paul and Silas were unjustly attacked by an angry crowd, unjustly beaten, and unjustly thrown into prison.

Miracles! Out these repeated acts of injustice, God brought forth miracles and conversions.

At midnight in the jail, Paul and Silas, instead of lamenting their unjust treatment, were engaged in prayer and praise. Then there was an earthquake which caused the doors of the prison to open and the chains to fall off the prisoners!

Paul reassured the terrified jailer that they were still there. The jailer immediately asked Paul and Silas what he had to do in order to be saved.

Believe! Trust! Paul and Silas simply told him to trust and believe in Jesus and he and his entire household would be saved.

So, in the middle of the night, Paul and Silas became guests in the home of the jailer. The jailer carefully bathed the wounds of the apostles. Then the jailer and all his household were baptized. There was a meal accompanied with great rejoicing!

Lord Jesus, let us meet injustice with trust and expectation that you will bring forth good. Thank you that you are at work in the lives of everyone in the particular situation which concerns us. Let us be ready to intercede, to forgive, and to tell others about you. Alleluia!

Wednesday, April 30, 2008 St. Pius V
Acts 17, 15,22 - 18, 1
Paul in Beroea; Paul's Speech at the Areopagus; Paul in Corinth

"Then Paul stood in front of the Areopagus and said, 'Athenians, I see how extremely religious you are in every way. For as I went through the city and looked carefully at the objects of your worship, I found among then an altar with the inscription, 'To an unknown god.' What therefore you worship as unknown, this I proclaim to you (vv. 22-23)."

Paul opened himself to be used by God in the city of Athens, a city filled with idols. He spoke and debated with the Athenians both in the synagogue and in the city square.

Paul acknowledged where the people were spiritually. He understood their underlying fear and superstition manifested in the ways in which they sought God and made shrines. There was even an altar to a God who was unknown.

Bingo! That was the entry Paul needed. He now had an opportunity to proclaim Jesus. He told the Athenians what God was really like.

Paul also referred to the "Man." Jesus! Jesus whom God raised from the dead. Some scoffed. Some believed.

Lord Jesus, let us respect each person we encounter. Let us learn to be more sensitive to the guidance of the Holy Spirit about how we are to speak. Let us speak forth the words you give us to speak. Let us be open to being used in your service wherever you send us. Alleluia!

Thursday, May 1, 2008 St. Joseph the Worker
Acts 18, 1-8
Paul in Corinth

Paul was in ministry, active ministry, intense ministry, almost hyperactive ministry during this time in Corinth. At first, he lived and worked with fellow tentmakers Aquila and Priscilla. On the Sabbath, he was in the synagogue, ready to proclaim Jesus to both Jews and Greeks.

With the arrival of Timothy and Silas, Paul devoted himself completely to proclaiming to the Jews that Jesus was the Messiah. When they rejected Paul and his message about Jesus, he knew it was time to go and proclaim Jesus to the Gentiles.

Paul moved to a house, belonging to Titus Justus, next door to the synagogue. His presence must have livened up that neighborhood!

The official of the synagogue, Crispus, and his whole household believed in the Lord. Many others in Corinth also came to believe in Jesus and were baptized.

Lord Jesus, let us be willing to serve you among many different kinds of people and to live where you call us to live. Let us be active in serving you and in proclaiming you. Alleluia!

>Friday, May 2, 2008 St. Athanasius
>Acts 18, 9-18
>Paul in Corinth; Accusation before Gallio;
>Return to Syrian Antioch

Look to the LORD for guidance. Look to the LORD for wisdom in knowing when to speak and when to be silent. Look to the LORD alone for vindication.

We can't be looking this way and that to see what we think we should say or what we think others want us to say. We can't expect understanding or vindication from any source but the Lord.

Lord Jesus, help us not be become so political and cynical that we no longer truly trust you. Let us learn to seek you and to be so filled with your life and your love that we are content to speak or to remain silent, according to your plan. Alleluia!

>Saturday, May 3, 2008 Sts. Philip and James
>1 Corinthians 15, 1-8
>The Gospel Teaching

The result of Paul's preaching was the ongoing working out of the salvation of the Christians in Corinth. What did he preach?

Simple! Paul simply relayed to the Corinthians what he himself had received.

"For I handed on to you as of first importance what I in turn had received: that Christ died for our sins in accordance with the scriptures, and that he was buried, and that he was raised on the third day in accordance with the scriptures, and that he appeared to Cephas (Peter) then to the twelve (vv. 3-5)."

Jesus! For our sins, Jesus died. Jesus was buried. Jesus was raised from the dead the third day. All for us. All according to the sacred scriptures.

Jesus appeared to many others after his resurrection. Peter. The Twelve. More than five hundred. James. The apostles. Paul.

Lord Jesus, thank you for helping us to keep it simple. Let us learn to be simple and pure of heart as we proclaim you with our lives and our words. Alleluia!

Sunday, May 4, 2008   Ascension of the Lord
Acts 1, 1-11
The Promise of the Spirit; The Ascension of Jesus

Mission accomplished! Back home to our heavenly Father, our Abba!

Before Jesus was taken back to his Father in heaven, he carefully instructed the apostles to wait. They were to wait for the promised Holy Spirit. The Holy Spirit would bestow upon them the necessary power needed to witness to Jesus in Jerusalem, in Judea, in Samaria, and all over the world.

The time had come. Jesus was taken from their sight. Even as they stared up at the sky, they were assured that Jesus would come back in the very same way.

Lord Jesus, you have not forsaken us. The Holy Spirit is here to tell us what to do during the rest of our time here on earth. You triumphantly completed your mission on earth. Let us complete ours by following you in love and in trust. Alleluia!

Monday, May 5, 2008
Acts 19, 1-8
Paul in Ephesus

Paul met the group of Ephesian disciples where they were spiritually. He asked them if they had received the Holy Spirit.

Since they had so far been baptized only with the baptism of John the Baptist, a baptism for repentance, Paul gave them further instruction. They received baptism in the name of Jesus. After this, they received the Holy Spirit, began to speak in other languages, and began to prophesy.

Lord Jesus, thank you that you know where we are spiritually. You know when and how to lead us to the next step in our walk with you. Open us to receive the fullness of the Holy Spirit. Let us be filled to overflowing with the Holy Spirit. Alleluia!

Tuesday, May 6, 2008
Acts 20, 17-27
Paul's Farewell Speech at Miletus

Humility. Tears. Trials.

In Paul's final meeting with the church leaders of Ephesus, he summarized his own experience of ministry. In humility, he had served the Lord.

In his many trials, Paul had wept and suffered. Still, he had been steadfast in speaking forth words to benefit the Ephesians. He had faithfully taught both in public and in various homes.

To both Jews and Greeks, Paul had borne witness to the Lord. It was now time to travel to Jerusalem where he knew further suffering awaited him. His priority was to complete, with joy, the ministry entrusted to him by the Lord.

Lord Jesus, let us complete the mission you have entrusted to us. Let us be faithful to do what we know you have called us to do. Let our lives be a witness to your mercy and your grace as you transform our suffering into joy. Alleluia!

Wednesday, May 7, 2008
Acts 20, 28-38
Paul's Farewell Speech at Miletus

First things first! Paul earnestly entreated the Ephesian church leaders to maintain close watch over themselves as well as over Christ's flock. He reminded these leaders that the Church belongs to God and was purchased by the blood of Christ.

There is an anecdote about Pope John XXIII (Angelo Guiseppe Roncalli) staying awake, unable to sleep, in his deep concern for the Church. The Lord called him little Angelo and told him to go to sleep because the Holy Spirit was running the Church.

Paul understood all about wolves and hirelings (John 10, 12-13). Tragically, there would be those, even within the ranks of these church leaders, those who would attempt to pervert the truth for their own purposes. Constant vigilance was required.

There is an old saying about how easy it is gradually to begin to serve the work of the Lord rather than the Lord of the work. It is even possible and very dangerous to worship the work of the Lord rather than the Lord of the work.

That is a form of idolatry. When that happens, all sorts of evils follow, to the harm of the flock of Christ.

Lord Jesus, help us to be vigilant to pray for all leaders in the Church to stay close to you. Forgive us when we criticize and gossip rather than intercede. Thank you that you are our Good Shepherd and that we belong to you. You are guarding us and guiding us. Alleluia!

Thursday, May 8, 2008
Acts 22, 30; 23, 6-11
Paul before the Sanhedrin

Tried for hope! In his appearance before the Sanhedrin, composed of both Pharisees and Sadducees, Paul addressed them all as "brothers," but clearly identified himself as a Pharisee.

Uproar! Paul proclaimed that he was on trial because of his firm hope in resurrection.

The Pharisees believed in the resurrection of the dead and also in the existence of spirits and angels. Their Sadducee colleagues on the Sanhedrin believed in none of these.

Stuck in the middle? Was Paul just a pawn?

No. Paul clung to the Lord who spoke words to cheer and to encourage him.

Lord Jesus, sometimes we are stuck in the middle of others' disputes. We may even feel like helpless pawns. We are not helpless because we are in your strong hands. The mighty Holy Spirit is our Helper and is right here beside us. You are our risen, victorious Lord. Thank you that you will honor our trust in you. Alleluia!

Friday, May 9, 2008
Acts 25, 13-21
Paul before King Agrippa

Ensnared in the political plots and issues of others, Paul was passed from one leader to another like a hot potato! How people treated the apostle Paul spoke volumes about these rulers.

Their basic cowardice and greed quickly surfaced. They were dedicated, not to truth and justice, but to self-preservation and self-promotion.

Lord Jesus, thank you that you are with us and you will lead us safely Home. Help us not to be overly concerned with how others perceive us and how others treat us. Let us remain focused on you and on completing the work you have given us to do. Alleluia!

Saturday, May 10, 2008 Bl. Damien de Veuster
Acts 28, 16-20,30-31
Arrival in Rome; Testimony to Jews in Rome

Paul was faithful to his vocation, difficult though it was. For two years, he continued to bear witness to the Jews in Rome.

"He lived there two whole years at his own expense and welcomed all who came to him, proclaiming the kingdom of God and teaching about the Lord Jesus Christ with all boldness and without hindrance (vv. 30-31)."

Lord Jesus, thank you for strengthening us to continue to trust you and to be faithful to our vocation. Alleluia.

Sunday, May 11, 2008 Pentecost, Year A
Acts 2, 1-11
The Coming of the Spirit

Time. Place. Unity.

It was the appointed time. The followers of Jesus were gathered together in Jerusalem on the Feast of Pentecost. The Holy Spirit came in power, as rushing wind and flames of fire. ALL were filled with the Holy Spirit. ALL spoke in other languages about God's majesty. ALL in the huge crowd heard and understood God's message.

Lord Jesus, help us to be patient to wait your timing for your purposes in our individual lives and in the whole Church to be fulfilled. Let us learn how to live in unity with other Christians. Thank you for the Holy Spirit who teaches us how to speak of you so that all come to know you. Alleluia!

Monday, May 12, 2008 St. Nereus, St. Achilleus, St. Pancras
James 1, 1-11
Perseverance in Trials

"My brothers and sisters, whenever you face trials of any kind, consider it nothing but joy, because you know that the testing of your faith produces endurance; and let endurance have its full effect, so that you may be mature and complete, lacking in nothing (vv. 2-4)."

Are we there yet? Are we ready to embrace our trials with trust?

Our trials are frustrating, but also temporary. They can be used of God to expand our capacity to trust.

If we are baffled and don't know what to do, all we have to do is, with trust, to ask God for wisdom. God is delighted to give us the wisdom we need. As we receive God's wisdom and act on it, our level of trust rises.

Lord Jesus, we become so weary trying to avoid trials. We worry and try to figure everything out on our own. Let us learn to trust you as our wise and loving Shepherd. You are leading us through this valley into a place of light and peace. Alleluia!

Tuesday, May 13, 2008
James 1, 12-18
Temptations

Subtle. Temptations become much more subtle as we draw closer to God.

We are beginning to see ourselves in a new light, in the light of God's purity and holiness. We are becoming more aware of our complex motives and of our inner poverty.

Lord Jesus, when we realize we are about to act from a wrong motive, let us stop and ask for your help. Thank you that you stand ready to forgive us, to purify our hearts, and to redirect our actions.

Wednesday, May 14, 2008 St. Matthias
Acts 1, 15-17,20-26
The Choice of Judas' Successor

Let God vote! Let God choose.

Crude though the method may have been, a successor for Judas was indeed chosen.

The apostles were not a polished group of church professionals. They simply believed that another apostle was meant to take the office of Judas. They prayed that God would choose this person.

Lord Jesus, thank you that you see our hearts. Although our reasoning may seem good to us, let us pray, in humility, for your guidance. We leave matters of ministry and methodology in your hands. Alleluia!

Thursday, May 15, 2008 St. Isidore
James 2, 1-9
Sin of Partiality

A clergy friend from my hospital ministry days actually saw this passage in James lived out in her church. Her husband, a computer programmer, dressed neatly, but simply.

One Sunday morning, however, he got all dressed up and wore a suit! Several people in the church made a big fuss over him and said, "Oh, HELLO! Are you a visitor?"

God actually chooses those the world considers poor to be wealthy in what matters, faith! They are heirs of God's kingdom.

Lord Jesus, we are poor when we do not honor others. We are poor when we do not live for you and love others. Let us learn to trust in your love for us. Then we will be secure enough to realize that we are rich. Alleluia!

Friday, May 16, 2008
James 2, 14-24,26
Faith and Works

BELIEVE! When the people in Capernaum asked Jesus what they should do to accomplish God's work, Jesus told them to BELIEVE!

In his Bread of Life discourse, Jesus told the crowd following him that God's work is to believe in him (Jesus) who was sent by God. Jesus said, "This is the work of God, that you believe in him whom he has sent (John 6, 29)."

Jesus later told his disciples, at the Last Supper, to believe that he is in the Father and that the Father is in him or, at least, to believe because of his works (John 14, 11). Believing in Jesus will lead us to do the works Jesus did and even greater works (John 14, 12) Amazing!

Bearing in minds these words of Jesus helps us when we encounter these strong words in today's first reading in James. James doesn't mince words.

Ignoramus! James says that anyone is an ignoramus for not believing that it's futile to have faith and not to have works also.

"You see that a person is justified by works and not by faith alone. For just as the body without the spirit is dead, so faith without works is also dead (vv. 24,26)."

Even Abraham, the great Abraham, was justified when he was willing to offer his son, Isaac, to the Lord. His faith and trust in God was truly put to the test. His faith and trust were proven by his actions.

Rahab, who was a harlot, helped to protect the Israelites back in the time of Joshua. She, too, was justified, by her deeds (James 2, 25, Joshua 2, 1-21).

Both! We need both. We need faith and we need to live out our faith in the work God gives us to do.

Lord Jesus, thank you for the Holy Spirit who teaches us how to illustrate our faith by our actions. Let us trust in you and live out our trust. Alleluia!

Saturday, May 17, 2008
James 3, 1-10
Power of the Tongue

The tongue is very small. The tongue is very powerful.

Our tongue can defile us and destroy us. It can defile and destroy others

No one except God can tame our tongue. We must learn to surrender both our hearts and our tongues to God. This is crucial, since Jesus told us that "… out of the abundance of the heart the mouth speaketh (Matthew 12, 34 KJV)."

Lord Jesus, forgive us when we have given free rein to our wild tongues. Heal our hearts and tame our tongues to speak your words of peace and gentleness. Alleluia!

Sunday, May 18, 2008 Most Holy Trinity
Exodus 34, 4-6,8-9
Renewal of the Tablets

From a cloud, God actually came and stood with Moses on Mt. Sinai. Bowing in worship, Moses asked the Lord to accompany the stubborn Israelites, to forgive them, and to count them as the Lord's own people.

Lord Jesus, thank you for renewing us in your love. Thank you for your presence among us and with us in the Person of the Holy Spirit. Alleluia!

Monday, May 19, 2008
James 3, 13-18
True Wisdom

From heavenly wisdom comes humility. From heavenly wisdom comes true humility.

From mere earthly wisdom and craftiness come suspicion and ambition. From mere earthly wisdom comes disorder.

"But the wisdom from above is first pure, then peaceable, gentle, willing to yield, full of mercy and good fruits, without a trace of partiality or hypocrisy. And a harvest of righeousness is sown in peace for those who make peace (vv. 17, 18)."

Lord Jesus, thank you for helping us to face ourselves and to acknowledge our lack of true wisdom. Thank you for forgiving us and filling us with gentleness and wisdom in facing ourselves and others. Alleluia!

Tuesday, May 20, 2008 St. Bernadine
James 4, 1-10
Causes of Division

The gentle Holy Spirit within us is grieved and wounded when we long for the world to give us what God alone can bestow. St, Paul warns, "… do not grieve the Holy Spirit of God, with which you were marked with a seal for the day of redemption (Ephesians 4, 30)."

Gradually, in subtle and not so subtle ways, we may begin to align ourselves with the world's way of doing business. We begin to distance ourselves from God and indeed we are at enmity with God.

"Do you not know that friendship with the world is enmity with God? Therefore whoever wishes to be a friend of the world becomes an enemy of God (v. 4)."

For our own good, the Lord will then oppose us. When we humble ourselves before the Lord, the Lord will lift us up again.

"Submit yourselves therefore to God. Resist the devil, and he will flee from you. Draw near to God, and he will draw near to you (vv. 7-8)."

We are called to submit ourselves to God and then to resist the devil. As we draw near to God, God draws near to us. When we have been double-minded and two-faced, we may come to our Lord for forgiveness and cleansing.

Lord Jesus, let us look to you and not to the world. Let us live in honesty and simplicity before you this day. Alleluia!

Wednesday, May 21, 2008 St. Christopher Magallanes
James 4, 13-17
Warning against Presumption

St. James reminds us that we do not know what tomorrow will bring. Constantly we are to submit our bright ideas and our projects to the Lord.

We have no idea where the Lord may decide to lead us. We have no idea what may be required of us.

We are held to strict accountability. "Anyone ... who knows the right thing to do and fails to do it, commits sin (v. 17).

Lord Jesus, let us live today in simplicity and trust. Thank you that you will lead us and direct us. Thank you that you will strengthen us to follow your plan. Alleluia!

Thursday, May 22, 2008 St. Rita of Cascia
James 5, 1-6
Warning to the Rich

The wealthy who refuse to share their wealth are judged severely. They are unworthy of the enormous responsibility which accompanies all of our resources.

The Lord listens to the poor. The Lord is aware of the way the poor have been mistreated by the irresponsible wealthy.

"Listen! The wages of the laborers who mowed your fields, which you kept back by fraud, cry out, and the cries of the harvesters have reached the ears of the Lord of hosts You have lived on the earth in luxury and in pleasure; you have fattened your hearts in a day of slaughter. You have condemned and murdered the righteous one, who does not resist you (vv. 4-6)."

Lord Jesus, let us joyfully share what we have with others. Let us treat others, not with condescension or condemnation, but with respect, courtesy and compassion. Alleluia!

Friday, May 23, 2008
James 5, 9-12
Patience and Oaths

God is my point of reference. I am not to complain about others.

Expectations. When I complain about others, I am living out of my own unrealistic expectations.

I am not the judge of others. God alone is the Judge of us all and is full of tender compassion.

We are called to remember the prophets who spoke forth the Lord's messages. The prophets suffered for their fidelity to the Lord.

Lord Jesus, let us be truthful and simple in our thoughts and in our words. Let us speak, with courage, the words you call us to speak. Alleluia!

Saturday, May 24, 2008
James 5, 13-20
Anointing of the Sick; Confession and Intercession;
Conversion of Sinners

Prayer is powerful! A compact course in prayer is packed into this short passage.

Are we suffering? What do we do? Pray.

Are we cheerful? We praise God and sing.

Are we sick? We are to call for the elders of the church. They are to pray over us and to anoint us with oil in the Lord's name.

There is a promise. The prayer prayed in faith and trust will indeed be answered. The Lord will save us and raise us up. Our sins will be forgiven.

What do we do with our sins? We are told to confess our offenses, our sins, and our faults to one another and to pray for one another that we may be healed

Prayer is powerful. Your prayer is powerful. My prayer is powerful.

The prophet Elijah, a human being like us, prayed about rain. He prayed that it would not rain. It did not rain for three and a half years! Then he prayed again that it would rain and the rain fell.

We pray for another's conversion. God will hear the prayer from our heart about the one who concerns us so much.

"My brothers and sisters, if anyone among you wanders from the truth and is brought back by another, you should know that whoever brings back a sinner from wandering will save the sinner's soul from death and will cover a multitude of sins (vv. 19-29)."

Lord Jesus, we look to you in trust and we pray! Thank you for the Holy Spirit who instructs us in the way to bring wanderers back to you, the Good Shepherd. Thank you for answering our prayers for ourselves and for others in the very best way. Alleluia

Sunday, May 25, 2008 Most Holy Body and Blood of Christ
Deuteronomy 8, 2-3,14-16
God's Care; Danger of Prosperity

"Remember the long way that the LORD your God has led you these forty years in the wilderness, in order to humble you, testing you to know what was in your heart, whether or not you would keep his commandments. He humbled you by letting you hunger, and then by feeding you with manna, with which neither you nor your ancestors were acquainted, in order to make you understand that one does not live by bread alone, but by every word that comes from the mouth of the LORD (vv. 2,3)."

A good land! Through a desert of snakes and scorpions, the Lord led the Israelites to a good land.

"For the LORD your God is bringing you into a good land. a land with flowing streams, with springs and underground waters welling up in valleys and hills, a land of wheat and barley, of vines and fig trees and pomegranates, a land of olive trees and honey … (vv. 7-8)." Although they had been afflicted and tested, the Lord's intention was to make them prosperous.

What was the Lord trying to teach them? The Lord was teaching them that they lived, not merely by the bread (manna) they ate, but by every word of the Lord.

We still face the snakes and scorpions of life. We still need the Lord to lead us and to direct us. We still need the Lord to feed us.

Lord Jesus, thank you for being the Word of God, the Word made flesh. Thank you for feeding us with your own precious Body and Blood. Let us accept your discipline and continue in the strength you have given us for the rest of the journey.

Monday, May 26, 2008 St. Philip Neri
1 Peter 1, 3-9
Blessing

In! To! Through! From!

Within this dance of prepositions, we are reassured that we are sewn into God's care.

God is stretching us, stitching us, and fashioning us. God's purposes are being worked out in our lives.

In God's mercy, we were given a new birth. We are actually regenerated.

Our new birth in Christ leads us to a hope that is alive and active. Our hope is alive because it comes through the resurrection of our Lord Jesus Christ.

Our hope leads us to our inheritance, which is kept safe for us in heaven. By God's power we are being safely led through our trust and faith to the ultimate revelation of our salvation.

We rejoice in the midst of our sufferings and in the midst of our trials. If even gold is tested, so must our precious faith be tested.

These trials are temporary and are being used of God to stretch us and to test us. This will all work out for our good and for God's glory.

We are growing closer and closer to the true goal of our faith. Our goal is our salvation. Our goal is to be conformed to the image of Christ (Romans 8, 29).

Lord Jesus, thank you that the Holy Spirit is teaching us about our salvation. We are saved, but we don't yet understand all that is implied in our salvation. There is so much more than we imagined. Thank you that, in the midst of our questions and in the midst of our suffering, we are safe in your care as you lead us to the house of our Father. Alleluia!

Tuesday, May 27, 2008 St. Augustine of Canterbury
1 Peter 1, 10-16
Blessing; Obedience

Live! Because of the grace that is ours, we are to live. We are to live lives of holiness.

The prophets knew about us. Long ago, before the birth of Christ, the prophets recounted the grace that was to be given to us.

The prophets were serving us as they were given insight by Christ's Spirit into our future. Even the holy angels longed to know about these matters.

Lord Jesus, we fix our hope on the grace that awaits us when we, at last, see you as you really are. Let us pray that every aspect of our lives reflect the holiness to which we are called. Let our thoughts, our words, and our actions show that you are at work within us. Alleluia!

Wednesday, May 28, 2008
1 Peter 1, 18-25
Reverence; Mutual Love

We are valuable! We have been ransomed at a huge cost.

We are not cheap, worthless objects in Satan's dirty pawn shop. We are of inestimable value to Almighty God.

It cost God everything to ransom us. It cost God his only Son, Jesus.

Jesus. Jesus, the Lamb of God, took away our sins. Where did he take them?

Jesus took our sins into himself. He took the poison of our sins and drank it!

When he died on the Cross, our sins died! They no longer exist. Do we believe this?

If we know our value, we will conduct ourselves accordingly. We will not think that we are worthless, because we know we are of supreme value to GOD.

We will resist the temptation to despair. We will not think that everything is futile and that nothing we do matters.

Everything we think, say, and do matters to God, because we matter to God. We are invited to take every concern, big or little, to our loving God, who has all the time in the world to listen to us and to help us.

We are like newborns. We are newborns who will live forever because we are born from a seed that will never die.

We are born through God's word and God's word endures forever. Forever and ever.

Lord Jesus, let us, from this moment, view ourselves in a different light. We are valuable to you. Let us also learn to look upon every person we encounter today as of great worth and value. Alleluia!

Thursday, May 29, 2008
1 Peter 2, 2-5,9-12
God's House and People; Christian Charity; Christian Examples

Ongoing! Our salvation is an ongoing process.

Yes, we are saved. However, our salvation is not stagnant.

We are growing into our salvation (v. 2) We are being built into a temple in which we offer sacrifices of praise and worship to God.

Rejected! Rejected, and yet chosen.

Jesus, our Lord Jesus Christ, was the stone rejected by the human builders, but chosen by God. Jesus, the stone rejected, was chosen by God to be the cornerstone of the Church (1 Peter 2, 6-7).

Chosen! We are chosen to worship God.

We don't need to be overly concerned about rejection. God will never vote us off the island.

Lord Jesus, let us remember that we are aliens and nomads here on earth. We are your people and we are traveling Home to you. Let us be patient in this process of living out and growing into our salvation. Let us remember that we have been called out of darkness to live in your glorious light. Alleluia!

Friday, May 30, 2008 Sacred Heart of Jesus
Deuteronomy 7, 6-11
Destruction of the Pagans

Chosen! The Israelites were chosen by God, not because they were so great, but because God was so great and God loved them.

God brought this tiny nation out of captivity and ransomed them from the tyrannical rule of Pharaoh. God was and is faithful to his people. God is committed to keeping his covenant with his people.

Lord Jesus, thank you that you chose us to follow you. Let us live confidently in the freedom you died to give us. Alleluia!

Saturday, May 31, 2008 Visitation of the Blesssed Virgin Mary
Zephaniah 3, 14-18
Reproach and Promise for Jerusalem

Shout and sing! There is a time for rejoicing, a time for loud rejoicing.

There is a time for shouting. Elizabeth, filled with the Holy Spirit and pregnant with John the Baptist, was loud in expressing her joy when her pregnant cousin Mary came to visit her (Luke 1, 41-45).

Elizabeth had lived in sorrow and silence long enough. Now it was time for a SHOUT OUT!

Life is hard. Sometimes we become quieter and quieter as we are seemingly silenced.

We have forgotten that this life is not all there is. This life is very important, but it is not all there is.

We may have forgotten who we are. We may have forgotten whose we are.

We belong to God. We are conquerors, indeed, we are more than conquerors through Christ (Romans 8, 37).

SHOUT! Jerusalem was instructed to shout and to rejoice because the Lord was in her midst as victorious King.

Lord Jesus, you are in our midst and you are our victorious King. Let us rejoice even now. Let us shout and sing, regardless of our circumstances and regardless of our feeling. You are our King. You are rejoicing over us even now. Thank you for reviving us and renewing us. Alleluia!

> Sunday, June 1, 2008 Ninth Sunday in Ordinary Time
> Deuteronomy 11, 18,26-28,32
> Reward of Fidelity; A Blessing and a Curse

We are to take God's words into our very heart and soul. We are blessed when we obey God, regardless of our feelings. We invite God's curse when we rebel against God and disobey God.

Lord Jesus, let us learn to listen to your voice and obey your words to us. Forgive us when we insist on our own way. Heal whatever it is in us that keeps us from fully trusting in your love your us. Alleluia!

> Monday, June 2, 2008 Sts. Marcillinus and Peter
> 2 Peter 1, 2-7
> Greeting; The Power of God's Promise

Through. Through. Through!

Everything we need to live for God is available to us. Everything we long for is waiting for us. Everything is available through the knowledge of God.

Peace? It's ours. Everything that makes for true life is ours. through knowing God's power.

We have trouble trusting people, don't we? Do we have trouble trusting God?

God is completely worthy of our trust. God has our best interests at heart.

So, for a summer project, we may begin to build blocks. Upon our block of faith (trust), we build virtue, knowledge, self-control, endurance, devotion, loving concern for others, and finally LOVE!

Lord Jesus, let us stop our timid tiptoeing through life. Let us know your power at work within us, changing us to brave, bold disciples and apostles. Alleluia!

> Tuesday, June 3, 2008 St. Charles Lwanga and Companions
> 2 Peter 3, 12-15,17-18
> Exhortation to Preparedness

The Lord will come in glory! We are growing in the knowledge of the Lord as we await his return. We are eager, yet patient.

Lord Jesus, thank you for this time to grow in grace. You are with us and you are teaching us stability in our faith. Alleluia!

Wednesday, June 4, 2008
2 Timothy 1, 1-3,6-12
Greeting; Thanksgiving; The Gifts Timothy Has Received

You are a witness to the Lord. You have a testimony of the Lord to share with others.

Paul instructed Timothy not to be ashamed of testifying to the Lord. Timothy was to stir up and to kindle into action the gifts the Holy Spirit had bestowed upon him.

Like Paul and Timothy, we are called to bear hardships for the sake of the Gospel. This is part of our discipleship package. Timothy and Paul had hardships to bear and so do we.

God has given us all we need. "For God hath not given us the spirit of fear; but of power, and of love, and a sound mind. (2 Timothy 1, 7 KJV) We need these gifts in order to live a life of holiness, wisdom, and self-control.

Lord Jesus, you lived, you died, and you defeated death. You are watching over us and you will complete the plans and purposes you have for us. Let us learn to live in your love and to exult in your strength and power within us. Show us how to stir up the gifts entrusted to us, as we bear witness to you. Alleluia!

Thursday, June 5, 2008 St. Boniface
2 Timothy 2, 8-15
Timothy's Conduct; Warning Against Useless Disputes

Although the one who proclaims the Gospel may suffer and even be imprisoned, God's word can never be imprisoned. God's word will never return void or without accomplishing God's purpose.

"For as the rain cometh down, and the snow from heaven, and returneth not thither, but watereth the earth, and maketh it bring forth and bud, that it may give seed to the sower, and bread to the eater: So shall my word be that goeth forth out of my mouth; it shall not return unto me void, but it shall accomplish that which I please, and it shall prosper in the thing whereto I sent it (Isaiah 55, 10-11 KJV).

Paul instructed Timothy not to allow the people in his care to dispute about words. This harms those who listen to such harangues.

Instead, Timothy was instructed to pay careful attention to himself. Timothy was instructed to impart God's word with integrity.

Lord Jesus, our lives are speaking even when we are silent. Speak through us today as you choose, in our silence and in our words. Alleluia!

Friday, June 6, 2008 St. Norbert
2 Timothy 3, 10-17
Paul's Example and Teaching

Paul was straightforward and truthful. He made it clear that all who really live for Jesus Christ will be persecuted.

We are called to stay faithful to what we have learned from the Holy Scriptures. God has inspired all scripture to teach us and to train us.

Lord Jesus, let us be confident as we proclaim you word. Let us be honest with others about the joys and the struggles of following you as Lord. Alleluia!

Saturday, June 7, 2008
2 Timothy 4, 1-8
Solemn Charge; Reward for Fidelity

Fulfill your own ministry! We are called and charged to be faithful to the ministry entrusted to us.

Paul continued to instruct Timothy to proclaim God's word. He reminded Timothy to be patient and to persevere in the face of opposition and apathy.

Lord Jesus, it's hard to keep on. We grow weary and discouraged with the world, the Church, and with ourselves. Energize us today to abandon ourselves entirely to you and to your plan for our ministry, especially when we do not completely understand. Thank you that you are coming in glory and you will reward us. Alleluia!

Sunday, June 8, 2008 Tenth Sunday in Ordinary Time
Hosea 6, 3-6
Insincere Conversion

After the darkest night, dawn will come! There will be light again.

The Lord's coming is just as certain. Like the dawn, the Lord Jesus Christ will return in glory as our King.

Lord Jesus, thank you for pouring out your love upon our parched lives and reviving us. Let us now love others with the overflow of the abundant love you have poured into us. Alleluia!

Monday, June 9, 2008 St. Ephrem
1 Kings 17, 1-6
Draught Predicted by Elijah

Hidden! The prophet Elijah was hidden within the circle of God's providence. Elijah delivered the prophecy about the draught and then God hid him away for a period of time.

The prophet dwelt beside the brook called Cherith. At Cherith, God supplied all Elijah needed for this period of seclusion.

Lord Jesus, you speak to us, you speak through us, and then, sometimes you hide us. We are safely within your care and you provide all we need. You are giving us a time of respite and shelter before sending us out again into visible service. Let us be content in this time of seclusion, knowing that we are still serving you in silence and solitude. Alleluia!

Tuesday, June 10, 2008
1 Kings 17, 7-16
Elijah and the Widow

Time to move! It was time for the prophet, Elijah, to leave the brook Cherith for another assignment.

It was the Lord who had sent Elijah to Cherith. It was the Lord who had provided for the prophet during this time by the brook.

The Lord was now sending Elijah to another assignment. in a town called Zarephath. The Lord had already arranged provision for Elijah in this new place. A widow, who lived there with her son, would provide for Elijah.

This woman was about to experience God's miraculous provision in a time of scarcity. With only small amounts of flour and oil, she was expecting death for both herself and her son.

The Lord had other plans. She was told not to be afraid.

The prophet Elijah first spoke words of encouragement to her. Next he spoke words of challenge. She was to provide for Elijah even before providing for herself and her son. Elijah assured her of provision during the drought.

For a whole year, the flour container and the oil jug were not empty! The Lord's word, spoken forth from the prophet, Elijah, proved true.

Lord Jesus, when it's time for us to leave our present assignment, let us continue to trust in your presence with us and your provision for us. Thank you that you will direct us, guide us, and provide all we need to serve you in our new assignment. Alleluia!

Wednesday, June 11, 2008 St. Barnabas
Acts 11, 21-26; 13, 1-3
The Church at Antioch; Mission of Barnabas and Saul

A new assignment! Barnabas had proved faithful and true in his work in the church in Jerusalem.

He was now being sent to the believers in Antioch. He was full of joy as he recognized that the Lord was at work in this community of believers. He encouraged them to stay close to the Lord.

Meanwhile, Barnabas took the initiative to seek out Saul (Paul) in Tarsus and to bring him to Antioch. There followed a year of instruction in the faith for the Christians in Antioch from Barnabas, Paul, and other teachers.

Time to move again! In Antioch, while worshipping the Lord and fasting, the Holy Spirit made it clear that Barnabas and Paul were to be sent on another mission.

Lord Jesus, help us when we begin to feel dispirited in our current assignment. Let us work and serve you as you direct. Let us be content to stay here as long as you direct and let us be joyful and full of trust when you call us to another assignment. Alleluia!

Thursday, June 12, 2008
1 Kings 18, 41-46
Elijah and the Prophets of Baal

Speak! Speak the word of the Lord and then look for the Lord's response. It may take awhile, but the Lord will answer!

The prophet Elijah boldly spoke forth the word of the Lord. Elijah told the wicked King Ahab about the sound of a torrential rain even before there was even a little cloud in sight.

Over and over, Elijah's servant checked for clouds. Nothing.

Finally, at the seventh search for a cloud, the servant reported seeing a tiny cloud. That was enough for Elijah!

Darkness. Clouds. Wild blowing of the wind. Rain descended!

Lord Jesus, speak your word to us and then let us boldly speak forth your word as you direct. Thank you that you will honor your word and bring your word to pass. Alleluia!

Friday, June 13, 2008 St. Anthony of Padua
1 Kings 19, 9,11-16
Flight to Horeb

A new mission! Elijah was depleted and depressed after the dramatic confrontation with those who worshipped idols. Poor dear, he even prayed to die (1 Kings 19, 4).

The Lord knew how to take care of Elijah. The Lord gently spoke to his exhausted servant.

The Lord spoke, but not in a dramatic way. The Lord spoke, not in an earthquake, not in the tempestuous wind, not in the fire. The Lord spoke in a whisper to Elijah,

The Lord listened to the laments of Elijah, who was feeling seriously burned out and very isolated. The Lord directed Elijah to a new mission.

Elijah was to travel back to the desert and to anoint Hazael as king of Aram and Jehu as king of Israel. Elijah was to anoint Elisha as his own successor.

Lord Jesus, you understand that the onslaughts are the fiercest after the greatest victories. Shield us and shelter us. Thank you that you renew us, refresh us, and redirect us. You are victorious in our lives! Alleluia!

Saturday, June 14, 2008
1 Kings 19, 19-21
Call of Elisha

The mantle. Elijah placed his own mantle (cloak) over Elisha. Elisha was being called to be a prophet.

The mantle. At the Last Supper, Jesus told his disciples that they would do the works he did and that they would do even greater works (John 14, 12) After his resurrection, Jesus told his disciples that, just as the Father had sent him, so he was sending them (John 20, 21).

Lord Jesus, thank you for your mantle placed upon us. This mantle may be invisible, but you see it. Thank you that the Holy Spirit strengthens us to do your will. Thank you that the Holy Spirit gives us your words to speak and to live. Alleluia!

Sunday, June 15, 2008 Eleventh Sunday in Ordinary Time
Exodus 19, 2-6
Arrival at Sinai

Who were they? Who were the Israelites?

After the years of slavery in Egypt and after years on the wilderness journey, the Israelites were now at the desert in Sinai. Moses was going to deliver to them the word of the Lord.

Identity. The Israelites were assured of their true identity.

They were to keep the covenant of the Lord and to be the Lord's own, dear people. They were called to be holy. They were to considered as an entire kingdom of priests. The entire nation was to be holy.

What about us? Who are we?

As Christians, we are also chosen by the Lord to be holy, to be a royal priesthood, a holy nation, God's own people. We have been called from darkness into God's light (1 Peter 2, 9).

Lord Jesus, thank you that we are your lambs. Let us follow you as our Good Shepherd. We are also your priests and you are our Great High Priest. Let us live out our true identity as you direct us. Alleluia!

Monday, June 16, 2008
1 Kings 21, 1-16
Seizure of Naboth's Vineyard

Selfishness. Greed. Anger. Pouting.

King Ahab of Samaria indulged in all these simply because he could not have one particular vineyard. This was Naboth's ancestral vineyard.

Manipulation. False pretenses. False accusations. Death.

Through the schemes of the king's wicked wife, Jezebel, Naboth was falsely accused. Then, he was murdered.

Lord Jesus, let us be aware of our raging emotions and learn to submit all our emotions to you. Calm us. Restrain us. Let us not continue to indulge emotions that will harm us and harm others. Forgive us, heal us, and let us rejoice in your present provision for us. Alleluia!

Tuesday, June 17, 2008
1 Kings 21, 17-29
Seizure of Naboth's Vineyard

Confrontation. Judgment. Repentance. Mercy.

The Lord confronted wicked King Ahab through the prophet Elijah. Elijah predicted the Lord's judgment on both Ahab and Jezebel for the murder of Naboth.

The judgment was very graphic and gruesome. Dogs would lick Ahab's blood and would devour Jezebel.

Ahab had truly been a terrible king. a wicked king, a king who followed idols. No one had yielded to evil more than this king (v. 25).

And yet, when Ahab humbled himself, fasted, and donned sackcloth, the Lord changed the situation. The Lord decided not to inflict the terrible judgment in Ahab's time.

Truly, the Lord's way are beyond our understanding. The Lord's mercy is beyond our understanding (Isaiah 55, 7-9).

Lord Jesus, please purify our thoughts. Let us be aware of the progression of our thoughts into words and actions. Thank you for

stopping this cycle. Thank you for the Holy Spirit who reminds that we have your mind (1 Corinthians 2, 16). Alleluia!

Wednesday, June 18, 2008
2 Kings 2, 1,6-14
Elijah and Elisha; Elisha Succeeds Elijah

Elisha asked for something big! Elijah cautioned him that this would be hard.

"Is anything too hard for the Lord (Genesis 18, 14a KJV)?" Absolutely not!

Elisha had asked for a double portion of the powerful, prophetic spirit that had been Elijah's. A bold request.

The request was granted. Elisha saw Elijah taken to heaven in a chariot of fire!

Elisha then reached for Elijah's mantle. Very soon, Elisha experienced the power of the Lord for his own ministry and mission.

Jesus told us to ask, to seek, and to knock (Matthew 7, 7). Jesus also instructed us to ask and to receive so that we would be filled with joy (John 16, 24).

Lord Jesus, forgive us when we are timid and when we do not ask for much. Forgive us when we become frustrated and passive. Let us be bold to ask for everything you know we need to fulfill your call on our lives. Alleluia!

Thursday, June 19, 2008 St. Romuald
Sirach 48, 1-14
Elijah and Elisha

Purity. Prayer. Power.

Elijah and Elisha, imperfect human beings, were still consecrated to God's service. Both were zealous for God's glory.

They could not tolerate infidelity to the Most High God. They were filled with the power of God. When they prayed, God acted.

The letter of James reminds us of the power of prayer and cites Elijah. The power of a righteous person is very powerful.

Elijah was "… a man subject to passions as we are, and he prayed earnestly that it might not rain: and it rained not on the earth by the space of three years and six months. And he prayed again, and the heaven gave rain and the earth brought forth her fruit (James 5, 17,18 KJV)."

Lord Jesus, purify us in our thought lives, prune our words, and direct our actions. Thank you for the power of the Holy Spirit within us at this moment. Let us be bold to pray as you direct us to pray and then to rejoice at your answer. Alleluia!

Friday, June 20, 2008
2 Kings 11, 1-4,9-18,20
Rule of Athaliah

Sheltered. Sheltered in the temple during the reign of a wicked ruler.

In the midst of the murderous plots of Athaliah, mother of the late King Ahaziah, the Lord protected Joash, the future king. For six years in the temple, the future king was hidden and protected.

Finally, under the leadership of the priest, Jehoiada, the wicked queen mother was removed from power. Joash was anointed king, a covenant was made with the Lord, and the pagan temples were destroyed. There was now rejoicing and quiet peace.

Lord Jesus, thank you that you shelter us in your presence. Let us rejoice, even when we are surrounded by evil, knowing that you are in control of our lives. Alleluia!

Saturday, June 21, 2008 St. Aloysius Gonzaga
2 Chronicles 24, 17-25
Apostasy of King Joash; Retribution

Constant vigilance. Constant fidelity.

King Joash, who had become king at age seven (2 Chronicles 24, 1) pleased the Lord as long as the priest, Jehoiada, was alive. The king, who ruled for forty years, and the priest, who lived to be 130, restored the temple.

However, when the priest Jehoaida died, the king listened to his advisors who were beginning to serve idols. The warnings of the prophets were ignored.

Then, the priest, Zechariah, son of Jehoiada, spoke the truth to the people. He told them that they had broken the Lord's commands and had even abandoned the Lord. That was the reason they were not prospering. For speaking the truth, the priest, Zechariah, was murdered in the court of the temple.

The Lord then allowed a small number of Arameans to invade Judah and Jerusalem and to send the spoil to the King of Damascus. King Joash's own servants murdered him while he lay sick. This king was not buried in the royal tombs.

Lord Jesus, help us to be vigilant over ourselves. Let us seek your honor over any earthly honor. Let us remain faithful to you regardless of the behavior of others. Every day, let us entrust ourselves to you. Alleluia!

Sunday, June 22, 2008 Twelfth Sunday in Ordinary Time
Jeremiah 20, 10-13
Jeremiah's Interior Crisis

Jeremiah. The poor prophet was experiencing great suffering.

Deceived and denounced. Jeremiah even came to feel that the Lord had deceived him. Jeremiah was indeed being denounced even by his friends.

There seemed no escape. If Jeremiah spoke forth the word of the word of the Lord, he was derided. If he tried to remain silent, the word of the Lord smoldered in his very heart and bones (Jeremiah 20, 9).

The Lord had not deceived Jeremiah and had not forsaken him. Jeremiah eventually reminded himself that the Lord was still with him. He trusted himself and his mission to the Lord.

Lord Jesus, help us to sing to you and praise you even in the midst of our suffering. Let us continue to acknowledge your presence with us. You have called us to follow you and you will lead us through this time of suffering. Alleluia!

Monday, June 23, 2008
2 Kings 17, 5-8,13-15,18
Hoshea of Israel

King Hoshea of Israel committed evil in the sight of the Lord. He became the servant of the king of Assyria and was imprisoned.

The people of Israel, having served idols and having committed many abominable deeds, were sent to Assyria. Their choices had sent them back into captivity.

The people had become what they had pursued. They had forsaken the Lord and "…followed vanity, and became vain, and went after the heathen that were round about them, concerning whom the Lord had charged them, that they should not be like them (2 Kings 17, 15b KJV)."

This is a warning to us. Whom are we pursuing? What are we pursuing?

We are not called to fit into the corrupt, heathen culture around us. We are called to follow the Lord Jesus Christ.

Lord Jesus, we choose to pursue you. We long to become like you. Thank you for strengthening us to follow and to pursue your will for us.

> Tuesday, June 24, 2008 The Nativity of John the Baptist
> Isaiah 49, 1-6
> The Servant of the Lord

"The Lord called me before I was born, while I was in my mother's womb he named me. He made my mouth like a sharp sword, in the shadow of his hand he hid me; he made me like a polished arrow, in his quiver he hid me away. And he said to me, 'You are my servant ... (vv. 1b, 3a)."

Called and concealed. Hidden and revealed.

The Lord was at work in the life of Isaiah. The Lord is at work in your life and in my life, regardless of what we think or what we feel.

The Lord called the prophet Isaiah even before his birth. Isaiah was concealed and hidden away while the Lord was preparing him for his ministry. The time would come for the Lord's message through Isaiah to be revealed.

Isaiah reflected on the Lord during times of exhaustion. Isaiah acknowledged his feelings of futility. What was the use of it all?

"I have labored in vain, I have spent my strength for nothing and for vanity; yet surely my cause is with the LORD, and my reward with my God (vv. 3b-4)."

Isaiah knew, deep down, that his reward was ultimately with the Lord. The Lord still had important work ahead for his servant.

Lord Jesus, you have called us to follow you. Sometime we become exhausted, cynical, and dispirited. Refresh us when we feel exhausted and when we feel that our work has all been futile. Thank you for reminding us that you alone are the judge. Let us rejoice in your love for us and strengthen us to complete the work you have given us to do. Alleluia!

Wednesday, June 25, 2008
2 Kings 22, 8-13; 23, 1-3
The Book of the Law

Do you ever read the Bible and then tear your clothes? That's what King Josiah did!

King Josiah was an earnest young king, a good, conscientious king. He listened attentively as the scribe Shaphan read to him from the book of the law, which the priest Hilkiah had found in the temple of Jerusalem. This was during a time of repair in the temple, following the reign of a previous wicked king.

As he listened to the book of the law being read to him, the king was seized with the understanding that his ancestors had not lived according to the Lord's teaching. The king instructed the high priest, the scribe, and several others to seek the Lord for direction in this serious matter.

Huldah! The high priest, the scribe, and several other leaders sought the Lord's counsel through the ministry of a woman, a prophet named Huldah.

She lived in a newer area of Jerusalem, called the Second Quarter. Huldah assured the king that, because he had humbled himself, he would be spared the judgment pronounced against the idolaters (2 Kings 22, 14-22).

The king then gathered all the people in Jerusalem together and had the complete book of the covenant read to them. King Josiah then revived the covenant. The king and the people would keep the commands of the Lord.

Lord Jesus, sometimes our heart is torn within us as we study the sacred Scripture. We realize that we have not followed you as you have called us to follow. you. Thank you that you long to speak to us and give us specific, as well as general, direction for our lives. You are greater than our sins and you are greater than the sins of those who went before us. Let us humble ourselves before you, ask for and receive your forgiveness, and then continue joyfully in your service. Alleluia!

Thursday, June 26, 2008
2 Kings 24, 8-17
Reign of Jehoiachin

King Josiah! It is tragic to read of the kings following good King Josiah.

"And like unto him was there no king before him, that turned to the Lord with all his heart, and with all his soul, and with all his might, according to all the law of Moses; neither after him arose any like him (2 Kings 23, 25 KJV)."

King Josiah's father, King Amon and his grandfather, King Manasseh had both done great evil during their reigns. Now, after King Josiah, there would be another tragic period of kings who did not honor the Lord and rule with wisdom.

King Jehoichin continued the pattern of committing evil in the sight of the Lord. He was taken captive by the king of Babylon.

All of Jerusalem was deported. Only the poor remained.

Lord Jesus, thank you that you are our true King. You will return in glory. Help us to remain faithful to you and to honor you with our trust and obedience. Alleluia!

Friday, June 27, 2008 St. Cyril of Alexandria
2 Kings 25, 1-12
Reign of Zedekiah

Jerusalem! How could it get any worse in Jerusalem?

King Zedekiah, who committed evil in the eyes of the Lord, fled from his palace as King Nebuchadnezzar of Babylon seized starving Jerusalem. King Zedekiah's own army deserted him.

The King of Babylon murdered King Zedekiah's sons and then blinded King Zedekiah before taking him to Babylon.

Jerusalem. Jerusalem. Jerusalem was on fire!

The Babylonian king burned the Temple, King Zedekiah's palace, and other major buildings. The walls of Jerusalem were torn down.

The poor. Some of the poor survived in Jerusalem. They were left to work as farmers and vinedressers.

As the Lord had promised, good King Josiah was spared seeing the Lord's judgment on Jerusalem (2 Kings 22, 20). The Lord's judgment, which had been delayed because of King Josiah's repentance, humility, and reforms, was now a reality (2 Kings 24, 3-4).

Lord Jesus, you wept over Jerusalem. As we read of all those kings of old who committed evil, let us remember to intercede for all leaders. You will not remove their freedom of action. You will not remove our duty to intercede for them. As we weep and as we intercede, let us also remember the reality of the heavenly Jerusalem. You are leading us closer each day to the heavenly Jerusalem. Alleluia!

Saturday, June 28, 2008 St. Irenaeus
Lamentations 2, 2,10-14,18-19
The Lord's Wrath against Zion

Wrath! The Lord's anger was the grief of an outraged lover, whose love had been trampled and whose heart was crushed.

Silence. The silence of old men who sat in despair.

Hunger. The hunger of starving infants and children whose mothers had no food to give them.

Death. The starving little ones died in the arms of their mothers.

Deception. The false prophets led the Lord's people astray.

Weeping. Crying.

Hope! Even now, in the midst of all this desolation, Jerusalem was exhorted to turn to the Lord.

Lord Jesus, we come to you and pour out our hearts in your presence. Let us trust in you and in your mercy. You will forgive us, renew us and restore us. Alleluia!

Sunday, June 29, 2008 Sts. Peter and Paul
Acts 12, 1-11
Herod's Persecution of the Christians

Prison. Prayer. Which is greater?

The apostle Peter was chained in prison, under heavy guard. King Herod had no intention of letting him escape.

Prayer! King Herod's soldiers and chains were no match for the power of prayer. The church was praying for Peter's release.

The sleeping Peter was awakened in the night. Light from heaven flooded his cell!

An angel awoke him and led him past the guards to the city gates, which opened before them. Freedom!

Lord Jesus, let us exult in you and in the power of prayer. Let us expect light and freedom for ourselves and for those for whom we pray. Alleluia!

Monday, June 30, 2008   Holy Martyrs of Rome
Amos 2, 6-10,13-16
Israel

A dual vocation. Amos was both a shepherd and a prophet. He did not hesitate to proclaim, with boldness, the words the Lord gave him to speak.

Through Amos, the Lord confronted his people Israel for their crimes. Through Amos, the Lord reminded Israel of their former slavery and their present prosperity. Through Amos, the Lord warned of coming judgment upon Israel for their abominable behavior.

Lord Jesus, no matter if we are students, shepherds, sales reps, or whatever, you long to speak through our lives to others. Let us look to you, trust you, love you, and follow you. Let your life within us speak to others the message you choose to impart. Alleluia!

Tuesday, July 1, 2008
Amos 3, 1-8; 4, 11-12
First Word; Second Word

Confrontation! The Lord continued to confront Israel through the shepherd/prophet Amos.

Prophets! The Lord does not act without first of all revealing his intention, his secret counsel, to the prophets.

"Surely the LORD GOD does nothing, without revealing his secret to his servants the prophets (v. 7)." Through Amos, Israel was warned to prepare to meet GOD!

"The lion has roared; who will not fear? The LORD GOD has spoken; who can but prophesy (v. 8)."

Lord Jesus, let us be alert to hearing you speak through unlikely prophets. Let us discern your word to us and then respond to you with trust and obedience. Alleluia!

Wednesday, July 2, 2008
Amos 5, 21-24
First Woe; Second Woe

God detests mechanical, superficial, hypocritical worship. God is concerned with how we treat people.

Lord Jesus, let us pursue goodness and justice. Let us live for you and worship you with purity and integrity. Alleluia!

Thursday, July 3, 2008
Ephesians 2, 19-22
One in Christ

As I read this passage, I was reminded of a song made popular by the Fisherfolk, "Come and Go with Me to My Father's House." Joy abounds in the Father's house!

We belong inside the house! We are not to live as beggars at the gate nor as mere tenants in the house. We belong!

We long to belong and the Lord has made provision for this longing. We belong to the Lord. We belong to one another in the Body of Christ.

The Lord's house is safely built upon the Lord Jesus Christ as the cornerstone. We are standing upon the foundation of the prophets and the apostles.

"Now therefore ye are no more strangers and foreigners, but fellow-citizens with the saints, and the household of God (Ephesians 2, 19 KJV)."

Lord Jesus, thank you that you are holding us together as we grow up in God's household. Let us invite others into relationship with you. Let us bring others to your Father's house, where joy abounds. Alleluia!

Friday, July 4, 2008 St. Elizabeth of Portugal
Amos 8, 4-6,9-12
Against Greed

Famine! Quite an antidote to greed.

God had become quite fed up with Israel. Time was up.

God would no longer tolerate perversion of justice and oppression of the poor. "Hear this, you that trample on the needy, and bring to ruin the poor of the land (v. 4)."

Famine! This famine would be far more frightening than a mere physical hunger. This famine would involve being famished for the Lord's word.

"The time is surely coming, says the LORD GOD, when I will send a famine on the land; not a famine of bread, or a thirst for water, but of hearing the words of the LORD (v. 11)."

Lord Jesus, you call us not to oppress others but to care for others. You call us to seek justice for all. You call us to light, not to darkness. You call us to be filled with your word, to live your word, and to give your word to others. Thank you for the Holy Spirit who strengthens us to fulfill your call to serve. Alleluia!

Saturday, July 5, 2008 St. Anthony Mary Zaccaria
Amos 9, 11-15
Epilogue; Messianic Perspective

Sifted! Then a sword.

Then a raising up and a rebuilding. Restoration.

God is very just and thorough. Evil will not be tolerated.

God is also very merciful. There is a promise of restoration of the ruins. Promises of gardens and vineyards. A promise of security.

"I will restore the fortunes of my people Israel, and they shall rebuild the ruined cities and inhabit them; they shall plant vineyards and drink their wine, and they shall make gardens and eat their fruit. I will plant them upon their land, and they shall never again be plucked up out of the land that I have given them, says the LORD your God (vv. 14-15)."

Lord Jesus, your word sifts us. Your word slices through our lives like a sword. Your word purifies us and lifts us up to new life. Thank you that you will restore us. Alleluia!

Sunday, July 6, 2008 Fourteenth Sunday in Ordinary Time
Zechariah 9, 9-10
Restoration under the Messiah

Jesus, who will return in glory, came first as the just and humble savior. He entered Jerusalem mounted on the colt of a donkey.

Jesus will return to us as KING! There will be peace at last.

Lord Jesus, thank you that you are our King and our Savior. You understand us completely. Let us come to you and be refreshed and renewed. Let us live in the confidence and certainty of your presence with us now as we wait for your coming in glory. We rejoice in you! Alleluia!

Monday, July 7, 2008
Hosea 2, 16-18,21-22
Israel's Punishment and Restoration

From the desert wilderness and the valley come clarification. It is dry in the desert and dark in the valley.

We begin to see ourselves more clearly. We acknowledge ourselves as we are. We have sinned and we now know our need for forgiveness.

We learn to see the Lord more clearly. We learn again of the Lord's faithful, tender love for us. We learn again to rest in the Lord.

The Lord, who drew us into the wilderness, will care for us. "Therefore, I will now allure her, and bring her into the wilderness, and speak tenderly to her. From there I will give her her vineyards, and make the Valley of Achor a door of hope. There she shall respond as in the days of her youth, as at the time when she came out of the land of Egypt (Hosea 2, 14-16)."

Lord Jesus, thank you that we belong to you. We are espoused to you and you are caring for us tenderly. Let us know again in our hearts, wounded as they are, that you love and are eager to forgive us and to restore us. Alleluia!

Tuesday, July 8, 2008
Hosea 8, 4-7,11-13
Perversity of Israel

"They made kings, but not through me; they set up princes, but without my knowledge. With their silver and gold they made idols for their own destruction. For they sow the wind, and they shall reap the whirlwind (vv. 4,7a)."

Innocence. Israel, in worshipping idols and acting in defiance of the Lord, lost innocence.

Innocence. In frantic, futile attempts to worship the Lord in their own ways, Israel lost innocence. Israel stood defiled.

Lord Jesus, we lose our innocence when we wander from you and choose our own ways. Have mercy on us. Forgive us. Cleanse us. Restore us. Let us worship you in clarity and truth. Alleluia!

Wednesday, July 9, 2008
St. Augustine Zhao Rong and Companions
Hosea 10, 1-3,7-8,12
Punishment of Idolatry; Time to Seek the Lord

"Israel is a luxuriant vine that yields its fruit. The more his fruit increased the more altars he built; as his country improved, he improved his pillars. Their heart is false; now they must bear their guilt. The LORD will break down their altars, and destroy their pillars (vv. 1-2)."

Israel prospered and said "thank you!" Alas, Israel gave the credit to idols.

Israel even built altars to idols. This did not settle well with the Lord, Israel's outraged Lover.

Thorns. Thistles. The Lord promised that thistles and thorns would grow over these idolatrous altars his own people had erected.

The Lord, through the prophet Hosea, told Israel that it was time for planting a fresh field, a time for sowing justice. It was time, overtime, for seeking the Lord and returning to the Lord.

"Sow for yourselves righteousness; reap steadfast love, break up your fallow ground; for it is time to seek the LORD, that he may come and rain righteousness upon you (v. 12)."

Lord Jesus, our idols and altars may be subtle or even invisible. You see them, however. You see the thistles and thorns growing over them. Thank you for the Holy Spirit who reveals to us the real objects of our devotion. In your mercy, forgive us, heal us, cleanse us, and let us serve you again in holiness and purity. Alleluia!

Thursday, July 10, 2008
Hosea 11, 1-4,8,9
When Israel Was a Child; End of the Exile

The Lord is grieved and angered over Israel's infidelity and idolatry. However, uppermost in the heart of the Lord is tender compassion for Israel.

"When Israel was a child, I loved him, and out of Egypt I called my son. The more I called them, the more they went from me; they kept sacrificing to the Baals, and offering incense to idols. Yet it was I who taught Ephraim to walk, I took them up in my arms; but they did not know that I healed them. I led them with cords of human kindness, with hands of love. I was to them like those who lift infants to their cheeks, I bent down to them and fed them (vv. 1-4)."

Israel! The Lord had rescued Israel from slavery in Egypt only to watch Israel choose another form of slavery. This was the slavery of idolatry.

Lord Jesus, forgive us when we sin against you and do not trust in your love for us. Forgive us when we give our time, our attention, and our devotion to modern equivalents of idols. Have mercy on us. Forgive us and draw us back to you. Let us rejoice in the cords of your love binding us to your heart. Alleluia!

Friday, July 11, 2008   St. Benedict
Hosea 14, 2-10
Sincere Conversion

"Return O Israel, to the LORD your God, for you have stumbled because of your iniquity. Take words with you and return to the LORD; and say to him, 'Take away all guilt; accept that which is good, and we will offer the fruit of our lips (vv. 1-2)."

A fresh start! No more stumbling in the darkness because of sin and guilt.

The Lord pours mercy upon Israel. The Lord reaches out to Israel. The Lord heals Israel.

The Lord says, "I will be like the dew to Israel; he shall blossom like the lily, he shall strike root like the forests of Lebanon. They shall again live beneath my shadow, they shall flourish as a garden; they shall blossom like the vine, their fragrance shall be like the wine of Lebanon

The Lord is as the morning dew to parched Israel. As a beautiful lily, Israel will blossom. Israel will be as majestic as an olive tree and as fragrant as a cedar from Lebanon.

There will be a fresh harvest of grain. There will be fragrant wine from the new vineyards.

Lord Jesus, thank you for refreshing us with your presence this hot, dry, summer. Thank you for giving us wisdom and discernment to understand your message to us. Let us come to you with honesty about ourselves. Have mercy on us. Forgive us. Heal us. Let us rest in you. Let us praise you. Let us again, in your time, bear fruit for you. Alleluia!

Saturday, July 12, 2009
Isaiah 6, 1-8
Call of Isaiah

Seeing God. Seeing yourself. Purification. Service.

Seven centuries before the birth of Christ, Isaiah saw the Lord.

"... I saw the LORD sitting on a throne, high and lofty; and the hem of his robe filled the temple. Seraphs were in attendance above him .... And one called to another and said: 'Holy, holy, holy is the LORD of hosts; the whole earth is full of his glory (vv. 1-3).' "

This manifestation of the Lord to Isaiah occurred in the Temple in Jerusalem. The Lord's holiness was continually proclaimed by the flaming seraphim. The Lord's glory filled the Temple.

Isaiah saw himself. He comprehended the depth of his sinfulness and the impurity of his words. He realized he was unclean and yet he had seen the great King.

"Woe is me! I am lost, for I am a man of unclean lips, and I live among a people of unclean lips; yet my eyes have seen the King, the LORD of hosts (v. 5)."

From the altar, a seraph flew to Isaiah, touched his lips with a coal, and proclaimed that Isaiah's wickedness was taken away!

" 'Now that this has touched your lips, your guilt has departed and your sin is blotted out (v. 7).' "

The Lord then inquired about who to send on a mission. Isaiah offered himself for the Lord's service.

"Then I heard the voice of the Lord saying, 'Whom shall I send, and who will go for us?' And I said, 'Here I am; send me (v. 8).' "

Lord Jesus, before we may truly serve you, we must be overwhelmed by your holiness and our own unworthiness. Then, and only then, are we able to go through the fires of purification which are essential in our preparation for ministry. Only then are you able to release us for the mission you have assigned to us. Alleluia!

Sunday, July 13, 2008 Fifteenth Sunday in Ordinary Time
Isaiah 55, 10-11
An Invitation to Grace

"For as the rain and the snow come down from heaven, and do not return there until they have watered the earth, making it bring forth and sprout, giving seed to the sower and bread to the eater, so shall my word be that goes out from my mouth; it shall not return to me empty, but it shall accomplish that which I purpose, and succeed in the thing for which I sent it. For you shall go out in joy, and be led back in peace; the mountains and the hills before you shall burst into song, and all the trees of the fields shall clap their hands (vv. 10-11)."

Lord Jesus, sometimes we simply close up shop. We hear your word, believe it, and expect you to act to fulfill your word.

Time goes by. More time.

What is happening? Have you forgotten us?

We may lose hope. We still live, but we don't really live, because hope has died within us.

This summer day, let us read again and believe again your word to us. Your word is never without effect. Your word does not return to you without effect and without accomplishing your purposes. Breathe new life into us. Let us live again and rejoice that your word will be fulfilled in us, for us, and through us. Alleluia!

Monday, July 14, 2008 Blessed Kateri Tekakwitha
Isaiah 1, 10-17
Israel's Sinfulness

Stop! Israel, rebuked for insulting the Lord with phony worship, is commanded to stop.

This kind of worship, phony worship, is an offense to the Lord. It is also without effect.

The Lord cares nothing for phony worship and meaningless sacrifices. The Lord will not even bother to listen to the meaningless droning of the prayers of those who commit grievous sins and then refuse to repent.

"Wash yourselves; make yourselves clean; remove the evil of your doings from before my eyes; cease to do evil, learn to do good; seek justice, rescue the oppressed, defend the orphan, plead for the widow. Come now, let us argue it out, says the LORD; though your sins are like scarlet, they shall be like snow; though they are red like crimson, they shall become like wool (vv. 16-18)."

Israel, entrenched in evil, is commanded to learn how to do what is right and good. Israel is to seek justice, to come to the aid of those who have been wronged, and to defend the widows and orphans.

Lord Jesus, we need constantly to heed these words of Isaiah. Thank you that you invite us to pour out our hearts before you and tell you everything that troubles us. You know how to cleanse us, to purify us, and to heal us. Let us be real before you and before others. Let both our worship and our way of life honor and glorify you. Alleluia!

Tuesday, July 15, 2008 St. Bonaventure
Isaiah 7, 1-9
Birth of Immanuel

Tranquil! The Lord instructed the prophet Isaiah to encourage the king of Judah to be tranquil and not to be afraid even with this latest threat of imminent attack.

What about the two kings who were planning to attack Jerusalem? The king was instructed to look upon them as mere smoldering stumps of firewood!

Why worry? The Lord was in charge!

Trust! The king was cautioned, however, that unless his own confidence in the Lord was firm, he himself would not be firm in this time of trial.

Lord Jesus, you are greater than any trial we encounter. Let us recall your mighty presence within us and remain tranquil and filled with firm trust. Alleluia!

> Wednesday, July 16, 2008 Our Lady of Mt. Carmel
> Isaiah 10, 5-7,13-16
> Assyria the Unconscious Instrument of God

Bliss! Ignorance may not be bliss, but it does have its advantages. Many times God uses people who are totally unaware that they are being used.

That's good! If we knew all the times we were being used by God, we might become either terrified or full of pride.

We might become fearful of not saying or doing what God would have us say or do. On the other hand, we might become so full of ourselves that God could not longer use us.

Lord Jesus, let us offer ourselves for your service and then go out and live this day in childlike trust! You are in charge! We don't have to be perfect, only to be yielded to you and willing to be invisible in your service. Glory to YOU, Lord Jesus! Alleluia!

> Thursday, July 17, 2009
> Isaiah 26, 7-9,12,16-19
> The Divine Vindicator

Restoration! The Lord Jesus Christ will bring new life and peace.

Vigil! We long for the Lord. We wait for the Lord. We keep vigil for the Lord.

Vindication! The Lord will vindicate the poor and guide the just.

Lord Jesus, thank you that in the new Jerusalem there will be light. There will be joy and singing. There will be peace. Let us trust you as we pray for your kingdom to come on earth and for your will to be done on earth as it is in heaven. Alleluia!

Friday, July 18, 2008 St. Camillus de Lellis
Isaiah 38, 1-6,21-22,7-8
Sickness and Recovery of Hezekiah

Practice! King Hezekiah had practiced. He knew what to do in a crisis.

Pray! He prayed. He went to the temple. On at least one occasion, he had gone to the temple, spread out an alarming letter before the Lord, and prayed.

King Hezekiah acknowledged the Lord's sovereignty. He himself was merely an earthly king. The Lord was the true King. The Lord, who had created heaven and earth, was in charge of his situation.

The poor king was very frightened with the news of his terminal illness. He prayed. He also wept.

Hearing Hezekiah's prayers and seeing Hezekiah's tears, the Lord intervened and healed him. He even mercifully granted a sign to reassure Hezekiah that he would recover.

In three days, Hezekiah would be able to go back to the temple! The Lord added fifteen years to his life.

Lord Jesus, no matter how frightened we are in our current situation, you are in charge. You are the Lord who works wonders on our behalf. Let us practice each day honoring you with our prayers and with our trust. Thank you for the gift of life, health, and peace. Alleluia!

Saturday, July 19, 2008
Micah 2, 1-5
Social Evils

Plan! Whose plan will succeed?

The Lord promises woe to those who plan and plot evil. The Lord will not tolerate mistreatment of others.

The Lord has plans for those who mistreat others. The Lord plans ruin for them.

Lord Jesus, you told us to treat others as we would choose to be treated. Let us plan good for others! Let us be full of compassion in our thoughts, our words, and our actions. Let our lives reflect your life within us. Alleluia!

Sunday, July 20, 2008 Sixteenth Sunday in Ordinary Time
Wisdom 12, 13,16-19
Digression on God's Mercy

"Although you are sovereign in strength, you judge with mildness, and with great forbearance you govern us; for you have power to act whenever you choose (v. 18)."

God cares for us all. God is in charge of us all. God, who is all-powerful, is free to be merciful to all.

Lord Jesus, thank you that you are the judge and that you are righteous. Aware of our constant need for your mercy, let us gladly extend mercy to all. Alleluia!

Monday, July 21, 2008
Micah 6, 1-4,6-8
Accusation and Answer

What is the Lord really like? What does the Lord really want?

The Lord, the Lord Almighty, is pleading. The Lord pleads with Israel. The Lord is grieved over the behavior of the people of Israel.

What more could the Lord have done for them? The Lord rescued them and released them from their terrible slavery in Egypt. The Lord sent them Moses, Aaron, and Miriam to serve them.

What does the Lord really want? Some splendid sacrifice that will feed our egos?

We already know what the Lord really wants. In case we've forgotten, it's spelled out for us again in this passage.

We are simply to do what is right. We are to love what is good. We are to live in humility with our God.

Lord Jesus, it may be simple, but it is not always easy. Our fears, our insecurities, our hidden agendas, and our pride all get in the way of simplicity. Forgive us. Heal us. Free us to serve you with simplicity, humility, boldness, and joy this day. Alleluia!

Tuesday, July 22, 2008 St. Mary Magdalene
Micah 7, 14-15,18-20
Condemnation and Prayer

"Who is a God like you, pardoning iniquity and passing over the transgression of the remnant of your possession? He does not retain his anger forever, because he delights in showing clemency. He will again have compassion upon us; he will tread our iniquities under foot. You will cast all our sins into the depths of the sea (vv. 18-19)." Corrie ten Boom delighted in saying that the Lord then put up a sign saying "No Fishing!"

God forgives our sins, but where do they go? God removes them completely.

What about our guilt? Where does our guilt go? It's gone! God completely removes our guilt.

Lord Jesus, you are the Lamb of God who takes away our sins. You are the Good Shepherd leading us today into fresh, green meadows. Let us receive the wonders you have for us and live with joy. Alleluia!

Wednesday, July 23, 2008 St. Bridget of Sweden
Jeremiah 1, 1,4-10
The Call of Jeremiah

Go and speak! There is a time to stay still and silent. There is also a time to go where God leads and to speak the words God gives us.

If our heart is pure before God, watch out! Our presence and our words may not be welcome. We recall the prophecy that Jesus would be a sign of contradiction and that he would be opposed (Luke 2, 34,35).

Lord Jesus, we are not here to blend in or to be politically correct. We are here for your purposes. We are here to bear your presence and to speak your message. Let us trust you in the midst of the mission for which you sent us, especially when we are discouraged because of our inadequacy or when we don't even understand the implications of our mission. You are the Lord, you are in charge, and you have sent us. Alleluia!

Thursday, July 24, 2008 St. Sharbel Makhluf
Jeremiah 2, 1-3,7-8,12-13
The Infidelity of Israel

From tender trust to outright betrayal. Israel, beloved of the Lord, betrayed the Lord.

In the beautiful land of gardens and promise, the people of Israel tragically forsook the Lord. The Lord was their source. The Lord was their fountain of life.

They forsook the Lord. They betrayed the Lord.

They tried to dig their own cisterns, incapable of holding water. They did this by choosing idols.

Lord Jesus, when we turn from you we are digging cisterns which are already broken. Forgive us. Have mercy on us. You are our source. Let us return to you. Let us honor you with our trust. You will purify us, renew us, and release us again to serve you in holiness. Alleluia!

Friday, July 25, 2008 St. James
2 Corinthians 4, 7-15
The Paradox of the Ministry

Life outruns death! The life of the Lord Jesus Christ within us is greater than our despair, our defeats, and even our death. The light of Christ shines through us!

Lord Jesus, thank you that the same Holy Spirit who raised you from the dead is alive and active in us today. Let us not become overly discouraged in our present trials. They are temporary. You are eternal. Thank you that you have already won the victory for us. Alleluia!

Saturday, July 26, 2008 Sts. Joachim and Anne
Jeremiah 7, 1-11
The Temple Sermon

The temple. God stated definite conditions to the people of Israel about their behavior and about the temple.

Only if the people reformed their ways would God remain with them in the temple. They could not commit evil and then chant empty words about the temple, presuming they were exempt from God's judgment.

The house of God bears the name of God. God will not permit impurity and wickedness to continue unchecked in his house.

What was Israel to do? What are we to do?

We are to deal in honesty and justice with others. We are not to oppress others. We are not to follow false gods.

Lord Jesus, help us to speak and to live with humility and respect. Let us be humble before you and others. Let us respect you as God and respect all people including ourselves. Alleluia!

Sunday, July 27, 2008 Seventeenth Sunday Ordinary Time
1 Kings 3, 5,7-12
Wisdom of Solomon

The fast track! Humility is the fast track to the heart of God.

King Solomon had the opportunity to ask ANYTHING of God. Solomon was painfully aware of his youth and his inadequacies as he succeeded his father, David, as King.

What did Solomon ask of God? He asked for wisdom and for understanding in governing the people. He understood that they were God's people.

God gave to the young king his request. He promised Solomon extraordinary wisdom. In addition, God gave to Solomon riches beyond comprehension (v. 13).

Lord Jesus, we can never lose when we come to you in humility. You know how to give us what we need to serve you and to serve others. No matter what our position is, let us remember that we serve you at your pleasure and we are completely dependent upon you to serve your people as you direct us. Alleluia!

Monday, July 28, 2008
Jeremiah 13, 1-11
Judah's Corruption

Cling or rot? Which do you choose?

The Lord, in order to make a point, trusted Jeremiah to do the craziest things. The Lord told Jeremiah to buy a loin cloth of linen.

Instead of wearing it, Jeremiah was to bury it. How crazy is that?

Jeremiah obligingly buried the linen cloth. A long time later, the Lord told Jeremiah to dig up the cloth. The cloth had rotted.

What in the world? The Lord wanted to give a graphic illustration of how pride rots.

The Lord's beloved people had been fashioned to cling to the Lord as an undergarment clings to our skin. They were the God's own people made for God's praise. Instead, they were rebellious and stubborn. They worshipped idols.

Lord Jesus, let us cling to you, praise you, and trust you. Let us, like Jeremiah, serve you faithfully, no matter what you ask us to do. Alleluia!

Tuesday, July 29, 2008 St. Martha
Jeremiah 14, 17-22
The Great Drought

The Lord had had it with Judah! The Lord even told Jeremiah not to bother to intercede for these stubborn people (Jeremiah 14, 11). They had brought death and destruction upon themselves.

Jeremiah called on the people to recognize their own wickedness and also the sins of their ancestors. They were to implore the Lord to remember the covenant.

Lord Jesus, we look to you alone. We are like those people in Jeremiah's time. We grow careless in our prosperity and begin to trust in ourselves and in the worthless things of this passing world. Have mercy on us. Let us return to you and look to you alone. We trust in you and in your mercy. Alleluia!

Wednesday, July 30, 2008 St. Peter Chrysologus
Jeremiah 15, 10,16-21
Jeremiah's Complaint

"Woe is me, my mother, that you ever bore me, a man of strife and contention to the whole land! I have not lent, nor have I borrowed, yet all of them curse me (v. 10)."

Desolation! Poor Jeremiah. He had suffered in his vocation as prophet and he was lashing out even at the Lord.

The Lord loved Jeremiah and was well aware of his situation. The Lord spoke stern, strong words to Jeremiah because those words were necessary in order to restore him.

"Therefore thus says the LORD: If you turn back, I will take you back, and you shall stand before me. If you utter what is precious, and not what is worthless, you shall serve as my mouth. It is they who will turn to you, not you who will turn to them. And I will make you to this people a fortified wall of bronze; they will fight against you, but they shall not prevail over you, for I am with you to save you and to deliver you, says the LORD (vv. 19-20)."

Repentance. Jeremiah, even the prophet Jeremiah, was called to repentance. This was necessary in order for him to continue to speak forth the Lord's words with a pure heart.

When Jeremiah's words were again pure, the Lord reassured him that the stubborn people would be the ones to come to him. He would not have to go to them.

Even though the people fought against Jeremiah, they would not be able to prevail against him. How could they? The Lord was with Jeremiah to free him from their schemes.

Lord Jesus, thank you that you are with us even when we are in a time of desolation. Forgive us for our wild words. You understand us and you know why we said those words. Forgive us. Purify us. Comfort us. Restore us. Let us again speak forth your pure words. Alleluia!

Thursday, July 31, 2008 St. Ignatius of Loyola
Jeremiah 18, 1-6
The Potter's Vessel

Get up! Get going!

The Lord sent Jeremiah on yet another interesting mission. Jeremiah was to go on a field trip for the Lord. He was to go to visit a potter and watch the potter at work.

The potter stayed at the wheel. When his clay project did not go as he intended, he stayed at the wheel and kept working.

Israel! Israel was as clay in the hands of the Lord. The Lord was in charge.

Lord Jesus, thank you for the Holy Spirit who teaches us how to listen to you. Let us know when we are to stay still and be silent. Let us also know when to get up and go where you tell us. Thank you for your loving presence with us always. You are in charge. We rest in you and trust in you. Alleluia!

Friday, August 1, 2008 St. Alphonsus Liguori
Jeremiah 26, 1-9
Jeremiah Threatened with Death

Stand. Stand up and speak!

This was not a time for silence. This was a time for bold proclamation of the truth.

Jeremiah did indeed speak for the Lord. Jeremiah was faithful to the Lord.

Jeremiah omitted nothing that the Lord had instructed him to say to the people entering the temple. Not one single syllable did he omit.

After Jeremiah obediently proclaimed the word of the Lord to the people of the Lord in the house of the Lord, there was opposition. So what else is new?

"And when Jeremiah had finished speaking all that the LORD had commanded him to speak to all the people, then the priests and the prophets and all the people laid hold of him, saying, 'You shall die! Why have you prophesied in the name of the LORD, saying, 'This house shall be like Shiloh, and this city shall be desolate, without inhabitant?' And all the people gathered around Jeremiah in the house of the LORD (vv. 8,9)."

The priests, the prophets, and the people seized Jeremiah and declared that he should die. WHY!

Jeremiah had prophesied, in no uncertain terms, about the ruin of Jerusalem, as the Lord had directed him. Jerusalem and the temple would be destroyed if the people did not repent.

Lord Jesus, you warned us of the price to pay in order to follow you. We cannot expect to follow you faithfully and to be popular. Let us choose to continue to follow you, to stand for you, and to live and speak as you direct us.

Saturday, August 2, 2008 St. Eusebius of Vercellis,
St. Peter Julian Eymard
Jeremiah 26, 11-16,24
Jeremiah Threatened with Death

It was the Lord! Jeremiah made it clear to the leaders and to the people that the Lord had sent him to prophesy these hard words about the destruction of Jerusalem and the temple.

The people still had a choice. They could listen to the Lord's message delivered by Jeremiah. They could reform their evil ways. There was still time for repentance.

Jeremiah was a realist. He acknowledged he was in the hands of his accusers.

He warned them, however, that he had spoken as the Lord had directed him. If he was killed, his blood would be upon them and upon Jerusalem.

The people and the officials then warned the priests and the prophets that Jeremiah had indeed spoken in the Lord's name. They said he should not be killed.

Lord Jesus, there is never a dull moment when we truly live for you. Thank you for the privilege of following you and living for you. Let us not be overly concerned about how others perceive us and treat us. What matters is that we remember that you love us and are with us. Let us trust you and persevere in the work you have given us to do. Alleluia!

Sunday, August 3, 2008 Eighteenth Sunday Ordinary Time
Isaiah 55, 1-3
An Invitation to Grace

Super sale! No, it's not the Anniversary Sale at Nordstrom. It's even better.

Free! To the hungry and thirsty, the Lord freely offers water, wine, milk, and grain. The Lord freely offers life, true life.

Listen! The Lord calls us to careful, attentive listening. When we listen to the Lord and then follow the Lord, we have life.

Lord Jesus, we run all over the place looking for free stuff, for bonus gifts, coupons, and all sorts of things we think we need. You offer us LIFE! When we breathe in the true life you offer us, we will be satisfied. Alleluia!

> Monday, August 4, 2008 St. John Mary Vianney
> Jeremiah 28, 1-17
> The Two Yokes

Be careful what you say. Remember the injunction, "...touch not my anointed, and do my prophets no harm (1 Chronicles 16, 22 KJV)."

The false prophet Hananiah prophesied a lie. He prophesied what would be popular. Jeremiah warned him that one who prophesies peace is only acknowledged as a true prophet when the prophecy is fulfilled (v. 9).

Hananiah did not like that at all. He grabbed the wooden yoke from Jeremiah's neck and broke it.

Not a good idea. The Lord stepped in and informed Hananiah, through Jeremiah, that, by breaking the wooden yoke, he had just forged an iron yoke.

Instead of the power of Babylon being broken, as Hananiah had falsely prophesied, the Lord would place an iron yoke on all who served King Nebuchadnezzar of Babylon.

In other words, Hananiah was toast! The Lord had not sent him.

Hananiah prophesied things that were not from the Lord. By his false prophecy, Hananiah had condoned rebellion against the Lord.

That happened? Hananiah died.

Lord Jesus, let us be careful as we listen and as we speak. Thank you for the Holy Spirit who is ready to give us wisdom and discernment. Alleluia!

> Tuesday, August 5, 2008
> Dedication of the Basilica of Saint Mary Major in Rome
> Jeremiah 30, 1-2,12-15,18-22
> The Restoration

Write! The Lord, who had given the prophet Jeremiah words to speak, now told him to write down the words in the form of a book.

The last word! The Lord had smitten faithless Israel and yet, the final word had yet to be spoken. The Lord always has the last word.

Judgment! The Lord promised judgment upon Israel's enemies.

Restoration! The Lord promised restoration to Israel. Health! Rebuilding. Praise. Laughter. A leader from among their own people.

These are the Lord's beloved people. The merciful Lord will never forsake them.

"And out of them shall proceed thanksgiving and the voice of them that make merry: and I will multiply them, and they shall not be few; I will also glorify them, and they shall not be small (v. 19 KJV)."

Lord Jesus, let us pray, think, speak, write, and act as you direct. Let the words you give to us to speak and to write fulfill your purpose. Alleluia!

Wednesday, August 6, 2008 Transfiguration of the Lord
Daniel 7, 9-10,13-14
Vision of the Four Beasts

Proscenium! Glory!

The curtain was drawn back for Daniel to receive an overwhelming glimpse of glory. Daniel endeavored to express what he saw in his visions.

Strange beasts. Terrifying creatures. Visions of great destruction.

Thrones! The Ancient, the Eternal God in dazzling white.

Fire! The One so Ancient is all-powerful and dictates the fires of judgment.

Clouds! Daniel saw the One we know as the Son of Man arrive from heaven's clouds.

Sovereignty! To the Son of Man the Ancient, the Eternal God bestowed permanent dominion.

Lord Jesus, you came as Son of Man in Daniel's vision. When you came, the puzzling vision of beasts was secondary to the glory of your presence. You came, transfigured, to Peter, James and John on a mountain. You came to us, you come to us, and you will return to us as our King who will reign forever. Let us worship you as our King. Alleluia!

> Thursday, August 7, 2008 St. Cajetan, St. Sixtus II and Companions
> Jeremiah 31, 31-34
> The New Covenant

Hand to heart. There is a new covenant with the Lord.

Hand. The Lord took the people of Israel by the hand, so to speak, to lead them out of Egypt, their place of bondage. He made a covenant with them which was plain to see. It was written on stone. They chose to disregard this covenant.

Heart. The new covenant is written on our heart. The Lord dwells within us. The Lord's laws are written on our heart. The Holy Spirit strengthens us to keep the Lord's commandments.

Lord Jesus, you are closer to us than we can imagine. You live within us and you feed us with your own Body and Blood. Let us listen to you and live from your Life within us. Alleluia!

> Friday, August 8, 2008 St. Dominic
> Nahum 2, 1,3; 3, 1-3,6-7
> The Lord's Coming in Judgment; Ruin Imminent and Inevitable

The arrival of the Lord on the scene meant destruction for evil Ninevah. Ninevah would be judged and would no longer commit atrocities against the Lord's people.

The Lord's coming meant something altogether different for suffering Israel. It meant restoration!

Lord Jesus, thank you that you will return in glory! Your coming will bring consternation for some and consolation for others. Let us live for you, intercede for all, and look with joyful anticipation for your return as King. Alleluia!

> Saturday, August 9, 2008 St. Teresa Benedicta of the Cross
> Habakkuk 1, 12 - 2, 4
> The Prophet's Complaint and Its Answer

Habakkuk was getting desperate! He had been crying out to the Lord about all the terrible things that were happening.

Why was the Lord silent? Why was the Lord not intervening?

After pouring out his heart to the Lord, Habakkuk waited. He waited for the Lord's answer.

The Lord did answer his anguished servant. The Lord instructed Habakkuk to write the vision so that it could be easily read.

"Then the LORD answered me and said: Write the vision; make it plain on tablets, so that a runner may read it. For there is still a vision for the appointed time; it speaks of the end, and does not lie. If it seems to tarry, wait for it; it will surely come, it will not delay (vv. 2-3)."

The Lord reassured Habakkuk the vision would be fulfilled. It was not the time, however. With the Lord, timing is everything.

Lord Jesus, thank you that we be may honest with you. We too grow weary of waiting for you to answer and to intervene on our behalf. Thank you that the promise you gave to us is real. It will come to pass. Let us stand and rejoice as we trust in you. Alleluia!

Sunday, August 10, 2009 Nineteenth Sunday in Ordinary Time
1 Kings 19, 9, 11-13
Flight to Horeb

Victory. Exhaustion. Flight. A new encounter with the Lord.

The great prophet Elijah had just been through a time of great crisis resulting in the Lord's amazing intervention. Even so, Elijah was unnerved and terrified by the threats from a wicked queen. He fled to the desert and prayed to die!

The Lord sent an angel to bring food and water to his exhausted servant. Strengthened, Elijah made the journey to God's own mountain, Horeb (Sinai) where the Law was given to Moses and where the covenant was made.

This mountain was definitely a place where the Lord had showed up in the past. Theophany!

The Lord was about to speak to Elijah on this mountain. How would the Lord speak?

The Lord directed Elijah away from his gloomy fixation on the sins of the Israelites and his own frustration. The Lord told Elijah to get out the cave and stand!

There was a mighty wind. There was an earthquake. There was fire.

The Lord was not speaking to Elijah through these mighty manifestations of nature. The Lord chose to whisper to Elijah.

Lord Jesus, thank you for your mercy when we are exhausted and feel like running away and hiding in a cave. Thank you for those you send to help us. Thank you for your presence and for preparing us to listen to your message to us. Alleluia!

Monday, August 11, 2008 St. Clare
Ezekiel 1, 2-5,24-28
The Vision: God on the Cherubim

Heaven while we are still in exile? It is possible to see the glories of heaven while we are still in our earthly exile.

Ezekiel, a priest, was in exile in Babylon when God granted him these majestic visions. The stunned priest could only use similes to attempt to describe what he had seen.

The winged creatures had whirring wings which sounded like powerful waters. Upon what appeared to be a throne was one who appeared to be a man. The splendor surrounding him was like a rainbow. How can the glory of God be described?

Lord Jesus, thank you for the reminders that come to us in myriad ways that this life on earth is not all there is. Let us live bravely for you as we long to see you come in glory. Alleluia!

Tuesday, August 12, 2008
Ezekiel 2, 8 - 3, 4
Eating of the Scroll

Eat your words! The priest Ezekiel, summoned to be a prophet, was told to eat God's words. Literally!

Ezekiel was to eat the scroll which had hard words on it. Then he was to go to Israel and to speak forth those hard words.

What were those words? On the scroll was written, "... lamentations, and mourning, and woe (Ezekiel 2, 10b KJV)." This would not be an easy message to deliver.

Lord Jesus, we put all our trust in you. We trust that you will convey your message through us, your followers. Thank you for giving us courage to live for you. Then, even when we are silent, you will speak through us. Alleluia!

>Wednesday, August 13, 2008 Sts. Pontian and Hippolytus
>Ezekiel 9, 1-7; 10, 18-22
>Slaughter of the Idolaters; God's Glory Leaves Jerusalem

Holiness! Glory! Judgment!

Enough already. God will no longer tolerate filth and idolatry in Jerusalem. Where there should be reverence and holiness, there is filth.

There is time for mercy and forgiveness. There is also a time when God will judge in no uncertain terms.

What about those who deplored living in the midst of moral and spiritual filth? From the altar of bronze, the man in linen with a writing instrument was told to mark, with a cruciform letter, the foreheads of those who were disgusted with the abominations. They would be spared when judgment was executed.

Judgment began at the Temple. The glory of the Lord departed from the Temple.

Lord Jesus, how can we read these verses without crying out to you for mercy in our own time? Forgive us. Forgive your Church. Forgive us all. Lord, have mercy. Thank you that we are marked with the sign of the Cross at our baptism and we belong to you forever. Alleluia!

>Thursday, August 14, 2008 St. Maximilian Kolbe
>Ezekiel 12, 1-2
>Acts Symbolic of the Exile

The Lord gave it to Ezekiel straight. The Lord told Ezekiel that he lived among rebellious people. Ezekiel needed these words of truth to sink in before the Lord gave him further instruction.

Lord Jesus, help us not to be impatient when you tell us what we think we already know. Forgive us for our pride and our presumption. If you are telling us something, it is something we need to hear and to assimilate before you give us further direction. Thank you for your patient tenderness as you continue to speak to us. Alleluia!

Friday, August 15, 2008
The Assumption of the Blessed Virgin Mary
Revelation 11, 19; 12, 1-6,10
The Seventh Trumpet; The Woman and the Dragon

"Then God's temple in heaven was opened, and the ark of his covenant was seen within his temple; and there were flashes of lightening, rumblings, peals of thunder, an earthquake, and heavy hail (v. 19)."

From heaven to heaven! This passage begins with the opening of heaven and the sight of the ark of God's covenant in the temple. Thunder! Lightening! Earthquake!

"A great portent appeared in heaven: a woman clothed with the sun, and with the moon under her feet, and on her head a crown of twelve stars (12, 1)."

The passage ends with the powerful proclamation that salvation has come. God's kingdom has come. Satan, our constant accuser, has been removed from the scene.

"Then I heard a loud voice in heaven, proclaiming, 'Now have come the salvation and the power and the kingdom of our God and the authority of his Messiah, for the accuser ... has been thrown down, who accuses them day and night before our God. But they have conquered him by the blood of the Lamb and by the word of their testimony, for they did not cling to life even in the face of death. Rejoice, then you heavens ... (vv. 10-12a)."

Lord Jesus, thank you that you will come to reign in glory. Thank you for the life of your Blessed Mother Mary, whose entry into heaven we celebrate today. In the midst of the terrors of the present time, let us rejoice! You are our victorious King. Alleluia!

Saturday, August 16, 2008 St. Stephen of Hungary
Ezekiel 18, 1-10, 13, 30-32
Personal Responsibility

We must not live in a state of constant remorse. No matter what we have done, we are invited to return to the Lord.

The Lord loves us and knows how to help us. We face the truth and the truth sets us free.

The Lord holds us accountable for our choices and yet invites us to turn away from our wrongdoing. The Lord is here to forgive us and to show us how to live.

Lord Jesus, help us not to fear your judgment, but to welcome it. Help us to see ourselves as you see us. Show us how to confess our sins. Thank you for the sacrament of reconciliation in which we are assured of your forgiveness. Thank you for freeing us and showing us how to live for you. Alleluia!

> Sunday, August 17, 2008 Twentieth Sunday Ordinary Time
> Isaiah 56, 1, 6-7
> The Lord's House Open to All

"Thus says the LORD: Maintain justice, and do what is right, for soon my salvation will come and my deliverance be revealed (v. 1)."

Present. Future. God's mighty power to save will be revealed both now and in the future.

The Lord's invitation is for all. All are invited to be made whole. All are invited to love the Lord and to minister to the Lord.

"And the foreigners who join themselves to the LORD, and minister to him, to love the name of the LORD, and to be his servants, all who keep the sabbath, and do not profane it, and hold fast my covenant – these I will bring to my holy mountain, and make them joyful in my house of prayer ... for my house shall be called a house of prayer for all peoples (vv. 6-7)."

Lord Jesus, thank you that your offer of salvation is for all. You call to all of us to come to you. Please help us to remember that your house is an open house, a house where all may pray. Alleluia!

> Monday, August 18, 2008 St. Jane Frances de Chantal
> Ezekiel 24, 15-24
> Symbol of the Destruction of the Temple

Priest. Prophet. Sign.

Ezekiel, in the midst of his personal suffering, was called to be a sign to the rebellious, idolatrous people of Israel. A priest and a prophet, he was now commissioned by the Lord to be a sign to those who had refused to repent.

The manner in which Ezekiel was told to deal with his beloved wife's sudden death was the manner in which the people of Israel were to deal with the impending, sudden destruction of the Temple in Jerusalem. There would be no time to observe the usual forms of grief.

No outer signs of mourning. No weeping.

Silence.

Lord Jesus, you were a sign of contradiction. You knew what it was to suffer as you lived out your vocation. As we go about our day, let us be signs of your presence. Alleluia!

Tuesday, August 19, 2008 St. John Eudes
Ezekiel 28, 1-10
The Prince of Tyre

Haughtiness! There are certain things the Lord really hates and haughtiness is one of them (Proverbs 6, 16).

The prince of Tyre had become haughty in his innermost heart because of his great wealth. Everything starts in the heart and haughtiness is no exception.

Through Ezekiel, the Lord confronted the prince. The haughty prince was confronted with his own mortality. He would be slain by barbaric foreigners and cast into the sea.

Lord Jesus, you know that we are tested and tempted in many ways in this life. As we grow closer to you, the temptations become extremely subtle. Thank you for the Holy Spirit who gives us discernment. Thank you for holding our hand, keeping us honest and humble, and leading us through our times of trial. Alleluia!

Wednesday, August 20, 2008 St. Bernard
Ezekiel 34, 1-11
Parable of the Shepherds

"Thus says the LORD GOD: Ah, you shepherds of Israel who have been feeding yourselves! Should not shepherds feed the sheep? You have not strengthened the weak, you have not healed the sick, you have not bound up the injured, you have not brought back the strayed, you have not sought the lost, but with force and harshness you have ruled them. So, they were scattered because there was no shepherd ....Thus says the LORD GOD, I am against the shepherds; and I will demand my sheep at their hand, and put a stop to their feeding the sheep; no longer shall the shepherds feed themselves. I will rescue my sheep from their mouths, so that they may not be food for them. For thus says the LORD GOD: I myself will search for my sheep, and will seek them out. I will rescue them from all the places to which they have been scattered ... I will feed them on the mountains of Israel, by the watercourses .... I myself will be the shepherd of my sheep.... I will seek the lost, and I will bring back the strayed, and I will bind up the injured, and I will strengthen the weak ... (vv. 2,4,5a,10-12,13,15-16)."

The Lord was outraged because the shepherds, the leaders of Israel, were more concerned with indulging themselves than they were with feeding and caring for the Lord's flock. They exploited the Lord's people and drove them away.

Leaders are called to protect and to guide. They are to feed, to strengthen, and to heal. Instead, these unworthy leaders had exploited those committed to their care.

The Lord promised to put a stop to this! The Lord personally would tend his flock.

Lord Jesus, thank you that you are our Good Shepherd. You are protecting us, guiding us, feeding us, strengthening us, and healing us. You are leading us today into fresh meadows. We entrust ourselves into your loving, wise care. Alleluia!

Thursday, August 21, 2008 St. Pius X
Ezekiel 36, 23-28
Regeneration of the People

The Lord is acting decisively on behalf of his people, Israel. For the honor of his name, the Lord is bringing his people back from exile to their own land.

In spite of the sins of the people of Israel, the Lord promises to manifest his holiness through them. How would the Lord do this?

A new heart! The Lord would cleanse them and then give them a new, fresh heart and a new, fresh spirit. The Lord's people would be empowered from within to live as the Lord directed them to live.

Lord Jesus, thank you for cleansing us from our sins. Thank you for the Holy Spirit living within us to accomplish your will in us and through us. Alleluia!

Friday, August 22, 2008 Queenship of Mary
Ezekiel 37, 1-14
Vision of Dry Bones

Speak! Speak the words that God tells you to speak! Life will follow Transformation will follow.

Speak! Ezekiel, in his vision, was told to speak life into a whole field of dry bones. The bones represented Israel. There seemed to be no hope for Israel, only dryness and death.

Speak! The Lord told Ezekiel to prophesy and to tell the bones, first of all, to hear the Lord's message to them.

Speak! The message Ezekiel spoke was a message of life and hope. The Lord showed Ezekiel sinews, flesh, and skin coming over the parched bones.

Speak! There were outer signs of life, but still no spirit.

Speak! Ezekiel was told to call the spirit to breathe new life into the bones.

Speak! Ezekiel spoke again and the bones came to life and stood.

Lord Jesus, thank you for speaking to us the words you want US to speak to ourselves and to our situation. You are alive and you are speaking LIFE to us today. Alleluia!

Saturday, August 23, 2008 St. Rose of Lima
Ezekiel 43, 1-7
The Return of the Lord

Glory! Ezekiel, priest and prophet, was granted a vision of the Lord's glory coming to the Temple, entering the Temple, and then filling the Temple. This vision was consistent with the previous visions Ezekiel had been given.

Lord Jesus, you bring us back again and again to the vision and to the words you gave us long ago. Although we may have forgotten and although all may seem lost and hopeless, you have not forgotten us for one minute. Your vision for us will be fulfilled. The words you spoke to us till be fulfilled. Come Holy Spirit, enter into our hearts in a powerful way, and fill us anew. Glory! Alleluia!

Sunday, August 24, 2008 Twenty-First Sunday in Ordinary Time
Isaiah 22, 19-23
Shebna and Eliakim

The Lord is in charge! The Lord knows how to deal with people in positions of responsibility.

The Lord promised he would personally thrust Shebna from his position in the royal palace. The Lord then promised to call his loyal servant, Eliakim, and to clothe Eliakim with the robe and the sash once worn by Shebna.

Eliakim would be given the authority formerly entrusted to Shebna. Eliakim would be as a father to the people in Jerusalem and in Judah. Great honor would be given to Eliakim.

Lord Jesus, thank you for our privilege and our responsibility to intercede for all in positions of responsibility. We trust you to place people where you choose. Alleluia!

Monday, August 25, 2008 St. Louis of France, St. Joseph Calasanz
2 Thessalonians 1, 1-5,11-12
Greeting, Thanksgiving, Prayer

Suffering! Suffering for the faith.

The Christians at Thessalonica were suffering for the sake of the kingdom of God. In the midst of their patient suffering, their faith flourished. Paul commends them for their steadfast trust in the Lord during this time of suffering.

Lord Jesus, when we suffer, let us continue to trust in you and to love others. Thank you that you are fulfilling your purpose in us and through us. Alleluia!

Tuesday, August 26, 2008
2 Thessalonians 2, 1-3,14-17
Christ and the Lawless One

Caution! Paul warns the Christians at Thessalonica not to be disturbed about prophecies of the return of the Lord Jesus Christ.

Yes, Jesus will return in glory. However, there are certain events which will precede his coming as King.

Stay steady! The Lord is in charge. Our part is to continue to trust the Lord and to live for the Lord.

Lord Jesus, in our day we see many evidences of apostasy and of lawlessness. Still, we do not know exactly the time of your return. Thank you for the Holy Spirit who teaches us how live in readiness for your return and how to be prepared to greet you as our King. Alleluia!

Wednesday, August 27, 2008 St. Monica
2 Thessalonians 3, 6-10,16-18
Neglect of Work

Work! We are to work as we wait for the Lord's return in glory.

Lord Jesus, thank you for your gift of peace. Although we do not know when you will return, we rejoice to persevere in the work you have given us to do. Alleluia!

Thursday, August 28, 2008 St. Augustine
1 Corinthians 1, 1-9
Greeting

Called! Called to holiness. Paul reminded the Christians at Corinth that they were called to live a holy life.

Called to holiness. If we seek to honor the Lord by living in holiness, all other aspects of the call of God on our lives will fall into place.

Lord Jesus, thank you for filling us with your love. Let our lives reflect your presence within us. Alleluia!

Friday, Augusts 29, 2008
1 Corinthians 1, 17-25
Groups and Slogans; Paradox of the Cross

Power! As a Gospel hymn tells us, there is indeed wonder-working power in the Blood of the Lamb. We know that there is true power associated with the Cross of the Lord Jesus Christ.

Do we know that there is also power in the crosses in our own lives? We are being conformed to the image of Christ (Romans 8, 29) and that image is in the form of a cross.

Lord Jesus, when we are discouraged, thank you for reminding us that our lives proclaim you. Thank you that the power of your Cross is flowing into us and transforming us more and more into your image. Alleluia!

> Saturday, August 30, 2008
> 1 Corinthians 1, 26-31
> The Corinthians and Paul

Get this! God will not share his glory (Isaiah 42, 8). All the credit for what God does must be given to God alone.

God delights in knocking the socks off the ones who think they are so smart. God shows them up by elevating the very people scorned by the power elite.

"For God hath chosen the foolish things of the world to confound the wise; and God hath chosen the weak things of the world to confound the things which are mighty .... (1 Corinthians 1, 27 KJV)."

It is because of what God did that we may now live in Christ and that Christ may live in us. This is God's doing.

It is because we live in Christ that the wisdom of Christ may be made manifest in our lives. We are cooperating with the work of the Holy Spirit, that's all.

Lord Jesus, we rejoice in you! We rejoice that you redeemed us and that you are imparting your righteousness to us. Thank you that day by day we are being sanctified. Let us rest in you and trust in your work in us. Alleluia!

> Sunday, August 31, 2008
> Twenty-second Sunday in Ordinary Time
> Jeremiah 20, 7-9
> Jeremiah's Interior Crisis

Lord Jesus, thank you that you are with us in all our crises, whether the crises are external or interior. We listen to you and we act on your word as well as we know how to act. Sometimes it seems that when we do this, things don't work out as we hoped. We live, but we don't live in the fullness to which you call us. We try to be quiet about our frustrations, but that doesn't work either. We are consumed interiorly with your word. We feel imprisoned and yet we know you are in control. Free us and release us to live in the fullness of the word you spoke to us. Alleluia!

Monday, September 1, 2008
1 Corinthians 2, 1-5
The Corinthians and Paul

Jesus! The crucified Lord Jesus Christ.

Paul was determined to concentrate on Jesus and his death on the Cross. Paul did not want the Christians who lived in Corinth to be dazzled by brilliant preaching. He earnestly longed for their faith to rest on God's power alone.

Lord Jesus, let us not worry if we are not as articulate as we'd like to be when we speak of you to others. We are not here to present and to proclaim ourselves but to present and to proclaim you. Let your power flow through us to others. In spite of our limitations, let others receive the message you are speaking through our lives. Alleluia!

Tuesday. September 2, 2008
1 Corinthians 2, 10-16
The True Wisdom

The Holy Spirit! The Holy Spirit generously gives us understanding of God's many gifts.

The Holy Spirit. The Holy Spirit teaches us how to discern spiritual realities and how to speak of spiritual realities to others.

The mind of the Lord Jesus Christ. Amazingly, we have the mind of our Lord Jesus.

Lord Jesus, how can we ever begin to absorb these wonders? We do not even have a glimmer of who we really are. Let us be brave and bold as we live this day in your presence. Let us remember that we have your mind. Alleluia!

Wednesday, September 3, 2008 St. Gregory the Great
1 Corinthians 3, 1-9
The True Wisdom; The Role of God's Ministers

Who's who? Paul is trying to enlighten the Corinthian Christians who seem fixated on personalities and allegiances.

The Christian life is not about fan clubs based on ministers. Ministers are God's servants to be used as God directs. God alone causes us to grow spiritually.

Lord Jesus, thank you for all ministers, whether their ministry is seen or unseen. Thank you for the privilege of serving you wherever you place us. Alleluia!

Thursday, September 4, 2008
1 Corinthians 3, 18-23
The Role of God's Ministers

Security! There is no need to boast or to stoop to name dropping if we are secure in our relationship with God.

Paul knew this. He taught the Christians in Corinth to view all as belonging to God. "So let no one boast about human leaders (v. 21)."

Lord Jesus, we belong to you and we are secure in your care. Let us serve you this day, knowing we are secure with you. Alleluia!

Friday, September 5, 2008
1 Corinthians 4, 1-5
The Role of God's Ministers

The judge! The Lord Jesus Christ is the judge. The Lord alone knows the motives hidden in the human heart.

Lord Jesus, forgive us when we presume to judge others or even to judge ourselves. Let us live for you and leave all matters of judgment in your hands. Alleluia!

Saturday, September 6, 2008
1 Corinthians 4, 6-15
Paul's Life a Pattern

Suffering! Look at the Church.

Foundation of prophets and apostles, with Jesus as the cornerstone (Ephesians 2, 20). The prophets suffered. Jesus suffered. The apostles suffered.

Paul was being very realistic and very graphic as he described the suffering of the apostles. For the sake of Christ, the apostles were considered fools.

They experienced hunger. They experienced thirst.

Vestments? They were vested in shabby clothing.

They worked hard. They were persecuted. They were slandered. They were considered garbage.

Paul, as a loving and wise father in Christ, was trying to correct the faulty thinking of the Christians in Corinth. He was trying to lead them from superficial pride in personalities to the reality of suffering for the sake of Christ and the Church.

Lord Jesus, let us learn to bless when we are ridiculed for our faith in you. Let us learn to endure when we suffer for our faith. Let us learn to be gentle in responding to those who slander us. You alone are the judge. We trust in you. In the midst of our suffering, which is temporary, let us look to you and rejoice. Glory! Alleluia!

Sunday, September 7, 2008
Twenty-third Sunday in Ordinary Time
Ezekiel 33, 7-9
The Prophet a Watchman

Keep watch! Speak only the message God tell you, personally, to speak.

The priest and prophet Ezekiel was charged by God to be a watchman for Israel. Ezekiel could not say just anything he chose.

Ezekiel was to speak God's words of warning to the wicked. He was held responsible only for speaking as God directed. He was to deliver God's message and then it was up to the hearer to respond.

Lord Jesus, help us to stay within the borders of our vocation. Let us be careful to speak as you direct. Let us not take inappropriate responsibility for others. We may intercede for them, but we are not responsible for their response to your message. Alleluia!

Monday, September 8, 2008
The Nativity of the Blessed Virgin Mary
Romans 8, 28-30
God's Indomitable Love in Christ

God will make it right. Whatever has happened, no matter how tragic, can still be transformed by God. God can mysteriously work it out for our benefit.

God is in the business of conforming us to the image of Jesus. Everything that life can throw at us can be used by God to make us more like Jesus, our Brother.

We may rest secure in God's wisdom and care. God is the one who calls us, justifies us, and ultimately glorifies us.

Lord Jesus, let us honor you with our trust. We say we are your followers and yet we shrink from suffering. Let us have a radical trust in your power to turn everything into our good and your glory. Alleluia!

Tuesday, September 9, 2008 St. Peter Claver
1 Corinthians 6, 1-11
Lawsuits before Unbelievers

We are told not to settle Church matters in the civil courts. If the Church is unwilling or unable to settle disputes, all is not lost.

Jesus is the Head of the Church. Jesus will set matters right. Jesus knows how to bring vindication.

Lord Jesus, how we long to lash out and to try to take matters into our own hands. You see the suffering of those who have been wronged. Let us trust you to bring healing and justice. Alleluia!

Wednesday, September 10, 2008
1 Corinthians 7, 25-31
Advice to Virgins and Widows

Camping out! Whatever our state in life is, we're still campers.

We're camping out here in this world. We are living in these little tent bodies for a relatively short time.

This world is temporary. Our real life, our life with the Lord, is forever.

Lord Jesus, let us live responsibility while we are here on your assignment for us on earth. Let us also enjoy our time in this beautiful world. We have the fragrant forests, the mountains, the meadows, the blue waters, and the marshmallows to roast during our time in "camp" Let us not consider earth our real home, however. Our real home is with you. Thank you for having gone ahead to prepare a place for us. Alleluia!

Thursday, September 11, 2008
1 Corinthians 8, 1-7,11-13
Knowledge Insufficient; Practical Rules

Do you want to puff yourself up or do you choose to build up others? Paul tells us that mere knowledge inflates our egos. Real love, on the other hand, edifies and builds up others.

It is not a matter of insisting that we are right and others are wrong or at least unenlightened. It is a matter of putting others first and not wounding their consciences by flaunting our freedom. We sin against Christ if we sin against our sisters and brothers.

Lord Jesus, help us to put you first by acting in gentleness and humility with others. Let us understand that true freedom is not doing as we wish and indulging every selfish whim. Forgive us when we have knowingly chosen self over others. You know why we have done the things we have done. Let us remember that our true freedom is found in loving you by serving others. Alleluia!

Friday, September 12, 2008 Most Holy Name of Mary
1 Corinthians 9, 16-19,22-27
Reason for Not Using His Rights; All Things to All

Bound and free! If we are bound to the Lord Jesus Christ, we are free to serve others in radical ways.

We are free to associate with all sorts of people with whom we may not always agree. Others may not understand and we may not understand either. The Lord who called us and is still calling us understands.

Lord Jesus, let us run our race with confidence that your purpose for us is indeed being fulfilled. Let us not look around at others and compare ourselves with others. Let us run straight to you and into your arms. Alleluia!

Saturday, September 13, 2008 St. John Chrysostom
1 Corinthians 10, 14-22
Warning against Idolatry

Participant! When we approach the altar to receive Jesus in Holy Communion, we are active participants.

We are actively participating in the Body and Blood of Christ. We are one with our brothers and sisters in Christ.

Lord Jesus, as we leave the altar, we do not leave you. You are always with us. We have received your Body and Blood in Holy Communion and you are with us in your Body, the Church. As you direct us, let us live out our participation in your Body and Blood. Alleluia!

Sunday, September 14, 2008 The Exaltation of the Holy Cross
Numbers 21, 4-9
The Bronze Serpent

Lift and live! Stop complaining and getting bitten by the various snakes of this life.

Moses interceded for the weary Israelites who complained about the Lord's provision for the wilderness journey to the Promised Land. The Lord really does not like complaining, so he sent fiery serpents to bite them!

Moses did as the Lord instructed. He made a serpent of bronze and mounted it on a pole. When the people lifted their eyes to the serpent, they recovered.

Lord Jesus, lifted on the Cross, you triumphed! Because of your triumph, we live. Let us praise you and trust you as we live out the remainder of our journey. Let us lift you up by the way we live. Alleluia!

Monday, September 15, 2008 Our Lady of Sorrows
1 Corinthians 11, 17-26,33
An Abuse at Corinth; Tradition of the Institution

The Lord sees. The Lord is present.

The Lord sees the state of the community gathered for Eucharist. The Lord sees the divisions. The Lord is present.

On the evening he was betrayed, the Lord Jesus gave instructions about the celebration of the Eucharistic meal. As we thank the Lord and partake of his Body and Blood, we are proclaiming his death until he comes in glory.

Lord Jesus, let us show respect and reverence for you, for your Body and Blood, and for your Body, your Church. Let us discern who you are and who we are and live accordingly. Alleluia!

Tuesday, September 16, 2008 Sts. Cornelius and Cyprian
1 Corinthians 12, 12-14,27-31
One Body, Many Parts; Application to Christ

Our baptism plunges us into the Body of Christ, the Church. We are not only individual believers, but we are also members of the Body of Christ, the Church.

No one can live out your particular vocation but YOU. The Church needs you to live fully your vocation, as well as you are able.

You and I belong. We are part of the Body of Christ on earth.

Lord Jesus, give to us a deeper understanding of how your Body, the Church, is truly one. Let us learn to relate to one another according to your plan and your purpose. Alleluia!

Wednesday, September 17, 2008 St. Robert Bellarmine
1 Corinthians 12, 31 - 13, 13
The Way of Love

LOVE! Without love, the more visible gifts and even noble acts of charity avail nothing. Nothing at all.

Paul does not disdain the gifts of the Holy Spirit or acts of self-sacrifice. However, he is pointing to the way of love, which is unfading and eternal.

Lord Jesus, at the present time I seem to be wandering in a wilderness. Please fill me with your love. This is what I need. Let me learn to be patient and kind. Help me not to become envious or rude in any way in my dealings with others. Help me not to put myself first by insisting on my own way. Help me not to allow my temper to flare or even to think evil thoughts. Help me not to brood over past grievances. Help me not to rejoice over what is wrong, but to rejoice and to exult in the truth. Lead me quietly to trust you more and more, to hope, and to endure. Let me learn to live out my trust in you as your love flows into me, replenishes me, and then flows through me to others. Alleluia!

Thursday, September 18, 2008
1 Corinthians 15, 1-11
The Gospel Teaching

Reminders! Paul reminds the Corinthians of the Gospel of Jesus Christ. They have already received the Gospel, but they still need reminders in order to stand fast and to live out their salvation.

Paul relays what he himself has received. It is good for us, also, to remind ourselves of what we already know.

The Scriptures teach us that Jesus died for us. He died for your sins and for my sins.

Jesus was buried as the Scriptures tell us and he was raised from the dead. He appeared to Peter, to the other apostles, to a group of five hundred, and to James.

At a later time, he appeared even to Saul, who had cruelly persecuted the Church. This man was chosen to become Paul, the apostle. With the Lord, nothing is impossible.

Lord Jesus, let us remember in an active way, what you have done for us. Thank you for those who remind us of what we have received. Let us joyfully live out the Gospel and relay the Gospel to others. Alleluia!

>Friday, September 19, 2008 St. Januarius
>1 Corinthians 15, 12-20
>The Resurrection of the Dead; Results of Denial

A little Easter holy card proclaims, "Christ is Risen! Rise we too!"

Lord Jesus, we trust in you and hope in you in this life, but not for this life alone. We trust in you and hope in you for the bright, new life ahead of us. Alleluia!

>Saturday, September 20, 2008 St. Andrew Kim Taegon,
>St. Paul Chong Hasang and Companions
>1 Corinthians 15, 35-37,42-49
>The Manner of Resurrection; Practical Arguments;
>The Resurrection Body

We live in a temporary body of flesh. This body is not meant to last forever. It is only our earthly body, our little tent.

We will one day live in a new body. This body will be our resurrection body, our heavenly body. Our new body will be strong, glorious, and eternal.

Lord Jesus, thank you that we shall be raised body, soul, and spirit. Thank you for the powerful new body in which we shall live forever with you. Alleluia!

Sunday, September 21, 2008
Twenty-fifth Sunday in Ordinary Time
Isaiah 55, 6-9
An Invitation to Grace

God does not think as we think. God does not act as we act.

God's ways are high above our ways. God's thoughts are high above our thoughts.

We are able to connect with God, however. We are free to seek God.

We are free to seek the mercy our loving God is freely offering us. We are free to ask for and to receive the forgiveness our gracious and generous God is offering us.

The Holy Spirit teaches us to understand the things of God (1 Corinthians 2, 12). Amazingly, we have the very mind of our Lord Jesus Christ (1 Corinthians 2, 16).

We are now free to do the deeds that Jesus did and to do even greater deeds (John 14, 12)! What an adventure awaits us when we truly believe this.

Lord Jesus, wonder of wonders! You come to us, knowing how we think and how we act. You forgive us and empower us to think as you think and to act as you act. Glory! Alleluia!

Monday, September 22, 2008
Proverbs 3, 27-34
Attitude Toward Fellow Men

The Lord "... blesses the abode of the righteous ... and to the humble he shows favor (vv. 33-34)."

Have you ever been invited to a house blessing? A time of joy, laughter, fresh flowers, refreshments, and the assurance of the Lord's benediction on one's home.

Have you ever been invited to a house cursing? Probably not.

God does not wait for an invitation. God openly promises to bless the homes of the just. God also promises to curse the places where the wicked dwell.

Lord Jesus, bless our homes with your presence. Let your love increase within us and within our homes. Let us learn to love others nearby and far away and to show them honor and kindness. Alleluia!

Tuesday, September 23, 2008 St. Pio of Pietrelcina
Proverbs 21, 1-6,10-13
First Collection of the Proverbs of Solomon

Doing what God considers right is more pleasing to God than our ideas of sacrifice. What we think is important. What we say is important. What we actually do is important.

Lord Jesus, in your mercy, purify our thoughts and our words. Thank you for directing our actions to manifest your love for others. Alleluia!

Wednesday, September 24, 2008
Proverbs 30, 5-9
The Words of Agur; Numerical Proverbs

We are to honor God and to live in truth. We are to have a healthy respect for God's words.

"Every word of God proves true; he is a shield to those who take refuge in him (v. 5)."

God's words are pure. We are never to add to God's words.

Agur, the writer of this proverb, prays, "Two things I ask of you; do not deny them to me before I die: Remove far from me the way of falsehood and lying; give me neither poverty nor riches; feed me with the food I need, or I shall be full, and deny you, and say, 'Who is the LORD?' or I shall be poor, and steal, and profane the name of my God (vv. 7-9)."

Lord Jesus, thank you for shielding us as we take refuge you in you. Let us honor you as we live in the light of your teaching. Alleluia!

Thursday, September 25, 2008
Ecclesiastes 2, 1-11
Vanity of Toil without Profit

"So I became great and surpassed all who were before me in Jerusalem .... Whatever my eyes desired I did not keep from them; I kept my heart from no pleasure .... Then I considered all that my hands had done and the toil I had spent ... and ... all was vanity ... (vv. 9-11)."

Downer! What's the use of it all? This passage, written hundred years before Christ, is a real downer.

Lord Jesus, thank you that we may come to you and pour out all of our feelings about the state of the world and the state of ourselves. You understand. You know what it is like to be human. Thank you that we don't have to continue to live with feelings of futility or fatalism. While we are on our pilgrimage to the heavenly Jerusalem, let us rejoice in you! Let us trust that your purpose for our lives is being worked out, even if the purpose is not completely clear to us. Alleluia!

Friday, September 26, 2008 Sts. Cosmas and Damien
Ecclesiastes 3, 1-11
Man Cannot Hit on the Right Time to Act

"For everything there is a season, and a time for every matter under heaven … (v. 1)."

Time! This passage assures us of God's control of the timing of all the events in our lives. God, the Eternal One, knows the appropriate time for everything.

In the fullness of time, when the time was ripe, God the Father sent Jesus, his Son, into our world to redeem us (Galatians 4, 4,5). We are free and secure in our identity as God's own, beloved children. We may take a deep breath and trust God, even when it is very difficult and when we do not understand.

Lord Jesus, let us trust you in all matters of timing in our lives. We don't have to try to force events before their time. When we feel that we have been stretched beyond endurance, thank you for strengthening us. Thank you for the wonders that will unfold before us as we wait patiently and joyfully for you. Alleluia!

Saturday, September 27, 2009 St. Vincent de Paul
Ecclesiastes 11, 9 - 12, 8
Poem on Youth and Old Age

"Remember now thy Creator in the days of thy youth …. (Ecclesiastes 12, 1 KJV)." As we grow older we are more and more aware that we will be held accountable for the way we have lived.

Lord Jesus, let us rejoice in the life we are given. Let us also realize that our life on earth is but for a short time, no matter how long we live. Let us live this day for you and trust you for the future. Alleluia!

JANIS WALKER　　　　　　　　　　　　　　　　　　FIRST READING

Sunday, September 28, 2009
Twenty-sixth Sunday in Ordinary Time
Ezekiel 18, 25-28
Personal Responsibility

Open door! The door is open for us to acknowledge that we have done wrong and to repent. The Lord freely offers us new life.

Lord Jesus, thank you that we are not held captive by our own sins or by the sins of others. Thank you for your power and your mercy. Thank you for forgiving us, cleansing us, and sending us out again to work in your vineyard. Alleluia!

Monday, September 29, 2009
St. Michael, St. Gabriel, and St. Raphael
Daniel 7, 9-10,13-14
Vision of the Four Beasts

Jesus! The Son of God.

Jesus! The Son of Man.

Jesus! The Son of Mary.

Angels! Clouds. A flaming throne. A fiery stream.

In the midst of the drama in heaven, we see Jesus, our Brother, who referred to himself as Son of Man. In Daniel's vision, the Son of Man is on a journey. He is traveling to the throne of Almighty God.

At God's throne, Jesus receives his kingship. Jesus receives glory. Jesus receives dominion that is forever.

Journey! We have a journey to make, also. Our journey is to Jesus, our Brother, who is also our Judge.

Judgment! The Father gave all matters of judgment into the hands of Jesus, his Son (John 5, 22). We will all stand before God (Romans 14, 10) and will be required to give an account of ourselves (Romans 14, 12).

Lord Jesus, help us not to be afraid to stand before you. Let us honor you and follow you as well as we are able. Thank you for your eagerness to forgive us. Thank you for your journey from heaven to the womb of Mary, your Virgin Mother. Thank you for your patient journeys in the land we call holy. Thank you for your journey to the Cross for us. Thank you for your journey, mission accomplished, to your Father in heaven to prepare a place for us. Thank you for the presence of Holy Spirit with us on each step of our journey. Alleluia!

>Tuesday, September 30, 2008 St. Jerome
>Job 3, 1-3,11-17,20-23
>Job's Plaint

Darkness. Bitterness. Grief

Job is in a state of such suffering that he wishes he had never been born. Longing for death, he is assigned to life.

Lord Jesus, thank you that we may cry out to you in our times of darkness and suffering. In the valley, we cannot imagine any future light or joy. Thank you for leading us safely through this dark valley to the sunlit meadows and the flowing streams of cool, refreshing water. Alleluia!

>Wednesday, October 1, 2008 St. Therese of Lisieux
>Job 9, 1-12,14-16
>Job's Second Reply

In the midst of his suffering, Job attempted, somehow, to honor God. He acknowledged God's wisdom, power, and sovereignty

Job was aware, painfully aware, of his own limitations. He was not yet aware of God's intentions to restore him and to bring him new joy.

Lord Jesus, thank you for warning us that in this world we will experience tribulation. Thank you for overcoming the world! Let us be of good cheer, knowing that you are Victor. Alleluia!

>Thursday, October 2, 2008 The Guardian Angels
>Exodus 23, 20-23
>Reward of Fidelity

God sent an angel to go before his people. The angel was to guide them and to guard them.

Where were they guided? To their enemies!

Before entering the promised land of milk and honey, the Israelites had to face their enemies. God promised to get rid of all these enemies, but the Israelites still had to face them.

Lord Jesus, you lead us, but sometimes you lead us to a difficult place. We are forced to face ourselves. We are forced to face others. We are forced to confront when we would rather run. Thank you that we are safe with you. Thank you for leading us safely through this wilderness into the place you have prepared for us. Alleluia!

Friday, October 3, 2008
Job 38, 1,12-21; 40, 3-5
The Lord's Speech

From storm to silence. From tempest to tranquility.

The Lord, the mighty Lord, the Creator of the universe, spoke to Job. Job was stunned into silence.

Lord Jesus, thank you for your incredible patience with us as we lash out in our terror. Let us enter now into silence as we wait for you. Alleluia!

Saturday, October 4, 2008 St. Francis of Assisi
Job 42, 1-3,5-6,12-17
The Lord's Speech; Job's Restoration

"Then Job answered the LORD: 'I know that you can do all things, and that no purpose of yours can be thwarted .... I have uttered what I did not understand, things too wonderful for me, which I did not know. I had heard of you by the hearing of the ear, but now my eye sees you ... I ... repent in dust and ashes (vv. 1-3,5-6)."

Before all his trials, Job had conscientiously served the Lord as well as he knew how. During his trials, he cried out in anguish to the Lord.

Now, after his trials, Job has a whole new perspective on his relationship with the Lord. He knows the Lord in a way he did not know the Lord before his suffering.

The Lord, before restoring Job's prosperity, referred to Job twice as his servant (vv. 7,8) The Lord also expressed anger with two of Job's so-called friends.

These two friends had misrepresented the Lord to Job. They were required to go to Job and Job would intercede on their behalf.

Job entered into a whole new life of exceedingly abundant joy and blessing. His restoration was sweet. His restoration was complete.

Lord Jesus, let us trust you to set matters right for us. Let us pray for those who misrepresent you. Let us be careful not to misrepresent you when we minister to the suffering. Alleluia!

Sunday, October 5, 2008
Twenty-seventh Sunday in Ordinary Time
Isaiah 5, 1-7
The Vineyard of the Lord

Israel! The Lord's lovely vineyard.

What more could the Lord have done for Israel? What more could the Lord have done for us?

Lord Jesus, we are your garden, your vineyard, your Church. What more could you have done for us? Let us lay down our lives by laying down our agendas. Be glorified and exalted in your Church, Lord Jesus. Alleluia!

Monday, October 6, 2008
St. Bruno; Bl. Marie-Rose Durocher
Galatians 1, 6-12
Greetings; His Call by Christ

Choose! Please people or serve Christ.

Lord Jesus, let us choose to follow you first and foremost. You know all about us. You know how frightened and insecure we can become. You know our need to fit in and to be approved. If we have been enslaved by an unhealthy need to please people, please free us and deliver us! The greatest service we can offer others is to follow you and to trust you with all our heart. Alleluia!

Tuesday, October 7, 2008 Our Lady of the Rosary
Galatians 1, 13-24
His Call by Christ

How did we get to where we are now? The Lord has been leading us and guiding us, in spite of our mistakes.

The Lord will continue to lead us and to guide us. It's not over, yet!

Paul recounted his former days as a zealous, almost obsessive observer of Jewish law. Paul realized that, although God had called him even before his birth to proclaim Jesus to the Gentiles, his living out of God's call was up to God.

Paul did not run around consulting people. Instead, he withdrew to the desert. After a period of years, he went to Jerusalem to meet with Peter and with James.

Lord Jesus, let us learn to be patient with ourselves and with your timing in our lives. You know how to use even our mistakes and our failings. Thank you for freeing us to follow you, with trust and joy, this day. You will lead us to the place of service you have designated for us. Alleluia!

Wednesday, October 8, 2008
Galatians 2, 1-2,7-14
The Council of Jerusalem; Peter's Inconsistency at Antioch

Another space of years. Fourteen years.

After this second interval, Paul went back to Jerusalem, accompanied by Barnabas and Titus. Established in his relationship with the Lord and secure in this relationship, Paul was free to present to the church leaders in Jerusalem the Gospel he proclaimed to the Gentiles.

Paul was also free to confront Peter. Peter, entrusted with proclaiming the Gospel especially to the Jews, was just wrong in a particular matter. It was necessary for Paul to confront him and to correct him.

Lord Jesus, let us learn to move and to speak in your time. Let us learn to speak forth your words, even if we are afraid. We choose to please you in all things. Alleluia!

Thursday, October 9, 2008 St. Denis and Companions;
St. John Leonardi
Galatians 3, 1-5
Justification by Faith

A daily challenge! Do we continue to progress in the real, yet unseen world of the spirit, or do we insist on seeing before believing?

Do we insist on serving God according to our desires or according to the desires of the Holy Spirit? Do we walk by trust or do we insist on walking by sight (2 Corinthians 5, 7).

Lord Jesus, we are indeed foolish to start out in trust, holding your hand, and then turning around in fear and mistrust. Thank you for the Holy Spirit who strengthens us to persevere in following you, knowing we are safe and secure in your keeping. Alleluia!

Friday, October 10, 2008
Galatians 3, 7-14
Justified by Faith

"Just as Abraham 'believed God, and it was reckoned to him as righteousness,' so, you see, those who believe are the descendants of Abraham. And the scripture, foreseeing that God would justify the Gentiles by faith, declared the gospel beforehand to Abraham, saying, 'All the Gentiles shall be blessed in you.' For this reason, those who believe are blessed with Abraham who believed (vv. 6-9)."

Abraham! He had to trust before he saw.

Abraham had to live in confident trust that God was trustworthy. What God had promised, God would deliver!

Jesus! What did Jesus do?

Out of the loop! Jesus took us out of the loop of the law.

Jesus died for us, removed us from the curse of the law, and inserted us into Abraham's blessing. We are now free to live on a new plane.

Lord Jesus, thank you for the gift of the promised Holy Spirit. Thank you that the Holy Spirit is teaching us how to live this day in joyful trust. Alleluia!

Saturday, October 11, 2008
Galatians 3, 22-29
The Law Did Not Nullify the Promise; What Faith Brought Us

School's out! For a time, we were in the care of teachers who tried to teach us how to live while we were still in that school.

That was only for a time, however. We are God's own children, now! We are able to live in a new way.

We have been plunged and baptized into the Lord Jesus Christ. We are now clothed with Christ. We will never be the same as before. We don't have to worry and fret about what makes us different. Jew of Greek? Slave or free? Male or female? We are one because we belong to Jesus.

We are also descendants of Abraham. We are heirs and heiresses because of God's promise to Abraham.

Lord Jesus, sometimes we are still living as helpless orphans without hope of ever having a real home. Thank you for making it possible for us to be your little sisters and brothers. Thank you that God is our loving Father. Thank you that the Holy Spirit is our Teacher. Thank you that you are leading us each day closer and closer to our real Home. Alleluia!

Sunday, October 12, 2008
Twenty-eighth Sunday in Ordinary Time
Isaiah 25, 6-10
Devastation of the World: A Remnant Saved

God is here! Here is the One for whom we have been waiting.

God is here! God is here to rescue us. We rejoice because of what God has accomplished for us.

Party! It's time to party! It's time to celebrate.

Our host at this celebration is none other than the Lord of Hosts. The Lord will provide for us on the mountain a feast of delicious food and choice wine.

No more death. God has destroyed death. God will remove all traces of our tears.

No more reproach. We belong to God and God has removed all reproach from us.

Lord Jesus, let us celebrate in advance the victory you have won for us. Thank you for the feast of the Eucharist which prepares us on earth for the feast in the heavenly Jerusalem, our true Home. Alleluia!

Monday, October 13, 2008
Galatians 4, 22-24,26-27,31 - 5,1
All Allegory on Christian Freedom The Importance of Faith

Don't go back there! Don't go back into slavery.

Christ has set us free! We are free to follow Christ. We are free to live for Christ.

Lord Jesus, sometimes we are enslaved by our own ideas of how to follow you. Thank you for setting us free to follow you as you call us to follow you. Alleluia!

Tuesday, October 14, 2008 St. Callistus I
Galatians 5, 1-6
The Importance of Faith

"For freedom Christ has set us free. Stand firm, therefore, and do not submit again to a yoke of slavery (v. 1)."

Freedom! Discipline is needed in order to live in true freedom.

Slavery! All that is needed to live in slavery is fear.

Lord Jesus, thank you for the Holy Spirit who instructs us in the discipline of following you this day in freedom. You are continually calling us to live on a new plane, a new level, a place of complete trust in you and a complete surrender to your glorious plan for our lives. Alleluia!

Wednesday, October 15, 2008 St. Teresa of Avila
Galatians 5, 18-25
Freedom for Service

The Holy Spirit. The Holy Spirit will lead us and guide us.

Then the fruit from our life will be good! The life of the Lord Jesus Christ will be evident in our life.

The fruit of the Holy Spirit is "love, joy, peace, patience, kindness, generosity, faithfulness, gentleness, and self-control. If we live by the Spirit, let us also be guided by the Spirit. Let us not become conceited, competing against one another, envying one another (vv. 22,23,25)."

Lord Jesus, thank you that we belong to you. Help us not to look so much at ourselves and become discouraged. Let us look to you and be encouraged because you haven't given up on us. Thank you for the Holy Spirit who will continue to guide us. Alleluia!

> Thursday, October 16, 2008
> St. Hedwig; St. Margaret Mary Alascoque
> Ephesians 1, 3-10
> The Father's Plan of Salvation, Fulfillment through Christ

Chosen! Chosen for holiness.

God our Father "…chose us in Christ before the foundation of the world to be holy and blameless in love. He destined us for adoption as his children … (vv. 4-5)."

Chosen for adoption! We are chosen for adoption by none other than God. That is our destiny.

In Christ and through Christ, our vocation and our destiny are realized. It is in Christ and through Christ that we are chosen.

It is in Christ and by the blood of Christ that we are redeemed. "In him we have redemption through his blood, the forgiveness of our trespasses, according to the riches of his grace … (v. 7)."

The will of God! We are informed about the will of God.

"With all wisdom and insight he has made known to us the mystery of his will, according to his good pleasure that he set forth in Christ, as a plan for the fullness of time, to gather up all things in him, things in heaven and things on earth (vv. 8-10)."

We are included in God's family. We live in God's house. We are insiders. We are secure in our identity.

Lord Jesus, everything is summed up in you and we are in you! Let us live today with a new confidence and purpose. Thank you for the work of the Holy Spirit to teach us how to live out our vocation. Alleluia

> Friday, October 17, 2008 St. Ignatius of Antioch
> Ephesians 1, 11-14
> Inheritance through the Spirit

Why do you exist? For the praise of the glory of the Lord Jesus Christ! For this you were chosen.

Lord Jesus, thank you that we have been sealed by the Holy Spirit. Thank you that the Holy Spirit is revealing to us the awesome nature of our inheritance as God's children. Let us live in a new way as we begin to comprehend who we really are. Alleluia!

Saturday, October 18, 2008 St. Luke
2 Timothy 4, 10-17
Paul's Loneliness

We are NOT alone. The Lord is standing beside us and strengthening us! The Lord will deal with all who wish to harm us.

Lord Jesus, thank you that we are safe with you. No matter how we are treated by others, you are with us. You will fulfill your plan for us and, in your time, bring us safely Home. Alleluia!

Sunday, October 19, 2008
Twenty-ninth Sunday in Ordinary Time
Isaiah 45, 1,4-6
Cyrus, Anointed of the Lord; Liberator of Israel

The Lord's instrument! The Lord chooses and uses many people in order to bring freedom.

King Cyrus was the Lord's unlikely instrument to bring freedom to exiled Israel. The Lord also sends people across our path to bring us to new life and liberty.

Lord Jesus, let us be willing to serve as your instruments. Use us to bring your life to others. Thank you for leading us and opening surprising doors before us. Alleluia!

Monday, October 20, 2008 St. Paul of the Cross
Ephesians 2, 1-10
Generosity of God's Plan

God stepped into our mess! We were living in a mess because we were living only for ourselves.

God stepped in and lifted us out of this futile way of living. The Holy Spirit breathed new life into us.

We are now living in a new realm. We have been raised to a new life with Christ.

Although we are still living on earth, we are also with our risen Lord Jesus Christ in the heavenly realm. A mystery, and yet a reality grounded on the truth of God's Word.

God's power has been at work in us. Although this power is beyond our comprehension, we trust God and thank God for the amazing gift of new life.

"For we are what he has made us, created in Christ Jesus for good works, which God prepared beforehand to be our way of life (v. 10)."

Lord Jesus, let us respond to you by living out our gratitude. While we trust you that your plan for our lives is unfolding, there is still so much that we do not see and do not understand. Let us live simply in the present moment and learn to give away the love you have poured upon us. Alleluia!

Tuesday, October 21, 2008
Ephesians 2, 12-22
One in Christ

You don't have to pay rent anymore. You're not a tenant. You're not an alien, either.

You live in God's house now. You belong.

Jesus! It's all about what Jesus accomplished for us. It's all about what Jesus is accomplishing in us right now. It's all about what Jesus is accomplishing and will accomplish through us.

Jesus brought in the outsiders! Jesus made it possible for outsiders to become insiders.

"But now in Christ Jesus you who once were far off have been brought near by the blood of Christ. For he is our peace; in his flesh he has made both groups[Jews and Gentiles] into one and has broken down the dividing wall, that is, the hostility between us. He has abolished the law with its commandments and ordinances, that he might create in himself one new humanity in place of the two, thus making peace ... So then you are no longer strangers and aliens, but you are citizens with the saints and also members of the household of God (vv. 13-15,19)."

By shedding his Blood and dying for us on the Cross, Jesus destroyed the hostile wall separating Jews and Gentiles. In Jesus himself, this hostility was destroyed completely. When Jesus died, the wall came down.

On the Cross, Jesus "... breathed his last. At that moment the curtain of the temple was torn in two, from top to bottom. The earth shook, and the rocks were split (Matthew 28, 50-51)."

One! Whether Jew or Gentile, free or slave, male or female, we are one in the Lord Jesus Christ (Galatians 3, 28).

We all live in one household because of Jesus. We are living in the household built on the foundation of the prophets and the apostles.

Jesus! Jesus himself is the cornerstone of our house. He is holding us all together as we grow up.

Lord Jesus, help us to remember today who we are, whose we are, and where we live. We are God's children. We belong to you. We live in your household. Secure in our identity, let us go out and bring others into your household, into your Body, into your Church. Alleluia!

Wednesday, October 22, 2008
Ephesians 3, 2-12
Commission to Preach God's Plan

Stewardship! Paul was entrusted as a steward of the grace of God. He had received an abundance of the grace of God and could generously give away what he had received.

Mystery! Paul was given deep insight into the mystery of the Messiah. The Gentiles are not low-life! The Gentiles are co-heirs with the Jews.

Lord Jesus, thank you have called us also to be stewards of your mystery. Let us live out your call to be one with other believers. Alleluia!

Thursday, October 23, 2008 St. John of Capistrano
Ephesians 3, 14-21
Prayer for the Readers

Inside! It's an inside job.

It is within our hearts that Christ dwells. It is within our hearts that we grow strong.

This is a strength beyond our usual comprehension of strength. This is not a strength with which we assert ourselves.

This is an interior strength with which we begin to grasp the immensity of the love of Christ. Breadth. Length. Height. Depth. This is a knowing beyond knowing.

Lord Jesus, let us cooperate with the Holy Spirit who is constantly teaching us about your love. Let your love within us radiate from us and through us to others. Alleluia!

Friday, October 24, 2008 St. Anthony Mary Claret
Ephesians 4, 1-6
Unity in the Body

If there is true humility, gentleness, and patience in the Church, there will be true unity in the Church. We will stop obsessing about image and turf.

We will finally begin to learn to love. We will love ourselves because Jesus indeed loves us.

Lord Jesus, thank you for freeing us to love you and to love others. Let us honor you by living in simplicity and humility with our brothers and sisters in the Church. Alleluia!

Saturday, October 25, 2008
Ephesians 4, 7-16
Diversity of Gifts

Group travel. Our gifts are for others.

Jesus Christ is the one who decides which gifts we have. These gifts are for us to give away in the service of our sisters and brothers in the Body of Christ, the Church.

We need each other in the Church. We do not have to compare ourselves with others. We do not have to compete with others.

We are traveling as a group. We need to grow up and to grow into the fullness of Christ.

Lord Jesus, let us be concerned first of all with honoring you and with offering ourselves to be used for your purposes in the Church. You know where you want us to serve you and how you want us to serve you. Let us rejoice in the gifts you have given to us. Let us also rejoice in the gifts you have given to others. Alleluia!

Sunday, October 26, 2008 Thirtieth Sunday in Ordinary Time
Exodus 22, 20-26
Social Laws

Aliens. Widows. Orphans. Neighbors in need.

Awareness. The Lord calls us to live with compassionate awareness of others.

Israel, the Lord's own chosen people, were once aliens in Egypt. The Gentiles were once considered aliens and outsiders with no share in the promise of God.

Jew and Gentile, we are now invited to live in the same household, God's household. We are invited to be filled with the love of Christ to reach out in active compassion to those who are suffering. The Holy Spirit will give us discernment.

Lord Jesus, thank you for the Holy Spirit who is teaching us to identify with aliens, widows, orphans, and needy neighbors. No matter what our passport says, no matter what the status of our family, no matter what the size of our bank account, we are always in need of compassion. Let us live today knowing that we are safe in your care. Let us manifest your love to all, regardless of their outer appearance. Alleluia!

Monday, October 27, 2009
Ephesians 4, 32 - 5, 8
Rules for the New Life; Duty to Live in the Light

As God's children, we are filled with power to live as God lives. The Holy Spirit fills us and frees us to be kind, to be tenderhearted, to be compassionate, and to offer forgiveness.

Jesus is our example! Jesus is God's own Son. Jesus gave away his own life as an offering for us, his little brothers and sisters.

We now live in the light! Our brother Jesus has transplanted us from the realm of darkness into his own brilliant, holy, light.

Lord Jesus, let our thoughts, our speech, and our actions all reflect your light. Let us remember that we are God's children and live accordingly. Let us offer ourselves daily for your purposes. Alleluia!

> Tuesday, October 28, 2008 Sts. Simon and Jude
> Ephesians 2, 19-22
> Generosity of God's Plan

Citizenship! We are again reminded of our true citizenship. As concerned as we are for our country, our true home is not here.

Heaven! Heaven is our true home.

We are citizens with the saints of heaven. Even here on earth, we are members of God's household, constructed on the foundation of the prophets and apostles with Jesus, our Lord, as the very cornerstone.

Lord Jesus, sometimes we live like little earthbound creatures without hope. Thank you for the Holy Spirit who delights to tell us about who you are, who we are, and where we are going. Thank you for lifting us to a new plane, a new level, today, in our thinking, our speaking, and in our actions. Alleluia!

> Wednesday, October 29, 2008
> Ephesians 6, 1-9
> Children and Parents; Slaves and Masters

Obedience. Honor. Service.

We're going to obey, honor, and serve someone every day of our lives. We may as well obey, honor, and serve in the way God directs. It is far easier to serve Christ than to serve ourselves, since we are often our own most difficult critic.

Lord Jesus, forgive us and heal us, especially when we have suffered injustice from those who abused their authority over us. Heal us and free us to live in a state of obedience and honor. We will then be prepared to serve wherever you lead us. Alleluia!

> Thursday, October 30, 2008
> Ephesians 6, 10-20
> Battle against Evil; Constant Prayer

Dressed for success! The Lord has endless reserves of strength from which we may draw. We're not up against human beings so much as up against the schemes of the devil and the powers of darkness. We need to know how to dress for battle.

We already know who will win the battle. Victory always belongs to the Lord! Victory also belongs to us since we belong to the Lord.

We are clothed in heavenly armor. We will stand our ground and see the Lord's victory on our behalf.

Lord Jesus, thank you for our battle wardrobe. Thank you for the armor of truth, righteousness, faith and salvation. Thank you for teaching us speak with the sword of the Holy Spirit, God's Word. Thank you for strengthening us to persevere and to pray for ourselves and for all who are engaged in spiritual battles. In the midst of the struggle, we walk in peace.

Friday, October 31, 2008
Philippians 1, 1-11
Greeting; Thanksgiving

Pray with joy! Paul did, even though he was in prison when he wrote this letter.

Reassure others! Paul did. He reassured the Christians in Philippi and he reassures us that God's work in us will indeed be completed on God's timetable.

Include others! Paul did. He referred to the Christians in Philippi as his partners in ministry. His was not an ego trip, but a God trip, a mission.

Intercede for others. Paul did. In the midst of his own suffering, Paul prayed for an increase of love and discernment among Christians.

Lord Jesus, let us pray with joy, knowing you are in charge. Let us do our part and continue to trust you to complete your work in us and in those for whom we pray. Alleluia!

Saturday, November 1, 2008   All Saints
Revelation 7, 2-4,9-14
The 144,000 Sealed; Triumph of the Elect

I once asked Christopher, my young son, what he thought was the meaning of the Book of the Revelation. He answered, "It's simple. God wins!"

God wins! God's people are signed, sealed, and saved.

Lord Jesus, thank you that we are signed with the sign of the cross and marked as your own forever. With the angels, the martyrs, and with all the saints, we worship you as the Lamb of God. Alleluia!

Sunday, November 2, 2008 All Souls
Wisdom 3, 1-9
The Hidden Counsels of God

Shine! Those who have trusted in the Lord will one day shine. They will be with their King and will live forever.

Lord Jesus, thank you that we are safe in your care whether in life or in Life. We trust in you and in your mercy. Alleluia!

Monday, November 3, 2008 St. Martin de Porres
Philippians 2, 1-4
Plea for Unity and Humility

Check, please! Before doing anything, we are to check.

We are to check our motives. We are to do nothing out of sheer selfishness or a desire to boast.

Lord Jesus, let us realize how secure we are in your love. You are in charge of our lives. We have need to prove anything. We do not need to drop names, degrees, or pedigrees of any kind, We are free to love and to serve others. Alleluia!

Tuesday, November 4, 2008 St. Charles Borromeo
Philippians 2, 5-11
Plea for Unity and Humility

Pattern! Jesus is our pattern. Jesus is the pattern for our attitude.

Who do we think we are? Jesus knew who he was. He was the Son of God. And yet, for us, he willingly humbled himself and died for our sins on the Cross.

Jesus chose not to assert his rights or his power. Knowing who he was, he chose to walk in loving, trusting obedience to his Father God.

As a result, God exalted Jesus. The name of Jesus is the name above all names!

So, who do we think we are? We know who we are. We are God's children.

As God's children, we are to have the same mental and emotional attitude that Jesus had. We are to be clothed with Christ (1 Peter 5, 5) and to remember that we have the mind of Christ (1 Corinthians 2, 16).

We are free to humble ourselves and to serve others. The Lord has promised to exalt those who will first humble themselves (1 Peter 5, 6).

Lord Jesus, sometimes we are afraid to lay down our agenda. Help us to trust you and to remember that we are here to fulfill your agenda for us. We humble ourselves before you, trusting in your mercy, and offer ourselves for your service. Thank you for being our pattern. Thank you for shaping our attitude into one of humility. Alleluia!

Wednesday, November 5, 2008
Philippians 2, 12-18
Obedience and Service in the World

A workout! A workout involving all the faculties of body, soul, and spirit. God is at work within us as we live out our salvation.

No complaining! Whining and fussing are unbecoming to God's children. We are living in a dark world and we are to shine as the stars of Christ in this world.

Lord Jesus, let us know the joy and exhilaration of cooperating with you as you work with us and work within us to manifest yourself through us. Alleluia!

Thursday, November 6, 2008
Philippians 3, 3-8
Against Legalistic Teachers; Paul's Autobiography;
Righteousness from God

Righteousness! Is your righteousness a result of your own efforts?

Before his encounter with the risen Lord Jesus Christ, Paul could boast quite readily of his Hebrew ancestry and his own meticulous observance of the law. He was a Pharisee of the Pharisee!

Jesus! After meeting Jesus, Paul was overjoyed to relinquish everything else. Everything else was as trash in comparison to knowing Christ Jesus as his Lord. He knew his righteousness came from his trust in the Lord.

Lord Jesus, whatever honor can be bestowed upon us or whatever honor is withheld from us in this transitory life is not that important. What matters is knowing you! No matter how long we have followed you, let us discover the freedom of knowing, truly knowing, that our righteousness comes from you. Alleluia!

Friday, November 7, 2008
Philippians 3, 17 - 4, 1
Wrong Conduct and Our Goal; Live in Concord

Mind! Whatever is occupying our mind will influence our actions.

Are we concentrating on following the Lord? Are we intent, instead, on following our own desires?

Heaven! Heaven is the realm of our true citizenship.

In heaven, we will live in a new body. Our new body will be a glorified body as is the body of our Beloved Lord.

Lord Jesus, let us conduct ourselves as citizens of heaven even as we go about the work you have given us to do in this world. Let our minds be transformed and renewed and let our actions be aligned with heaven. Alleluia!

Saturday, November 8, 2008
Philippians 4, 10-19
Joy and Peace

Contentment! Paul had learned how to be content, whatever the state of his personal finances.

Strength! Paul knew he had the strength for whatever curve was thrown at him. God gave him the strength and the power.

Gratitude! Paul graciously expressed his gratitude to those who had supported him financially. He assured them that God would, in turn, supply all their own needs.

Lord Jesus, thank you for teaching us how to live. Thank you for teaching us how to handle money and how to give to others. Let us be grateful to you, no matter the state of our finances. Thank you that, as we reach out and give to others, you will supply what we need. Alleluia!

Sunday, November 9, 2008
Dedication of the Lateran Basilica in Rome
Ezekiel 47, 1-2,8-9,12
The Wonderful Stream

Lord Jesus, let us remember that we are the temple of God and that the Holy Spirit dwells within us. Let the pure, cleansing waters of our baptism flow through us and bring freshness to those around us. Let us be as sturdy fruit trees, bearing food to feed and to heal others. Alleluia!

> Monday, November 10, 2008 St. Leo the Great
> Titus 1, 1-9
> Greeting; Titus in Crete

Servant. Apostle. Child.

Before instructing Titus about the appointment of church leader in Crete, Paul spoke of himself and his relationship with Titus.

Servant. Paul referred to himself as a servant, indeed a slave, of God. He called himself God's slave before he called himself Christ's apostle.

Child. Paul referred to Titus as his own child in the faith.

Paul gave specific instructions to Titus on the selection of church leaders, the predecessors of our priests and bishops. They were to have been married only once. Their children were to be believers. The leaders themselves were to be holy in all matters, faithfully proclaiming the Gospel.

Lord Jesus, thank you for all who serve in your Church. Thank you for those who serve as priests and as bishops. Let them trust you, put you first, and serve your flock in humility and holiness, as they courageously proclaim the Gospel. Alleluia!

> Tuesday, November 11, 2008 St. Martin of Tours
> Titus 2, 1-8,11-14
> Christian Behavior; Transformation of Life

Model. Paul charged Titus with being a model of good in the Christian community of Crete. Titus was to live and to teach with integrity and dignity as he instructed the various groups of believers in Crete how to live the Christian faith.

Lord Jesus, thank you for sacrificing yourself for us. Thank you for entrusting your Church into human hands. Let our lives bring you glory as we joyfully await your return in glory. Alleluia!

Wednesday, November 12, 2008 St. Josaphat
Titus 3, 1-7
Transformation

Lord Jesus, thank you for pouring out your love and kindness on us. Thank you for extending mercy to us and rescuing us. Forgive us for the times we have hated ourselves and then hated and mistreated others. Thank you for transforming us and making us heirs of eternal life. Let us now live in peace and integrity with you, with ourselves, and with others. Alleluia!

Thursday, November 13, 2008 St. Frances X. Cabrini
Philemon 7-20
Address and Greeting; Thanksgiving; Plea for Onesimus

Humility. Gratitude. Identification. Request.

Humility. Paul, in prison for his faith in Christ, approached Philemon, Apphia, and Archippus in humility before making his request to Philemon on behalf of Onesimus. Paul, the great apostle, simply referred to himself as an old man and a prisoner for Christ.

Gratitude. Paul offered thanks to God for Philemon, Apphia, Archippus, and for all the other Christians in their community. He acknowledged them as his partners.

Identification. Paul, a prisoner, referred to Onesimus, a runaway slave as his spiritual child.

Request. Paul wanted to send Onesimus back to Philemon, not as a slave, but as a brother in Christ, a fellow believer. Paul offered to make right any debt Onesimus may have owed Philemon.

Lord Jesus, thank you for giving us wisdom in matters of ministry. Let us humbly identify ourselves with those considered "little" by others. Let us learn to be bridges of reconciliation between Christians. Alleluia!

Friday, November 14, 2008
2 John 4-9

Safety net! God's safety net is one of love and truth.

Love. Love is living according to God's commandments.

Truth. Jesus himself is the way, the truth, and the life (John 14, 6). Jesus was truly divine and simultaneously truly human.

He truly came to us in the flesh. He truly was God clothed in human flesh. He truly came to us in the flesh to live among us and to die for us.

Lord Jesus, thank you that you are our Good Shepherd. Keep us safe in your care from the wolves and the hirelings who would lead your flock astray by distorting your teaching. Let us live in your love and walk in truth. Alleluia!

Saturday, November 15, 2008 St. Albert the Great
3 John 5-8

Support! Gaius was commended for his faithful support of Christian missionaries. He was asked to continue to assist them as they continued to travel and to proclaim the Gospel.

Lord Jesus, help us to remember that we may still support missionaries in the three classic ways. Pray! Give! Go! Let us pray, give, and even go as you direct us. The mission field you have for us may be closer than we realize. Let us offer encouragement and hospitality to all who proclaim the Gospel. Alleluia!

Sunday, November 16, 2008
Thirty-third Sunday in Ordinary Time
Proverbs 31, 10-13,19-20,30-31
The Ideal Wife

Heart and hands! This woman knows how to live and how to love.

She is worthy of trust. Her husband has confidently placed his heart in her care.

She knows how to work with her mind and with her hands. She extends her care to the poor.

She is worthy of recognition and reward. She has lived in reverence.

Lord Jesus, thank you for the example of all holy women who serve as our role models. Thank you for strengthening us to live out the vocation to which you have called us. Alleluia!

JANIS WALKER — FIRST READING

Monday, November 17, 2008
Revelation 1, 1-4; 2, 1-5
Prologue; Letters to the Churches of Asia; To Ephesus

Read aloud! Listen! The person who reads aloud this revelation of the Lord and listens to this prophecy will be blessed.

The Lord knows. The Lord knew what the Christians in Ephesus were going through and the Lord knows what we are going through, also.

The Lord commended the Christians in Ephesus for their endurance. The Lord reproved them for allowing their once-blazing love for him to be lost. They had apparently become so preoccupied with the work of the Lord that they had neglected the Lord himself.

Lord Jesus, as we work for you, let us grow in love for you. Let us not wound your heart by indifference. Let us daily make you first in our hearts and on our calendars. Alleluia!

Tuesday, November 18, 2008
The Dedication of St. Peter and St. Paul Basilicas in Rome;
St. Rose Philippine Duchesne; To Sardis; To Laodicia
Revelation 3, 1-6,14-22

Reputation! Our true reputation is known to God alone.

The church in Sardis had the appearance and even the reputation of life. Not so! The church in Sardis was dead.

Hope! A bit of hope remained for the church in Sardis. The Lord commanded the church to be alert, to repent, and to strengthen whatever remained.

Remnant. There was a remnant in Sardis deemed by the Lord to be worthy. They were promised that they would be clothed in white and walk with the Lord.

The Lord promised that the victor would wear white. Jesus would acknowledge the victor in the presence of God and the angels. The victor's name would never be erased from God's book.

The church in Laodicia was another matter altogether! This church was wishy-washy, not hot and not cold. The Lord does not tolerate politically correct fence-sitters. The Lord promised to vomit this church out of his mouth.

Appearance. The church in Laodicia appeared to be rich and self-sufficient. Not so. The Lord knew all about this church and saw it as it truly was. This church was pathetic. It was pitiful. It was naked and blind.

Hope! There was still hope even for the church in Laodicia. The Lord still loved the people in this church and called them to repentance. Jesus said that he was standing and knocking, awaiting entrance. He promised to enter if the door was opened.

Lord Jesus, thank you for pouring the fire of your grace upon the Church. You are calling us to repentance. You are calling us to reality. You are calling us to see ourselves as you see us. We open our lives to you and invite you to come to us. Purify us and send us out to proclaim the Gospel, in integrity, to all. Alleluia!

Wednesday, November 19, 2008
Revelation 4, 1-11
Vision of Heavenly Worship

A vision! In a vision, John, the writer of the Revelation saw a door opening. The door was opening into heaven!

A voice! The same voice. John heard the same voice that had spoken to him before. This voice sounded like a trumpet.

John was transported into the heavenlies. He observed worship beyond his ability to describe. He described it as well as he could, with dazzling images.

A throne! A halo. Sparkling jewels. Elders wearing white with crowns of gold. Thunder. Lightening. Torches. Amazing living creatures.

Praise! Constant praise and adoration of God.

Lord Jesus, you are worthy of all praise and honor and glory. We worship you as well as we know how to here on earth. Thank you for giving us these previews of worship in heaven. Let us remember that we are truly joining with angels and with all the company of heaven as we sing of your holiness. Alleluia!

Thursday, November 20, 2008
Revelation 5, 1-10
The Scroll and the Lamb

Your prayers! Do you ever wonder where your prayers go? They go to God, of course.

John, the writer of the Revelation, saw, in his vision, the elders holding golden bowls of incense. The incense was described as the prayers of God's holy people.

Our prayers did arrive! The answers will arrive on God's timetable.

We will understand more when we see what John saw. We will see the Lamb of God. The Lion of Judah, the triumphant Lamb who had been slain, was found worthy to open the scroll with the seven seals.

Lord Jesus, we are overcome by these glimpses into the reality of heaven. Thank you for hearing and receiving all our prayers. You are the Lion. You are the Lamb. You have called us to serve you as kings and priests who will reign one day on earth. When we are weighted down by the sorrows and trials of this world, let us look to you. You are with us and you are leading us to our true Home. Alleluia!

Friday, November 21, 2008
Revelation 10, 8-11
The Presentation of the Blessed Virgin Mary

Eat the scroll! We've heard that before.

Who ate the scroll long ago? The priest and prophet Ezekiel, who lived six hundred years before Christ, received amazing visions. Once, he was instructed to eat a scroll and then go speak to Israel (Ezekiel 2-3, 1-4). He had a hard message to deliver.

John, the writer of the Revelation, was also told to eat a scroll. The scroll, at first, tasted as sweet as honey. Then it turned bitter. John was then told to go and prophesy about many nations and kings.

Lord Jesus, let us consume your words and then go and speak as you direct. Let us be faithful to speak as you direct us. Alleluia!

Saturday, November 22, 2008
Revelation 11, 4-12
The Two Witnesses

Commissioned to prophesy! The two mysterious witnesses in this passage were to wear sackcloth and to speak forth God's words for a fixed period of time.

Invincible! The two witnesses seemed invincible. If anyone desired to harm them, fire issued from their mouths. They were given power to prevent rain from falling. They could also bring other forms of distress on the earth.

Glee! When the beast from the abyss killed the two prophets, after their proclamation was complete, there was great glee all over the earth.

Invincible! The glee of the wicked was not to last. God breathed life into the two and they arose. God took them at once into heaven, as their enemies stared.

Lord Jesus, thank you for the presence of the powerful Holy Spirit within us. Help us to live for you, to bear witness to you, and to speak your words. Let us not be terrified, but full of trust. You are victorious! You are in charge of our lives. Alleluia!

Sunday, November 23, 2008 Christ the King
Ezekiel 34, 11-12,15-17
Parable of the Shepherds; Separation of the Sheep

The shepherd tends. The shepherd judges.

The Lord was thoroughly fed up with the bad shepherds who were leading Israel (Ezekiel 34, 1-10). They cared only for themselves and not for the sheep committed to their care.

The Lord had one word for these bad shepherds. WOE!

The Lord would tend his sheep himself, since the shepherds were unworthy to lead. The Lord would rescue the scattered sheep. The Lord would provided good pasture for the sheep.

The Lord would seek the lost sheep. The Lord would retrieve the strayed sheep. The Lord would heal the sick and injured sheep.

The Lord would also judge the sheep. The Lord would judge between the sheep, the rams, and the goats. The Lord's purpose was still to protect and to save (Ezekiel 34, 22).

Lord Jesus, thank you that we may trust you as our Good Shepherd. Heal us and lead us to the still waters and fresh meadows where we may live and serve you as you call us to serve you. Alleluia!

Monday, November 24, 2008 St. Andrew Dung-Lac
Revelation 14, 1-5
The Lamb's Companions

Be with the Lamb. Follow the Lamb. Worship and sing to the Lamb.

Lord Jesus, you are the Lamb of God. You offered yourself as our Lamb of sacrifice. We follow you now as our Good Shepherd. Let us live in purity as we follow you. Let us speak the truth and live the truth. Alleluia!

Tuesday, November 25, 2008 St. Catherine of Alexandria
Revelation 14, 14-19
The Harvest of the Earth

The time will come. The time will come for God to make final judgment.

Lord Jesus, thank you for your amazing mercy. Let us remember that you are also our Judge. Let us live in a manner worthy of you. Alleluia!

Wednesday, November 26, 2008
Revelation 15, 1-4
The Seven Last Plagues

Victory! Praise! Singing!

In John's vision, those who had been victorious over the beast were singing. They were singing of God's deliverance.

Lord Jesus, you are holy, you are powerful, and you are leading us in your victory procession. Let us practice living as victors today. Alleluia!

Thursday, November 27, 2008
Revelation 18, 1-2,21-23; 19, 1-3,9
The Fall of Babylon

Whatever is holding you captive and is caging you in will be destroyed. As God's child, you cannot be contained and you cannot be destroyed.

Lord Jesus, let us learn to live as victors. Thank you for summoning us to your wedding feast. You are the glorious Lamb of God who won the victory for us. Alleluia!

Friday, November 28, 2008
Revelation 20, 1-4,11 - 21, 2
The Thousand Year Reign; The Large White Throne;
The New Heaven and the New Earth

Books! THE BOOK.

Some say they want to be judged only on the basis of their deeds. There will be just such a judgment at the white throne. Their deeds have been recorded in a book.

There is another Book, however. This is the Lamb's Book. This is the book of life. Only those whose names are in the Lamb's book will enter into the joy of the new Jerusalem (Revelation 21, 27).

Lord Jesus, it does seem overwhelming to read of beasts, thrones, books, judgment, fire, the abyss, the devil, and on and on. Help us to place all our trust in you and in the power of your mercy to forgive us. You said you would never reject anyone who came to you. Let us now be strong in bearing witness to you this day and trust you to lead us into our new life. Alleluia!

Saturday, November 29, 2008
Revelation 22, 1-7
The New Jerusalem

"Then the angel showed me the river of the water of life, bright as crystal, flowing from the throne of God and of the Lamb through the middle of the street of the city. On either side of the river, is the tree of life with its twelve kinds of fruit, producing its fruit each month; and the leaves of the tree are for the healing of the nations. Nothing accursed will be found there any more. But the throne of God and of the Lamb will be in it, and his servants will worship him; they will see his face, and his name will also be on their foreheads. And there will be no more night; they need no light of lamp or sun, for the LORD GOD will be their light, and they will reign forever and ever. And he said to me, 'These words are trustworthy and true, for the Lord, the God of the spirits of the prophets, has sent his angel to show his servants what must soon take place.' 'See, I am coming soon! Blessed is the one who keeps the words of the prophecy of this book.' The one who testifies to these things says, 'I am coming soon.' Amen. Come, Lord Jesus (Revelation 22, 1-7,20)."

Lord Jesus, let us continue to trust you as we work and as we wait to see you face to face. Let us be worthy of the trust you have placed in us. Alleluia!

About the author

Janis Walker was born in Louisiana and grew up in Oklahoma and Texas. As an Episcopalian, she served in hospital ministry, parish ministry, ecumenical prayer group ministry, and retreat ministry. She is a member of the ecumenical Order of St. Luke the Physician. In 1991, she received a Master's degree in Theology from St. Patrick's Seminary. She also studied at Fuller Theological Seminary and at the Graduate Theological Union in Berkeley. Janis was received into the Roman Catholic Church in a Chrism Mass for Christian Unity on May 13, 1998, in Rossi Chapel at the Jesuit Retreat Center in Los Altos, California. She lives with her family in California, enjoys visiting a village in Vermont, and swimming in the Atlantic Ocean by the Jersey shore. Janis has a continuing interest in the ecclesial effects of the Oxford Movement and the legacy of Cardinal Newman.

A.M.D.G.

You may order additional copies of this book

from www.amazon.com, www.barnesandnoble.com,

or at your favorite independent bookstore.